Banking on Basel

The Future of International Financial Regulation

Daniel K. Tarullo

Peterson Institute for International Economics
Washington, DC
August 2008

Daniel K. Tarullo is a professor of law at Georgetown University Law Center. He has taught at Harvard Law School (2005) and Princeton University (2004). He held several senior positions in the Clinton administration, ultimately as assistant to the president for international economic policy, responsible for coordinating the international economic policy of the administration. From 1993 until early 1996, he was assistant secretary of state for economic and business affairs. In March 1995, President Clinton appointed Tarullo as his personal representative to the G-7/G-8 group of industrialized nations, with responsibility for coordinating US positions for the annual leaders' summits. He continued this assignment after he moved to the White House, participating in four summits. He serves on the editorial advisory board of the *International Economy* and the Advisory Committee of Transparency International.

PETER G. PETERSON INSTITUTE FOR INTERNATIONAL ECONOMICS
1750 Massachusetts Avenue, NW
Washington, DC 20036-1903
(202) 328-9000   FAX: (202) 659-3225
www.petersoninstitute.org

C. Fred Bergsten, *Director*
Edward Tureen, *Director of Publications, Marketing, and Web Development*

Typesetting by Xcel Graphic Services
Printing by Edwards Brothers, Incorporated
Cover by Barbieri & Green, Inc.
Author photo by Jeremey Tripp

Printed in the United States of America
10 09 08   5 4 3 2 1

Library of Congress Cataloging-in-Publication Data

Tarullo, Daniel K.
   Banking on Basel : the future of international financial regulation / Daniel K. Tarullo.
       p. cm.
   Includes bibliographical references and index.
   1. Banks and banking, International—State supervision. 2. Banks and banking, International—Standards. 3. Bank capital. 4. Banking law. I. Title.

   HG1725.T37 2008
   332'.042—dc22

                                    2008037233

To VT

Contents

Preface

The financial distress that followed the implosion of markets for securitized mortgages in 2007 has raised profound doubts about the adequacy of supervision of financial markets—in the United States and in other countries. One question in the ensuing public policy debate has been whether financial institutions would have been in sounder condition had the capital regulations agreed upon internationally in the Basel II accord, negotiated between 1999 and 2004, already been in place. Basel II marks a dramatic change in capital regulation of large banks in the countries represented on the Basel Committee on Banking Supervision, composed of 13 of the most important financial centers, by using banks' own credit risk models in setting minimum capital requirements.

In this book Daniel Tarullo considers the Basel II approach both as a paradigm for domestic banking regulation and as the basis for an international cooperative arrangement. While highly skeptical of Basel II as a domestic regulatory system, he does not definitively reject some use of banks' own risk models in setting minimum capital requirements. Although he is troubled by the theoretical and practical problems in relying on the value-at-risk credit models used by large banks, he finds no clearly superior alternative approach to capital regulation.

As to the Basel II agreement that each participating country implement the same "internal ratings" method of minimum capital regulation for its large banks, however, Tarullo is unequivocal in his criticism. He concludes that the shortcomings of this method as the foundation for domestic regulation will only be magnified at the international level. The details of this very complicated set of regulations are unlikely to be appropriate for the different circumstances of participating countries. Yet the very negotiation of such detailed rules invites the banks and supervisors from their home countries to seek national competitive advantage, at the possible expense of the common goal of a more stable international banking system. At the same time, the complexity of the rules will make effective monitoring of their implementation very difficult.

Although Tarullo is dubious that the internal ratings method of capital regulation is well-advised for either an international agreement or national banking regulation, he recognizes that the Basel Committee is unlikely to abandon that approach after nearly a decade of effort in negotiating and implementing Basel II. Thus his recommendations, while defining a significant change of course, do not require supervisors in the Basel Committee countries to cast aside its work on using internal risk ratings as an element of supervisory requirements. While recommending much simpler rules and more emphasis on supervisory principles at the international level, he includes as one of those principles that each large bank be required to maintain a validated credit risk model as part of its risk management system.

While this book is careful to limit its specific conclusions to the best modes of national and international capital regulation of large banks, it has several important broader implications. First, as a matter of sound prudential banking regulation, it casts considerable doubt on the wisdom of relying on capital requirements to the extent supervisors have in recent years. Second, it suggests that stronger and more innovative international institutions may be necessary if arrangements to contain transnational financial problems are to be effective. Third, in recounting the history of Basel Committee activities, the book contains valuable lessons on how the interaction of domestic politics and international negotiations may shape the outcome in a way that, depending on the circumstances, may either advance or hinder the cause of effective and efficient regulation. This last point has relevance well beyond the area of financial regulation.

The Peter G. Peterson Institute for International Economics is a private, nonprofit institution for the study and discussion of international economic policy. Its purpose is to analyze important issues in that area and to develop and communicate practical new approaches for dealing with them. The Institute is completely nonpartisan.

The Institute is funded by a highly diversified group of philanthropic foundations, private corporations, and interested individuals. About 22 percent of the Institute's resources in our latest fiscal year were provided by contributors outside the United States, including about 9 percent from Japan.

The Institute's Board of Directors bears overall responsibilities for the Institute and gives general guidance and approval to its research program, including the identification of topics that are likely to become important over the medium run (one to three years) and that should be addressed by the Institute. The director, working closely with the staff and outside Advisory Committee, is responsible for the development of particular projects and makes the final decision to publish an individual study.

The Institute hopes that its studies and other activities will contribute to building a stronger foundation for international economic policy around the world. We invite readers of these publications to let us know how they think we can best accomplish this objective.

C. FRED BERGSTEN
Director
August 2008

Acknowledgments

My first note of thanks goes to Fred Bergsten, who was willing to commit to a book proposal that was somewhat atypical for the Peterson Institute. In researching this book, I spoke with dozens of past and present officials from national bank supervisory agencies, central banks, and international institutions, all of whom had been involved in the Basel II process. I am grateful to each of them for taking the time to discuss, analyze, and sometimes argue the history and merits of Basel II with me. I also profited enormously from two peer review sessions organized at the Peterson Institute and from comments received from participants at a session of the FDIC's Annual Bank Research Conference. Finally, I extend special thanks to Mark Carey of the Federal Reserve Board and Ted Truman of the Peterson Institute. Each carefully read and critiqued successive drafts of this book and spent considerable time helping me work through both my major themes and important details. It goes without saying that neither is responsible for—and should not be associated with—the content, conclusions, or ultimate quality of the book. But their generosity and insight made the book a much better informed policy analysis than it otherwise would have been.

1

Introduction

The completion in June 2004 of the Revised Framework on International Convergence of Capital Measurement and Capital Standards, popularly known as Basel II, was a milestone in two respects. First, it brought about a major change in the basic method of banking regulation applied in financially significant countries by completely overhauling the minimum capital requirements that have become central to prudential supervision. Second, it was unprecedented as an exercise in international regulatory coordination and harmonization.[1] Even by the standards of the Basel Committee on Banking Supervision[2] (box 1.1)—already the exemplary case of international regulatory convergence—it is extremely ambitious. The capital rules and associated supervisory provisions run nearly 300 pages. Successful implementation will require extensive ongoing cooperation among national banking supervisors.

Both as a regulatory model and as an international regulatory convergence arrangement, Basel II moves far beyond the original 1988 framework (Basel I). Indeed, it has come to dominate the work of the Basel

---

1. There is, of course, even more extensive harmonization and coordination among the member states of the European Union.

2. Up until 1999, the committee called itself the *Basle* Committee, using the French spelling. In 1999, apparently in response to the expressed preferences of the predominatly German-speaking residents of the city, the committee began calling itself the *Basel* Committee. The committee's website now uses standard indexing for "Basel," but specific documents from the 1980s and most of the 1990s have the old spelling, "Basle." For the sake of consistency, the name is spelled "Basel" throughout the book.

Box 1.1   Basel Committee on Banking Supervision

The Basel Committee on Banking Supervision states its objective as "improv[ing] supervisory understanding and the quality of banking supervision worldwide" (Basel Committee 2007a). Originally the Committee on Regulations and Supervisory Practices, it was created by the Group of Ten Countries (G-10) at the end of 1974, after the failure of Herstatt Bank caused significant disturbances in currency markets throughout the world.[1] National representation on the committee comes from central banks and other agencies with responsibility for supervision of banks.

The committee has no formal legal existence or permanent staff, and the results of its activities do not have the force of international law. It provides a forum for exchanges of views several times a year in Basel, Switzerland, where it is housed at the headquarters of the Bank for International Settlements (box 1.2). Its proceedings are neither open to the public nor—as with some entities like the Executive Board of the International Monetary Fund—memorialized in publicly available summaries. However, it releases and maintains on its website a steady stream of documents on standards, recommendations, guidelines, and best practices for supervision of internationally active banks. The committee describes its activities as "encourag[ing] convergence towards common approaches and common standards without attempting detailed harmonisation of member countries' supervisory techniques" (Basel Committee 2007a), an accurate characterization of its first 20 years of work but belied by the Basel II exercise.

The first major and ongoing effort undertaken by the committee was to close gaps in the supervision of internationally active banks, while assuring that the supervision provided was adequate. In 1975, shortly after its creation, the committee released a paper that eventually became known as the "Concordat," a set of principles for sharing supervisory responsibility for bank activities between host and home countries. These principles were subsequently elaborated or revised in light of further deliberations or obvious supervisory failures such as that involving the Bank of Credit and Commerce International in the late 1980s. This ongoing activity has led to a number of related initiatives, such as those dealing with the problems posed for consolidated supervision by offshore banking centers.

A second strand of Basel Committee activity has been the promulgation of standards for bank supervision generally. This effort was made more comprehensive at the behest of the leaders of the Group of Seven (G-7) following their

(box continues on next page)

Committee. The policy implications of Basel II are correspondingly far-reaching. Its impact on domestic banking regulation and on international cooperation in supervising internationally active banks is self-evident. Less obvious, but perhaps of equal importance, is its possible role as a trailblazer for international arrangements covering other financial institutions and activities. The global reach of large financial institutions and the substantial global integration of financial markets mean that serious problems originating in one country are apt to spread quickly to other countries, just as extensive interbank lending has long served as an international transmission mechanism for bank stress.

Experience with Basel II will inevitably shape the future of all international financial regulation, a future that is likely to arrive sooner than the

Box 1.2 Bank for International Settlements

The Bank for International Settlements (BIS) is the institutional home of the Basel Committee on Banking Supervision. Headquartered in Basel, Switzerland, the organization's mandates are to promote international monetary and financial cooperation and to serve as a bank for central banks. The BIS also houses the secretariats of several committees and organizations focusing on the international financial system, including the Basel Committee, although these entities are not formally a part of the BIS. BIS membership currently totals 55 central banks.

The BIS was created in 1930 within the framework of the Young Plan to address the issue of German reparations. Its focus soon shifted to the promotion of international financial cooperation and monetary stability. These goals were initially pursued through regular meetings of central bank officials and economic experts directed toward promoting discussion and facilitating decision-making processes, as well as through the development of a research staff to compile and distribute financial statistics. The BIS also played a role in implementing and sustaining the Bretton Woods system.

Throughout its history, the BIS has retained its role as a bank for central banks, acting as an agent or trustee in connection with international financial operations and a prime counterparty for central banks in their financial transactions and providing or organizing emergency financing to support the international monetary system (including as part of stabilization programs such as those for Mexico in 1982 and Brazil in 1998 led by the International Monetary Fund). The BIS assists central banks in their management of foreign currency reserves and itself holds about 6 percent of global foreign exchange reserves invested by central banks.

Basel Committee might have thought when it released the revised framework. The search for additional or alternative regulatory mechanisms assumes greater urgency in the wake of the subprime mortgage crisis that began in 2007, which revealed massive failures of risk management by financial institutions and of supervision by government authorities. Basel II had not been in place during the years in which banks accumulated subprime mortgage assets on their balance sheets and, in some cases, sponsored off-balance-sheet entities that served as investment vehicles for those assets. Even in the midst of the crisis, however, debate began as to whether a fully implemented Basel II would have mitigated or exacerbated the bank problems that gave rise to the financial turmoil.

By the spring of 2008, the Basel Committee itself had implicitly acknowledged that the revised framework would not have been adequate to contain the risks revealed by the subprime crisis and needed strengthening. However, that crisis has highlighted two more basic questions about Basel II. First, is the method of capital regulation incorporated in the revised framework fundamentally misguided? Second, even if the basic Basel II approach has promise as a paradigm for domestic regulation, is the effort at extensive international harmonization of capital rules and supervisory practices useful and appropriate? This book provides extended and, on balance, reasonably negative answers to both questions.

Summary of Argument

The core policy issue is whether an international effort at regulatory convergence around Basel II's bank capital rules will produce net benefits for the United States greater than those that could be gained through viable policy alternatives, including the status quo.[3] Narrowly framed, the conclusion of this book is that Basel II's detailed rules for capital regulation are not an appropriate basis for an international arrangement among banking supervisors. As suggested by its wording, this conclusion is supported by three interrelated analyses, which themselves have broader implications both for US banking regulation and for international cooperation among banking supervisors.

First, and most important, is an evaluation of the rules for domestic bank capital regulation contained in Basel II. An international arrangement grounded on a badly flawed bank regulatory model is obviously unlikely to be worthwhile. Yet even theoretically sound rules may be suboptimal because of administrative factors such as compliance costs and supervisory limitations.

Until Basel II, capital requirements were based on relatively simple rules that required a capital set-aside for each bank asset based on the "risk-bucket" approach—a somewhat arbitrary categorization of the riskiness associated with various types of credit exposures. For most banks, such rules will continue to apply, though the risk weighting of a bank's assets may be determined by the assessments of external credit rating agencies where applicable ratings are available. Debatable as this change may be, particularly in light of the shortcomings of external credit ratings exposed by the subprime crisis, the focus here will be on the entirely new method for determining minimum capital requirements that will be applicable to very large banks.

---

3. This book takes a US perspective on Basel II. However, most of its analysis is equally relevant to policymakers in other countries. There may, of course, be somewhat different balances of gains and costs for other countries or, more accurately, for specific policymakers. For example, any policymaker in the European Union—whether in a member state or in the Commission—will consider how an arrangement like Basel II will affect a broader set of policy dynamics within the European Union.

Basel II's internal ratings–based (IRB) approaches to capital regulation will allow large banks to use their own credit risk models to generate key inputs into the formulas that determine how much capital they must hold. The advantage sought from an IRB approach is the increased risk sensitivity of regulatory capital requirements, to be achieved through the use of the sophisticated risk assessment techniques of major banks. Unlike the regulatory methods and rules resulting from most exercises in international convergence, the IRB approaches were developed entirely during the international negotiation itself, rather than adapted from regulatory systems already in use in one or more countries. Insofar as capital requirements are central to contemporary banking regulation and the IRB approaches are essentially untested, the regulators adopting them are taking at least a leap of faith and, critics fear, possibly a leap off a cliff. The manifold conceptual and practical problems associated with the IRB approach make it a questionable basis for domestic banking regulation, though many regulators continue to believe it can be fine-tuned adequately after some period of adaptation to be a sound regulatory paradigm.

Second is an assessment of the contribution of the specifically international character of Basel II in achieving various national policy goals. Even if an underlying bank regulatory design is flawed, perhaps significantly so, adherence to those rules by other countries may produce important benefits for each participating country. On the other hand, even if detailed harmonized regulatory rules produced in an international arrangement rest on a conceptually sound foundation, they will necessarily differ from rules tailored to the economic circumstances, legal environment, and policy preferences in each participating country. From the standpoint of any one country, then, the key question is whether the gains from having other countries subscribe to the Basel II rules will offset the losses from following rules different from those that would have been generated in a purely domestic process.[4]

Specifying the gains from cooperation is considerably less straightforward than it might first appear. One familiar difficulty is that the potential gains are of different types, and the more complete realization of one goal may come at the expense of others. Moreover, the relative importance of these various gains will be evaluated differently by groups within each country. There is, in other words, no unitary national interest on the basis of which to judge the arrangement; choices must be made on the basis of one's own relative policy emphases. Large banks, small banks, legislators, regulators, and self-identified advocates of the public

---

4. It is possible that an international regulatory convergence process could yield rules better suited to the public interest in one or more countries than those that would be produced in a purely domestic process. This could happen, for example, if the migration of the rule-making to an international forum reduced the influence of certain interests that had dominated the domestic process.

interest regard Basel II very differently. The two most prominently stated aims of Basel II—to enhance the safety and soundness of internationally active banks and to promote competitive equality among banks from different countries—are not difficult to reconcile in theory. But in practice, one or the other aim may have the upper hand during critical points of a negotiation. Unfortunately, as will be explained in the history of Basel II, the important but abstract general interest in effective and efficient banking regulation was subordinated at key moments in the negotiations by commercial and bureaucratic interests.

Apart from the absence of a single national interest implicated in the Basel II arrangement, another difficulty for a policy evaluation is that the theoretical plausibility of gains from an IRB approach may not translate into actual gains within the particular institutional structure of the Basel Committee. Misaligned incentives of the relevant actors, monitoring difficulties, or other factors may limit the effectiveness of the arrangement. Critical as the choice of regulatory model is, and intriguing as the operation of the Basel Committee may be, it is the interaction between the two that will determine the impact of Basel II. Assessment of this interaction leads to the conclusion that the international character of Basel II does not redeem the deficiencies of the IRB approach. On the contrary, the infirmities of the IRB approach as a basis for domestic regulation are multiplied as more countries adopt it, while the difficulties in effective monitoring of its implementation will limit any benefits arising from common adoption of the regulatory model.

The third analysis is explicitly comparative. Since virtually any initiative will have drawbacks as well as merits, reasonable policy analysis looks not for the perfect arrangement but for the best among practical alternatives. Even significant shortcomings of a proposal do not necessarily make it a bad policy choice. Other proposals might have even greater unintended negative consequences or have fewer negative effects only at the cost of poorly realizing the original policy aims. Comparing the benefits and faults of Basel II with those of other options, including the status quo ante, indicates that there is no single alternative that would be superior to the IRB approaches as the basis for an international arrangement. However, a combination of uncertainty as to the optimal substantive approach for capital regulation and the institutional limitations of the Basel Committee suggests that a simpler and more eclectic international arrangement would be preferable to Basel II. The final chapter of the book provides recommendations for such an alternative.

Outline of the Book

The evaluation of Basel II and its implications begins with some background on the role of bank capital regulation and then recounts the history of Basel I and Basel II. It turns next to the core analysis of Basel II as a bank regulatory paradigm and as an international arrangement, followed by consideration of some possible alternatives, before ending with recommendations for significant changes in the arrangement.

Chapter 2 reviews the rationale for, and history of, minimum bank capital requirements in the G-10 countries. Two points are key to understanding why the stakes in Basel II are exceedingly high. First, there has been a secular shift in the nature of bank regulation over the past quarter-century in the United States and, to a lesser degree, other financial centers. The symbiotic effects of the evolution of the financial services industry and the relaxation of many restrictions on bank activities have placed capital regulation at the center of bank regulation. Second, however sophisticated and quantified the assessment of risks may become, the setting of bank capital requirements involves a trade-off between financial stability and moving capital to productive uses throughout the economy. Accordingly, capital regulation cannot be a purely mechanistic task but necessarily requires the exercise of policy discretion.

Chapter 3 describes the origins, characteristics, and history of Basel I. It provides some background on the creation of the Basel Committee and the dual motivations of the United States and United Kingdom in seeking an arrangement on capital adequacy in the late 1980s. The chapter also recounts the notable adjustments made to the Basel Accord and other supervisory cooperative arrangements of the Basel Committee prior to the launch of the major redrafting. Even as the Basel Committee was modifying the original Basel I framework, the United States unilaterally supplemented the rules as applied to its own banks, in order to take account of emerging issues such as the credit risks associated with securitization. However, with Basel I in place, national regulatory systems adjusted only at the margin to the perceived imperative for regulatory change. Despite widespread awareness that there was a growing gap between the science and practice of credit risk management, on the one hand, and the regulatory regime, on the other, no national bank supervisors initiated an overhaul of capital adequacy requirements.

The chapter also assesses the merits and shortcomings of Basel I. The most important criticisms of Basel I were that it had gaps in its coverage and that the opportunities it created for regulatory arbitrage became progressively more serious as the mix of bank activities shifted toward securitization, writing derivatives, and other financial products that had comprised much smaller segments of major bank activity during the period in which Basel I was drafted. These criticisms formed much of the motivation for the launch of Basel II.

Chapter 4 recounts the tortured negotiation of Basel II and describes the 2004 revised framework, including its implementation and modification in the subsequent four years. Although the committee decided in 1998 to undertake a thorough revision of the accord, it seems to have had little sense of direction. Particularly in light of the regulatory shortcomings revealed by problems associated with subprime mortgage lending and securitization, there is a case to be made that the opportunity costs of this effort were substantial. For example, the supervisory resources and energy devoted to the Basel II process necessarily delayed efforts to address liquidity risks, which were realized with a vengeance during the subprime crisis.

The Basel Committee's first effort, in 1999, introduced the "three-pillar" approach to capital regulation that remains in the revised framework. Pillar 1 includes the minimum capital rules themselves, pillar 2 consists of guidance for supervision of banks beyond the minimum capital rules, and pillar 3 addresses market discipline. Pillar 1 of the 1999 draft did not depart from the basic risk-bucket approach of Basel I. It proposed using external credit ratings, such as those developed by Moody's or Standard & Poor's, as the basis for defining risk categories. Widespread dissatisfaction among large banks with the failure to incorporate up-to-date risk management ideas in the proposal sent the committee back to the drawing board. Attention was redirected toward an approach that relied on banks' own, internally generated credit ratings as the basis for regulatory capital calculations. However, the banks' credit risk ratings for specific exposures were to be inputs into capital formulas devised by supervisors. Thus the IRB approach is a hybrid form of regulation.

Development of a satisfactory proposal for using internal ratings was not easy. Two comprehensive drafts and numerous discrete modifications produced progressively more complexity, as the Basel Committee attempted to respond to objections from many quarters, most importantly including banks in their countries. In its attempts to respond to problems in successive proposals, the Basel Committee became so preoccupied with constructing a viable IRB approach that it neglected to adequately develop pillars 2 and 3. The result is a somewhat unbalanced final version of Basel II.

The major changes from Basel I effected by Basel II were to

- refine the risk buckets for the capital adequacy calculations to be used by smaller banks and make certain other changes but maintain the basic 1988 approach, as contemplated in the original 1999 proposal;
- permit larger, sophisticated banks to base their minimum capital requirements on inputs from their own internal credit risk models through the use of either a "foundational" internal ratings–based approach (F-IRB) or an "advanced" internal ratings–based approach (A-IRB);
- require certain disclosures by banks in an attempt to incorporate modest market disciplines into the regulatory scheme;
- augment the supervisory process; and
- require capital set-asides for operational risk.

Of these elements, the proposal for using banks' internal ratings was, by a substantial margin, both the most difficult and the most controversial, with operational risk a clear second.

The revised framework was controversial even before it was issued. Even as some large banks were reassured by trial runs of the Basel II IRB formulas showing that bank capital would decline, many academics and policy commentators—and even a few legislators—had concluded that the whole enterprise was significantly deficient, if not wholly misguided. Some US regulators had second thoughts as well, leading to a semi-public interagency struggle over the degree to which US implementing regulations would require more safeguards against capital declines than are present in the revised framework. The subprime crisis of 2007 reinforced the case made by at least some of the skeptics and induced the Basel Committee to propose significant modifications to Basel II before it had even been fully implemented. These post-2004 developments suggest the possibility that the revised framework will be subject, if not to continuous revision, then at least to continuous debate over whether changes are needed.

Chapter 5 evaluates Basel II as a domestic regulatory model. It begins by discussing the important questions of why and how capital regulation matters, given that banks regularly hold capital well in excess of minimum regulatory requirements. While a reduction in capital is obviously not inherent in an IRB approach as such, the Basel II formulas appear to produce this result. The chapter then turns to the potential advantages of the IRB approaches, with emphasis on the A-IRB approach applicable to the very largest banks. These include greater risk sensitivity; the prod given to large and complex banks to improve their internal risk management systems; and the creation of a "common language" of risk profiles that will enhance both the supervision and market discipline of banks' extension of credit. Numerous problems, including the unproven character of value-at-risk (VaR) models for assessing credit risk and the significant administrative difficulties in monitoring bank implementation of IRB requirements, raise significant doubts that these advantages will be substantially realized. The chapter also considers two negative effects of the A-IRB regulatory paradigm: exacerbation of the countercyclical macroeconomic effects normally associated with risk-sensitive bank capital requirements and the systematic advantage provided A-IRB banks over smaller banks in certain forms of lending.

The conclusion to be drawn from the chapter is that the potential benefits of the A-IRB approach are likely outweighed by its risks and shortcomings. Thus, as a regulatory model standing outside an international arrangement, its desirability is at best uncertain. Indeed, there is a significant possibility that the Basel II paradigm might eventually produce the worst of both worlds—the enormous complexity associated with the supervisory capital formulas without the advantages of customized, state-of-the-art risk modeling techniques available to banks.

Chapter 6 asks whether the A-IRB model is redeemed by its status as the basis of an international arrangement. It first considers the potential benefits of the arrangement. These include enhanced safety and soundness of internationally active banks around the world (in both Basel Committee and non–Basel Committee countries), increased competitive equality among banks from different countries, facilitation of supervision of internationally active banks, and reductions in the costs imposed on banks or investors by the existence of multiple regulatory and disclosure regimes. None of these potential advantages is both substantial and likely to be realized.

There are significant doubts as to the efficacy of this approach in the many countries in which supervision is considerably less hands-on than in the United States. Moreover, there are substantial monitoring problems for regulators attempting to confirm that their counterparts in other Basel Committee countries have successfully validated and supervised the internal ratings models of banks in those countries. Finally, the chapter considers the deleterious effects on safety and soundness regulation of the national opportunism created by the negotiation and implementation structure of Basel II.

Chapter 7 considers alternatives to Basel II—both substitute paradigms for domestic capital regulation that could be incorporated into an international arrangement and different approaches to international cooperation. In the first category are three options: maintaining a modified standardized approach for all banks; moving toward a predominantly market-oriented basis for regulation, such as by requiring each bank to maintain special issues of subordinated debt; and a "precommitment" approach. The second category poses two fairly dramatic possibilities: eliminating international efforts to harmonize capital regulation and—perhaps even more controversial—moving beyond harmonized national regulation toward direct regulation of internationally active banks by a supranational authority. The conclusion here is that none of these alternatives presents either a substantive approach or a mode of international cooperation preferable to Basel II, at least not at present. However, elements of several of these alternatives may be usefully engrafted onto the modified Basel II suggested in the final chapter.

Chapter 8 offers conclusions and recommendations. One important conclusion from an analysis of Basel II is that capital regulation cannot bear as much of the weight of prudential regulation as has been placed upon it. Uncertainty about the efficacy of capital regulation—whether based on an IRB, standardized, or some other approach—counsels greater attention to other prudential tools. The subprime crisis has dramatically reinforced this conclusion by revealing the extent of liquidity and reputational risks associated with certain banks that were, under prevailing regulations, "well capitalized." The crisis has also raised at least the question of whether regulation of certain bank *products*, in addition to bank risk management *processes*, may be necessary. Perhaps most significantly, the cumulative experience of the subprime crisis and other instances of financial distress in recent years suggests that more attention must be paid to the systemic risks that arise from the interactions among financial actors and that cannot be measured or contained solely by a focus on each individual institution's balance sheet (US Department of the Treasury 2008). While this book does not address these other issues, the reader should not mistake its concentration on capital adequacy with an endorsement of the unbalanced supervisory focus on that regulatory tool over the last decade.

As to Basel itself, although there is no self-contained alternative approach ready to substitute for Basel II, the problems with that arrangement counsel quick mitigating steps. While a case can be made that the IRB approach would best have been abandoned some years ago, that is not a realistic starting point for policy recommendations at present. The Basel II rules have been incorporated into domestic banking regulation in the Basel Committee countries and will be implemented by many non-committee countries as well. Thus, the recommendations here begin from this fact but urge changes to both the substantive capital rules and to the institutional mechanisms for overseeing those rules. The focus should be on principles, straightforward common rules, peer review, and coordinated procedures for enforcement of domestic laws. Specifically with respect to capital regulation, the Basel Committee should

- *accelerate its work on redefining capital.* Capital regulation means little if the definition of capital is not limited to the kinds of buffers that will actually protect a bank from insolvency. As explained in chapter 3, the definition of capital was a subject of compromise in the original Basel I negotiations and has been subsequently expanded—probably excessively—since then.

- *adopt a simple leverage ratio requirement, such as that included in US law.* This admittedly blunt measure of capital is highly transparent and not subject to easy evasion. It provides a kind of regulatory safety net, even though it is not highly risk sensitive. The committee should also consider implementing a minimum ratio of capital to income in order to take account of off-balance-sheet bank activities in a similarly blunt but transparent fashion.

- *institute a requirement that complex, internationally active banks issue subordinated debt with specific, harmonized characteristics.* While not an assured outcome, there is a reasonable chance that the market pricing of this debt would serve a "canary in a coal mine" role in alerting supervisors to potential problems at a bank.

- *remove the detailed rules of pillar 1 in favor of augmenting the current pillar 2 principles that guide national agencies' supervision of complex, internationally active financial institutions.* These would include (a) some form of risk-based capital requirement, (b) a requirement that banks maintain a credit risk model for use in calculating internal capital requirements and an operational risk system, and (c) more detailed expectations for supervisory intervention when capital requirements fall below minimum levels. National implementation of these principles would be subject to regular and sophisticated peer review. While less detail is needed in the minimum capital rules, more detail would be needed on the information that banks adopting the IRB approach would have to disclose.

- *strengthen the monitoring role of the Basel Committee.* This should include regular and substantially more robust peer review of national regulatory activity to implement Basel rules and principles. The committee should regularly report on bank capital positions and capital supervision. Finally, and most importantly, the committee should establish a special inspection unit—a supranational team of experts that conducts in-bank validations of the credit risk models used by internationally active banks in the Basel Committee countries. This unit would serve both to disseminate expertise among the various national supervisors and to provide some monitoring of their own validation of their banks' models and attendant risk management.

Chapter 8 concludes with some tentative observations on its implications for such efforts in other areas. Although the examination of Basel II itself shows that the effects of international regulatory convergence are highly specific to particular circumstances and regulatory choices, the case study does provide a starting point for assessing the promise of this form of international cooperation in other regulatory areas, financial and nonfinancial.

A Note on Timing

One further introductory point is necessary. After six years of negotiations and another three years before the United States adopted implementing measures, Basel II was finally completed. But implementation is only beginning. One might argue that any judgment on Basel II should now await some accumulated experience after it has been made fully operational. However, there are good reasons for a more immediate assessment, notwithstanding the obvious absence of data on Basel II in practice.

First, there have been serious and persistent doubts about Basel II throughout its negotiation and implementation. Although the technical nature of the undertaking helped keep it from attaining general political salience, it was marked by controversy at each step of the way. For a time, dissent was generated by banks that feared stricter regulation and higher compliance costs and by legislators who feared competitive disadvantage for their own country's banks. Many academics from across the ideological spectrum thought the entire enterprise misguided as a matter of sound regulatory policy. A handful of bank supervisory officials expressed concerns with the complexity of the effort—usually privately, but in at least one case very publicly. By the time the negotiations were completed, some members of Congress had concluded that the academics may have been right.

Second, if a thorough analysis of Basel II as enacted reveals the persistence of serious questions concerning its dependability, both as a regulatory model and as an international arrangement, then there will be a strong case for maintaining or establishing mechanisms to complement or support it. More specifically, conclusions on the likely efficacy of Basel II will be relevant for determining whether the transitional safeguards established for the arrangement should be broadened or extended.

Third, doubts raised during the negotiation and implementation of Basel II have only been strengthened by the circumstances surrounding the subprime mortgage crisis. Key features of Basel II include reliance on the internal risk models of large banks to determine minimum capital requirements, the use of external credit-rating agencies to help set capital requirements for most banks, and an overall reduction in the risk weighting assigned to residential mortgages. The irony is inescapable, as the events of 2007 called into question the reliability of risk modeling, the usefulness of external agency ratings, and the benign view of residential mortgage riskiness. If a conscientious appraisal reveals that earlier implementation of Basel II would have done nothing to prevent these problems or might even have exacerbated them, then a relatively quick change in policy might be warranted.

Fourth, even if such an exercise is not conducted by regulators or proves inconclusive, the possibility that Basel II will prove seriously flawed is great enough that an early assessment of alternatives—including analysis by those outside the official sector—is advisable. Insofar as decisions on whether to retain or abandon a policy approach are greatly influenced by whether viable alternatives have been developed, consideration of options now may ease policy decisions the future.

Finally, precisely because both the substantive model and international arrangement associated with the revised framework stand as a kind of prototype for similar initiatives in other areas of financial regulation, it is important to learn from Basel II sooner rather than later. If any reminder was necessary, the global repercussions of the subprime crisis underscore the imperative, and the tardiness, of adjustment by financial regulators to far-reaching changes in financial markets.

2

Role of Capital Regulation

Over the past 25 years, banking regulation in the United States and to some extent in other G-10 countries has been characterized by two noteworthy trends. First, capital adequacy requirements have become the most important type of regulation designed to protect bank safety and soundness. Basel I both reflected and accelerated this growing emphasis on capital adequacy. Second, there has been a shift away from a bank regulatory system that rests principally on generally applicable rules toward a "supervisory" approach that emphasizes particularized review of the activities of a specific bank. Especially with respect to large, complex banking institutions, this regulatory technique relies increasingly on assuring the sophistication and integrity of a bank's own risk management systems (DeFerrari and Palmer 2001).[1]

For a time these trends were in some conflict with one another, as Basel I applied the same minimal capital requirements to all banks.[2]

---

1. Then-chairman of the Federal Reserve Board Alan Greenspan summed up this trend in remarks on banking regulation to the Independent Community Bankers of America National Convention, March 11, 2005: "Over the past 15 years or so, supervision has focused on ensuring that bank management has in place policies and procedures that will contain such risk and that management adheres to those policies and procedures. Supervision has become increasingly less invasive and increasingly more systems- and policy-oriented. These changes have been induced by evolving technology, increased complexity, and lessons learned from significant banking crises, not to mention constructive criticism from the banking community."

2. Still, within a few years after Basel I took effect, influential regulators were already urging a shift away from traditional bank regulation. In 1994, Fed Chairman Greenspan said that banks and other financial institutions would have to be increasingly "self-regulated largely

Now, however, the two trends have converged in the advanced internal ratings–based (A-IRB) approach of Basel II. The new accord increases the centrality of capital regulation but does so principally by promoting the adoption of highly developed risk assessment capabilities by the banks themselves. That an international arrangement should so influence bank regulation in the United States and other G-10 countries is remarkable. Yet the very centrality of the A-IRB approach to bank regulation in the coming years means that any limitations of that approach could have serious repercussions. As a prelude to examination of the two Basel frameworks on minimum capital requirements, this chapter provides an introduction to the rationale for regulating bank capital levels and a brief account of how capital requirements assumed rapidly increasing importance in the years prior to Basel I.

Rationale for Capital Regulation

Policymakers and commentators often begin a discussion of bank capital adequacy requirements by citing their role in providing a buffer against bank losses, protecting creditors in the event a bank nonetheless fails, and creating a disincentive to excessive risk taking or shirking by bank owners and managers.[3] The first two effects exist almost by definition, though they are no less important for that; the important issue is *how much* of a buffer and protection are provided. A firm with no capital will become insolvent upon an unexpected loss, potentially leading to bankruptcy proceedings and consequent losses to some or all creditors. A capital buffer, on the other hand, reduces the chances that the firm will fail. This is obviously important to creditors. Where the firm is a bank, it is also important to society to the degree that failure will result in the loss of economically valuable relationships, investments, or knowledge.

The justifying principle that capital requirements contain risk taking is of more recent vintage.[4] In fact, it is questioned from time to time by

---

because government regulators cannot do that job." See John Gapper, "Fed Chief Sees Need for Self-Regulation," *Financial Times*, June 9, 1994, 1.

3. Policymakers and commentators frequently list half a dozen or more purposes of capital. Some, such as providing a ready source of financing for new activities, are undoubtedly important but of only marginal importance to the subject of capital regulation. Others, such as protecting a government deposit insurance fund or counteracting the inefficiencies in capital allocation resulting from the government safety net, are derivative of, or at least closely related to, one of the basic functions noted in the text.

4. Discussions of bank capital regulation dating from the 1960s and 1970s generally omit any mention of the risk-confining role of capital requirements. However, by the time of adoption of Basel I in 1988, the rationale was not only well developed, but emphasized (Bank for International Settlements 1989).

various academics who have devised models suggesting that capital requirements may under some circumstances *increase* risk taking (Kim and Santomero 1988).[5] Still, regulators and many academics now seem to accept the proposition that well-conceived capital requirements will generally discourage undue risk-taking (Santos 2001).[6] In any case, as explained more fully below, the role of capital in containing risky business behavior has become a key element of prevailing explanations of why private creditors are concerned with capital levels of the firms to which they lend.

Of course, the magnitude of these salutary effects depends on the level of the capital required, the establishment of which requires a trade-off between these stabilizing effects and the opportunity costs of restricting use of the capital. But this exercise is necessary only after the decision to regulate capital. Why should capital standards be imposed in the first place? This question is best answered by following the lead of Berger, Herring, and Szego (1995), who first specify why market actors demand that their counterparties hold certain capital levels and then consider why the resulting market-generated demands may produce socially suboptimal levels in banks, as opposed to other corporations.

In the absence of a dependable third-party guarantee, lenders want assurance that a borrower will be sufficiently solvent and liquid to repay its debt in accordance with the contractual terms of the loan, bond, or other extension of credit. Owners and, at least presumptively, managers of the enterprise have an incentive to use debt capital for projects that have the potential for very high profits. Of course, projects that may yield big returns are also more likely to be risky and to result in losses that will threaten the ability of the borrower to repay its loans. The incentive for risk taking increases as a firm approaches insolvency: the limited liability of the shareholders means the owners have increasingly

---

5. As, indeed, there continue to be academic challenges to the benefits of capital regulation more generally. See, for example, Allen and Gale (2003).

6. There may nonetheless be circumstances where capital requirements might encourage risk-taking by banks. For example, Blum (1999) has argued that an increase in capital requirements can lead to short-term increases in risk taking by banks attempting to increase their equity base before the tighter regulation takes effect. Calem and Rob (1999) find a U-shaped relationship between capital position and risk taking, in which severely undercapitalized banks take the most risk. As capital rises, the bank takes less risk, but as capital reaches higher levels, it will resume taking on more risk. Calem and Rob (1999, 336) conclude "that a minimum capital standard has a favorable effect on risk of failure to the extent that banks are required to be well removed from the range of maximal risk taking," but that significant reductions in the probability of insolvency for banks out of that range can be achieved only with stringent capital standards. Jeitschko and Jeung (2005) explain how relevant actors—deposit insurers, shareholders, and managers—have varying proclivities toward bank assumption of risk in differing circumstances. Thus the risk-assumption behavior of a bank will depend in part on which actor is exercising the most influence.

little to lose through a high-risk strategy. If things turn out well, the risky ventures will have saved the company and increased the equity of the owners. If things do not turn out well, the firm goes bankrupt, leaving the owners not much worse off. Because creditors generally do not share in the profits of an enterprise, and thus do not gain when a risky venture pays off, their preference is that their debtor be managed relatively conservatively.

A related problem is that, all else being equal, a debtor has an incentive to leverage its enterprise as much as possible so that potentially high profits from its ventures will be spread over a narrower equity base. A creditor, on the other hand, wishes to maximize the chances that the enterprise will have adequate resources to service *all* its debt, and thus wants limits on the total amount of debt assumed by the borrower.[7] The potential for opportunistic behavior by debtors will cause lenders to charge a higher risk premium unless their concerns can be allayed through devices such as covenants, priorities, and limits on total debt. A capital cushion can be understood as just one such device, but a particularly useful one, insofar as it helps guard against all kinds of opportunistic behavior, not just those kinds anticipated ex ante by the lender.

A debtor's capital also provides a buffer against economic reversals that do not result from its opportunistic behavior but from bad business judgments or bad luck. In the case of banks, the potential for both bad judgment and bad luck to affect asset values is obvious. Loan officers may fail to accurately gauge the creditworthiness of their borrowers, or unexpected exogenous shocks may diminish the value of whole categories of bank assets. A company whose assets just equal its liabilities is vulnerable to insolvency whenever an asset declines in value for any reason. A company perceived as vulnerable to insolvency will have a more difficult time retaining employees, maintaining relationships with suppliers and customers, and otherwise protecting the value of its franchise as an ongoing business. Hence bankruptcy becomes more likely (Berger, Herring, and Szego 1995). An insolvent company's assets will usually depreciate even further for the same reasons, as well as because of the transactions costs that bankruptcy entails. Again, in the absence of protective devices, lenders will respond to the anticipated risk of their debtor's insolvency by demanding a higher premium for their credit.

The possibility for opportunistic behavior and vulnerability to insolvency can significantly raise the cost of debt capital to borrowers. The un-

---

7. More precisely, a specific creditor will be concerned both that the debtor be able to service all its debt so as to avoid the insolvency costs discussed below and that, if insolvency should nonetheless occur, there will be sufficient assets to pay off all the debt having the same bankruptcy priority as the creditor's. For creditors holding subordinated debt of a borrower, the two considerations essentially merge.

certainties detailed above may be particularly acute in lending to financial institutions, whose assets are notoriously difficult for outsiders to evaluate. Thus the asymmetry of information between corporate insiders and lenders that exists in any situation is compounded in the case of banks. One would, accordingly, expect even higher risk premiums to be charged. A bank wishing to access credit can reduce the risks of lending to it by maintaining the value of its assets above the sum of its liabilities. The difference between these two amounts is, of course, the company's net worth, a concept roughly equivalent to that of a company's "core" capital. Any company, including a bank, should seek to optimize its capital structure by increasing its capital until the point at which the cost of additional equity is greater than the anticipated benefit in reduced risk premia on its borrowings (assuming, of course, that the company has projects that will yield sufficient returns to justify the costs of obtaining additional capital).[8] Thus, while lenders may be unwilling to advance credit at *any* price to a company with zero or negative capital, generally the market does not so much "demand" that borrowers maintain certain capital levels as it does price credit based on the amount of capital actually maintained by the borrower.[9]

The salutary effects of a capital cushion on the cost of debt apply to *all* corporations, not just banks. However, governments generally do not impose capital requirements, except on companies in the financial sector, where special circumstances are thought to necessitate this form of regulation. Although the conventional justifications for capital requirements vary among industries within the financial sector, they rest on some combination of information problems, moral hazard, and systemic risk.[10]

The rationale for bank capital requirements begins with the fact that as deposit insurer or lender of last resort, or both, the government is

---

8. Berger, Herring, and Szego (1995) also factor in the impact of the tax advantage of debt capital and the divergence of interests between shareholders and managers on a firm's optimal capital structure.

9. A different, though not incompatible, rationale for creditors to demand certain capital levels is developed by Rochet (2004), who suggests that bank owners and managers will, as the bank's equity shrinks, lose their incentive to monitor the performance of the bank's own assets—that is, the loans it has made—since they no longer have anything to lose. Capital requirements assure that they retain the monitoring incentive. This is a particularly interesting theoretical justification for capital requirements insofar as it builds on one important economic explanation for the existence of banks—their ability to monitor users of debt capital more effectively than either nonspecialists or markets possessed only of publicly available information.

10. Traditionally, capital requirements for securities firms are a kind of sophisticated consumer protection device that assures full and quick repayment of all counterparties in the event of the firm's insolvency. The celebrated 1998 bankruptcy of Long-Term Capital Management (an unregulated hedge fund rather than a securities firm regulated by the Securities and Exchange Commission) led to some concern over the impact of a large security holder's insolvency on markets generally, as well as on its counterparties. The existence of systemic-type risks attendant to a securities firm failure, while contested by others, was

potentially the largest creditor of a bank. It thus shares the interests of other creditors in avoiding the costs of financial distress and preventing the exploitation of opportunistic behavior by shareholders and management of the bank. However, the government's extensions of credit differ significantly from those of private lenders. As to the lender-of-last-resort function, actual extensions of credit are rare. When they do occur, the central bank (or other lenders of last resort) should theoretically be able to set the terms for its lending. In practice, the lender-of-last-resort function is most likely to be exercised in exigent circumstances that include the possibility of contagion in other parts of the banking system should the troubled bank fail. Thus the central bank may believe it has little practical choice, in either financial or political terms, but to provide the credit needed to keep the bank afloat. At least for those banks considered too big to fail, the government's lender-of-last-resort role can be understood as providing a vaguely specified, but still significant, guarantee of the bank's obligations.

With respect to deposit insurance, the government is an explicit guarantor of the bank's debt to insured depositors. Precisely for this reason, an insured depositor will generally not care whether the bank is adequately capitalized. The depositor's relative indifference to the bank's condition essentially negates the possibility of runs and panics, of course. But the resulting moral hazard also expands the scope for opportunistic bank behavior and exposes the government insurer to loss, because depositors will neither demand levels of capital commensurate with the bank's ability to pay its deposits nor monitor the bank's financial condition.

Two features of deposit insurance systems further complicate the situation. First, the guarantee automatically attaches to new deposits. That is, the government has no opportunity to decide whether to extend its guarantee as new deposits are made. Second, despite a strong theoretical case for establishing a premium schedule for deposit insurance that closely tracks the riskiness of the bank, actual deposit insurance systems only weakly reflect the actual risk that the bank will not be able to repay its depositors in a full and timely fashion.[11] The government's credit exposure to its banks is thus created more or less automatically, without the particularized evaluation of the bank's capital and risk profiles that a pri-

---

obviously believed by the Federal Reserve when it acted to support Bear Stearns in March 2008. Capital requirements for insurance companies are generally secondary to provisioning requirements. Here, too, though, the principal rationale is one of consumer protection; policyholders are assumed to have neither an adequate incentive to expend the resources necessary to monitor the financial condition of the insurance company nor, even if they did, the ability to discern the actual value of the company's often opaque assets. Comparisons of the rationales and operation of capital requirements in the securities, insurance, and banking industries are presented in Basel Committee on Banking Supervision Joint Forum (2001).

11. Comparing estimates of actuarially fair deposit insurance prices with actual premiums, Laeven (2002) concludes that deposit insurance premiums are generally underpriced. Cull, Senbet, and Sorge (2004) conclude that, even in countries with risk-adjusted premia,

vate lender is assumed to make in setting the terms on which it will offer credit. The government's recourse is to regulate the bank's safety and soundness on an ongoing basis. Historically, of course, safety and soundness regulation has taken many forms. As explained in the next part of this chapter, though, capital adequacy regulation is increasingly central to safety and soundness regulation. This trend has created a closer conceptual link between one important rationale for bank regulation and the dominant regulatory paradigm.[12]

Although the justification for capital regulation begins with the government's credit exposure to commercial banks, it may not end there. Note first that the preceding account highlighted the effect of the government safety net on the perceptions and incentives of a bank's private counterparties. If the result is a belief that the bank will be bailed out by the government should it face serious liquidity or solvency problems, then private market actors may not demand that the bank hold as much capital as the terms of their credit exposures would otherwise require in order to yield an appropriate risk-adjusted return. In that event, the government's capital requirements might have to compensate for the moral hazard created with respect to all of a bank's creditors.[13]

An additional rationale is that the government can use capital regulation to reduce the chances of bank failures that cause significant negative externalities. Most obvious is the potential for systemic risk. A bank failure could endanger another bank that has extended credit to the first bank through the interbank lending market or is expecting funds from the

---

there is no effective deterrence of risk taking. These studies appear to confirm theoretical arguments, such as that of Chan, Greenbaum, and Thakor (1992), which suggested the impossibility of implementing incentive-compatible, fairly priced insurance. Freixas and Rochet (1995) conclude that fair pricing *is* feasible but that it is not desirable from a welfare perspective.

12. There is another interesting parallel in US law between the protective devices adopted by private creditors and the regulatory techniques used by government. The Federal Deposit Insurance Corporation Improvement Act of 1991 added to US banking regulation an elaborate mechanism for "prompt corrective action" by banks to bring capital levels that have fallen below requirements back up to the regulatory minimum. Although intended principally as a device to force early intervention by bank supervisors suspected of regulatory forbearance during the savings and loan debacle of the 1980s, the prompt corrective action mechanism is roughly analogous to action by bondholders or other lenders under covenants contained in their indentures or loan agreements. Acharya and Dreyfus (1989) had previously suggested that governments should price deposit insurance in the same way that private creditors would establish closure rules and covenants in their lending agreements. Similarly, Rochet (2004) suggests that his proposal for regulators to close a bank when subordinated debt prices fall below a certain level is analogous to the action a private lender would take in accordance with relevant covenants.

13. In fact, as discussed in chapter 5, nearly all banks in G-10 countries hold capital substantially in excess of current regulatory requirements. Commentators dispute, and speculate over, the reasons for this practice.

first bank for the accounts of its customers through the payments system. Since the social costs of widespread financial instability would be substantial and would not be borne solely by the shareholders and creditors of the bank whose failure triggered the crisis, the government might justify requiring higher levels of capital as an effort to align the social benefits and costs of the bank's operations more closely.

Although some academics have questioned the significance of systemic risk, particularly as credit exposure in the payments system has been progressively reduced,[14] bank regulators all appear to believe that it is real, if indeterminate.[15] Nonetheless, regulators generally seem not to invoke this justification for capital requirements, at least not explicitly.[16] To the contrary, former Federal Reserve Chairman Alan Greenspan expressly disclaimed any such justification. In his view, stated while he was chairman, the "management of systemic risk is properly the job of the central banks" and "banks should not be required to hold capital against the possibility of overall financial breakdown" (Greenspan 1998, at 167). Not all regulators have taken so clear a position, but the extensive official Basel Committee commentary on the Basel II process has not cited prevention of systemic risk as either a rationale for the existence of capital adequacy requirements or as a factor in setting them. As discussed below, systemic concerns should perhaps not be dismissed so readily in framing capital adequacy requirements, but as a factual matter they are not invoked in official justifications for Basel II.

Another negative externalities argument is that bank failures can lead to the dissipation of information on borrower creditworthiness that is costly to develop. This argument builds on an important economic explanation for the existence of financial intermediaries: that they develop information on potential borrowers and borrower projects that allows them to distinguish good loans from ill-advised ones. The costliness and often proprietary character of this information lead banks to keep much of it nonpublic, other than the signal of creditworthiness that the extension of the loan itself conveys. Banks also develop expertise in monitoring particular borrowers to protect their loans. The resulting information and ex-

---

14. For examples of such skepticism, see Scott (2005) and Benston and Kaufman (1995).

15. Indeed, the anxiety of regulators over the potential for systemic risk was dramatically illustrated in March 2008, when the Federal Reserve Bank of New York provided certain financial guarantees to facilitate the sale of Bear Stearns to JPMorgan Chase. Bear Stearns was not a commercial bank, and thus, under conventional understandings, would have had no access to the Fed's discount window or similar sources of financial assistance. The Federal Reserve Bank of New York's action, taken in the midst of the subprime crisis, has far-reaching implications for the scope and reach of financial regulation.

16. Sometimes, though, it is invoked indirectly. See, for example, the remarks of Howard Davies, then chairman of the UK Financial Services Authority, at the Basel Capital Accord Conference, London, April 10, 2001.

pertise may be lost when banks fail. In extreme circumstances, the result may be negative macroeconomic effects (Bernanke 1983).

Short of genuine systemic risk, then, bank failures can still create social costs that are not internalized to the bank and its stakeholders. Of course, whether the bank information and expertise are actually lost depends on the mode of resolving bank failures. If the bank is simply liquidated, such a consequence will follow. More often, though, bank failures result in acquisition by a stronger bank of at least the performing assets of the insolvent bank. To the degree the acquiring bank also takes on the loan officers and records of the failed bank, these informational assets should be preserved (though in practice some fraction of borrower relationships is usually lost). Even if the informational consequences are significant, then, it is possible that the more efficient way to deal with them may be through the resolution process, rather than by requiring higher capital levels to prevent insolvency.[17]

The merits of the theoretical case for capital adequacy regulation cannot in themselves justify the pivotal role it has come to play in contemporary banking law and international cooperative arrangements. For purposes of fashioning a sound regulatory system, the question of *how much* capital banks should be required to hold is as important as the question of whether they should be subject to capital requirements at all. Answering this question involves both identifying the principle for making this calculation and determining whether that principle can be implemented in a workably feasible fashion that can bear the reliance now being placed on it by banking supervisors throughout the world. Succeeding chapters will consider certain practical and administrative considerations in some detail. The remainder of this section first deals with the conceptual issue of a principle for deriving the required levels of capital and then examines the overarching practical question of how to measure the risk assumed by banks.

At first glance, the standard for regulatory capital levels looks relatively easy to set, at least as a conceptual matter. As Santomero and Watson (1977) suggested well before the Basel I process was even under way, the government should establish minimum capital requirements that equalize

---

17. Bank regulators have, in part for this reason, traditionally favored resolution of bank failures through merger or acquisition of most of the failed bank's assets, even at a higher cost to the public than would have been incurred under a simple liquidation. In the United States, such a preference is technically no longer permitted. As part of the Federal Deposit Insurance Corporation Improvement Act of 1991, one piece of reform legislation following the 1980s savings and loan debacle, Congress enacted the "least cost alternative" rule, under which the FDIC may not opt for a resolution that costs taxpayers more than would a basic deposit payout. This provision is codified in Title 12 of the United States Code §1823(c)(4). Because relatively few banks have failed in recent years, there is not an adequate basis on which to judge whether more failed banks will end up being essentially liquidated. Although experience to date is limited, most failures still result in at least partial asset acquisitions by other banks.

the marginal returns from bank capital requirements (i.e., the social benefit of reduced risk of costly bank failures) and the marginal cost of capitalization (i.e., the social cost of the reduced financial intermediation resulting from higher capital requirements). Writing in the context of a public
policy debate over the decline in bank capital, Santomero and Watson
pointed out that bankers tended to overlook the noninternalized costs of
bank failure, while regulators tended to overlook the opportunity costs of
higher bank capital levels.

If the regulator regards systemic risk or other negative externalities
associated with bank failures to be both significant and appropriately addressed through capital requirements, then required capital levels should
be set such that the present value of the expected return from an additional dollar of lending would just exceed the reduction that would be
achieved in the risk of all losses attendant to bank failure (also discounted
to present value) by adding that dollar to the bank's capital. On the other
hand, if the regulator is convinced by the academic skeptics of systemic
risk or, like Greenspan, believes systemic risk is best insured directly by
the central bank as lender of last resort, then the marginal social cost/
benefit calculus should be similar to that of the marginal costs and benefits to private actors.[18] Indeed, Greenspan has said that "a reasonable principle for setting regulatory soundness standards is to act much as the market would if there were no safety net and all market participants were fully
informed" (Greenspan 1998, at 167).[19] From the lender's perspective, the
capital "demanded" is that which provides a buffer against insolvency at
the level of probability associated with a competitive return on its investment at the contractual price of the capital (i.e., the interest rate). Thus, for
example, if a bank held capital sufficient to reduce the probability of insolvency within a year to less than 0.1 percent, the approximate level associated with an "A" rating from Standard & Poor's, then credit to the
bank would be priced as an A-rated bond would be.

The difficulties in calculating the amount by which additional capital
in a particular bank would reduce systemic risk are self-evident. This
alone might argue for Greenspan's standard. Whether or not an additional
amount is to be added to reduce the possibility of the negative externali-

---

18. Of course, social costs of bank failure other than those associated with systemic risk
might be regarded as relevant by some regulators. They are omitted from the formula in the
text because they are likely to be less significant in most instances than systemic risk and
because, as suggested earlier, some of these costs might be better addressed in the procedures for resolving failed banks rather than through capital requirements.

19. As will be discussed more fully below, the Greenspan standard is not necessarily a theoretically sound one. Nor does it necessarily reflect official thinking at all times or of all supervisory agencies. In its comprehensive review of the banking system following the savings
and loan crisis of the 1980s, the Treasury Department indicated that judgments about systemic risk were an essential part of capital regulation (US Department of the Treasury 1991).

ties associated with a systemic banking crisis, the regulatory standard would have to require *at least* the amount of capital that an uninsured private market actor would demand were it faced with the credit exposure borne by the government. Counterfactual analysis is always problematic, of course. Yet even in theory, the Greenspan standard does not provide a basis for setting capital levels as readily as one might have thought.

As already observed, the government's credit exposure to its banks is unlike that of private market actors. The latter extend funds to a firm in exchange for a promise to repay those funds, with an agreed amount of interest, at some later date. As noted earlier, the "demand" of a private creditor that the firm hold a particular amount of capital is really only a condition for charging a lower risk premium or, in some instances, for being willing to lend money at *any* rate. In seeking a competitive, risk-adjusted return, the private lender sets the interest rate it charges in light of what the firm's capital position suggests about the risk of nonpayment. However, the credit exposure of the government insurer of deposits is not a loan but a guarantee that a bank will repay depositors their principal and accrued interest should the bank fail. Hence the government cannot simply mimic the behavior of private lenders who take the capital position of the bank into account in extending credit with, or counterfactually, without, the safety net in place. The Greenspan standard of "acting much as the market would" must instead be applied by reference to what a private guarantor or insurer would do.

A private insurer would presumably price its service so as to provide it with funds that, when invested, would yield sufficient returns both to cover losses from insured events and to produce a competitive rate of return on the insuring company's own capital. Because government insurers of deposits do not—for a combination of technical, policy, and political reasons—set premiums in this way, capital requirements serve at least in part as a surrogate for a risk-sensitive premium structure. By this reasoning, a capital requirement mimicking private market behavior would require banks to hold capital at a level that reduced the probability of losses to the insurance fund such that returns on investment of the premiums actually charged would cover those losses and provide a reasonable rate of return.

Needless to say, no regulator sets capital requirements this way.[20] Governments are not in the business of insuring deposits in order to earn a competitive return on their investments. The government is the appropriate

---

20. Note also that, were a government to set capital requirements based solely on its interests as a guarantor of bank deposit liabilities, it would have to require different capital levels of banks with identical portfolios of assets but different ratios of deposits to total liabilities. Although the first-best preference of a guarantor is that the insured firm not fail at all—a point that argues for similar capital levels for similarly risky banks—the second-best preference of a guarantor is that the insured firm have sufficient assets at insolvency to pay off higher-priority debt such as deposits.

insurer of deposits largely because private insurers lack the information necessary for them to price the insurance efficiently. The risks of an "extreme" event, in the form of a banking crisis resulting in massive losses to a deposit insurance fund, defy the sort of probabilistic quantification based on experience that insurers conduct to anticipate losses from insured events. In the face of this uncertainty, an insurer cannot calculate the resources it may need and thus cannot price efficiently. If it charges very high premia, the insurance will be little used and vulnerable to severe adverse selection effects. But if the pricing is such as to produce the level of insured deposits that exist in G-10 countries today, a banking crisis would likely bankrupt an insurer, except of course an insurer that is also the government lender of last resort. If depositors are aware that the insurer may be unable to pay off all deposit losses, they may revert to the depositor behavior associated with bank panics and runs in the absence of insurance. In either case, the outcome will be problematic. Hence the strong case for government involvement in the deposit insurance system, notwithstanding the moral hazard distortions attendant to it.

Thus, as with safety and soundness regulation more generally, a government's decision on required capital levels necessarily involves a trade-off between the cost of capital to firms and individuals, on the one hand, and the possibility of disruptive bank failures, on the other. This trade-off may be implicit or explicit. The point, though, is that setting a target probability of bank insolvency within a year at, for example, less than 0.1 percent cannot be justified on the grounds that this is the level at which a firm earns an "A" rating from Standard & Poor's. Instead, it must be defended on the grounds that it produces the optimal social trade-off between the cost of capital and the economic risks of bank failure.[21] The kinds of data relevant to such a calculation obviously include the probability density functions of bank insolvencies, but they do not determine the outcome, as, in theory, they determine the interest rate to be charged on credit privately extended to the bank.[22]

---

21. There can certainly be private participation in a deposit insurance system, as, for example, in Germany. The nominally insured amount of deposits is much lower in Germany than in most other G-10 countries. Moreover, public authorities are involved in the management of the system. Most importantly, of course, the safety net does not disappear just because a deposit insurance system is nominally private. The lender-of-last-resort and discretionary powers of government authorities provide a critical backstop to deposit insurance schemes, whether public or private. In Germany, there are guarantees applicable to certain financial institutions, as well as deposits. Thus, even if a country were to have a fully privatized system of deposit insurance, in all probability the private insurer and the banks would understand that the government would provide assistance in a full-blown crisis. The pricing of deposit insurance would clearly be affected by the shared perception that the government would step in during an extreme tail event.

22. As mentioned earlier, the magnitude—and perhaps existence—of systemic risk is questioned by some academics. However, for purposes of setting a conceptual standard for capital

All this has three implications for capital regulation. First, it undermines conceptually the Greenspan standard of doing what market actors would do in dealing with the bank in the absence of a safety net. Second, it suggests that regulators cannot, in setting capital regulations, avoid taking at least implicit positions on the relative seriousness of systemic risk and the socially optimal trade-off between capital costs and bank failures.[23] These factors are very hard to quantify. But that fact just emphasizes that no financial model, whatever its sophistication, can provide an unassailable formula for capital requirements. Third, precisely because of the difficulties in making such determinations, *minimum* regulatory capital requirements should not be confused with *optimal* capital levels.[24]

The foregoing mention of probability functions of bank insolvencies returns us to the second issue identified at the beginning of this section—the measurement of risks that have been, or might be, assumed by banks. The trade-off between bank stability and reduced financial intermediation can only be assessed if one knows how much stability (i.e., reduction in chances of bank insolvency) one will buy with a particular capital requirement. While regulators have been generally vague or evasive on the first question of how much stability they want to achieve (and why), they have become progressively more focused on accurate assessments of what it will take to achieve a given level of stability. In fact, Basel II is almost entirely an effort to more accurately calibrate the risks faced by banks.

A bank is exposed to various risks that could spell serious trouble for its continued solvency. The taxonomy of bank risks is extensive and can vary among analysts. Most obvious and, traditionally at least, most important is the credit risk that its borrowers will not repay their loans in a full and timely fashion. Market risk, the potential for decline in the market value of assets, becomes more significant as a higher proportion of a bank's assets is traded rather than lent, whether in a universal bank or as a result of a commercial bank's business in financial instruments such as derivatives. The concept of operational risk has been characterized in

---

requirements, the actual extent of systemic risk is considerably less important than what relevant market actors *believe* about both the extent of systemic risk and the likely response of government officials confronted with one or more large bank insolvencies. The generally lower capital levels of large banks may, for example, reflect market beliefs that these banks are considered too big to fail by the government and will thus be kept liquid and solvent during periods of stress.

23. This fact has been recognized by regulators in the past. Consider, for example, the following observation in a study by the US Department of the Treasury (1991, at II-17): "The question of the appropriate level for minimum capital ratios for insured depositories is essentially the question of what is the maximum level of depository system risk that society is willing to tolerate."

24. See Estrella (1995) for an explanation of the differences between optimal and minimum capital levels.

somewhat different ways but, as defined by the Basel Committee itself, it is the risk of loss resulting from "inadequate or failed internal processes, people and systems or from external events [including] legal risk" (Basel Committee 2004d, 144). Thus the current notion of operational risk includes everything from the physical disruption of a bank's operations by natural or human agents to a massive liability judgment entered against the bank. Interest rate risk refers to the problems that ensue for banks when rising interest rates result in nearly immediate increases in the bank's cost of capital, while most of its assets (in the form of previously extended loans) will continue to provide only the lower rate. Liquidity risk refers to the possibility that a bank will have inadequate cash or other liquid assets available to it to meet the demands of depositors or other short-term debtors, even though the bank is solvent on a balance-sheet basis. Liquidity risk is inherent in the maturity mismatching that characterizes the bank's economic role of financial intermediation. Attention is sometimes also paid to reputational, political, and other risks.

If one can quantify the risks that the banks themselves face, then regulators can better judge how much capital will be needed as a buffer to contain the chances of bank insolvency below a specified level. Of course, quantifying with precision the risks that banks face is a daunting task. Some risks, such as political risk, seem to defy any reasonable quantification. Credit and market risk, which both refer to the value of assets held by the bank, have been the strongest candidates for quantification. More controversially, as will be seen later, Basel II also attempts to quantify capital requirements for operational risk.

As the next section describes, even before Basel I most countries computed capital requirements or guidelines by reference to the amount of assets held by the bank. The simple ratio of capital to assets is a crude but, in its own way, comprehensive measure that covers all risks—or at least all risks that are susceptible to significant mitigation through the maintenance of higher capital levels. Two obvious problems with this simple approach are, first, that it does not cover off-balance-sheet items, and, second, that it does not account for the very different risks of loss that inhere in different portfolios of assets. A bank that lends exclusively to start-up companies without established income streams is exposed to significantly higher risks of loss than a bank with the same amount of assets that lends exclusively to AAA-rated governments and corporations. Thus, the sustained regulatory tendency of the last few decades has been in the direction of a "risk weighting" of assets to reflect better the chances of loss to the bank. Technology has had an enormous impact here, first with the regulatory embrace of value-at-risk models for calculating capital requirements for market-traded assets and, with the coming of Basel II, credit risk models for calculating capital requirements for loans. The results of this tendency are seen most starkly in the A-IRB approach; thus, analysis of the reliability of the new metrics will be deferred until chapter 5, where Basel II is considered in detail.

Evolving Role of Capital Regulation

Capital levels of credit institutions have long been subject to some form of supervisory scrutiny. Many jurisdictions traditionally required a minimum capitalization before promoters of a new bank could obtain a charter and begin business. Regulatory monitoring of capital levels at operating banks has existed in the United States since at least the early years of the 20th century. The relative sophistication of that monitoring evolved fairly steadily thereafter, particularly following World War II. Despite this long-standing concern with bank capital, explicit minimum capital requirements were not imposed by US bank supervisory agencies until the 1980s. Until almost that same time, formal capital regulation was either undeveloped or wholly absent in the other Basel Committee countries. In the intervening decades, capital requirements have not only been formalized, they have also become the most important form of prudential regulation.[25] This steady shift in regulatory approach has occurred as, and to a considerable extent because, the banking industry itself has been substantially transformed.

From about 1900 to the late 1930s, the most frequently cited measure of capital among US regulators was the ratio of capital to deposits, rather than the now familiar ratio of capital to assets or risk-weighted assets. A number of state banking regulators required this capital/deposit ratio to be at least 10 percent (Orgler and Wolkowitz 1976). The Office of the Comptroller of the Currency adopted the same minimum ratio for national banks in 1914 and even proposed amending the National Bank Act to make this a statutory requirement. This may seem a peculiar requirement, insofar as losses to banks arise from deterioration in *asset* quality, not from deposits. However, this ratio does give a rough idea of a bank's leverage and, until the federal deposit insurance system was established in 1933, it accordingly gave a rough indication of how well depositors would be protected should the bank fail. By the late 1930s, the newly created Federal Deposit Insurance Corporation (FDIC) had shifted emphasis to the ratio of capital to total assets that is still used today as the basis for one of several US capital requirements (though no longer in most other Basel Committee countries).

During World War II, US banking agencies essentially suspended application of administrative guidelines for capital ratios, in recognition of

---

25. While a host of supervisory practices and requirements arguably equals capital requirements in importance, it is clear that the latter are the most important set of prudential *rules*.

the fact that banks were purchasing massive quantities of US government securities to help fund the war effort (Hempel 1976). Application of a capital/assets requirement would obviously have constrained those purchases. After the war, a prolonged period of experimentation with capital ratios began, during which there was substantial divergence in practice among the federal banking agencies. The Office of the Comptroller of the Currency and the Federal Reserve Board shifted their focus to the ratio of capital to "risk assets," in recognition of the now commonplace observation that the optimal amount of bank capital varies with the riskiness of its assets. "Risk assets" were defined as total assets less cash and government securities. The FDIC, meanwhile, returned to its use of the capital-to-total-assets ratio.

The discrepancies in agency practice actually increased as time went on. During the 1950s, the Federal Reserve Board further refined its approach to capital requirements. It began assigning risk weights to major categories of items on the asset side of a bank's balance sheet before calculating the capital ratio (Orgler and Wolkowitz 1976, Hempel 1976). The Office of the Comptroller of the Currency, however, did not adopt this rough precursor to the Basel I approach to risk-weighted capital adequacy.[26] To the contrary, the comptroller's office actually disclaimed reliance on capital ratios until 1971 and, throughout the 1970s, insisted that it used capital ratios only as a helpful indicator of potential problems at national banks. It emphasized the importance of a variety of nonfinancial factors in assessing the adequacy of a bank's capital.[27] The FDIC, meanwhile, continued to use several variations on the total-capital-to-assets ratio.

Obviously, capital adequacy was unlikely to play a central role in bank regulation in the United States or elsewhere, so long as there were such basic differences between regulators themselves over the appropriate use and characteristics of capital ratios. However, three interrelated developments combined to produce a focus on capital levels that became progressively more important in banking regulation within the Basel Committee countries and eventually in the rest of the world as well: first, a decline in capital ratios; second, the upheaval in the finan-

---

26. During this period, the role of the Federal Reserve in bank regulation was actually quite circumscribed. It was the primary federal regulator only for state banks that were members of the Federal Reserve System. However, the Federal Reserve also has regulatory authority over all bank holding companies. As that corporate form became the dominant mode of bank ownership in the 1960s and 1970s, the Federal Reserve's influence on bank regulation increased.

27. The practice of the Office of the Comptroller of the Currency, more fully explained in Orgler and Wolkowitz (1976, 70–71), was itself a precursor to the system for evaluating banks that is now used by all US bank examiners. Thus, the comptroller's office examined— among other factors—the quality of management, the liquidity of assets, the history of bank earnings, and the liquidity of assets. Eventually, the comptroller's office began experimenting

Figure 2.1   Equity as a percent of assets for all insured commercial banks, 1840–1989

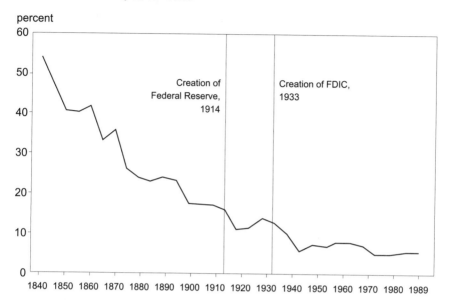

percent

FDIC = Federal Deposit Insurance Corporation.

Note: Ratio of aggregate dollar value of bank book equity to aggregate dollar value of bank book assets.

Source: US Department of the Treasury (1991).

cial services industry; and third, the modification or outright abandonment of many traditional regulatory devices for assuring bank safety and soundness.

Figure 2.1 shows that bank capital levels had been in decline for well over a century. Most of the decline in the late 19th century was the result of wholly salutary developments such as the growing efficiency and transparency of the US financial system. The decline in the 1930s and 1940s was probably due in significant part to the establishment of the federal deposit insurance system, though the general economic environment of the Depression and then war undoubtedly played a part as well.

---

with classifying assets before calculating the ratio even within the context of its use as a guideline rather than a rule. In 1978, Congress established the Federal Financial Institution Examination Council, composed of the federal agencies with responsibility for regulating depository institutions, and instructed the agencies to establish uniform standards for bank examination. The council adapted the comptroller's list of factors and instituted the CAMEL system, which provided for an evaluation of a bank's capital level, asset quality, management, earnings, and liquidity. Subsequently the council added sensitivity to market risk, hence the current acronym of CAMELS.

Table 2.1 US bank capital ratios, 1970–81

Year	All banks	Banks with assets over $5 billion	17 largest banks
1970	6.58	5.34	5.15
1971	6.32	5.10	4.91
1972	5.95	4.71	4.43
1973	5.67	4.14	3.82
1974	5.65	3.82	3.49
1975	5.87	4.13	3.94
1976	6.11	4.51	4.00
1977	5.92	4.32	3.86
1978	5.80	4.13	3.76
1979	5.75	4.03	3.61
1980	5.80	4.12	3.69
1981	5.83	4.21	3.83

Note: All figures are percentages of equity capital to total assets.

Source: Board of Governors of the Federal Reserve System (1983).

There followed a plateau in overall capital levels that lasted a quarter century. Capital levels began to decline again in the 1970s, ultimately provoking the concerns that led, among other things, to Basel I.

As shown in table 2.1, the capital levels of US banks as a whole actually declined only modestly during the 1970s—by about 11 percent. Indeed, the capital ratios of the smallest banks (less than $300 million in assets) actually *increased* significantly. The decline in overall US capital levels was predominantly due to significant declines in the capital levels of the biggest banks. The last column in table 2.1 shows that the capital levels of the 17 largest multinational banks, which as a group had been identified for special concern by banking supervisors, declined by about 25 percent. The capital levels of the somewhat larger group of all banks with assets in excess of $5 billion had declined almost as much, by about 21 percent. The distribution pattern of capital declines thus reinforced systemic fears, since the failure of a very large bank is far more likely to trigger a banking crisis.

The risks to the banking system resulting from lower capital levels did not appear purely hypothetical. In the space of a few months in 1974, the Herstatt Bank failed in Germany and the Franklin National Bank failed in the United States. Because it had massive foreign exchange exposure, Herstatt's failure threatened the payments systems of other countries. Franklin, the 20th largest bank in the United States, posed less of a threat, but only because the Federal Reserve provided lender-of-last-resort assistance, including to the bank's London branch (Dale 1984, Spero 1980). These failures spurred creation later that year of the group of banking regulators that has become known as the Basel Committee on Banking Supervision, as national authorities saw the need for increased cooperation to prevent further banking problems that could cross national boundaries.

The decline in capital levels was due in significant part to the changed environment in which commercial banks were operating. They faced both turbulent macroeconomic circumstances and a structural change in competitive conditions within their own industry. The world economy was turned upside down in the 1970s. First, the Bretton Woods system collapsed. The resulting volatility in foreign exchange rates was something contemporary bankers had never faced and, until they developed the requisite expertise and financial hedging instruments, something that could play havoc with the profitability of foreign lending. Then came the oil embargo and worldwide recession of 1974–75, which resulted in increased defaults on loans and an across-the-board decline in credit quality. The stagflation of the late 1970s was the third of this harsh trio of developments. Even as credit quality continued to deteriorate, double-digit inflation eroded the profitability of loans that *were* being serviced.

Within their own industry, commercial bankers were caught in a kind of business pincer, squeezed by more competition on both the buy and sell sides of their business. On the sell side, companies that had historically been among the most important purchasers of bank credit found other, cheaper sources of capital. Most important were the burgeoning public capital markets, whose growth and consequent increased liquidity made them attractive to more and more companies. The maturation of the commercial paper markets, for example, gave large companies an alternative to bank loans for a source of short-term operating capital. Domestic banks were also facing more competition in meeting the borrowing needs of the largest corporations, both directly from foreign banks and through the expanding euromarkets.

On the buy side, net savers found more lucrative destinations for their money than bank accounts. The period of prolonged high inflation in the 1970s accelerated the flight of funds from traditional savings and checking accounts to money market funds organized by investment companies as part of their families of mutual funds. The money market funds were able to grow so rapidly because of the increasing supply of commercial paper, which was a principal investment of the money market fund managers because of its high credit quality and short duration to maturity. The resulting increased liquidity further expanded the commercial paper market. Thus, the competition to banks on the buy and sell sides was mutually reinforcing. From 1976 to 1982, the assets of US mutual funds rose from less than $3 billion to about $230 billion.[28] The days when most of

---

28. Later, middle- and upper-middle-class Americans would begin investing in equities through broadly diversified mutual funds. Thus, even after interest rate caps on depository institution accounts were lifted, prospects for recapturing the funds that had fled to money market funds were limited.

the savings of most Americans could be found in commercial and savings banks were fast becoming history. As a result, the time when banks had access to a vast pool of capital, the cost of which was arguably suppressed by the federal deposit insurance system, was also drawing to a close.

Faced with increased competition, and thus decreasing margins, in their established customer base, many banks looked for new sources of revenue. In part, they simply tried to lend more, placing downward pressure on their capital ratios. They also sought permission to engage in new lines of business such as data processing and leasing. They asked the Federal Reserve for a liberal interpretation of the Glass-Steagall Act's restrictions on commercial bank affiliation with investment banks. Even within their traditional business of extending credit, they looked for new borrowers. The most attractive new borrowers were those without access to public capital markets who would presumably be willing to pay a higher premium for loans. Of course, borrowers without access to public capital markets are usually less creditworthy. Thus banks were taking on more risk in a search for higher returns. One source of much new business for the largest multinational banks was sovereign borrowing, which would have disastrous consequences for both debtors and creditors in the 1980s. In short, banks responded to competition by extending more credit to riskier borrowers, a development that reduced capital ratios immediately and exposed the banks to more losses down the line, as a result of which capital ratios would decline further.

The competitive squeeze on banks was related to some of the traditional prudential rules that had restricted their activities. Since World War II, the US bank regulatory paradigm had significantly restricted competition in banking. The Federal Reserve's Regulation Q, which limited the interest rate banks could pay on deposits, restrained price competition among banks. Prohibitions on interstate branching protected banks from incursions by large out-of-state banks. The Glass-Steagall Act forbade investment banks from engaging in the "business of banking." For several decades the result had been a fairly quiet and predictably if unspectacularly profitable industry. Beginning in the 1960s, however, and more obviously in the 1970s, technology, competition, regulatory relaxation on nonbanks, and a growing public financial sophistication were fast eroding the insulation that protected commercial banks. Now the same regulations that had protected banks appeared to remove many options for a competitive response. In an inflationary environment, the Regulation Q cap of 5 percent on interest rates left banks vulnerable to the money market funds. The restrictions on branching foreclosed realization of economies of scale by the more efficient banks. Restrictions on affiliations between commercial and investment banks barred the former from realizing what many believed to be a potentially important source of earnings diversification. Reserve requirements put domestic banks at a disadvantage in competing with offshore banks.

Citing these developments, commercial banks urged relaxation of these and other constraints on their ability to enter new markets and new lines of business.[29] The regulatory agencies, concerned that the banking system itself could be weakened if banks were handicapped in responding to the new forms of competition, were receptive to at least some of the calls for change. Thus began a 20-year period during which many traditional bank regulatory devices were relaxed or removed.[30] In 1980 Congress passed legislation phasing out the limits on interest rates. Two years later, the Garn-St. Germain Act authorized depository institutions to establish the equivalent of money market deposit accounts. Limitations on the activities and investments of banks were relaxed in significant ways, such as the 1980 administrative ruling that banks could compete directly with securities firms in selling commercial paper. The political heft of investment banks offset that of commercial banks in the latter's campaign for Glass-Steagall reform in the Congress and produced a stalemate that would not be broken until 1999. However, the Federal Reserve Board authorized by regulation some affiliations between commercial banks and firms engaged in investment banking—first in a quite limited way, but progressively more generously. Reserve requirements were applied to a narrower range of deposits and reduced.

Since the Depression era reforms, banking law in the United States had been based on restricting the activities, investments, and businesses of banks. Removal of so many elements of the old regulatory approach freed the banks to compete with other banks and with nonbanks making inroads into traditional banking markets. It also freed banks to fail in these new endeavors. Some of the resulting failures were quite spectacular, provoking concerns about systemic stability and costing taxpayers hundreds of billions of dollars. While the efficiency gains from the deregulatory steps promised to be substantial, the potential gap in prudential regulation was worrisome to some regulators and members of Congress. Capital regulation was the most obvious candidate to fill that gap. It appeared to be a more flexible mode of safety and soundness controls, one that could be a shock absorber for whatever difficulties banks might encounter in the new competitive environment. Since the modification and repeal of traditional constraints on banks continued after Basel I—as, for example, through the effective elimination of restrictions on geographic expansion by banks in the United States—the centrality of capital regulation in banking regulation has only increased.

---

29. For example, in responding to an argument for continuity in bank regulation put forth by then-president of the Federal Reserve Bank of New York Gerald Corrigan, an executive of Chase Manhattan Bank relied heavily on the new forms of competition faced by commercial banks in arguing for deregulation in the early 1980s (Aspinwall 1983).

30. For one comprehensive account, see Wilmarth (2002).

By 1980 the foregoing considerations led regulators in many of the Basel Committee countries to place more emphasis on capital regulation. In the United States, as in some of the other countries, the various capital ratios employed by banking regulators had not been freestanding, independent requirements so much as guidelines for supervisory scrutiny. Even where the Federal Reserve or the FDIC informally communicated the ratios they found to be generally acceptable or made known the specific levels that would trigger closer inspection, they had not published regulations with required ratios. In 1981 the banking agencies took the first of several steps that would, in the years prior to the first Basel Accord, formalize and risk-weight capital requirements.

Stating that they were "increasingly concerned about the secular declines in the capital ratios of the nation's largest banking organizations, particularly in view of increased risks both domestically and internationally," the Office of the Comptroller of the Currency and the Federal Reserve jointly published numerical capital ratios applicable to all but the largest banks (Board of Governors of the Federal Reserve System 1982, at 34). The agencies used only simple ratios of primary capital and total capital to total assets, rather than some form of risk-weighted ratio. Although the specific ratios were still characterized as guidelines for administrative action rather than independent requirements, the agencies made clear that banks with capital below a specified level would create "a very strong presumption that the bank is undercapitalized." In effect, the agencies had adopted a minimum primary capital/assets ratio of 5 percent (6 percent for small banks). The 17 banks with assets in excess of $15 billion were not covered by the guidelines, though the Board of Governors and the Office of the Comptroller of the Currency indicated that their policies with respect to these institutions "would be modified to insure that appropriate steps are taken to improve over time the capital positions of banking organizations in this group" (Board of Governors of the Federal Reserve System 1982, at 34).

The FDIC issued a separate statement establishing a "minimum acceptable level" of primary capital at 5 percent of assets for the banks for which it was the primary federal supervisor (FDIC 1981). The FDIC did not include a total-capital-to-assets ratio requirement. While observers also noted the FDIC's disagreement with the Board of Governors and the Office of the Comptroller of the Currency on the issue of whether different-sized banks should have different minimum ratios, the more important point was that all three federal regulators of commercial banks had converged around a presumptive minimum capital requirement.

The Latin American debt crisis accelerated the trend toward a central role for capital adequacy requirements in US banking regulation (Kapstein 1994, Reinicke 1995). The significant exposure of several large US banks to defaulting sovereign debtors such as Brazil and Mexico called into question the adequacy of their existing capital levels to absorb the losses they would incur on these assets. This lending was itself a response by the banks to the competitive squeeze mentioned earlier. Developing-country lending commanded a substantial premium over other significant categories of bank lending, and in the 1970s, few if any developing countries had access to public capital markets. Between 1978 and August 1982 (when Mexico defaulted), the total developing country debt held by the largest money-center banks had increased from $36 billion to $55 billion. This portfolio of assets was more than twice the total capital and loan loss reserves of the largest banks (FDIC 1997). So critical was the problem that a quick resolution of the crisis through restructuring and write-downs might have rendered one or more of these banks technically insolvent.

In May 1984, the problems in US banking reached a new stage with the crisis faced by the Continental Illinois National Bank, at that time the seventh largest commercial bank in the country. Continental was a poster child for the threats to banking safety and soundness posed by changes in the industry and its regulation. Despite the challenging environment confronted by commercial banks in the 1970s, it had grown quickly, in part by engaging in considerable high-risk lending (FDIC 1997). It had substantial exposure to Mexican sovereign debt and had $1 billion in participations originated by Penn Square Bank, itself a now-notorious example of a bank that had financed its aggressive (and imprudent) lending in part by taking advantage of the deregulation of interest rates to purchase high-cost deposits. Concerns about its financial condition turned quickly into an electronic run on Continental Illinois, as large domestic and foreign account holders shifted their deposits elsewhere. Regarding the bank as too big to fail and unable to find a healthy merger partner, the FDIC kept the bank afloat through a de facto nationalization.

These unhappy developments prompted regulators to reconsider their exemption of the largest money-center banks from the minimum capital ratios applied to all other banks in 1981. In June 1983, the Board of Governors and the Office of the Comptroller of the Currency jointly announced application of the capital requirements to those 17 multinational banks.[31] However, this belated action was not enough to assuage influential members of Congress who believed that more rigorous capital regulation of large banks could have mitigated the effects of the crisis on the US economy (FDIC 1997). Indeed, the June extension of capital rules to the "big 17" was regarded as an effort to stave off congressional action.[32]

---

31. Based in part on an internal Federal Reserve Board memorandum, Reinicke (1995) hypothesizes that the banking agencies took this step not only because of congressional pressure but also because 12 of the 17 large banks had improved their capital ratios to at least the minimum levels set by the guidelines.

32. In fact, compliance turned out not to be difficult for most of the 17. By year's end, only Citicorp and Manufacturers Hanover had ratios below the 5 percent minimum level. See Robert Trigaux, "Multinationals Raise Primary Capital Ratios: Only Citicorp, Hanover Fall Below 5% Minimum," *American Banker*, December 1, 1983, 3.

When the large banks bluntly opposed both congressional calls for additional capital regulation and the banking agencies' five-point plan for strengthening supervision of international lending, their resistance actually increased the likelihood that Congress would legislate on the topic (Reinicke 1995).

Meanwhile, the shift toward more generally applicable and binding capital ratios was abruptly called into question in 1983, when a federal court overturned a 1980 order by the Comptroller of the Currency requiring a national bank to increase its capital ratio to 7 percent. The court itself was not altogether clear as to the limits it was imposing on the discretion of regulators to require banks to maintain specific capital levels. However, it implied that the promulgation of industrywide capital requirements, detached from an analysis of the condition of a particular bank, might not be within the powers of the bank regulatory agencies.[33]

Already exercised over the banking agencies' failure to implement tighter capital regulation, Congress now had additional incentive to legislate, and an occasion for action had already presented itself. The Reagan administration had requested an increase in the US quota at the International Monetary Fund (IMF) as part of the general augmentation of the institution's quotas initiated to shore up its resources in the face of the Latin American problems. As would be the case a decade later during the Mexican and Asian crises, legislators of both parties reacted negatively to a request for additional US government resources that would be seen, at least in part, as intended to bail out the large banks. As Senator Jake Garn (R-UT), chairman of the Senate Banking Committee put it, "[T]he price of an $8.4 billion increase in the IMF authorization in Congress is going to be legislation so that lawmakers can go home and report that 'we did not bail out the banks'" (quoted in Reinicke 1995, 46). Thus, a variety of factors galvanized the Congress later in 1983 to pass legislation that not only expressly permitted but *required* the federal banking agencies to establish minimum capital levels for banks and bank holding companies.[34]

Following passage of the 1983 legislation, the three banking agencies moved quickly not only to apply mandatory capital levels to all US banks but also to bridge the differences among them that had marked (or marred, depending on one's perspective) previous supervisory practice in

---

33. The judicial decision in question was *First National Bank of Bellaire v. Comptroller of the Currency*, decided by the United States Court of Appeals for the Fifth Circuit in 1983. Ironically, the comptroller's office appears to have been overturned partly because of its explicit reliance on both quantitative and qualitative measures in assessing the adequacy of bank capital. The comptroller's office had given high ratings on the qualitative measures such as quality of management.

34. Later that same year, Congress included the new authority for capital regulation in §908 of the International Lending Supervision Act. The provision can now be found in §3907(a) of Title 12 of the United States Code.

the area of capital ratios. The Federal Reserve, Office of the Comptroller of the Currency, and FDIC published parallel final regulations in early 1985. Although these regulations were similar to the Fed/Comptroller guidelines of 1981 in their definitions of capital and other components of the capital calculation, they raised the minimum primary capital/asset ratio to 5.5 percent and the minimum total capital/asset ratio to 6 percent (as compared with 5 and 5.5 percent, respectively, for noncommunity banks in the 1981 guidelines).[35]

Almost as soon as the agencies had published these regulations, they turned their attention to developing risk-based capital requirements. As indicated by the Federal Reserve in its preliminary proposal, the agencies were responding to a series of worrisome developments: the growth in off-balance-sheet assets that were not covered by the simple capital ratios,[36] the apparent regulatory arbitrage of some banks in shifting toward higher-risk assets in the face of the simple capital ratio requirements, and "the growth and change in the nature of risks to which banking organizations have become exposed" (Board of Governors of the Federal Reserve System 1986, 3977). The Fed was first to issue a proposal, which would have added an "adjusted capital measure" to the existing two capital ratio requirements. This measure divided a bank's assets into four categories based on risk and assigned different percentage weights to those assets in calculating a capital requirement. The Fed proposal also covered, for the first time in US regulatory practice, certain off-balance-sheet items such as letters of credit. This regulatory proposal never became operative, as it was subsumed into the Basel I exercise. But it reflected a convergence and evolution of views among US supervisory agencies in the direction of a risk-weighted capital requirement as a central component of banking regulation.

The increasing emphasis on capital ratios and, as noted by the Fed, risk-based ratios was not unique to the United States, with its particular combination of industry structure and regulation. However computed, bank capital ratios had declined in other Basel Committee countries. While no other country had the combination of highly developed capital markets and restrictions on bank activities that created such a severe squeeze on the business of commercial banks in the United States, the effects of adverse macroeconomic conditions, increased competition, and financial innovation were felt in banking industries everywhere (Pecchioli

---

35. One version of the parallel regulations may be found in US Department of the Treasury Office of the Comptroller of the Currency (1985).

36. Examples of these growing risk exposures included (1) an increase in standby letters of credit issued by the 10 largest banks from 7.6 percent of total assets at year-end 1981 to 11.6 percent of assets by mid-1985; and (2) interest rate swaps, introduced only in 1981, but which had grown to 14 percent of total assets by mid-1985 (Bardos 1987, 88). The latter example overstates the actual risk, since the 14 percent figure is based on the notional amounts of the swaps, rather than the amount actually at risk.

1987). As in the United States, the economic upheavals of the 1970s and early 1980s led to deteriorating asset quality. Although savers in most countries may have had fewer alternatives than in the United States, large borrowers throughout the world could seek financing from foreign banks or, increasingly, from public debt issues through the euromarkets or elsewhere. Again, as in the United States, many banks responded to the competitive pressures by offering new financial instruments that, by virtue of their novelty, posed significant risk management challenges.

The regulatory response to these developments in other Basel Committee countries was less dramatic than in the United States. But the trend was similar—removing constraints that had originally protected the competitive position of banks but now handicapped them in responding to market developments. One example was the legal separation of the banking industry based on the duration of assets and liabilities. In countries such as France, Italy, and Japan, banks were in either the short- or long-term segment.[37] Between the late 1960s and the early 1980s, France essentially eliminated these restrictions and the latter two countries significantly reduced them (Pecchioli 1987). The separation between commercial and investment banking was under pressure everywhere. Where the separation was the result of legal barriers, as in Canada and Japan, there was pressure for change. In countries that permitted banks to underwrite securities—such as France, Germany, and the United Kingdom—there was a noticeable shift in banks' business toward those activities.[38] The result was another supervisory challenge, insofar as the greater concentration of nonlending activities created a different mix of risks to be managed.

Historically, the other Basel Committee countries had placed even less emphasis on bank capital than had the United States. Norton (1995) attributes the earlier attention to capital adequacy by the Federal Reserve Board and Office of the Comptroller of the Currency to the revealed utility of capital ratios in the US practice of extensive, on-site examinations for all banks. Whatever the reason, the other Basel Committee supervisors attached little importance to capital ratios as a supervisory device. Yet just as competitive pressures and other developments in the rest of the world paralleled those affecting US banks, supervisors in the rest of the Basel Committee countries responded with a parallel elevation of capital adequacy to a key position in bank regulation during the late 1970s and early 1980s. As a group, in fact, the European supervisors had leapt well ahead of their US, Canadian, and Japanese counterparts in moving toward a risk-based standard for capital ratios.

---

37. Actually, the segmentation scheme was considerably more complicated in many instances, particularly in Japan, which traditionally limited banks' activities not just to a particular duration of assets and liabilities but also to particular kinds of borrowers.

38. See David Lascelles, "Survey of World Banking: Why the Transatlantic Deal Must Be Extended," *Financial Times*, May 7, 1987.

In 1979 France introduced a risk-related capital standard. In 1980, Switzerland and the United Kingdom both thoroughly overhauled their approaches to capital ratios. The changes effected by Swiss banking authorities were particularly striking, in a single stroke shifting Switzerland from the anachronistic capital/liabilities approach to a capital/risk-based assets ratio requirement with 15 different risk categories. German capital rules weighted certain risks differently in calculating the overall capital/ assets ratio under its Banking Act (as amended in 1985). In fact, of the nine European countries with representation on the Basel Committee in 1985, seven had already adopted some form of risk weighting in the capital ratios they had issued as requirements or supervisory guidelines.[39]

To some degree, the similarities in European regulatory evolution were the results of similar circumstances and shared analyses of the implications of changes in the banking industry. In addition, though, the trend toward convergence had been accelerated by the activities of the European Economic Community (EEC). Beginning in 1973, the European Council adopted a series of directives that required member states to harmonize various elements of bank supervision. The Banking Coordination Directive of 1977 provided, among other things, for the establishment of capital ratios.[40] Though only for "observation purposes," this directive began the process that eventually led to the post-Basel I directives that set capital requirements for all credit institutions and investment banks in the European Union. As we will see, the harmonization efforts of the Basel Committee and the European Community/Union have, in significant ways, reinforced one another ever since.

By 1985 all but two of the other 11 countries represented on the Basel Committee had formal capital adequacy ratios in place.[41] In 1986 Japan published ratios for supervisory guidance, probably motivated by what turned out to be a vain effort to resist British and US pressure for mandatory measures. Thus, only Italy had no specified ratios for capital levels by the time the Basel Committee began discussions in earnest on a harmonized set of capital requirements. Regulatory authorities in Japan and, as already noted, the United States soon thereafter issued their own proposals for some form of risk-based asset capital requirements.[42] Canada, although

---

39. Luxembourg was still using the capital/liabilities ratio that had been abandoned decades before in the United States. As noted below, Italian supervisors did not use any specific ratios—general or risk-based—either as supervisory guidelines or as requirements.

40. This directive may be found in the EEC's *Official Journal*, no. L322, of December 17, 1977, Document Number 77/780/EEC.

41. In the 1980s, there were only 12 Basel Committee member countries. Spain was invited to join in 2001.

42. Japan's 1986 policy innovation involved a simple capital/assets ratio, whose value varied from 4 percent for banks without overseas branches to 6 percent for banks that did have an international presence (Pecchioli 1987).

not using a risk-weighting system, took off-balance-sheet items into account in its guidelines for overall capital ratios, thereby covering the second principal purpose of moving from simple to risk-weighted capital ratios. In six countries the capital ratios were binding regulatory requirements: Belgium, France, Luxembourg, Netherlands, Sweden, and Switzerland.[43] In Germany, if a bank's capital ratio fell below the published guideline, it created a rebuttable presumption that capital levels should be raised. In the United Kingdom and Canada, the published capital ratios were not technically binding but were used by supervisors in assessing banks under their jurisdiction.

Excessive significance should probably not be attached to whether the ratios were, by their own terms, mandatory. While the Bank of England's guidelines were not mandatory, supervisors were quite fastidious in their reviews of capital levels and, in many instances, insisted on higher levels of capital than those indicated by the published ratios. Conversely, it was not clear how rigorously some of the countries with nominally mandatory guidelines actually interpreted and enforced them. The required ratios varied. So too did the number of "risk buckets"—the weighting categories for assets posing different levels of presumed riskiness—vary from four in Germany to 15 in Switzerland. There were also important differences in the operative definition of capital for purposes of calculating the numerator in the ratios, notably on the issues of whether subordinated debt and unrealized capital gains on bank assets would qualify. Beyond these differences, however, the pattern of capital ratio requirements revealed a common trend, both toward attaching more importance to capital regulation and in converging around a risk-weighted ratio approach. This conceptual convergence was very significant in setting the stage for the harmonization of capital requirements in Basel I.

Conclusion

As has recently become apparent, the supervisory trend toward dominant reliance on capital requirements for prudential regulation has been at least in part misguided. The problem arises partly from the shortcomings of regulatory models in achieving accurate risk sensitivity and partly from the importance of liquidity, reputational, and other risks not captured by capital regulation. Still, the theoretical case for bank capital requirements as an important part of national prudential regulation is broadly accepted among regulators and most academics. Even at the level

---

43. Descriptions of capital adequacy requirements as they stood in the 1980s in the Basel Committee countries and certain other countries may be found in Dale (1984) and Pecchioli (1987).

of theory, however, the optimal level of capital requirements depends on judgments about the trade-off between the social benefits of efficient capital allocation and the social costs of bank failure or financial crisis. The practical task of setting minimum capital requirements depends on a similar set of judgments.

Those who believe the actual degree of systemic risk is small must still, in considering the optimal level of capital requirements, take into account the beliefs of market actors as to the likelihood that government authorities will rescue a specific bank whose failure is imminent. That is, the widespread assumption that regulators consider certain banks too big to fail may affect the pricing of private credit extended to those banks.[44] The importance of this consideration is that optimal capital requirements cannot convincingly be set solely through the use of even the most sophisticated institution-specific formula. It also suggests an argument for capital requirements being set higher for banks likely to be regarded as too big to fail. It is unclear to what extent this factor might offset the traditional presumption that the greater degree of portfolio diversification at large banks argues for lower capital requirements at larger banks.[45] Of course, the preceding observations do not preclude the possibility that, as a practical matter, minimum capital requirements might best be set through a formula-based approach. They simply remind us that, even at a conceptual level, capital regulation is necessarily part art as well as part science. As W. P. Cooke, the first chair of the Basel Committee, once wrote: "There is no objective basis for ex-cathedra statements about levels of capital. There can be no certainty, no dogma about capital adequacy."[46]

The evolution of capital adequacy regulation in Basel Committee countries in the late 1970s and early 1980s reveals two points of some significance in evaluating the Basel II approach as a substantive regulatory paradigm for an international arrangement. First, the movement toward risk-based capital/asset ratios was widespread even before the United States and the United Kingdom began their campaign for an international arrangement based on this method. Indeed, although the Federal Reserve Board had tentatively moved in that direction in the 1950s, the United States was a laggard rather than a leader on risk-based approaches in the

---

44. The reasons why banks may be considered by government regulators as too big to fail are not limited to classic fears of a domino-like collapse of the whole banking system. For example, the fact that there are only two banks that offer a full range of settlement services on US Treasury securities may make those banks too important to fail in the eyes of the Treasury Department (Stern and Feldman 2004).

45. It is also worth noting that bank regulators, including the Basel Committee, have not been explicit about the trade-off between bank stability and increased financial intermediation that is necessarily made in any capital requirement.

46. W. P. Cooke, "Banking Regulation, Profits and Capital Generation," *The Banker*, August 1981.

1970s and early 1980s. In at least one respect, then, the time was ripe for an international arrangement.

Second, however, there was substantial variation in the required capital levels, the definition of capital, and other features of the capital/risk-based asset ratios. As will be seen in the next chapter, this variance may have arisen in part in the search for competitive advantage by national banking authorities for their own banks. Yet it may also have been explained by variations in the nature of the banking industries, the regulatory and accounting context in which banking regulation existed, and other factors peculiar to each country. If any such differences remain important today, they may call into question the appropriateness of a highly detailed harmonized approach to capital adequacy. Conversely, if the highly detailed approach nonetheless allows for substantial national variation in implementation, then one may question exactly what purpose is served by such a high degree of harmonization.

3

Basel I

By 1985 nearly all the Basel Committee countries placed substantial regulatory reliance on specific capital ratio calculations that were increasingly based on a risk-weighting of assets. However, there was considerable variation in the mode and details of capital regulation among the 12 countries and little apparent interest among most supervisors in harmonizing their capital regulations. Yet within just a few years, the parallel national regulatory threads had been tied together in an international arrangement that set forth a unified approach to capital adequacy. This chapter briefly recounts the origins of the first Basel capital accord, the political economy of which provides a valuable basis for comparison with Basel II. The chapter goes on to discuss the structure, effectiveness, and shortcomings of Basel I, which together define the starting point for the Basel II process of revision. For all the continuity in the Basel Committee itself, there are substantial differences in the political circumstances at the time the two processes began and in the relative complexity of the capital rules in the two frameworks. These differences help explain why the Basel II exercise produced a flawed outcome.

Origins of the Accord

Basel I was motivated by two interacting concerns—the risk posed to the stability of the global financial system by low capital levels of internationally active banks and the competitive advantages accruing to banks subject to lower capital requirements.[1] These interacting concerns made the Basel I process a kind of hybrid of an international trade negotiation and a regulatory exercise. Although national competitiveness concerns became more dominant as time went on, the Basel I process never departed from the premise that capital ratios of internationally active banks needed to rise. The Basel I accord and its implementation largely fulfilled this intention.

The same 1983 legislation by which Congress mandated that capital requirements be set for US banks also prodded the Federal Reserve Board and the Treasury Department to seek an international agreement on capital standards.[2] The US banks whose travails had triggered congressional scrutiny had realized fairly quickly that they were in no position to stop legislation on capital adequacy. In the midst of the Latin American debt crisis and the necessary replenishment of International Monetary Fund resources by the United States and other industrialized countries, most members of Congress were not receptive to objections that increased capital levels would be costly and/or unnecessary for large multinational banks. They were more receptive to complaints that the stricter capital regulation contemplated by Congress would seriously disadvantage the competitive position of those banks. The banks could argue, with some justification, that explicit or implicit government safety nets in other countries allowed foreign banks to maintain lower capital levels than comparable US banks.

Of particular concern were the Japanese banks, which had grown rapidly in the preceding decade and would continue to do so during the negotiations that produced Basel I. Their pace of asset accumulation was astonishing. In 1974, the year in which the Basel Committee was created, only one of the 10 largest banks in the world (based on total assets) was Japanese (table 3.1), and in 1981 this was still the case. By 1988, however, nine of the 10 largest banks in the world were Japanese. Equally striking was the growth in the proportion of assets of the world's largest banks accounted for by Japanese institutions. In 1981 Japanese banks held just over a quarter of the total assets of the world's 20 largest banks; by 1988 the Japanese share had swelled to over 70 percent.[3]

The rise of Japanese banks had been mirrored by a decline in the position of US banks. In 1974 Bank of America, Citicorp, and Chase Manhat-

---

1. For chronological narratives of the origins and negotiation of Basel I, see Kapstein (1994), Norton (1995), and Reinicke (1995).

2. Specifically, §908(b)(3)(C) of the International Lending Supervision Act read: "The Chairman of the Board of Governors of the Federal Reserve System and the Secretary of the Treasury shall encourage governments, central banks, and regulatory authorities of other major banking countries to work toward maintaining and, where appropriate, strengthening the capital bases of banking institutions involved in international banking."

3. The national shares of the top 20 banks' assets were as follows, with the figure for 1981 followed by the 1988 figure in parentheses: Japan, 26.6 percent in 1981 (71 percent in 1988); France, 23.2 (12.8); United States, 18.2 (4.4); United Kingdom, 15.3 (8); Federal Republic of Germany, 8.6 (3.7); Canada, 4.2 (0); Brazil, 3.9 (0).

Table 3.1   The world's 10 largest banks, 1974, 1981, and 1988

Year/rank	Bank	Assets (billions of dollars)
1974		
1	Bank of America (US)	56.7
2	Citicorp (US)	55.5
3	Chase Manhattan (US)	41.1
4	Group BNP (France)	34.7
5	Barclays (UK)	33.3
6	Crédit Lyonnais (France)	32.8
7	Deutsche Bank (Germany)	32.4
8	National Westminster (UK)	31.9
9	Dai-Ichi Kangyo (Japan)	28.9
10	Société Générale (France)	27.7
1981		
1	Bank of America (US)	115.6
2	Citicorp (US)	112.7
3	BNP (France)	106.7
4	Crédit Agricole (France)	97.8
5	Crédit Lyonnais (France)	93.7
6	Barclays (UK)	93.0
7	Société Générale (France)	87.0
8	Dai-Ichi Kangyo (Japan)	85.5
9	Deutsche Bank (Germany)	84.5
10	National Westminster (UK)	82.6
1988		
1	Dai-Ichi Kangyo (Japan)	352.5
2	Sumitomo (Japan)	334.7
3	Fuji (Japan)	327.8
4	Mitsubishi (Japan)	317.8
5	Sanwa (Japan)	307.4
6	Industrial Bank of Japan (Japan)	261.5
7	Norinchukin (Japan)	231.7
8	Crédit Agricole (France)	214.4
9	Tokai (Japan)	213.5
10	Mitsubishi Trust (Japan)	206.0

Source: *The Banker*, various issues.

tan were the three largest banks in the world. Although Citigroup and Bank of America remained the top two in 1981, Chase had fallen to 15th. By 1988 the three largest US banks—Citigroup, Chase, and Bank of America—were only the 11th, 39th, and 41st largest banks in the world, respectively. The US share of assets of the world's top 20 banks declined from 18.2 percent in 1981 to 4.45 percent in 1988.

In fact, this was a period of significant overall growth in the assets of all international banks, with the largest banks growing extraordinarily

Table 3.2 Capital ratios of selected large banks, 1981 and 1988

Bank	1981 rank	Capital ratio (percent)	1988 rank	Capital ratio (percent)
Dai-Ichi Kangyo (Japan)	8	3.26	1	2.41
Sumitomo (Japan)	11	3.13	2	2.55
Fuji (Japan)	13	3.51	3	2.75
Mitsubishi (Japan)	14	3.25	4	2.58
Sanwa (Japan)	17	3.36	5	2.46
Citicorp (US)	2	3.54	11	4.84
BNP (France)	3	1.28	12	2.83
Barclays (UK)	6	4.66	14	5.57
Crédit Lyonnais (France)	5	0.95	16	3.02
National Westminster (UK)	10	5.10	17	6.11
Deutsche Bank (Germany)	9	3.10	19	3.78
Chase Manhattan (US)	15	4.77	39	4.34
Bank of America (US)	1	3.54	41	4.45

Note: The capital ratios are simple leverage ratios of capital to total assets.

Source: The Banker, various issues.

rapidly. From 1974 to 1988, the assets of the top 300 banks in the world grew nearly sevenfold, from \$2.2 trillion to \$15.1 trillion (de Carmoy 1990).[4] But during these 15 years the assets of the Japanese banks in this category increased by a factor of greater than 13, while the assets of the US banks represented among the top 300 did not even triple. The attention of US bankers and some policymakers was directed toward this divergence in relative growth rates and the market share changes that came along with it. Notably, the capital ratios of both Japanese and American banks had moved inversely to their market shares. Table 3.2 shows that, while the market rank of the top five Japanese banks rose from between 8th to 17th worldwide in 1981 to first through fifth in 1988, their capital ratios all declined from well over 3 percent to roughly 2½ percent. Meanwhile, the capital ratios of the largest US, French, British, and German banks all increased during this same period, as their market shares all fell.[5]

---

4. Given the depreciation of the dollar, the global numbers are in real terms less impressive than the nominal dollar figures. However, the growth was still substantial.

5. As discussed in more detail below, Japanese supervisors allowed banks to include in their calculations of capital most of their unrealized gains from their holdings of equities and real estate, a practice that would become a key point of contention in the Basel negotiations. If those unrealized gains are taken into account, the capital levels of the Japanese banks were calculated at around 5 percent, not much different from those of US banks when elements of capital idiosyncratic to the United States were included (IMF 1989). Of course, the concerns of German and other supervisors about the Japanese practice were borne out when the asset bubble burst and the assets held by Japanese banks declined dramatically in value.

US concerns about Japanese banks were, in fact, very much of a piece with contemporaneous complaints about Japanese steel, autos, and semiconductor companies. Increases in market share were often attributed to unfair advantages that the Japanese firms enjoyed. In the case of banks, the most important of these advantages was the presumed support afforded them by the tight safety net provided by the Bank of Japan. But other complaints about the supposed competitive advantages of Japanese banks echo those heard with respect to other industries. *Keiretsu* relationships between banks and industrial concerns assured the former of much of the financing business for the latter as they expanded rapidly abroad.[6] The country's high savings rate—alleged by some critics to be the consequence of intentionally suppressed domestic demand—made capital cheaper in Japan than elsewhere. US banks charged that their access to the Japanese market was impaired, providing protection for domestic banks (US General Accounting Office 1988). There were even complaints that Japanese banks, in their quest for market share, had engaged in dumping in the euro markets by offering loans to customers at rates that could not be matched profitably by their European and US competitors (de Carmoy 1990, 125).

The similarities to a trade dispute reflected in these complaints extended to the US domestic political dynamic that eventually led to Basel I. Congressional responsiveness to the bankers' complaints that they would be competitively disadvantaged by higher capital requirements meant that, even as the regulatory agencies proceeded to implement the statutory mandate for stricter capital standards at home, they were under complementary pressure to extend those standards abroad (Reinicke 1995). Indeed, at least judging by hearings, letters, and other public expressions, congressional concern over 1983–88 was less focused on the safety and soundness of US banks (with consequent implications for taxpayer liability) and increasingly centered on issues of competitive equality between US and foreign banks. Only in the early 1990s, after the full impact of the savings and loan debacle had been absorbed, would congressional attention revert to prudential considerations and supervisory efficacy.

The international initiative undertaken by the US regulators unfolded in a way familiar to those who have studied or lived through trade policy problems. First, the imperative for an international initiative required the US agencies to resolve their own differences, so as to be able to take a unified position with supervisors from other countries. The ensuing process differed from the usual interagency meetings in preparation for a trade negotiation in that the banking agencies were changing domestic regulatory practice to reflect their converging views, rather than simply working out a negotiating position. But conceptually the two processes were similar.

---

6. Readers who lived through this period of US-Japan trade conflict may recall that the industrial companies were also said to have an unfair advantage in their access to financing. That is, both the borrower and the lender were thought to have gained unduly from the transaction.

Second, even as the initial stage of the process was under way, the regulators prodded their foreign counterparts to begin discussions on possible international convergence. When faced with a trade-related problem that has elicited pressure from business and Congress, trade officials regularly initiate consultations to see if the problem can be resolved in a relatively low-key fashion. In March 1984, Federal Reserve Chairman Paul Volcker made a presentation at the Basel Committee seeking convergence in international capital standards. This proposal was reported to have been "greeted with a yawn," notwithstanding concerns over capital adequacy that existed in other countries (Kapstein 1994, 108). The potential for negative domestic political reaction, as well as the considerable technical difficulty that a harmonization effort would entail, made supervisors in other countries reluctant to commit to more than the work they had already commissioned to study possibilities for a common framework for measuring capital ratios.[7]

A third similarity with the dynamic of many trade issues is that, faced with a sluggish international process, US officials sought leverage with recalcitrant negotiating partners by threatening unilateral measures against firms from countries that were not sufficiently forthcoming. In the trade arena, this well-known course of action is associated with the use of Section 301 of the Trade Act of 1974 and its various offshoots, such as "Super 301" and "Special 301." The banking agencies played an analogous card, specifically directed—as so many such measures were in the 1980s—against Japan.

In late 1986, the United States and United Kingdom delayed further elaboration of their own capital adequacy standards in favor of developing a common approach. This bilateral initiative bore fruit within a matter of months, a result both of their shared strong interest in an international agreement and extensive prior interaction on capital adequacy policies between supervisors from the two countries (Reinicke 1995). Once this agreement had been concluded,[8] the two countries turned up the pressure on others by intimating that they might require these capital standards of foreign banks seeking to acquire banks, or perhaps even

---

7. The study is described in Committee on Banking Regulation and Supervisory Practices (1984).

8. The Federal Reserve published the US-UK agreement as part of a proposed rule making that was based in significant part on the bilateral agreement (Board of Governors of the Federal Reserve System 1987). However, it never took effect, since it had the desired consequence of prodding the Basel Committee negotiations to a successful conclusion. This bilateral gambit worried other members of the Basel Committee, who feared that it might become a "substitute . . . for internationally negotiated compromise" (Reinicke 1995, 169). In other words, it raised the prospect that the United States and United Kingdom would determine between them the proper standards for international banking regulation and then effectively impose them on the rest of the world. This, of course, is roughly what the United States and European Community did in the earlier days of trade negotiations. It also, in a way, prefigures the trade strategy of the United States in the early 1990s, when it reactivated

doing business, in their countries.[9] Operationally, the Federal Reserve Board stated publicly that it would use a US-Japanese agreement on disclosure for banks establishing subsidiaries in host countries to require certain Japanese banks active in the United States to supply capital adequacy data in conformity with the categories and definitions in the US-UK agreement. Within a few months, and despite the opposition of many Japanese banks, the Japanese Ministry of Finance had agreed in principle to subscribe to the agreement. However, as we shall see, Japanese officials obtained an important concession from the rest of the Basel Committee as the price of their acquiescence.

With Japan on board, the United States and the United Kingdom turned their attention back to the Basel effort. The process that followed reveals a fourth set of similarities with trade negotiations, in that there was sustained attention by both the negotiators and domestic constituencies to the competitive impact of the proposed standards on *their* banks. The discussions within the Basel Committee in 1987 could decidedly be described as negotiations. The major sticking points involved disagreement over what items could be included in the definition of "capital." To some degree, the issue was a lack of congruence in definitions used by national bank regulators. Thus, for example, the meaning of loan loss reserves (or "provisions") varied among the Basel countries. In particular, French banks employed a concept of "country risk" provisions, whereby provisions might be made for potential problems with loans to a particular country, even where no loan-specific risks had been identified.[10] The Basel Committee had to sort out whether, and to what extent, these kinds of provisions should count as capital. Not surprisingly, though, these differences generally pitted a country whose banks held considerable amounts of the questionable capital component against others whose banks did not.[11] So

---

the moribund Uruguay Round of multilateral negotiations in part by negotiating the North American Free Trade Agreement and enhancing the profile of the Asia Pacific Economic Cooperation forum. These steps signaled to Europe in particular that the United States believed it had other options for expanding trade—options that could leave Europe behind if the Uruguay Round failed.

9. Reinicke (1995, 169) quotes Chairman Volcker's April 1987 congressional testimony suggesting that the United States could "move in the direction" of "mandated reciprocity," as well as comments by the head of banking supervision at the Bank of England containing a subtle threat directed specifically at Japan.

10. See George Graham, "French Win Country Risk Argument: Moves Toward a Bank Capital Adequacy Standard," *Financial Times*, March 30, 1988, 30.

11. One notable exception was Germany, whose supervisors took the position that only retained profits and paid-in shareholder funds ought to count as regulatory capital. Thus, the Germans opposed most, if not all, of the additions to the definition of regulatory capital sought by others. Germany reserved its special interest pleading for the debate over which assets should be included in which risk buckets. See Haig Simonian, "Bundesbank Chafes at Cooke Report: Reactions to a Common Definition of Capital," *Financial Times*, March 15, 1988, 35.

Japan continued to argue that most of the unrealized capital gains on bank assets should qualify as capital, while the United States argued that certain kinds of preferred stock should qualify.

Of course, these kinds of questions had to be addressed in national regulatory contexts, quite apart from Basel Committee deliberations. So, in and of itself, the consideration of such matters does not render the Basel discussions more a "trade" negotiation than a regulatory process. Questions of political economy are, in any case, as relevant for the latter as for the former. However, the Basel Committee proceedings did have some attributes that are regularly associated with trade negotiations. While the *outcome* of a trade negotiation may be cooperative in the sense that countries collectively lower their trade barriers, the negotiating process itself is not "cooperative." Domestic concern tends to be with an "us-versus-them" assessment defined by the nationality of the affected firms, rather than by the position of all affected actors. That is, it becomes a matter more of whether Japanese firms are getting advantages over US banks (or vice versa) than whether US taxpayers and the financial system generally are being adequately protected.[12]

This shift in emphasis is well illustrated by congressional attention to capital adequacy issues. As noted in chapter 2, the passage of the International Lending Supervision Act (ILSA) in 1983 was driven both by concern over the risks posed by inadequately capitalized banks and, to a somewhat lesser extent, by concern that US banks not be competitively damaged by the needed remedial measures.[13] By the time hearings on the proposed Basel Accord were held by the Banking Committee of the House of Representatives in April 1988, not a single member of the committee inquired into whether the proposal was adequate to protect the safety and soundness of the financial system. Nearly every question was focused on whether US banks (or those such as government-sponsored enterprises whose assets were held by the banks) would be competitively disadvantaged.[14]

---

12. In traditional trade negotiations, there was a presumed unity of interest between consumers in each country and exporters in all other countries: Lower tariffs would redound to the benefit of both groups. Accordingly, the negotiating dynamic that may have directly reflected the concentrated influence of significant exporting interests and import-sensitive industries would also indirectly reflect the interests of consumers. When trade negotiations extend to include domestic regulatory measures such as health or safety regulations, the unity of interests between exporters and consumers can no longer be assumed. The danger in such circumstances is that the dispersed interests of consumers will then be effectively subordinated to the concentrated interests of exporting and import-sensitive industries.

13. "To a lesser extent" because ILSA required more or less immediate action by US regulators to develop capital standards and enforcement for US banks, while urging later development of an international arrangement.

14. The single exception was Representative Paul Kanjorski's (D-PA) question whether the Fed had adequate authority to instruct securities affiliates in bank holding companies to hold more capital. This issue was less about the Basel Accord itself than about changes in domestic rules governing the affiliation of banks with nonbank financial institutions.

The importance of competitive equality concerns in prompting US and UK officials to seek an international capital adequacy arrangement thus parallels certain negotiating dynamics in trade negotiations. Yet prudential considerations also played a motivating role. Moreover, whatever the relative weights of the two factors in motivating the negotiations, it is clear that safety and soundness concerns were important once the discussions were under way. Accordingly, while the Basel Accord cannot correctly be understood solely as a cooperative exercise among national regulators, it likewise cannot accurately be characterized solely as a trade arrangement by another name.

Experience with failures of internationally active banks in the 1970s and with the more recent failure of Continental Bank in 1984 provided ample reason to be concerned with the stability of foreign banks. Linkages through the interbank lending market or the payments system meant that a foreign bank's failure could create problems for domestic banks as well. As early as 1980, the G-10 central bankers had issued a communiqué that, among other things, affirmed the importance of capital adequacy (Reinicke 1995, 160). Competitive considerations were mentioned, to be sure, but so was the fear of a financial crisis arising from deteriorating capital buffers. The annual reports of the Basel Committee in the early 1980s consistently mentioned the supervisors' concern over the erosion of bank capital levels worldwide (Committee on Banking Regulation and Supervisory Practices 1981, 1982, 1983a). Moreover, the two concerns were closely tied together in committee statements on capital adequacy. Supervisors had apparently anticipated the risks of what has since, in various contexts, become known as a "race to the bottom," whereby one country's lower regulatory standards make it more difficult for other countries to maintain rigorous but necessarily more costly standards (Reinicke 1995, 162). Thus, the competitive equality factor was understood in a more nuanced way that implicated the ability of supervisors to implement policies they considered important for safety and soundness in their own banking systems.[15]

All this, of course, took place well before the US Congress had focused on capital adequacy, much less prodded US supervisors to negotiate an international arrangement. At the end of 1982, the Basel Committee began work on a common "general framework" for measuring capital (Committee on Banking Regulation and Supervisory Practices 1984). Although the committee explicitly disclaimed an intention to harmonize substantive standards, a common set of categories and definitions would obviously facilitate comparisons of banks' relative positions and thus the ability of supervisors to evaluate the capital positions of all banks having a potential impact on their domestic financial systems. When that

---

15. This point is covered more thoroughly in chapter 6, which discusses the purposes of international arrangements on capital adequacy.

measurement framework was completed and released, the committee explicitly linked the two incentives for convergence.

> The significance of this framework is that it allows members of the committee not only to monitor trends in capital ratios over time but also to coordinate objectives and to work toward reducing disparities in capital standards. In an increasingly global marketplace, both prudential and competitive considerations argue strongly for closer coordination of standards and policies. (Committee on Banking Regulation and Supervisory Practices 1987b, 5)

Similarly, in the final version of the accord itself, the committee identified the "two fundamental objectives" of the arrangement as strengthening the "soundness and stability of the international banking system" and "diminishing an existing source of competitive inequality among international banks" (Basel Committee 1988, paragraph 3).

The precise mix of motivations for US and UK officials to seek an international capital adequacy arrangement remains subject to debate. There is a plausible, though far from unassailable, case to be made that competitive equality was the more important impetus. Even so, the international initiative was motivated in the context of a strong push to raise the capital levels of domestic banks, and prudential concerns were demonstrably important during the negotiations. As it became clear that a reasonably detailed set of harmonized capital adequacy standards would emerge from the negotiations, the national banking supervisors could not avoid evaluating those nascent standards from both competitive equality and prudential perspectives. The Basel Committee had spent its first dozen years trying to improve the system for supervising internationally active banks. It would have been an abrupt turnaround for those same supervisors to have forgotten their shared prudential concerns in negotiating a capital adequacy arrangement. The national supervisors participating in the Basel Committee have obviously regarded it as an important locus (and, during the Basel II process, the *most* important locus) for developing and refining their own approach to capital regulation. If Basel ever was a venue for US and UK regulators simply to impose their preferred standards on other financial centers, it ceased to be so very quickly. Indeed, there is more than a bit of irony in the 1980s focus on the supposed competitive advantages of Japanese banks. In light of the devastation of the Japanese financial system just a few years later and the consequent impact on Japanese (and thus global) macroeconomic performance, one suspects in hindsight that more attention might better have been paid to the risks, rather than the advantages, lodged in Japanese banks in the late 1980s.

Elements of the Accord

Once negotiations had begun in earnest, the Basel Committee reached agreement relatively quickly on Basel I (another point of difference from most multiparty trade negotiations). In December 1987, the committee released what it termed a "consultative paper" on proposed international capital adequacy standards (Committee on Banking Regulation and Supervisory Practices 1987a). The paper elicited the predictable domestic complaints that various interests of each country's banks had been inadequately taken into account. However, like trade negotiators defending an agreement that admittedly fell short of realizing all of a country's negotiating aims, banking supervisors from the Basel Committee countries defended the proposal and warned against seeking changes that could undo the compromises struck during the negotiations. In July 1988, the committee released its final version of the accord (Basel Committee 1988), which reflected only modest changes from the December proposal.[16]

The structure of Basel I followed that of the US-UK agreement of early 1987, which in turn was based on the capital adequacy measures instituted by several countries in the early 1980s and reflected the common framework of capital measurement developed by the committee in the mid-1980s. The accord, by its own terms, addressed only credit risk, while acknowledging that banks must guard against other kinds of risk as well.[17] The basic approach was to assign each asset or off-balance-sheet item held by a bank to one of five risk categories, calculate the capital required for each asset or item based on the risk weighting, and then add all these amounts together to produce the total minimum capital to be held by the bank. The accord created two minimum capital ratios: a bank's core capital, called "tier 1" capital by the committee, which was to be at least 4 percent of risk-weighted assets, and a bank's total capital, which included so-called tier 2 components and was to be at least 8 percent of risk-weighted assets.[18]

---

16. The two most important changes were to include perpetual noncumulative preferred stock within the definition of core or "tier 1" capital and to assign the same risk weighting for a bank's credit extended to all banks in member countries of the Organization for Economic Cooperation and Development (OECD), not just those in a bank's own country. These were concessions to the United States and France, respectively. There were several discrete changes in the risk-weighting categories, such as one permitting loans to owners of certain residential properties to be risk-weighted identically with similar owner-occupied housing. The changes from the consultative paper to the capital accord are described in Committee on Banking Regulation and Supervisory Practices (1988).

17. The committee pointed out that it had addressed country transfer risk as an incident of credit risk through its assignment of governments and banks into different risk categories based upon their country (Basel Committee 1988, paragraph 31).

18. While many readers are doubtless familiar with the Basel I approach, a simple example may be useful. Suppose a bank had only three assets on its balance sheet—a $1 million loan to a corporation, $2 million of US government securities, and a $500,000 mortgage on the borrower's principal residence. The corporate loan would be risk-weighted at 100 percent, the government securities at 0 percent, and the mortgage at 50 percent. Thus, the risk-weighted capital would be $1million + 0 + $250,000, for a total of $1.25 million. The bank would have to hold at least $50,000 in tier 1 capital (4 percent of $1.25 million) and $100,000 in total capital (8 percent of $1.25 million).

Thus, the key elements of the accord were the definition of the two capital measures, the allocation of assets among the risk categories, and the conversion factors by which off-balance-sheet items were made equivalent to assets for risk-weighting purposes. Of these, the definition of capital was the most contested during the negotiations. The approach of using dual definitions of tier 1 and tier 2 capital had been developed during the common measurement framework exercise that had been completed in September 1986. At that time, the committee had agreed that shareholders' equity, retained earnings, and other disclosed reserves satisfied the essential conditions for regulatory capital—that it be paid up, freely and permanently available, able to absorb losses in the course of ongoing business, represent no fixed charge on the earnings of the bank, and rank below the claims of all creditors in the event of liquidation (Committee on Banking Regulation and Supervisory Practices 1987a, 12). The committee went on to note that some of its member countries included other items in their definitions of regulatory capital:

> This diversity in national capital definitions reflects differences in accounting practices as well as in supervisory policies. While members of the committee recognize that these additional elements, where they exist, may contribute to the underlying strength of a bank, they would not necessarily have the same view of the relative quality of each element. Nor is each of these additional constituents of capital found in every national system. As [a] result it is not possible to recommend one single, generally accepted definition of capital. (Committee on Banking Regulation and Supervisory Practices 1987a, 12–13)

Consequently, the committee adopted a tiered approach to capital measurement. Core, or tier 1, capital consisted of the universally recognized elements of shareholders' equity, retained earnings. The accord added noncumulative perpetual preferred stock to this list after persistent advocacy by the United States. Other elements—such as revaluation reserves, subordinated debt, general loan-loss reserves, and certain hybrid capital instruments—were designated as tier 2 capital. In retrospect, the most important of these accommodations to various national interests was the provision permitting up to 45 percent of a bank's unrealized gains from securities it holds to be included in tier 2 capital. This provision was considered crucial for Japanese banks, with their extensive holdings of securities that had, on paper, appreciated far beyond their purchase prices. The fact that this appreciation was the result of a massive asset bubble would become painfully evident within a short time of the framework's release.[19] The uneasiness with which these tier 2 elements were accepted by some Basel Committee members (particularly the German authorities,

---

19. Though Japanese government officials had originally proposed that 70 percent of the appreciated value of the securities be counted as tier 2 capital, even the 45 percent outcome was considered a major negotiating victory.

Box 3.1 Definition of capital in Basel I

Capital Elements

Tier 1

- paid-up share capital/common stock
- disclosed reserves

Tier 2

- undisclosed reserves
- asset revaluation reserves
- general provisions/general loan-loss reserves
- hybrid (debt/equity) capital instruments
- subordinated debt

Limits and Restrictions

- total of tier 2 elements limited to a maximum of 100 percent of the total of tier 1 elements
- subordinated term debt limited to a maximum of 50 percent of tier 1 elements
- loan-loss reserves limited to a maximum of 1.25 percentage points
- asset revaluation reserves that take the form of latent gains on unrealized securities subject to a discount of 55 percent

Source: Basel Committee (1988).

who argued for the most rigorous definition of capital) is reflected in the limitations placed on them (box 3.1). The use of two separate capital ratios maintained a focus on core capital while accommodating many idiosyncrasies resulting from characteristic national capital structures, political pressures from banks, or both. Though initially created simply as a flexible metric for the common measurement framework, the dual capital definition was thus conveniently available as the basis for a substantive regulatory compromise.

The accord ratified and consolidated the movement toward risk weighting of assets that had been advancing in the preceding decade. As can be seen by examining the Basel I risk categories (box 3.2), the assignment of assets was based principally on the generic nature of the borrower, rather than the borrower's specific financial characteristics or credit history. Thus, all loans to nonbanking corporations were risk-weighted at 100 percent, regardless of whether the borrower was General

Box 3.2   Risk-weight categories in Basel I

0 Percent

- cash
- claims on central governments and central banks denominated in national currency and funded in that currency
- other claims on OECD countries, central governments, and central banks
- claims collateralized by cash of OECD central government securities or guaranteed by OECD central governments

0, 10, 20, or 50 Percent (at National Discretion)

- claims on domestic public sector entities, excluding central governments, and loans guaranteed by securities issued by such entities[1]

20 Percent[2]

- claims on multilateral development banks and claims guaranteed or collateralized by securities issued by such banks
- claims on, or guaranteed by, banks incorporated in the OECD
- claims on, or guaranteed by, banks incorporated in countries outside the OECD with a residual maturity of up to one year
- claims on nondomestic OECD public-sector entities, excluding central government, and claims on guaranteed securities issued by such entities[1]
- cash items in process of collection

50 Percent

- loans fully secured by mortgage on residential property that is or will be occupied by the borrower or that is rented

100 Percent

- claims on the private sector
- claims on banks incorporated outside the OECD with a residual maturity of over one year
- claims on central governments outside the OECD (unless denominated and funded in national currency)
- claims on commercial companies owned by the public sector

(box continues on next page)

Box 3.2   Risk-weight categories in Basel I *(continued)*

- premises, plant and equipment, and other fixed assets
- real estate and other investments
- capital instruments issued by other banks (unless deducted from capital)
- all other assets

---

1. Amended in 1994 to include claims collateralized by securities of public-sector entities other than central governments.
2. A 1998 amendment added to the 20 percent risk-weight category claims on securities firms incorporated in the Organization for Economic Cooperation and Development (OECD) subject to comparable supervisory and regulatory arrangements.

Source: Basel Committee (1988).

Electric or a startup firm with no proven cash flow. Blunt as this approach seemed even in 1988, it did embed in bank supervisory practice around the world the concept that capital adequacy depends on the riskiness of a bank's portfolio. A certain limited amount of national discretion was permitted in the assignment of assets to risk categories, notably in the case of claims on public-sector entities other than central governments.

The inclusion of off-balance-sheet items in the total assets of a bank for purposes of capital calculations is one of the enduring contributions of the accord. As noted earlier, the growth of lines of credit, letters of credit, underwriting facilities, and other contingent obligations had rendered simple capital/asset ratios an increasingly misleading measure of a bank's capital position. With banks having written so many such contingent obligations, the odds increased considerably that enough of those contingencies would become assets as to change the bank's capital ratio abruptly. The accord dealt with off-balance-sheet items in a two-step process. First, a conversion factor was used to "transform" the item into the equivalent of an asset. Essentially, the factor applied a discount that reflected the likelihood that the contingency would become an asset and create credit exposure for the bank. Thus a performance bond was assigned a factor of 50 percent (table 3.3), meaning that the face amount of the bond was reduced by 50 percent. Then, in the second step, this "asset equivalent" would be assigned to one of the risk categories based on the generic type of the customer/borrower, just as a balance-sheet asset would be. So, for example, a trade-related letter of credit in the amount of $1 million issued on behalf of a private company would be converted to $200,000 in the first step (20 percent conversion

Table 3.3   Credit conversion factors for off-balance-sheet items in Basel I

Instrument	Credit conversion factor (percent)
1. Direct credit substitutes, e.g., general guarantees of indebtedness (including standby letters of credit serving as financial guarantees for loans and securities) and acceptances (including endorsements with the character of acceptances)	100
2. Certain transaction-related contingent items (e.g., performance bonds, bid bonds, warranties, and standby letters of credit related to particular transactions)	50
3. Short-term, self-liquidating, trade-related contingencies (such as documentary credits collateralized by the underlying shipments)	20
4. Sale and repurchase agreements and asset sales with recourse, where the credit risk remains with the bank	100
5. Forward asset purchases, forward deposits, and partly paid shares and securities, which represent commitments with certain drawdown	100
6. Note issuance facilities and revolving underwriting facilities	50
7. Other commitments (e.g., formal standby facilities and credit lines) with an original maturity of over one year	50
8. Similar commitments with an original maturity of up to one year or that can be unconditionally cancelled at any time	0

Note: The Basel Committee provided special and extensive guidelines, not reproduced here, to deal with interest rate and foreign exchange contracts and derivatives.

Source: Basel Committee (1988).

factor) and then assigned to the 100 percent risk category (private borrower) in the second step.

Amendments

The accord provided for a transition period until the end of 1992 for full implementation by national supervisors of the minimum capital requirements. Even before the transition period had run its course, the committee had made a modest revision, clarifying the characteristics of general provisions or loan-loss reserves necessary for those items to be included in tier 2 capital (Basel Committee 1991).[20] Later the committee made several

---

20. In the aftermath of the Latin American debt crisis, the status of loss provisions was a matter of considerable importance and dispute. One element of the 1991 amendments was intended, after a transitional period ending in 1993, to exclude provisions earmarked against country risk from the calculation of tier 2 capital.

modest changes in the risk-weight categories.[21] It also twice amended the accord to permit broader recognition of netting in calculating the exposure associated with certain off-balance-sheet items (Basel Committee 1994c, 1995a). These latter changes were very important as a business matter to large banks with substantial involvement in trading derivatives. However, like the discrete alterations of the risk categories, they did not represent any evolution in the committee's conceptual approach to capital regulation.

In contrast, the 1996 amendment to incorporate market risk reflected an important departure in the committee's substantive approach to capital regulation, one that emerged from a process unlike that which had produced the original accord. In both respects, the market risk amendment exercise foreshadowed Basel II. As to substance, in addressing market risk, the committee extended its reach beyond credit risk for the first time. Moreover, the amendment provided for the calculation of capital charges for market risk using the internal value-at-risk (VaR) models employed by financial institutions, though only within certain parameters set by the supervisors. As to process, the committee engaged in a multi-year exercise that involved significant interaction with internationally active banks.

The Basel Committee's effort on market risk had been prompted in significant part by the European Union's work on its capital adequacy directive (CAD), which was issued in final form in March 1993. Because some member states permitted commercial banking and other financial activities to be conducted within the same firm, the CAD applied to financial institutions generally and covered market risk as well as credit risk. While market risk was obviously highly relevant for a universal or quasi-universal bank, it was also increasingly important to large US banks, for which derivatives trading in particular accounted for a growing proportion of their business. The persistent volatility of foreign exchange markets rendered this form of market risk more important for all internationally active banks. The creation of market risk capital requirements by different jurisdictions and the potential for differential requirements depending on the nature of the institution holding the security was an obvious challenge to the committee's goal of consistency in treatment of

---

21. These included an addition to the risk category covering claims on domestic public sector entities of claims collateralized by securities of public sector entities other than central governments (Basel Committee 1994a), an amendment to exclude from the zero-risk category any government that has rescheduled its external sovereign debt in the preceding five years (Basel Committee 1994b), and an addition to the 20 percent risk category of claims on securities firms incorporated in the OECD subject to comparable supervisory and regulatory arrangements (Basel Committee 1998). The second of these changes, though not mentioning any country, was directed at Mexico, which had joined the OECD just before the 1994–95 peso crisis.

Table 3.4   Capital charges for debt instrument market risks in the Basel Committee 1993 proposal

Issuer	Capital charge (percent)
Government	0.00
Qualifying	0.25 (residual maturity of 6 months or less)
	1.00 (residual maturity of 6 to 24 months)
	1.60 (residual maturity of over 24 months)
Other	8.00

Source: Basel Committee (1993).

internationally active banks.[22] Accordingly, in April 1993 the Basel Committee released a consultative proposal to cover market risks.

Under the proposal, banks that held securities on their "trading book," as opposed to their "banking book," would substitute the capital charge generated by the market risk amendment for the capital charge generated by the original Basel credit risk calculation. The rationale for this substitution was that items on the trading book were far more likely to be sold prior to maturity.[23] The committee followed the CAD in proposing standardized measures for quantifying risks resulting from changes in price of traded debt instruments, equity, and activities involving foreign exchange.[24] For example, in calculating specific risk, debt securities were to be divided into three categories: government, "qualifying," and "other." Qualifying securities—those of higher investment quality from private issuers—were further subdivided based on the residual maturity of the instrument. Each category was to be assigned a capital charge (table 3.4). Similarly, general market risk capital charges were to be calculated based on the allocation of net open positions (long or short) into 13 different time bands ranging from less than one month to over 20 years. Each time band had an assigned risk weight. For traded debt and equity, the market risk charge was to apply in lieu of a credit risk charge.[25]

---

22. In fact, the committee originally tried to develop a common approach to market risk with the International Organization of Securities Commissioners in order to ensure that the capital treatment of a security did not vary depending on whether it was held by a commercial bank or an investment bank. That effort failed after the US Securities and Exchange Commission objected that the emerging proposal was too lax.

23. Furthermore, of course, some securities have no maturation date at all. Also, some securities, such as equity shares, present credit risks only in an extremely broad sense of the term.

24. Thus, the market risk capital charges apply only to instruments held in a bank's "trading book," as opposed to the "banking book," on which its loans are kept.

25. A capital charge for foreign exchange risk was to apply to assets in the banking book, as well as in the trading book.

The committee styled its April 1993 paper as a "consultative proposal," noting that the "primary purpose" of the consultative process was "to seek market reactions to the specific methodologies" set forth in the paper (Basel Committee 1993, paragraph 7).[26] This invitation for comment was, to say the least, accepted. In the words of the US banking agencies, the 1993 proposal was "strongly criticized," particularly by US banks.[27] Much as they would later argue during the Basel II process, the banks complained that the proposed approach did not take account of the correlations and portfolio effects across instruments and markets, was inconsistent with their own risk measurement systems, and did not provide an incentive for banks to improve those systems through adoption of risk measurement innovations (Basel Committee 1995b). The large banks were essentially unanimous in urging the committee to permit the use of the so-called VaR models—proprietary risk management models that calculated the amount at risk for traded instruments to within a specified level of statistical certainty, based on past market movements. The committee responded by delaying its initiative in order to develop an internal model alternative to the standardized approach. A full two years passed between the initial proposal and the April 1995 consultative proposal that incorporated the alternative approach (Basel Committee 1995b).

Although the committee accepted the use of internal models for calculating the VaR in trade instruments, it insisted on a range of quantitative parameters, as well as qualitative standards to assure the integrity of the model and supporting risk management practices (Basel Committee 1995b). Most notably, the committee proposed to apply a "multiplication factor" of three times the VaR identified by the model. The committee justified this requirement based on the limitations of even the best models: Past market experience did not necessarily predict future market patterns. Moreover, VaR models by their own terms establish the amount that could be lost in a specified period of time with a certain degree of statistical confidence. By definition, then, larger losses would occur in a small

---

26. Reflecting a continuing measure of uneasiness over the legal status of committee activities, the April 1993 paper indicated that comments would be solicited by the national authorities of the Basel Committee countries and then coordinated by the committee (Basel Committee 1993, paragraph 8). This rather formalistic distinction between the committee process and the various national regulatory systems was not followed in Basel II. For each of its consultative papers as part of that exercise, the committee solicited and received comments directly and, beginning with reaction to the second consultative paper, posted all the comments it had received on the Bank for International Settlements website. This practice resembles the notice and comment administrative process required for agency rule making in the United States and other countries.

27. The banks were not assuaged by the committee's proposal, which remained in the final amendment, to create a new category of "tier 3" capital that could be used for market risk amendment purposes only. See John Gapper, "Banks Criticise New Basle Committee Plan," *Financial Times*, December 13, 1993, 23.

number of instances, which are likely to be precisely the periods of stress that could endanger a bank's liquidity or solvency. The banks criticized the constraints on their flexibility, particularly the multiplication factor.[28] In the 1996 final version, the committee provided some additional flexibility on the quantitative parameters used in the calculations, but did not budge on the multiplication factor (Basel Committee 1996). Since the VaR for market risk was to be calculated based on trading losses anticipated over only a ten-day period, the committee obviously thought its cautious approach essential.

Thus, the market risk amendment exercise prefigured not only Basel II's substantive focus on banks' internal risk management systems and risk models but also the process by which the committee arrived at its final action. Although the original capital accord had been vetted in a consultative paper, and comments received from the banking industry, the changes between consultative paper and final framework were mostly details, and the accord was finalized within seven months. The July 1988 framework was recognizably the output of the process begun by the joint US-UK proposals based on their 1987 bilateral agreement. The market risk amendment, by contrast, was completely overhauled following the April 1993 proposal, with two years elapsing before the next consultative proposal was issued, and another nine months before the amendment was issued in January 1996. As would be the case in Basel II, this conceptual overhaul was prompted by the loud and persistent complaints of internationally active banks. Moreover, while the European Union's Capital Adequacy Directive provided a precedent for the idea of a discrete market risk measure, the path-breaking 1995 proposal was developed within the committee itself.

Assessment of Basel I

The Basel Accord, like any international economic arrangement, can be judged in two ways. One basis for evaluation is whether the arrangement has been implemented and observed by states in accordance with its terms. The other basis for evaluation is whether the arrangement, as implemented, has been effective in achieving its stated ends. Basel I appears to have been quite successfully implemented, although, as noted below, the data necessary for a thorough assessment are not readily available. With respect to the efficacy of the accord in achieving its stated ends of enhancing the soundness and stability of the international banking system and reducing competitive inequality, the picture is decidedly more mixed.

---

28. See Richard Lapper, "Banks Suggest Alterations to Proposed Rules," *Financial Times*, September 7, 1995, 4; and Justin Fox, "Banks Say Trading Set-Asides Tilt Field in Nonbanks' Favor," *American Banker*, September 22, 1995, 3.

In fact, widely shared criticisms of Basel I led to the revision process that eventually yielded the new advanced internal ratings–based (A-IRB) approach in Basel II. An assessment of Basel I is particularly difficult to make with confidence at present, since the subprime crisis has yet to run its course. The crisis has revealed shortcomings of Basel I that were previously more hypothesized than observed. At the same time, though, the events of 2007 and 2008 have raised additional questions about the efficacy of the Basel II regime that replaced it.

Implementation and Compliance

Basel I provided a four-year transition period, at the end of which the minimum capital ratios were supposed to be met by internationally active banks. In assessing an arrangement such as the Basel Accord, in which states agree to certain rules or policies for regulating economic activity, the first question is whether those states have taken the requisite steps to make the rules or policies binding on private actors within their domestic legal systems. By the beginning of 1990, the necessary laws, regulations, or guidance had been enacted in Canada, France, Germany, Japan, Sweden, Switzerland, the United Kingdom, and the United States (Basel Committee 1990a). The four other G-10 countries substantially implemented the Basel rules and completed the process during 1990 in conjunction with their adoption of relevant European Community directives. The importance of implementation lay not only in the setting of specific capital ratio floors, but also in bringing into the capital ratio exercise many of the off-balance-sheet assets referred to earlier.

Timely implementation of an international arrangement is noteworthy in itself. The Basel Accord, however, was also broadly implemented by states not in the G-10, a process encouraged by the Basel Committee and facilitated by the web of relationships established by the committee with various other international groups of banking supervisors (Norton 1995, 229–33; Heyward 1992, 792–93). The committee reported in 1992 that "[v]irtually all countries outside the membership . . . with international banks of significant size have introduced, or are in the process of introducing, arrangements based on the capital agreement" (Basel Committee 1992a, 21). Like the United States and many other Basel Committee countries, numerous non-Basel countries have applied the accord's capital requirements to all their banks. The voluntary implementation of an arrangement to which these states were not party appears to have been motivated by the expectation that both capital markets and other banks would look less favorably upon banks that did not meet the Basel minimum ratios. Thus, in a development that is unusual if not unprecedented, domestic regulatory standards elaborated in a non-legally binding international arrangement among a dozen countries have been adopted by more than 100 countries that did not participate in the formulation of the standards.

The second implementation question is whether the regulations, once enacted, are effectively enforced. In other words, by the end of the transition period in 1992, were risk-weighted capital ratios in the banks of Basel Committee countries at least 4 percent and 8 percent for tier 1 and combined capital, respectively? The answer provided by the Basel Committee based on reports from the various national supervisors was affirmative. By December 1991, a full year before the end of the transition period, the 8 percent standard was said to have been met "with few exceptions" (Basel Committee 1992b, 20). Since one of the exceptions was Citicorp and the situation of many Japanese banks was becoming increasingly shaky, the tone of this appraisal by the committee of its own work may have been a bit on the cheery side.[29] However, the improvement in G-10 economies generally, and real estate markets in particular, helped lift capital levels in the succeeding few years.[30] The Basel Committee (1994d) reported that all internationally active banks met the required ratios by the end of the transition period. Contemporaneous reports at the start of the transition period reveal, sometimes with considerable specificity, the efforts of banks in the Basel Committee countries to improve their ratios.[31] The improvement in capital adequacy was ascribed by the committee "mainly" to increases in capital, though the rate of growth of risk assets had also declined. In the succeeding years, reported capital ratios for most banks in most countries continued to climb (Jackson et al. 1999). A review of IBCA Banking Analysis (and, since 1997, FitchIBCA) reports shows that, with occasional exceptions, the requisite capital levels have been maintained.[32]

The rise in capital ratios and the absence of serious banking problems in committee countries other than Japan are points in the accord's favor, but disentangling the impact of Basel from other factors that produced

---

29. Major losses incurred by Citicorp in 1991 reduced its core capital to 3.64 percent. See Alan Friedman, "Citicorps's Own Remedy Fails to Work," *Financial Times*, October 17, 1991, 27. Since tier 2 capital may not count toward total capital in an amount greater than tier 1 capital, by definition Citicorp was also below the 8 percent threshold.

30. For example, by 1993 Citicorp had improved its tier 1 ratio to 6.6 percent (IBCA Banking Analysis 1994).

31. See David Lascelles, "Banking Without Borders: The New Worldwide Capital Adequacy Rules," *Financial Times*, July 19, 1988.

32. Of the approximately 90 banks that ranked among the global top 50 in assets, only three reported tier 1 ratios falling below the mandated 4 percent level—the Shokochukin Bank in 1995, the Norinchukin Bank in 1999, and Resona Holdings, Inc. (formerly Daiwa Bank Holdings, Inc.) in 2003 and 2004. However, as explained more fully below, there are serious questions as to the accuracy of reporting by Japanese banks and regulators during this period.

these outcomes is difficult.[33] To the degree the accord *has* led to higher capital ratios, the question would remain whether societal trade-offs between banking system stability and allocation of capital to productive uses have been made at optimal levels. Similarly, the existence of a certain level of banking system stability does not tell us whether it has been reached at significantly higher cost than might have been incurred while achieving the same stability under a different regulatory approach. There has been little empirical work on any of these issues, both because relevant data is generally not publicly accessible and, in all likelihood, because of the analytical complexity that would persist even were bank records completely available. Thus, the assessment of the accord that follows is necessarily largely suggestive. Of course, the same can be said of the assessments upon which policymakers have based their decisions to supplant Basel I.

There is little question but that the risk-adjusted capital ratios of banks in committee member countries rose following adoption of Basel I. A Working Party on Bank Capital and Behavior established to evaluate the impact of Basel I as the committee began the Basel II exercise concluded that the average capital level had risen from 9.3 percent in 1988 to 11.2 percent in 1996. Furthermore, the greatest increases were seen in countries whose banks had the lowest ratios in 1988 (Jackson et al. 1999, 6). These relatively high levels of capital have been generally maintained in the intervening years, as evidenced in particular by the reported ratios of the world's largest banks. In general, then, the accord's capital standards appear to have been enforced by supervisors in the Basel Committee countries. However, this conclusion must be qualified in three respects.

First, the reports that formed the basis for this conclusion were submitted by the supervisors, who had in many instances relied on self-reporting by banks. Although the role of independent auditors assures some check on the banks, the detail and rigor of examination practices differ widely among the Basel Committee countries. The committee has never really monitored the supervisory practices of its members. To the contrary, the supervisors have resisted outside suggestions that they do so. When, for example, the US General Accounting Office (1994) proposed a peer review process within the Basel Committee, the Federal Reserve Board expressed reluctance to share sensitive bank-specific information with other national supervisory agencies. Without that information, of course, serious review of an agency's enforcement of capital standards would be next to impossible. The Federal Reserve and the Federal Deposit Insurance Corporation (FDIC) also expressed concern that a peer review process

---

33. Surveying empirical research on the impact of capital regulation, Wall and Peterson (1996) concluded that the mandatory regulation prevailing in the United States since 1981 (including, of course, the early years of Basel I) was correlated with increases in bank capital levels that actually increased the buffer against failure and were not simply cosmetic. The effects of Basel I were not specifically addressed.

might disrupt the "harmonious relationship" that had developed among the regulators. The rigor of each supervisor's enforcement of the capital standards is not directly appraised, and thus the validity of reported capital levels is potentially subject to question.

This is not to say that the Basel Committee process is a mere formal exercise. In discussing the enforcement and interpretive issues that arise in the course of supervision, the participants have an opportunity to gauge the approach and understanding of their counterparts.[34] Furthermore, supervisors who have participated in the Basel Committee are virtually unanimous in asserting that the process itself nurtures trust within the committee that both facilitates cooperation in moments of crisis and provides assurance that one's counterparts share a commitment to implementation of the capital standards. There is little reason to doubt the overall conclusion of the committee that capital ratios had been raised following adoption of the accord. But there *is* reason to wonder whether, in the context of a particular bank at a particular moment, a national supervisory agency may be entirely forthcoming with its counterparts.[35]

The absence of a reliable monitoring process may have been relatively unproblematic under Basel I. In the 15 years in which Basel I has been in effect, there is little indication that supervisors have discovered misrepresentations or systematic subversion of the capital standards by any of their Basel Committee counterparts. Even in the case of Japan— discussed more fully below—it appears that the rest of the Basel Committee was well aware of the fiction of adequate capital maintained by Japanese banking supervisors in their prolonged and ultimately misguided efforts to muddle through the banking crisis rather than take aggressive corrective action.[36] However, this institutional shortcoming in

---

34. Soon after publishing the Basel I Accord, the committee established a mechanism for addressing interpretive questions arising from the accord itself or from the creation of new financial instruments. This mechanism was explicitly designed to avoid significant competitive inequalities (Basel Committee 1990a). However, the discussions preceding the publication of an agreed interpretation would also give the supervisors considerable insight into the practices and thinking of their peers.

35. This reluctance need not be attributed to bad faith or parochialism. More likely a national supervisor fears that, should it divulge to its counterparts that one of its large bank's capital ratios have dipped dangerously low, the counterpart supervisors would quietly advise *their* banks to avoid large exposures to the troubled institution. The result could be a crisis for the institution in the interbank lending market that need not have arisen. Of course, this rational reluctance to divulge also means that a banking crisis might develop that could otherwise have been averted through a coordinated limitation of excessive exposures by any one bank to the troubled institution.

36. One piece of evidence for this proposition is that the Federal Reserve Board had not approved a Japanese bank application for any significant expansion in the United States for more than a year before Basel I even took effect. This posture was believed by many to be designed to force Japanese banks to charter separately capitalized bank subsidiaries in the

the Basel process has, as will be seen in chapter 6, more profound implications for Basel II.

The second important qualification to the conclusion that the accord has been effectively enforced relates to the ways in which national authorities may have stretched the meaning of the Basel I provisions in their own supervisory activities. Notably, in the 1990s numerous countries had authorized their banks to consider as tier 1 capital a range of what the committee described as "innovative capital instruments," some of which were hybrids that offered tax deductibility on payments made by the issuer while maintaining enough equity characteristics to qualify as capital. Needless to say, the assurance provided by a given capital ratio declines considerably if the meaning of "capital" is expanded sufficiently. By 1998 some members of the Basel Committee were concerned enough to provoke a discussion and, after a period of disagreement, eventually put together a consensus on guidelines for such instruments.[37]

In one respect, this outcome shows the potential effectiveness of the Basel process in identifying deviant or questionable national practices and producing an agreed upon interpretation. On the other hand, this experience underscores both the potential for such divergent national practices and the committee's continuing failure to address comprehensively the critical issue of the definition of capital. The former concern is underscored by reports soon after the committee's statement on acceptable forms of capital that Germany would continue to permit its banks to count as tier 1 capital a hybrid instrument that, contrary to the committee's guidelines, was not permanent.[38]

A third qualification centers on Japan. The protracted financial crisis and related stagnation of the Japanese economy for over a decade serve as a cautionary tale of the potential harm to a nation from inadequate banking supervision, regulatory forbearance, and the moral hazard effects of government support for banks. The resolution costs of the crisis likely exceed 20 percent of GDP, a figure several orders of magnitude larger than that associated with any other banking crisis in a mature economy during

---

United States, rather than have Japanese bank branches or offices dependent on the capitalization of the home bank. This tactic, in turn, was thought to be related to the undependability of data on the capital position of Japanese banks. See Karen Shaw, "Japan's Lax Regulation Backfiring," *American Banker*, December 22, 1992, 4.

37. See Bank for International Settlements, "Instruments Available for Inclusion in Tier 1 Capital," press release, October 27, 1998.

38. See George Graham, "German Banks Win Concession: Basle Committee Compromise Allows Germans to Continue to Raise Diluted Form of Capital," *Financial Times*, November 9, 1998, 4. It appears that Germany, having failed in its earlier efforts within the committee to maintain a narrow definition of capital, eventually decided to act upon the old adage "if you can't beat 'em, join 'em."

the past 30 years (Basel Committee 2004d).[39] The relevance of this experience for evaluating Basel I may seem limited, insofar as the onset of the crisis was in 1992, before the accord was required to be fully implemented into national regulatory systems. Moreover, the causes of the crisis, which reached back well before Basel I had been negotiated, implicated fundamental characteristics of Japanese macroeconomic and regulatory policies—the expansion and then bursting of equity and real estate asset bubbles, the traditional "convoy" regulation of banks, de facto public guarantees of bank solvency, and the destabilizing manner in which deregulatory steps were taken.[40] Indeed, one of many lessons that might be drawn from the Japanese experience is the importance of assuring that banks *do* maintain adequate capital levels.

Although two recent studies undermine the view that Basel I had no effect on the behavior of Japanese banks,[41] it is reasonably clear that the capital standards have never been fully enforced in Japan. To some degree, this is understandable. The very existence of a serious banking crisis presumes that significant numbers of banks are in a weakened or insolvent position. Forcing capital ratios up in such circumstances could further constrict credit and thus be counterproductive to the economy as a whole.[42] Moreover, the delays in resolving the crisis, while costly to the Japanese economy, are attributable more to larger political and policy failures than to a lack of enforcement of the Basel standards as such.

Beyond these larger issues, however, the *reported* capital positions of Japanese banks during the crisis period have never reflected accurately the capital actually available as a buffer against bank losses. Of course, the provision of the accord permitting inclusion of 45 percent of a bank's unrealized capital gains as tier 2 capital is partly responsible. The rapid

---

39. One hopes that the aftermath of the subprime crisis will not supercede the Japanese episode on this list.

40. Useful accounts of the origins and progression of the crisis may be found in Hoshi and Kashyap (2004); Basel Committee (2004d); Calomiris and Mason (2003); Fukao (2003); Shimizu (2000); and Cargill, Hutchison, and Ito (1997).

41. However, Peek and Rosengren (2005) find in their empirical study confirmation of the generally-held impression that Japanese banks continued lending to their most troubled borrowers so that they would not have to write off their earlier loans to these same customers. Their corollary finding that banks close to required minimum capital ratios were even more likely to engage in this "evergreening" behavior suggests that those requirements had *some* influence on bank behavior. Using a panel of Japanese bank balance sheets for the period 1982–99, Montgomery (2005) finds that asset portfolios were highly sensitive to tier 1 capital requirements, as manifested in such behavior as substitution of zero-risk assets for corporate loans.

42. Unfortunately, as described by the Peek and Rosengren (2005) article discussed in the preceding footnote, Japanese banks continued lending to their most troubled borrowers, rather than directing their available lending to sounder businesses.

decline in the Nikkei following its peak in 1989, and the consequent decline in nominal Japanese bank capital, surely confirmed the worst fears of the German authorities who had opposed permitting banks to include unrealized equity gains and other soft measures in their capital calculation. This point, however, goes more to the appropriateness of the standards in the accord—considered in the next section—than to whether it has been implemented and enforced. Of more concern for present purposes are the upward biases in Japanese bank capital figures brought about by accounting and regulatory practices that have not been sanctioned in Basel I. Three such practices have been identified by researchers.

First has been the enormous problem of bad loans. Japanese banks substantially underreserve against recognized bad loans (Fukao 2003). More importantly, throughout the prolonged crisis Japanese banks have badly underreported the number of bad loans that they held (Hoshi and Kashyap 2004). Accurate estimates of the number of bad loans and adequate provisioning against those loans would obviously reduce the amount of unimpaired capital held by the banks.

Second is the generous accounting treatment of so-called deferred tax assets, which are tax credits arising from past losses that can be used to offset future profits. Japan does not limit the use of these credits as balance-sheet assets even when—as has been the case—there is little chance of profits against which these credits can be taken during the five years until the deferred tax assets expire (Hoshi and Kashyap 2004).[43] Fukao (2003) has attempted to measure the impact of these biases on actual, as opposed to reported, capital levels. He finds that, by 1999, deferred tax assets accounted for over 15 percent of the book value of the capital of Japanese banks, a figure that rises to more than 40 percent by 2003 (Fukao 2003). Using the adjusted capital figures calculated by Fukao as the numerator in a ratio in which risk-adjusted assets of all Japanese banks is the denominator suggests that the risk-adjusted tier 1 capital levels of Japanese banks as a whole was only 2 percent.[44]

A third source of bias in capital figures is not taken into account in Fukao's calculations, which focus on tier 1 capital. In the transitional period between the conclusion of Basel I and its effective date of December 31, 1992, nonconforming banks in all the G-10 countries were forced to adjust by raising their capital ratios. Where possible, they issued new equity capital, though this became increasingly difficult as the global economy dipped into recession. Thus, most had to pursue a combination of measures

---

43. Hoshi and Kashyap (2004, 15) rightly question whether even limited tax-deferred assets should count as capital because they do not serve as a buffer for unexpected losses and, in their words, "they become useless exactly when the buffer is needed."

44. It should be noted that Fukao relies upon Bank of Japan reports for the risk-adjusted asset figures.

to reduce the size of their risk-weighted assets by converting higher-risk assets into zero-risk government securities and measures to increase tier 2 capital. Issuance of subordinated debt was one means of achieving the latter aim. Japanese banks pursued both approaches (Ito and Sasaki 2002). However, much of the subordinated debt issued by Japanese banks is held by insurance companies, much of whose debt is held in turn by the banks themselves (Hoshi and Kashyap 2004). In essence, the banks lent money to the insurance companies so that the insurance companies could buy subordinated debt from the banks. This practice is a variation on "double gearing," a practice whereby the same capital is used simultaneously as a buffer against risk in two or more legal entities. The Basel Committee and other international groups of financial supervisors have consistently warned of the need to prevent double gearing.[45]

As noted earlier, regulators around the world were hardly deceived by the practices just discussed into believing that Japanese banks were adequately capitalized. With its financial system enfeebled for a decade, the question was how bad the situation was, rather than whether there was a problem. Still, the persistence of what one former Japanese bank regulator has called the "obscured capital ratios of Japanese banks" (Nakaso 2001) leaves considerable doubt that reported capital ratios would have been reliable even in better times and, accordingly, that the Basel capital standards would have been well enforced.

Effectiveness

Even substantial compliance with the rules of an international arrangement may not achieve the stated purposes of that arrangement. Conversely, depending on the circumstances, full compliance may not be necessary to make considerable progress toward achieving those ends. How, then, did the reasonably good compliance with Basel I rules fare in promoting the soundness of internationally active banks and competitive equality among banks from different nations?

Safety and Soundness of Internationally Active Banks

Establishing a causal connection between the increased capital ratios and the Basel I requirements is considerably more difficult than demonstrating that those ratios have increased. The Basel working party surveyed empirical work comparing bank behavior with and without capital require-

---

45. The double-gearing problem is particularly likely to arise within financial conglomerates, where there is common ownership of the two entities, thus complicating the problem of determining consolidated capital (Joint Forum on Financial Conglomerates 1999). But regulatory concerns exist whether the entities are commonly owned or simply cooperating with each other to meet their own regulatory standards.

ments and concluded they did not "demonstrate conclusively" that the requirements led banks to hold higher capital ratios than they otherwise would have (Jackson et al. 1999, 15).[46] The problem is that it is very hard to isolate the effects of capital requirements from other variables such as market discipline, changed economic conditions, or increased supervisory scrutiny. However, it is quite plausible that capital requirements are themselves positively correlated with market discipline and enhanced supervisory oversight. The latter correlation is reasonably obvious: Supervisors may focus more intensively on capital levels if there are quantitative minimum requirements in place. The possible link between capital requirements and market discipline is more intriguing. As discussed in chapter 5, market demands on banks seeking the lowest risk premium on their borrowing may themselves be based on existing regulatory requirements. The market, that is, may be demanding some buffer above whatever regulatory requirements have been set. To the degree this explanation is valid, the increase in capital ratios may be fairly attributed—at least indirectly—to the Basel I requirements. At the least, Basel I can claim to have been an important piece of a broader set of supervisory and market changes that increased both the attention paid to capital levels and the levels themselves.

Similarly, the absence of banking crises in the Basel Committee countries between 1992 and 2007—with the important exception of the special circumstances in Japan—is consistent with the proposition that the accord has been effective but hardly proves it. The stability of the banks was particularly impressive during the two significant emerging-market financial crises and several other events that could have roiled one or more national banking systems. The contrast with the fallout from the Latin American debt crisis in the 1980s is self-evident. Of course, the record of Basel I was marred in its waning days by the severity of the subprime crisis. Although, as of this writing, outright bank failures have been limited, the stability of some US and European banks was called into serious question by their extensive recourse to special lending arrangements created by central banks in response to the deterioration of assets and consequent impairment of credit markets. Depending on events in the next few years, this crisis may in retrospect be cited as proof of the shortcomings of Basel I or, perhaps, of capital regulation more generally.

Yet even with respect to the stability of banks for that first 15 years, factors other than capital requirements made contributions; better risk management practices, including risk-based pricing of both corporate and retail lending, apparently played an important role. For example, Shuermann (2004) finds that spreads between syndicated bank loans and

---

46. Subsequent research calling into question the relationship between higher capital requirements and the increase in actual capital levels includes Ashcraft (2001) and Kleff and Weber (2005).

corporate bonds narrowed by about one-third between the 1990 recession and the 2001 downturn, evidencing more risk sensitivity in pricing. Banks also made increasing use of risk-spreading devices such as credit derivatives during this period. Another factor was a relatively benign interest rate environment, with inflation largely under control for over a decade, and with aggressive action by central banks to maintain market liquidity in the face of financial dislocations in emerging markets and the popping of asset bubbles. Finally, in the 15 years after the accord took effect, there was no serious recession in the Basel Committee countries (other than in Japan) on the order of those seen in the mid-1970s and early 1980s. Thus, neither the capital requirements nor risk management improvements were tested in as stressful a set of conditions as those faced by banks 25 years ago.

As has already been suggested, many causes of the Japanese banking crisis substantially predate the implementation of Basel I. Once the equity and real estate bubbles burst, Japanese banks suffered both from the greatly reduced value of their assets and from unfavorable market conditions within which to attempt raising additional tier 1 capital. Moreover, the ensuing travails of the Japanese economy, and thus the condition of the banks, were exacerbated by an ill-advised monetary policy. Nonetheless, the Japanese banking crisis and its aftermath do not reflect well on Basel I. Most importantly, these events revealed the flaws in the rule permitting 45 percent of unrealized gains on equities held in bank portfolios to be included in tier 2 capital. The Nikkei 225 stock average declined rapidly by over 60 percent from its peak in 1989, continued to decline through 1992, stabilized for a few years, and then declined by over a quarter in 1997. Thus, an important part of the supposed capital buffer of Japanese banks was wiped away just when it was most needed. It is, of course, uncertain whether, even in 1989, Japanese banks could have raised more core capital. But the political compromise permitting recognition of these "latent reserves" removed any chance that the actual buffer against losses could be augmented while times were still relatively good.[47]

It is unrealistic to think that an international arrangement could have been invoked in the midst of a national crisis to force a country to enforce bank capital standards. By definition, perhaps, a set of standards that is essentially preventive in nature may not be optimal once a crisis hits. It is

---

47. There was a report at the time (Holloway 1987) that the opposition of US regulators to permitting a part of unrealized gains to be included in capital rule was "softened" by the purchase by Japanese banks of $250 million of subordinated debt from the then-troubled Bank of America. This report does not seem to have been verified by other journalists and scholars. If true, it would be an example of the dangers of trading a concession on an international rule for a short-term favor. Even if the report exaggerated the influence on US regulators, the compromise on the 45 percent rule (compromise from the original Japanese position that 70 percent of unrealized gains should count as capital) underscores the potential for suboptimal rules to emerge from negotiations—commonplace in both domestic legislation and international negotiations but still of concern.

more reasonable to expect that other members of the Basel Committee would have at least been able to monitor and understand what the condition of internationally active Japanese banks actually was. As detailed earlier, Japanese banks and regulators used numerous questionable devices to obscure the true condition of the banks, doubtless out of the well-worn hope that regulatory forbearance would allow banks to strengthen as the economy improved. It appears that the Japanese authorities were attempting to hide the true circumstances of the banks from other regulators as well as the markets. While other regulators were, as previously noted, well aware that the balance sheets of Japanese banks did not reflect their actual condition, they had no better way than market participants of determining just what that condition was.

A final observation on the effectiveness of Basel I relates to profitability. During the period since 1992 when Basel I has been fully in place, profitability among large banks has been strong by historic standards, and has been particularly high in recent years.[48] Obviously one cannot know whether profits would have been even higher in the absence of capital requirements. Equally obviously, one cannot know how much of an impact on profits those requirements would have had in a less benign macroeconomic environment than that of recent years. Furthermore, higher bank profits as such are not necessarily desirable if they come at the expense of socially desirable safety and soundness—a possible explanation that seems increasingly stronger in light of the subprime crisis. Jackson et al. (1999) found mixed evidence from a limited number of empirical studies as to whether minimum capital requirements may have had an adverse effect on bank profitability.[49] In sum, perhaps the most one can say is that Basel I did not have a noticeable negative effect on bank profits or elicit a steady stream of complaints from bankers that it has had such an effect.

Competitive Equality

Given the importance of competitive equality concerns as an impetus for Basel I, the relative dearth of academic or policy analysis of this issue is

---

48. Based on the ratio of pretax profits to tier 1 capital, an article in *The Banker* calculated that each of the three most profitable years ever for the top 1,000 banks in the world has been in the last five years—2001 (17.9 percent return on capital), 2003 (17.56 percent return), and 2004 (a staggering 19.86 percent return). See Terry Baker-Self, Beata Ghavinmi, and Matthew Dickie, "The Top One Thousand World Banks," *The Banker*, July 4, 2005, 208.

49. None of the papers attempted a direct measure of the impact of capital standards on profitability. Instead, they used as surrogates market reactions either to supervisors' announcements of capital requirements applicable to banks or to equity issuance by banks in the face of capital requirements. Jackson et al. (1999, 37) also point out that, in theory at least, regulatory requirements for—and attention to—capital levels could be viewed positively by markets and thus reduce funding costs.

somewhat surprising. Harmonized capital requirements would certainly narrow preexisting competitive advantage if other salient factors are held constant. That is, if a bank were required today to hold more capital than yesterday, but nothing else changed, then its capacity to make profitable loans or investments would have been reduced. There are, then, two questions. First, *were* other factors held constant? Increasing capital requirements may not increase a bank's cost of capital if, for example, its home government simultaneously extends its safety net in such a way as to effectively guarantee the bank's obligations to counterparties. Second, even if other factors were held roughly constant, how much competitive advantage for a nation's banks rested on divergent capital requirements relative to other possible sources of advantage? That is, how significant a narrowing can occur simply by applying convergent capital standards?

Such work as has been done to answer these questions has focused on Japan. Of course, within a few years of Basel I implementation, global concerns had shifted from the possible competitive advantage of Japanese banks to the possible collapse of the Japanese banking system. Still, studies of the period during and immediately after negotiation of Basel I suggest that the competitive leveling achievable through harmonized capital standards may have been modest. Available studies do not generally distinguish between the two questions advanced in the preceding paragraph. Thus, they do not address whether, for example, Japanese regulators enhanced safety net protections in response to Basel I or whether the prevailing levels of safety net protection were so extensive that they continued to offset some of the cost of increased capital requirements. In any case, the Japanese safety net, forbearance, and "convoy" policies are found to have limited the impact of Basel I on Japanese banks.[50]

As suggested in the second question about competitive advantage, other elements of the background business and regulatory environment may have substantial effects on the competitive position of a country's banks relative to those of other countries. Scott and Iwahara (1994) focus on the advantages from tax and accounting policies that may accrue to Japanese banks and on the possible advantages from more developed capital markets that may accrue to US banks, particularly if subordinated debt becomes more important in bank balance sheets. Zimmer and Mc-Cauley (1991) note that the capital-cost advantage of Japanese banks com-

---

50. Scott and Iwahara (1994) explain the relationship most convincingly. Acharya (2003) elaborates the theoretical relationship between capital requirements and what he characterizes as "forbearance" policies—meaning government policies to provide assistance to the existing management of insolvent banks, rather than close the banks or effect a major management shake-up. Wagster (1996) argues, on the basis of observed wealth effects for bank shareholders, that Basel I itself did not significantly affect Japanese bank fund-cost advantages.

ported with the capital-cost advantage of all Japanese companies relative to their US counterparts. And, making an important point that has often been undervalued in these debates, Kane (1991) argues that the most important source of Japanese bank competitive advantage lay not in its cost of equity capital but in its cost of funds. Exclusion of foreign banks from Japan's highly regulated deposit market was thus a major source of competitive advantage.[51]

Jackson et al. (1999, 42) briefly echo Kane's conclusion in observing that "[u]ndue weight should probably not be placed on the cost of capital in terms of international competitiveness because overall cost of funding is probably even more important." They go on to point out that nonetheless, if banks in some countries need to produce higher returns on equity than those in other countries, banks in the first group will be constrained from engaging in certain low-margin activities if those activities do not carry proportionately lower capital charges. They end their survey without reaching any conclusions on this point, a reflection of the surprising circumstance that, 15 years after Basel I took effect, the degree to which it has achieved one of its principal stated purposes still cannot be gauged with precision.

Drawbacks

A final step in evaluating Basel I is to examine its drawbacks. Some of these drawbacks are obviously related to the preceding question of how successful the accord was in achieving its stated aims. Others, though, involve actual or possible problems that the Basel I rules may have created in trying to achieve its stated aims.

Macroeconomic Effects

Bank lending patterns are naturally procyclical. During economic expansions, more borrowers are likely to have strong cash flows and more borrower projects are likely to appear viable. Indeed, bank supervisors often worry that banks unwisely lower their lending standards at the peak of expansions, as both banks and their customers underestimate the risks that will appear as the business cycle turns down. Since defaults and provisioning for potentially bad loans both decline during good economic times, economic and regulatory capital requirements are less likely to constrain lending. During an economic downturn, by contrast, cash flows are pinched and fewer projects appear promising. At the same time, banks suffer higher defaults on existing loans and must make additional provisions for deteriorating assets.

---

51. See also Kane et al. (1991).

Minimum capital requirements may further constrict lending because, when a bank's capital declines after a surge in loan defaults, it must either raise additional capital or reduce its assets. Since raising additional capital is likely to be most difficult and expensive when a bank is already suffering capital losses that bring it closer to the regulatory minimum, reductions in total assets (and, perhaps, corresponding reductions in deposits) will be the more probable response. If, as is likely to be the case, those reductions are substantially achieved through forbearance from new lending, then companies or other borrowers dependent on the bank for their financing needs may be adversely affected. Classes of borrowers, such as small businesses, that lack practical recourse to other sources of financing may be unable to obtain credit, even though they remain creditworthy. If this phenomenon is sufficiently widespread, the inability of economic actors to obtain financing could have a noticeable negative effect on economic activity, thereby deepening or prolonging the recession. Thus, the regulatory capital requirements may themselves be procyclical.

If capital requirements are based on risk-weighted assets, the bank has a third option: It can reallocate its mix to include greater amounts of low-risk assets such as government securities. Again, it may either sell existing assets that have high-risk ratings and use the proceeds to purchase the low-risk assets or reorient its future lending away from high risk–rated borrowers toward low risk–rated borrowers. Some commentators argued that the 1990–91 recession was exacerbated by the "credit crunch" that resulted from banks shifting their asset mix away from lending to companies (100 percent risk rating) toward government securities (0 percent risk rating) in response to the just-implemented Basel I requirements.[52]

As a theoretical matter, then, lending decisions without regard to economic or regulatory capital considerations and capital considerations themselves both appear to have a procyclical bias.[53] Isolating the magnitude of the marginal impact of capital requirements has not been easy. While there has been a fair amount of empirical work on this question, no clear answer has emerged. There is now good evidence that sectors particularly dependent on bank lending may be adversely affected by the constriction on lending that follows reductions in bank capital. Peek and Rosengren (1997, 2000) demonstrated that the commercial real estate industry in the United States was adversely affected during the 1990s by a reduction in lending from US branches of Japanese banks. The lending of the branches appears to have been sensitive to the capital conditions of the Japanese parents. Since the commercial real estate markets were in

---

52. The literature making this claim is reviewed in Wagster (1999).

53. Some relevant models are reviewed in Pennacchi (2005).

the United States, which was not suffering a generalized recession through much of this period, it is easier to conclude that capital levels—rather than reduced opportunities for profitable lending—caused the contraction.[54]

The situation at the macroeconomic level is less clear. One recent paper found evidence that the Peek and Rosengren sectoral effects can be generalized (Van den Heuvel 2002). However, Jackson et al. (1999) conclude that, while some studies have demonstrated a link between pressure on capital requirements and output—particularly during Japan's travails in the 1990s—there is not convincing evidence that capital requirements have had an impact at the aggregate economy level.[55] Thus, while there is an intuitive case to be made—backed by sectoral evidence and considerable theoretical work—that capital requirements in general, and Basel I in particular, can have procyclical effects, the case does not seem sufficiently strong to constitute a serious shortcoming of Basel I. This tentative conclusion is reinforced by the fact that, as capital markets expand, dependency on bank lending alone should continue to decline. In addition, of course, the positive macroeconomic effects flowing from bank stability may outweigh such negative effects as capital requirements may entail. However, as will be seen in chapter 5, Basel II has raised anew the procyclicality issue.

Regulatory Arbitrage

Basel I has been criticized early and often for permitting, even encouraging, regulatory arbitrage. Opportunities for manifold forms of regulatory arbitrage are inherent in the Basel I approach of a limited number of "risk buckets," on the basis of which all bank assets are categorized and capital requirements are assigned. The simplicity of this structure results in many assets with dissimilar actual or "economic" risks being assigned the same risk weight. It also permits changes in the form of an asset or transaction to result in a different capital requirement being assigned to what is essentially the same risk. These features of the accord obviously raise prudential concerns that the risk weighting may diverge so substantially from the actual risks entailed by certain assets that the resulting minimum

---

54. Earlier work by Peek and Rosengren (1995) attempted to isolate the effects of lower capital levels by examining the behavior of New England banks during the 1990–91 recession. Assuming that these banks were subject to essentially the same exogenous shock and thus faced similarly situated borrowers, they found that banks whose capital declined the most also cut lending the most.

55. Jackson et al. (1999) review the literature examining the relationship between aggregate bank lending and GNP and find the evidence mixed. Not surprisingly, one key point of disagreement is whether reduced bank lending follows or precedes reduced output. A later study found that adoption of Basel I requirements in Latin American countries had not had a significant effect on credit growth (Barajas, Chami, and Cosimano 2005).

capital requirements are insufficient to achieve the desired level of safety and soundness. They also create an incentive for banks to adjust their activities to exploit opportunities to lower their minimum capital levels while maintaining their return on assets or to increase their returns while keeping their capital levels constant.

The most basic forms of regulatory arbitrage arise from the fairly arbitrary nature of many of the Basel I rules. Thus, as noted earlier, the assignment of all exposures involving a particular type of counterparty to a single risk bucket means that the same risk weight of 100 percent is assigned to a loan to a large, highly profitable firm and to a loan to a startup company.[56] All else being equal, a bank will have an incentive to cherry-pick assets that yield higher returns while requiring capital set-asides similar to those for lower-yielding assets (lower-yielding because of the higher creditworthiness of the borrower, which is recognized by capital markets). This cherry-picking can be effected either through ex ante discrimination among borrowers of a certain type (corporate, sovereign, etc.) or, more probably, through sales of loans previously made to borrowers of relatively high creditworthiness. The result is a decline in the average quality of the bank's assets.

Similar in effect is the binary character of some rules. The most frequently cited example is the provision that requires capital only for loan facilities with a maturity of one year or longer. Industry lore—backed by at least anecdotal information from supervisors—holds that 364-day loan facilities became commonplace (Saidenberg and Schuermann 2004). This arbitrage can have undesirable consequences beyond its immediate impact on bank safety and soundness. For example, staff at the Bank of England found that loan data conformed to the commonsense intuition that the maturity distribution of lending to banks in higher-rated non-OECD countries was distorted by this regulatory feature (Drage and Mann 1999). Thus, Basel I may have played a modest contributory role in the 1997–98 emerging-market financial crisis.[57]

Other opportunities for regulatory arbitrage are afforded by gaps in the coverage of Basel I that create incentives for banks to engage in new kinds of activities, rather than simply to reallocate the mix of existing activities. The exemplary case is securitization—specifically, where a bank either sells assets for securitization to an entity with which it will have a continuing relationship or initiates such a relationship with an entity

---

56. Basel I does not explicitly assign corporate exposures to one of its risk buckets; thus they fall into the "all other" default bucket, which carries a 100 percent risk weighting (which in turn translates into a requirement that 8 percent of the amount of the exposure be set aside as regulatory capital).

57. One cause of the financial crisis was a serious maturity mismatch on the balance sheets of some Asian banks, which made short-term borrowings in foreign currencies and lent long-term in either domestic or foreign currencies.

whose securitized assets were originated by a third party. Of course, securitization can be motivated by reasons other than regulatory arbitrage, such as extending and diversifying sources of debt financing or increasing fee-based income through multiplication of the number of loans serviced. Yet it also provides many avenues for regulatory arbitrage. A straightforward sale of assets for securitization, where there is no recourse or other retained risk by the bank, is likely to be a form of cherry-picking, since generally the bank will sell higher-quality assets for securitization and retain lower-quality loans. The more interesting situations arise where banks retain an interest in the securitized assets or otherwise seek to enhance their credit quality.

Despite its acknowledged contribution in bringing off-balance-sheet items more squarely within the ambit of capital regulation, Basel I did so only incompletely. Thus, although it required capital charges for asset sales with recourse and for direct financial guarantees, it did not address securitization head on. So, for example, a bank was able to lower its capital requirement by retaining a recourse position for only the least creditworthy tranche of a securitization because, even though there is a capital charge for that position, it may be lower than the charge that applied when all the loans were held on the bank's balance sheet. Yet the retained tranche will, in effect, bear all the credit losses associated with the original package of loans. As Jones (2000, 52–54) illustrates, this outcome may be obtained even where, as in the United States, bank regulators supplemented the Basel I rules with capital requirements designed specifically for securitization. In fact, securitization appears to present a case in which efforts to plug gaps in regulatory coverage are quickly and repeatedly overtaken by innovative arbitraging measures. Thus, for example, even if it had been feasible to change the Basel I rules to prevent the outcome just described, a bank might have been able to provide "indirect" credit enhancements to investors in the form of early amortization or fast-payout provisions, rather than providing a standard guarantee (Jackson et al. 1999, 24).[58] These devices, which obviously create risk for the bank, are not covered in Basel I and thus require no capital charge. As discussed in the next chapter, the subprime crisis tellingly exposed the flaws in Basel I, and in the quality of supervision more generally, with respect to bank securitization practices.

---

58. These forms of indirect credit enhancements are particularly important in connection with revolving credit arrangements such as credit card lending, where the maturity of the securitized instrument typically exceeds that of the specific loans that have been securitized. The originating bank is responsible for generating enough new loans of the requisite quality to replenish the collateral against which the securities have been issued. To provide assurance to investors that they will not be disadvantaged if the bank cannot meet this obligation, the bank may offer certain contingent provisions. Early amortization provisions force an accelerated repayment of principal to the investors; fast-payout provisions subordinate part of the bank's share of principal repayments to the investors in the securitized assets.

A third type of regulatory arbitrage under Basel I is enabled by inconsistencies within the accord itself. Most notably, the market risk amendment of 1996 opened the door for a bank to reduce its regulatory requirements by originating and holding a position on its trading book rather than its banking book. Jackson et al. (1999, 25) observe that a three-month loan to a highly creditworthy company would carry a capital requirement of 8 percent, but three-month commercial paper issued by that same company would carry a substantially lower specific risk capital requirement under the market risk amendment.

Although regulators, academics, and policy analysts repeatedly characterize arbitrage as a major Basel I problem, there is very little empirical work that quantifies the practice or, even more importantly, that assesses the degree to which it compromises the safety and soundness of banks. This unhappy situation is doubtless due in large part to the inaccessibility of the data that would be necessary to study the phenomenon. To some degree this is because the data are proprietary to banks and neither published nor, in some instances, even reported to regulators. Surrogate measures are very crude. So, for example, Jones (2000) reports that Federal Reserve Board staff estimated the amount of nonmortgage securitization by the largest US banks to be nearly half the amount of their risk-weighted loans. The Fed staff apparently believed that these forms of securitization are "motivated heavily" by regulatory arbitrage considerations (Jackson et al. 1999, 25). Evidence for the proposition that Basel I has distorted credit markets can be found in the fact that entities falling into higher-risk Basel I categories, but with ratings from external bond rating agencies identical to those of entities in lower Basel I categories, appear to pay a premium on their borrowing (International Swaps and Derivatives Association 1998).

However, because securitization is also motivated by business reasons, one should be cautious about drawing inferences as to how much of this activity resulted from an *intention* by bank managers to engage in arbitrage. The difficulties in separating business from regulatory arbitrage motivations in assessing bank securitization practices is illustrated by Ambrose, Lacour-Little, and Sanders (2005), who conclude an empirical examination by finding evidence consistent with either capital arbitrage or reputational concerns.[59] Even if one is concerned with the effect of securitization on capital levels for a given portfolio of risk exposures, these gross numbers do not even begin to permit a calculation of how much

---

59. Current questions about the importance of regulatory arbitrage under a risk-weighted capital requirement regime echo earlier inquiries into whether banks engaged in increasing amounts of off-balance-sheet activity in order to arbitrage capital requirements such as leverage ratios, where balance sheet assets were the denominator in a capital ratio. Jagtiani, Saunders, and Udell (1995) review the literature and report on new empirical work, on the basis of which they conclude that changes in capital regulation had no consistent effect on banks' adoption of off-balance-sheet products.

those levels have been reduced. Furthermore, Jones (2000) suggests that securitization and certain other regulatory arbitrage devices may actually be desirable, because the Basel I rules themselves arguably assign many of the assets appropriate for these transactions to a bucket with too high a risk weighting.[60] Of course, this suggestion underscores the degree to which current capital requirements may rest upon risk weightings that deviate from the actual risk entailed by a bank's operations—hardly a ringing endorsement of any regulatory system and a prelude to the shortcoming of Basel I addressed in the next section.

Divergence Between Risk and Capital Regulation

The most trenchant criticism of Basel I is not that it has permitted capital levels that are too low for the actual risk to which a bank is exposed but that its metric is only obliquely connected to that risk. Basel I may require capital levels that are higher or lower than warranted by the credit risks a bank faces, at least where a large portion of the bank's business involves securitization, collateralized debt obligations, credit risk derivatives, and other innovative financial instruments. After summarizing regulatory arbitrage practice under Basel I, former Federal Reserve Board Vice Chairman Roger Ferguson commented that it had "greatly reduced the usefulness of regulatory capital ratios at the largest banks and provides little useful information to the public or the supervisors."[61] This theme of the disutility of Basel I as a supervisory tool has been increasingly emphasized by US regulators, particularly as criticism of Basel II has mounted.[62] As with so many other features of Basel I, the subprime crisis has underscored this problem.

A related criticism of Basel I is that it discourages banks from adopting sophisticated but costly risk management systems because there is no regulatory payoff (Saidenberg and Schuermann 2004). This notion perhaps reflected the belief of banks, discussed in chapter 5, that in exchange for the investments necessary to make them compliant with the Basel II A-IRB approach, they would reap benefits in the form of reduced minimum capital requirements. While the cost of compliance with risk

---

60. Mingo (2000) regards regulatory arbitrage as a lose-lose proposition because of the transaction costs required of banks to set up the transactions that permit the reduction in capital requirements.

61. Roger W. Ferguson, Jr., testimony before the Subcommittee on Financial Institutions and Consumer Credit of the Committee on Financial Services, US House of Representatives, June 19, 2003.

62. For example, in response to questions at a November 2005 Senate Banking Committee hearing on Basel II, Comptroller of the Currency John Dugan repeatedly underscored the importance of, as he put it in one answer, going "in a direction to get our arms around the risks that our largest, most complex banks are likely to take in the coming years." This theme is also elaborated in Mingo (2000).

management systems should always be relevant in deciding on regulatory requirements, an implicit regulatory promise to reduce capital requirements *before* conclusions can be reached as to the actual risk profiles of the banks seems at best premature.

There is no doubt that, optimally, a capital regulatory system would prompt banks to adopt advanced risk management techniques, at least up to the point where the incremental cost of those techniques exceeded the anticipated benefits in enhanced bank stability. However, it is by no means clear how much of a regulatory incentive is necessary to bring about extensive bank investment in risk management techniques. The interest of management and shareholders in maintaining the bank's value should, at least for currently healthy banks, serve as an important incentive. One recent study has concluded that the significantly improved performance of US banks during the 2001 recession, compared with the 1990–91 recession, is in significant part due to the integration of improved risk management tools into bank business decisions.[63]

Conclusion

In purely institutional terms, Basel I was an impressive accomplishment. The bank supervisors of a dozen key financial nations agreed to what seemed, at least in 1988, a fairly detailed set of harmonized rules on capital adequacy. With the important exception of Japan—the sources of whose banking and macroeconomic problems predated the accord—these rules have been quite faithfully enforced, not only in the Basel Committee countries but in nearly a hundred others. Again with the exception of Japan, the Basel Committee country banks were generally stable and profitable in the intervening years, despite several global financial upheavals. While Basel I can hardly claim all, or even most, of the credit for this happy circumstance, the general supervisory emphasis of the last 15 years on capital adequacy has surely played a part. However, when the history of the subprime crisis is finally written, it will surely detract from Basel I's accomplishments to a greater or lesser degree.

Because of this success, Basel I has been touted by some international law and international relations scholars as the exemplary case of trans-

---

63. Schuermann (2004) finds evidence for the improved ability of banks to price risk in, among other things, the shrinking relative spreads of loans to corporate bonds in the syndicated loan market and the steeper pricing schedules in retail and small-business lending. Ironically, Schuermann is coauthor of the earlier-cited paper suggesting that banks lacked regulatory incentive to adopt sophisticated risk management systems (Saidenberg and Schuermann 2004). While the two papers are not inconsistent—since a different capital regulatory regime can draw forth even more investment in risk regulation—the former suggests that there are important business motivations for banks to make such investments.

national regulatory cooperation. Yet the history recounted in this chapter should inject a note of caution into the story of Basel I so enthusiastically told by these scholars. Behind that history lay a politically based push for higher capital levels—first in the United States and the United Kingdom for largely domestic regulatory reasons and later in the rest of the G-10 as a result of US and UK concerns about competitive equality. Even in the relatively brief negotiating period, national competitive considerations played an increasing role, in many instances at the apparent expense of sound bank regulatory policy. However, sufficient momentum remained from the original push to produce a result that raised capital ratios. Basel II, as we shall see, did not begin with this kind of momentum behind it.

A second reason for caution in extrapolating the success of Basel I to the Basel II exercise is that that success may have been due in no small part to the relative simplicity of the capital rules negotiated in 1988. The shortcomings of the original accord were, and are, real. In a sense, the strongest case against Basel I is that it provides a decreasingly useful supervisory window on bank operations and soundness—both for supervisors and for the banks themselves. However, the fact that Basel I has drawbacks as a comprehensive scheme of domestic capital regulation does not mean that a highly complex international arrangement is the best way to improve each country's domestic regulatory paradigm. As the next chapter shows, the differences of political economy and institutional competence between the process and substance of Basel I and that of Basel II raise serious doubts whether the latter is on net a benign development.

4

Negotiating Basel II

Despite the initial push from the US Congress and a few interventions by government officials in other countries, banking supervisors were generally left to implement Basel I as they saw fit, using their existing regulatory authority. The Basel II process has been an altogether different story. Even more than Basel I, it has resembled a trade negotiation, with extensive political and constituency involvement at times submerging the spirit of regulatory cooperation traditionally central to Basel Committee activities. And yet no national regulator knew at the outset exactly what outcome it wanted. Thus, there has at other times been a peculiarly experimental feel to the exercise, resembling more an innovative but halting domestic regulatory reform effort. As the history of the negotiation set forth in this chapter will illustrate, it is difficult to avoid the conclusion that key participants in the process made a series of technical and political misjudgments that have prolonged, complicated, and ultimately marred the Basel II enterprise.

Launching the Review Process

From the outset, banking supervisors were aware of many of the weaknesses of Basel I. Some resulted from compromises necessary to secure international agreement, as detailed in the preceding chapter. Another was that, even after the market risk amendment in 1996, important bank risks were not subject to capital regulation.[1] Still others, such as the arbitrary

---

1. Foreshadowing Basel II, operational risk was most frequently mentioned, although the use of capital charges to manage operational risk has been controversial.

nature of the number and weightings of risk categories, were accepted as a necessary feature for an administratively workable set of rules. The resulting potential for regulatory arbitrage was also anticipated, even if the most troublesome forms of that arbitrage were not specifically foreseen. Thus, while further refinements to Basel I would not have been surprising, one might not have expected a fundamental overhaul of the capital accord to begin less than a decade after the original rules took effect. However, the acceleration of two trends made the case for an overhaul seem reasonable to the Basel Committee as a whole and compelling to Federal Reserve officials.

One development was the rapid increase in securitizations of mortgages and other loans by US and, to a lesser degree, other developed country banks in the decade following negotiation of Basel I. As noted in chapter 3, many securitizations were undertaken primarily for nonregulatory reasons, such as reducing interest rate exposure. However, even these securitizations can have a regulatory arbitrage effect if, as was often the case, the assets retained by the bank bear a higher risk of loss than the securitized portfolio of loans as a whole. Once the Basel I rules were operative, banks recognized that the innovative securitization techniques originally devised for business reasons also provided a major arbitrage opportunity. Supervisors became increasingly concerned with the resulting divergence of regulatory capital requirements from actual credit risk. By the mid-1990s, regulatory arbitrage through the use of nontraditional financial instruments was regarded as a serious problem with Basel I, and securitization was identified as the most prominent form of this arbitrage.[2]

The second development was a series of advances in the internal risk management techniques of large banks. Most important among these was the increasing use of credit risk models for risk assessment purposes. As the proliferation of new instruments made the credit risk profile of banks more complex, the industry was devising new methodologies to mange

---

2. Laurence Meyer, a member of the Federal Reserve Board closely involved in bank supervision, explicitly identified regulatory arbitrage as the "bad news" about capital standards, because it was making them "increasingly less meaningful and progressively undermined." He specified securitization, along with credit derivatives, as his principal concerns. See Laurence Meyer, "Increasing Global Financial Integrity: The Roles of Market Discipline, Regulation and Supervision," remarks at the 16th Annual Monetary Conference, Money in the New Millennium: The Global Financial Architecture, Cato Institute, Washington, October 22, 1998. Alan Greenspan and William McDonough similarly pointed to securitization as presenting a major challenge to the Basel I rules. These officials acknowledged that a measure of regulatory arbitrage was not necessarily undesirable given the bluntness of the Basel I rules, but they noted that the arbitrage process itself entailed costs and, more importantly, that the arbitrage highlighted the inadequacy of Basel I as a regulatory device. See Greenspan (1998); and William McDonough, "Issues for the Basel Accord," remarks at the Conference on Credit Risk Modeling and Regulatory Implications, London, September 22, 1998.

this risk. The use of these new methods underscored the degree to which a risk weight assigned to an asset or asset equivalent under Basel I could diverge from the bank's best estimate of the actual risk created by that exposure. The effect was both to facilitate regulatory arbitrage and to erode confidence that Basel I was an effective regulatory tool.

During the mid-1990s, the Capital Subgroup of the Basel Committee, chaired by Claes Norgren of the Swedish Financial Supervisory Authority, examined the implications of these and related developments for the accord. Most members of the committee seemed content to let work proceed in this low-profile, deliberate fashion. However, Federal Reserve officials became increasingly outspoken in calling for significant change in capital regulation. As early as May 1996, Federal Reserve Chairman Alan Greenspan publicly stated that the weaknesses in Basel I were becoming "ever more evident" and suggested that credit risk models had implications for capital regulation.[3] In December of that year the *American Banker* published a story, based on information from unnamed Federal Reserve officials, reporting that the Fed was considering far-reaching changes in the Basel I rules.[4]

The growing impetus for change was both reflected and strengthened at a February 1998 conference hosted by the Federal Reserve Bank of New York and cosponsored by the Bank of England, the Bank of Japan, and the Board of Governors of the Federal Reserve.[5] Government officials and bankers pointed to the limitations of Basel I in their remarks at the conference, while economic staff from the supervisory agencies and academics delivered papers exploring alternative approaches to capital regulation, including the use of banks' credit risk models as a basis for regulatory capital.[6] Although officials from the Federal Reserve Bank of New York were more tentative in their comments, Chairman Greenspan made a very strong case for change, and throughout 1998, calls for change in Basel I became a regular theme in public statements of Federal Reserve officials concerning bank regulation.[7]

---

3. See Jaret Seiberg, "Greenspan Hints at Revision in Capital Rules on Credit Risk," *American Banker*, May 3, 1996, 1.

4. See Jaret Seiberg, "The Fed Considers Sweeping Changes In Risk-Based Capital Requirements," *American Banker*, December 13, 1996, 1.

5. Papers and speeches presented at the conference, entitled "Financial Services at the Crossroad: Capital Regulation in the Twenty-First Century," are reproduced in the October 1998 issue of the *Federal Reserve Bank of New York Economic Policy Review.*

6. Some officials also promoted as a possible alternative the so-called "precommitment" approach to capital regulation. This approach, evaluated in chapter 7, was eventually abandoned in favor of the internal ratings–based method.

7. See Greenspan (1998); Clay Harris, "Call to Revise Banks' Capital Adequacy Rules," *Financial Times*, September 22, 1998, 4; Laurence Meyer, "Increasing Global Financial Integrity:

Meanwhile important segments of the banking industry were also calling for change. Executives from individual banks and officials of trade associations such as the American Bankers Association and the Institute of International Finance (IIF) emphasized the contrast between the blunt Basel I approach and the increasingly sophisticated credit risk assessments generated by the models and other internal risk management techniques used by large banks. Shortly after the Fed conference, the IIF issued a report criticizing Basel I as "flawed" and calling for supervisors to move toward the use of banks' internal models as the basis for capital regulation (Institute of International Finance 1998).

Despite the growing agitation for change by banks, the Federal Reserve was still the only supervisory agency actively and publicly suggesting that modification—perhaps fundamental modification—of the Basel I standards was necessary. At the February 1998 Fed conference, Tom de Swaan, the Dutch chairman of the Basel Committee, delivered remarks on the reasons for considering major change in Basel I that, while not inconsistent with those of Fed officials, were considerably more guarded (de Swaan 1998). Indeed, de Swaan's principal emphasis was the need to maintain existing capital levels no matter what revisions were made, and he even hinted that higher levels might be necessary. He also sounded a note of caution on the degree to which supervisors could rely on market-generated capital levels.

Even in the United States, the other bank supervisory agencies had not joined the Fed's public calls for change. At a December 1997 conference, Comptroller of the Currency Eugene Ludwig gave a speech on capital regulation in which he made observations about the changing nature of banking, asked questions about the right approach to bank regulation, and provided a brief history of capital requirements, but did not call for a major change in Basel I.[8] Officials at the Federal Deposit Insurance Corporation (FDIC) and the Office of Thrift Supervision, the other two federal banking agencies, had not spoken publicly on the issue at all.

In early 1998, then, change in Basel I seemed nearly inevitable, but the pace and direction of change were quite unclear. Unlike prior major Basel Committee initiatives, this one was not impelled by a crisis specific to

The Roles of Market Discipline, Regulation and Supervision," remarks at the 16th Annual Monetary Conference, Money in the New Millennium: The Global Financial Architecture, Cato Institute, Washington, October 22, 1998; and Susan M. Phillips, remarks at the International Swaps and Derivatives Association, 13th Annual General Meeting, Rome, March 26, 1998. Federal Reserve staff, normally very circumspect in their public comments on policy issues, were unusually outspoken at this conference. Press accounts quoted a staff economist as having characterized Basel I as a "lose-lose proposition" and saying that "[w]e should begin yesterday to reconstruct the accord."

8. See Eugene A. Ludwig, remarks to the Federal Financial Institutions Examination Council, December 12, 1997.

banks in member countries.[9] When Federal Reserve Bank of New York President William McDonough succeeded de Swaan as chair of the Basel Committee in June 1998, the momentum for change strengthened. In July, at the first meeting chaired by McDonough, the committee agreed to a thorough review of the Basel Accord. In September McDonough laid out the rationale and process for what he characterized as a "major effort" to revise the accord.[10]

The process was clear enough: While McDonough set no timetable in his September speech, he reported that the committee recognized "the need to move expeditiously, and to make significant progress in the next one to two years." In another speech two months later, he revealed that Claes Norgrens' group, now renamed the Steering Group on the Future of Capital, was to report back to the full committee at its December meeting. Furthermore, the committee "was committed to undertaking substantial work in 1999 in order to be able to publish a consultative paper with its proposals toward the end of 1999."[11] In conducting its review, the committee would consult with banking supervisors in non–Basel Committee countries, with supervisors of nonbank financial institutions, and with financial institutions themselves.

The rationale for an overhaul of Basel I was also clearly stated. McDonough began by observing that competition in the industry had become even more intense and more global since Basel I. Like other supervisors, McDonough pointed to "sophisticated arbitrage strategies," notably securitization and credit derivatives, as having both complicated the task of understanding the risk positions of banks and undermined the utility of Basel I. He questioned the wisdom of reliance on quantitative capital

---

9. The creation of the Basel Committee was itself the result of the 1974 crises at a number of G-10 banks. Similarly, Basel I resulted from the series of events set in motion by the Latin American debt crisis of the 1980s, and revisions to the Basel Concordat were made after the failure of the Bank of Credit and Commerce International in 1990. Although the worldwide financial turbulence from July 1997 to March 1999 provided a dramatic backdrop for the beginning of the Basel II process and underscored some of the flaws in the Basel I rules, G-10 country banks had not generally been seriously affected. Still, the crisis underscored the important role of capital regulation in financially significant countries. Reductions in lending to Southeast Asian countries by troubled Japanese banks may have contributed to the onset of financial crises in those countries. Moreover, several large banks did have exposure to the highly leveraged Long-Term Capital Management (LTCM) when that firm failed in the fall of 1998. Because the Federal Reserve Board of New York adroitly orchestrated the equivalent of a debt workout so as to forestall the dumping of LTCM's assets in order to repay banks, a crisis was avoided. However, the banks' exposure to a highly leveraged hedge fund served as another reminder of just how much bank exposures had changed in the preceding decade.

10. See William McDonough, "Issues for the Basel Accord," remarks at the Conference on Credit Risk Modeling and Regulatory Implications, London, September 22, 1998.

11. See William McDonough, "Credit Risk and the 'Level Playing Field'," remarks at the Conference on the Challenge of Credit Risk, Frankfurt am Main, Germany, November 24, 1998.

regulation alone, suggesting that ongoing supervision and market discipline should play important roles in assuring the adequacy of bank risk management. Finally, he noted the need to attend to operational risk and "stress loss potential" (i.e., low-probability but high-severity events that could threaten a bank's viability).

As to what the Basel Committee review might actually yield, however, McDonough was vague. He mentioned only two elements of what he anticipated would be a revised capital framework: first, an approach to capital requirements that could apply across countries and types of financial institutions, and second, the integration of quantitative capital requirements with "a set of qualitative expectations for banks in managing their risk and evaluating their capital needs." He provided no blueprint for how these aims would be accomplished. Although he mentioned credit risk models several times, he did not propose that the revised accord use those models as the basis for establishing regulatory capital requirements.

Neither did McDonough indicate whether the new regulatory requirements—however determined—should result in bank capital being higher, lower, or about the same as existing levels.[12] In fact, in marked contrast to the explicit Basel I aim of raising capital levels, nearly all participants in the public discussion preceding the launch of the Basel II process had studiously avoided this question. Generally, advocates of change suggested that capital requirements might go up for some kinds of lending and down for others, in accordance with the idea that regulatory capital should better align with economic risk. While large banks might have assumed that any such realignment would reduce the total capital requirement for their individual institutions, no supervisor had predicted such an outcome, much less committed to it—at least not publicly. Whatever the private views of bank supervisors, the financial uncertainty engendered by the Asian financial crisis, Russia's default on certain of its sovereign bonds, and the collapse of Long-Term Capital Management made the fall of 1998 a less than propitious time to suggest that banks could safely hold lower levels of capital.[13] Indeed, the most direct

---

12. McDonough alluded to a trend "observed until recently" for spreads in lending to erode "to levels which were worrisome" and a consequent reemergence of concern about the capital adequacy of "banks in some countries." However, the fact that he used the past tense suggested that these worries had abated. Moreover, he suggested later in his speech that capital requirements might be too high for certain kinds of lending, such as to highly creditworthy corporations (ibid., footnote 11).

13. For similar reasons, those involved in the early stages of Basel II never thought seriously of changing the 8 percent capital requirement of Basel I. Of course, by altering risk weights, the committee could achieve the same end as by changing the percentage of those risk-weighted assets required to be held as capital. But the optics of the change would be less dramatic.

comments by supervisors on the issue of capital levels—from Claes Norgren and Tom de Swaan—suggested that prevailing capital levels might be too *low*.[14]

Curious Release of the First Consultative Paper

In light of the expectations for far-reaching change raised during 1998, the committee's consultative paper issued in June 1999 (Basel Committee 1999b) was something of an anticlimax. Indeed, paradoxical as it might sound, the paper managed to be both anticlimactic and contentious. Subsequently referred to as the first consultative paper, or CP-1, it disappointed those who favored using internal credit ratings or credit risk models as the basis for capital regulation. It did not put forward proposals for either of these new paradigms for capital regulation. Instead, it built on the basic methodology of Basel I.

Although it revised rather than overhauled the capital scheme for credit risk, the committee indicated its intention to extend capital charges to operational risk and, for banks whose interest rate exposure was significantly above average, to that risk as well. The committee placed all the quantitative capital requirements in the context of what it described as a "three-pillar" approach. The capital rules were to be the first pillar, a robust supervisory review process the second, and market discipline the third. The committee stated that, under the second pillar, supervisors should have the ability to require banks to hold capital above the regulatory minimum. Under the third pillar, banks would be required to disclose more information that would enable market actors to make better assessments of the banks' risk positions. Pillars 2 and 3 were more suggestive than fully realized. The committee's work had been focused principally on pillar 1, as it would continue to be right through completion of the revised framework. As a result, while the "three pillars" define Basel II, they support a rather skewed edifice.

The most prominent, and controversial, innovation in the Basel I methodology was the committee's proposal to use ratings from "external credit assessment institutions," such as Moody's or Standard & Poor's, as the basis for assigning rated borrowers to a risk bucket (see box 4.1 for a summary of the CP-1 proposal.) Only one additional risk bucket would be created (a 150 percent risk weighting), but the use of external credit ratings would allow differentiation of risk weightings among corporate, sovereign, and bank borrowers. (Table 4.1 outlines the relationship between

---

14. At the same September 1998 conference at which McDonough laid out the agenda for revision of Basel I, Norgren was quoted as having said "[w]e have learned that the minimum is often not enough when the times get rough." See Clay Harris, "Call to Revise Banks' Capital Adequacy Rules," *Financial Times*, September 22, 1998, 4.

specific agency credit ratings and regulatory capital requirements.) The aim, of course, was to align the capital requirement for a given exposure more closely with actual credit risk. CP-1 also proposed special rules to deal with retained interests following securitizations, adjustments to capital requirements for certain credit risk mitigation measures taken by banks, consolidation requirements intended to reduce "double gearing," and a number of discrete changes to address other deficiencies of Basel I.

Table 4.1   External agency ratings and risk weights in the first consultative paper (percent)

Claim	AAA to AA−	A+ to A−	BBB+ to BBB−	BB+ to B−	Below B−	Unrated
Sovereigns	0	20	50	100	150	100
Bank option 1	20	50	100	100	150	100
Bank option 2	20	50	50	100	150	50
Corporations	20	100	100	100	150	100

Note: Risk weights illustrated using Standard & Poor's rating categories. Bank option 1 is based on risk weighting of sovereign in which bank is located. Bank option 2 is based on a rating agency assessment of the individual bank.

Source: Basel Committee (1999b).

The issue of internal credit ratings was not ignored.[15] The paper declared that the committee intended to issue a proposal for the use of banks' internal credit ratings in the calculation of regulatory capital (Basel Committee 1999b, paragraph 7). Although it was a bit ambiguous on the point, the committee seemed to suggest that it would complete that proposal during the year 2000—that is, within the same time frame as it finalized changes to the more conventional approach set forth in CP-1. The committee devoted several pages to rehearsing the benefits, drawbacks, and challenges of an internal ratings–based (IRB) approach to capital regulation. Yet, even as it essentially promised that an IRB proposal would be forthcoming, it gave no hint of the specifics that would successfully overcome the challenges in order to realize the benefits.

The CP-1 release was puzzling. It was certainly not a surprise that the committee had been unable to fashion an IRB approach in the less than 12 months since it had begun a formal review of Basel I. On the contrary, in the intervening period it had become reasonably clear that, notwithstanding the enthusiasm of some policymakers and Federal Reserve staff for moving forward, regulators were not yet convinced that there was a sound basis for doing so. Summarizing the September 1998 conference at which McDonough had laid out the agenda for revising Basel I, Bank of England staff observed that there were "significant hurdles that will have to be overcome" before banks' own systems could be used to set regulatory capital requirements (Jackson, Nickel, and Perraudin 1999, 100).

Ongoing work by the Models Task Force of the Basel Committee (which included many of the participants in the London conference) was

---

15. Echoing the conclusions of its staff study, the committee noted briefly that the use of full credit models might someday have promise but that "significant hurdles" of data reliability and model validation precluded any near-term proposal for their use in capital regulation. It committed itself only to monitor developments in the credit risk modeling area and to maintain a dialogue with industry (Basel Committee 1999b, paragraphs 52–53).

reaching the same conclusion, as eventually reported in a study issued shortly before CP-1 (Basel Committee 1999a). Although, strictly speaking, this judgment was made with respect to the use of full credit models, rather than with respect to the more limited step of using internal credit risk ratings, the analysis implicated the latter as well. The paucity of reliable data, which along with model validation was identified as a key hurdle to be overcome, applied to internal credit risk ratings just as to full-fledged modeling. A contemporaneous study by two Federal Reserve economists on risk rating by large US banks had found the state of their ratings systems less advanced than had been widely assumed (Treacy and Carey 1998).

The authors of the papers cited in the preceding paragraphs were not pessimistic about the potential for using banks' internal systems for regulatory purposes. They did, however, imply that an extended period of study and validation would be needed before a regulatory application of the internal systems could be deemed feasible. How, then, could the Basel Committee commit to advancing within a year a proposal for just this kind of application? And why had it rushed out a proposal for modifying what was becoming known as the "standardized" approach to capital requirements? McDonough had suggested in the fall of 1998 that the committee's proposals would be released toward the end of 1999. Yet the committee was beating its own deadline by six months. Might not the additional time have been profitably used to determine whether an IRB approach was feasible in the medium term?[16]

Discussions with some who followed or participated in the committee's work in 1999 do not yield clear and consistent answers to these questions. It appears that the committee, under pressure (some of it self-generated) to make capital regulation more sensitive to the credit risk actually assumed by banks, was attempting to improve the method that would remain applicable to the vast majority of banks, while assuring large banks that the goal of using internal risk systems for regulatory purposes had not been abandoned. A related factor may have been a desire to provide regulators in emerging-market countries with rules appropriate for their banking systems, a number of which had been badly disrupted by the inadequate regulation prevailing before the Asian financial crisis (although reliance on external ratings would be particularly inapposite in emerging-market lending). One banking industry observer even suggested that CP-1 was rushed in order to be done in time for the G-7 finance ministers' meeting in preparation for the Köln Summit, presumably so the ministers

---

16. The committee had actually completed the bulk of its work on CP-1 several months earlier. A press conference to issue the paper was scheduled for April 9, 1999, but a disagreement between Germany and other committee members on the risk weight to be assigned to commercial mortgages delayed release of the proposal for two months.

could note progress in reforming this part of the financial system in the wake of the 1997–98 emerging-market financial crisis.[17]

Whatever the committee's reasoning for the timing and contents of CP-1, the paper was not well received. Public criticism, somewhat muted in the months immediately following the CP-1 release, picked up in the fall. By the time of the March 31, 2000 deadline for written comments to the Basel Committee, nearly 200 had been received. Although the committee chose not to publish the comments, enough were released by their originators to give a fairly good picture of the views presented.[18] The complaints were directed both at what the committee had included and what it had omitted.

Despite the obvious advantage of allowing differentiated risk ratings for borrowers of the same type (e.g., corporations, sovereigns), reaction to the committee's proposal to use external agency ratings was largely negative. Even some US regulators were skeptical. Just a few days after the CP-1 release, newly appointed Comptroller of the Currency John D. Hawke said he did "not believe that the external ratings approach alone will go very far in solving the problems of the current accord."[19] One problem was that most borrowers did not have agency credit ratings, presumably because they did not issue substantial amounts of debt in public capital markets. Thus, small borrowers were placed at a fundamental disadvantage. Even most corporate borrowers, at least outside the United States, were not rated by external agencies.[20] Since a borrower that did not have an external rating would be treated much as under Basel I, CP-1 promised little increased risk sensitivity for broad groups of borrowers. A second problem was that agencies rated borrowers, not specific loan facilities. The credit risk entailed in lending to a specific borrower can vary depending on the terms of the particular facility.

A third problem was that agency ratings for sovereign borrowers had recently proven less than reliable in the run-up to the Asian financial crisis.

---

17. The report to the leaders by the finance ministers, issued just a week after CP-1, did include the Basel Committee proposals on capital regulation among measures taken to improve the global financial architecture.

18. Comments submitted in response to later consultative papers were posted on the Bank for International Settlements website.

19. See John D. Hawke, remarks to the International Monetary Conference, Philadelphia, June 8, 1999.

20. The use of the term "external credit assessment institutions" indicated that the eligible group was not limited to the familiar rating agencies such as Moody's. As later became clear, it also included government export credit agencies. While this feature of the proposal might help sovereign borrowers, the principal objective of a government export credit agency rating, it would still leave virtually all smaller firms and most non-US larger firms without eligible ratings. Moreover, the larger the group of eligible credit assessment institutions, the greater the opportunity for "ratings shopping."

The basic critique was that the agencies had essentially followed market sentiment, rather than help to establish it. Before the crisis, ratings for Thailand and Korea were almost certainly too high. Yet once the crisis hit, the agencies rapidly and substantially downgraded them. In its report on international capital markets released in September 1999, the International Monetary Fund pointed out that, had the CP-1 proposal been in place in early 1997, banks would not have been required to hold any more capital against the risk of sovereign defaults in the countries afflicted by financial crisis later that year (IMF 1999, 225).

At the same time, financial officials from emerging-market countries joined some banks in complaining that the CP-1 changes would create an undue disincentive against lending to emerging markets. Of course, to some extent that was the (unstated) intention of the committee, insofar as lending to emerging markets prior to the onset of the financial crisis in 1997 was considered to have inadequately reflected the risks entailed. However, the virtual absence of rated banks and firms in many countries made the external ratings approach especially troubling for emerging markets. In the absence of a rating, there was no way for a bank in an emerging market to obtain a favorable risk weighting, no matter what its actual credit history and capacity.[21]

Arguably the most serious blow to the committee's proposal came from the rating agencies themselves. The three largest of the four recognized rating agencies expressed varying degrees of reservation with respect to the CP-1 plan, principally because of fears that the agencies' independence, and thus their credibility, might be compromised.[22] The Basel proposal created incentives for a certain degree of "ratings shopping" among the established agencies.

The committee's stated intention to develop a method for imposing a capital charge for operational risk also drew criticism from banks. Because CP-1 did not include a specific proposal, there was nothing more than the concept to criticize. But, in a preview of the dissent that would meet the operational risk proposal in the second consultative paper (CP-2), a number of banks commented that operational risk—while undeniably significant—was unlike credit or market risk in that it was not susceptible to quantification in any meaningful way.

Banks questioned other discrete features of the proposal. But their most elemental complaint was directed at the committee's failure to move more resolutely toward an IRB proposal. Bankers' criticism of the proposal to use external credit rating agencies was generally a prelude to advocacy

---

21. On the other hand, emerging-market sovereigns with investment-grade ratings, such as Chile, would benefit from the shift to reliance on external agency ratings.

22. See Rob Garver, "Top Ratings Agencies Unanimous in Basel Opposition," *American Banker*, April 4, 2000, 2.

of an IRB approach. The shortcomings of the former could be remedied by a shift to the latter. CP-1 added only one risk bucket, many borrowers were unrated and thus would still be arbitrarily assigned to a risk bucket, and the track record of ratings agencies was not encouraging. The banks argued that only through building regulatory capital requirements on their own assessments would those requirements reflect actual risk.

At a banking conference in October 1999, key officials in the Basel process were already sounding less committed to CP-1. Danielle Nouy, secretary general of the Basel Committee, emphasized that CP-1 was a "very open document" and promised that the committee's next draft would be "very different."[23] Other officials, including McDonough and Greenspan, emphasized the importance of a collaborative effort between supervisors and banks to develop the IRB approach. Greenspan explicitly invited banks to pay close attention to the work of the Basel Committee in order to "influence the eventual outcome of the deliberations."[24]

In fact, large banks had not waited for Greenspan's invitation. Following release of the Basel Committee's paper on credit risk modeling, the IIF had asked some of its member banks to evaluate that paper. In October 1999, the IIF Working Group on Capital Adequacy, which had released a 1998 report advocating the use of banks' internal risk management systems as the basis for capital regulation, issued a report suggesting that the Basel Committee paper was setting the bar too high for the use of credit models as a basis for capital regulation (Institute of International Finance 1999). The previous month the IIF had organized a group of 32 senior managers from some of the world's largest banks to work together to affect the Basel Committee's work.[25] The group, chaired by Jan Kalff of the Dutch bank ABN Amro, was clear in its view that capital regulation should be based on the risk management systems of banks. A similar group was formed under the auspices of the International Swaps and Derivatives Association.

This transnational organization of banking interests highlights the changes that had taken place in the Basel process since negotiation of the first accord in 1988. Recall that the Basel I process was initiated by the United States and the United Kingdom, which together sought adoption by the Basel Committee of the bilateral capital arrangement on which the two countries had agreed the previous year. The negotiation itself followed a familiar pattern: Countries exercised available sources of leverage to prod

---

23. See Barbara A. Rehm, "Regulators Support Bigger Role for Market in Curbing Banks," *American Banker*, October 7, 1999, 1.

24. See Alan Greenspan, "The Evolution of Bank Supervision," remarks to the American Bankers Association, Phoenix, October 11, 1999.

25. US banks represented in the group included Citigroup, Bank of America, Chase Manhattan, and Bank One.

other countries into agreement on the basic contours of their proposal; certain compromises for particularized national interests were made along the way; and the interests of banks were, to a greater or lesser extent, mediated through their own countries' supervisors on the Basel Committee.

The Basel II process, by contrast, began without any clear proposal from any country. Although officials of the Federal Reserve Board were the most committed to revamping Basel I, even they lacked a specific proposal at the outset. The committee thus began a collective effort to determine alternatives to the Basel I capital standards. The committee eventually issued a series of proposals on its own authority and solicited comments from banks in particular, but, more generally, from anyone who cared to take the time to respond. Thus emerged an international variant on the kind of notice and comment procedure for proposed regulations found in national legal systems.[26] Large internationally active banks, in turn, organized themselves to maximize their influence in pursuit of their shared interest in this international rule-making exercise.

The repeated calls for collaboration by Basel Committee officials would be answered as the IRB approach was developed. The consequence was a further transformation of the Basel process. As recently as the spring of 1999, shortly before the release of CP-1, reports that German banking authorities were leaking details of the draft to their banks had elicited criticism from other Basel Committee countries, which preferred to exclude banks from the discussions until a complete draft was ready for comment.[27] Now, however, banks were being invited into the process. Thus, the Basel II exercise had evolved into a collective effort by national supervisors and large banks to create an entirely new paradigm for capital regulation. Specific national interests did not disappear, of course. Divergent interests and preferences would emerge as the IRB approach took shape. But the nature of this new Basel process generated as many disagreements *within* committee countries as among those countries. In particular, smaller banks that would not likely qualify for either of the two IRB approaches feared they would be disadvantaged. Within the United States—with its peculiar allocation of federal banking supervisory authority to four different agencies—there was friction among national supervisors over the scope and nature of the Basel II exercise that has continued to the present.[28]

---

26. The evolution and implications of this procedure are discussed in Barr and Miller (2006). As discussed in chapter 6, the Basel II process was in fact an unusual hybrid of this variation on domestic administrative legal procedure and an international trade negotiation.

27. See George Graham, "Fresh Drive to Reform Bank Capital Rules," *Financial Times*, May 14, 1999, 5.

28. Through the early stages of Basel II, the other federal financial institution supervisors were either less enthusiastic about or, in at least one case, downright resistant to the use of more elaborate quantitative tools in setting capital requirements.

Some of the implications of this novel approach to an international arrangement will be explored in succeeding chapters. Before discussing the results of that approach, however, it is worth addressing the incentives and motivations of the principal participants. Those of the large banks are reasonably clear. They aimed, of course, to convince the Basel Committee supervisors that an IRB approach to regulatory capital requirements was feasible. Their reason for favoring an IRB approach almost certainly rested on the expectation that their required capital levels would decline.[29] To be sure, banks would prefer that a regulatory IRB approach converge with their internal approach to risk measurement. But, as evidenced by the fact that large banks accepted the final revised framework, which imposes its own requirements and formulas, they are willing to accept a divergent approach so long as their capital requirements decline.[30]

The incentives and motivations of the Basel Committee members are more difficult to pinpoint. Certainly they wished to rectify the key flaws of Basel I, and some were convinced that using banks' own risk assessment systems was the only viable route to this end. Officials from the Federal Reserve, who as a group were the most committed to an IRB approach among all Basel Committee supervisors, apparently also believed that the Basel II process could be used to prod large banks to improve their internal risk systems. Despite the publicly stated enthusiasm of Chairman Greenspan for banks' credit risk modeling,[31] some Federal Reserve staff were concerned that very large banks did not actually have a good grasp of the risks entailed in many of the nonlending activities that had become such a large part of their overall business. While this circumstance was in part a result of the technical challenges in measuring risk, it was also grounded in the incentive structure created within large banks. The various bank divisions had little interest in promoting clear and well-developed risk profiles of their activities, since this might mean more constraints on the very activities that—at least in the short term—were most likely to yield the highest profits. Just weeks after the CP-1 release, the Federal Reserve issued a supervisory letter that directed its examiners to evaluate the internal capital-management processes to judge their adequacy in determining financial institutions' capital needs (Board of Governors of the Federal Reserve System, Division of Banking

---

29. Large non-US banks had the additional incentive that many of their corporate customers did not have external credit ratings.

30. Chapter 5 will attempt to explain why banks have sought reductions in their regulatory capital requirements even as they maintained capital levels well above existing requirements.

31. As early as 1996, Greenspan praised the internal credit risk models being used by some banks and looked forward to their widespread adoption. See Alan Greenspan, "Banking in the Global Marketplace," remarks at the Federation of Bankers Association of Japan, Tokyo, November 18, 1996.

Supervision and Regulation 1999). The letter followed a review by Federal Reserve staff that concluded there was significant room for improvement in these processes.

Some Federal Reserve officials suggested at the time, as they have since, that the most effective way to incentivize banks to make the desired improvements was to tie the banks' internal processes to regulatory capital requirements. Additionally, they believed that the only way to focus adequate supervisory and bank attention on the challenges of achieving a viable IRB approach to capital regulation was simply to move forward, regardless of how many technical and policy questions were unanswered. Only if banks believed that the end point of an IRB capital requirement would be reached would they invest the resources necessary to refine their IRB methods. And only through this commitment would the considerable difficulties be better understood and overcome. Finally, only through such a process would the risk management officials of the banks obtain both the resources and the internal stature to engage in the informed and sophisticated risk management desired by the supervisors. From this perspective, close involvement of the banks in development of the IRB methodology was not only inevitable as a means to an end; it was a goal in itself.

It is unclear whether the supervisors as a group—or at least those who led the Basel II process—intended a significant reduction in capital for banks that adopted an IRB approach. The committee had stated its intention in CP-1 that "the new framework should at least maintain the overall level of capital currently in the banking system (Basel Committee 1999b, paragraph 10). Once it had committed itself to an IRB approach, the Basel Committee clearly intended *some* decline for banks qualifying for that approach. In CP-2, described in the next section, the committee explicitly stated its goal for IRB capital requirements as "covering the underlying risk at a reasonable level of confidence and providing a modest incentive to adopt more sophisticated risk management systems" (Basel Committee 2001a, paragraph 53). It suggested a decline of 2 or 3 percent in capital requirements, an amount presumably considered a sufficient incentive (Basel Committee 2001a, paragraph 48).

The committee's changes in, or omission of, this stated goal in subsequent releases combine with persistent but undocumented reports of an understanding between certain Federal Reserve officials and large US banks to raise the question of whether supervisors intended larger reductions in capital requirements to result from application of an IRB approach.[32] Some participants in the Basel II process have suggested as

---

32. The suggestions by Governor Susan Bies that the leverage ratio requirement for US banks should be removed following full implementation of Basel II can be read as sympathetic to significant capital reductions for A-IRB banks, insofar as the leverage ratio only begins to place a floor under regulatory capital if there are significant reductions from current risk-weighted capital levels. See Michele Heller and Todd Davenport, "Congressional Pressure for Consensus

much, mentioning numbers as high as 20 percent. That figure may have its origins in the committee's suggestion in CP-2 that capital charges for operational risk should be approximately 20 percent of credit risk capital charges. Since the committee had already indicated that aggregate capital was to remain about the same, one might fairly have concluded that credit risk capital charges would decline by approximately the same amount as the operational risk charges that would be imposed.[33] Later, when the Basel Committee significantly lowered the intended level of capital charges for operational risk, some banks apparently continued to expect substantially reduced credit risk capital requirements.

It may also be that the intentions of Fed officials changed over time. Officials may have underestimated the potential resistance of banks, and, in order to complete the Basel II process, they may have acquiesced in significantly lower capital requirements. Another possibility, not inconsistent with the first, is that the change in the composition of the Board of Governors during the Basel II process may have brought into positions of authority individuals considerably more disposed to permit banks to hold lower levels of capital. The issue of overall capital levels, obviously central to the entire Basel II exercise, remained contested—both in the technical sense of predicting what the advanced internal ratings–based (A-IRB) methodology will yield and in the normative sense of whether required capital levels should be generally and significantly lower.

In any case, by the end of 1999 it was already obvious that many large and even some not-so-large banks were intent on having an IRB foundation for their regulatory capital requirements. The US members of the Basel Committee, particularly the Federal Reserve, were advocating more strongly than ever a far-reaching shift to an IRB approach. While some European members, particularly German supervisors, had misgivings, the Basel Committee agreed at a meeting in early 2000 to forge ahead with such an approach. In June 2000, with the committee well on its way to developing its first IRB proposal, McDonough stated publicly that "we are more committed than ever to an internal ratings–based approach" and that the committee could "now envision extending the applicability

---

on Basel II," *American Banker*, March 15, 2005, 4. Banks might also have seen such signals even where they were not intended. For example, in a March 2001 speech, Federal Reserve Board Governor Laurence Meyer suggested that "many institutions may desire to migrate directly to the advanced approach so as to achieve the largest possible reductions in regulatory capital." Although Meyer made this prediction in the context of emphasizing the high threshold standards that would be applied to banks wishing to elect the advanced IRB approach, banks may have drawn the inference that substantial capital reductions were likely for advanced IRB banks. See Laurence Meyer, remarks at the Annual Washington Conference of the Institute of International Bankers, Washington, March 5, 2001.

33. One contemporary account mentions this logic and the hope of banks for its realization. See "Capital Cushion Fight," *The Economist*, June 9, 2001.

of the internal ratings method approach to banks of varying sizes, including small and medium-sized institutions."[34]

Little had changed in the state of the art of quantitative risk assessment in the months since June 1999. What, then, *had* changed? First, widespread criticism of the external ratings approach revealed it to be an uncertain route to any of the various goals of the Basel II process. Second, Federal Reserve officials—particularly members of the Board of Governors—had become more assertive in championing the IRB approach. Third, the large international banks with potentially the most to gain from a change of regulatory paradigm to an IRB approach had organized themselves both at national and international levels in an effort to influence the final Basel II rules.

Shift to an Internal Ratings–Based Approach

In January 2001, the Basel Committee issued CP-2, which set forth the promised IRB approach (Basel Committee 2001a, 2001b). In fact, it set forth *two* IRB methodologies, reflecting the committee's new view that small and medium-sized institutions should have the option, if they were willing and able to invest the necessary resources, to elect such an approach. The committee indicated that it would "finalize" the new accord by the end of 2001, for implementation by 2004. As it turned out, the release of CP-2 was only the first step down what has been an arduous path to the committee's goal of implementing an IRB regulatory paradigm in its member countries.

CP-2 changed the nature of the Basel II exercise. In place of the approximately 60-page CP-1 and the 30-page Basel I was a package of over 450 pages, including the proposal itself and seven supporting documents. The proposal was not just long and detailed but technically complex, characteristics that have carried over into the final version of Basel II. Despite its length and complexity, however, CP-2 was fundamentally incomplete. Several key issues were left for later elaboration.[35] Furthermore, the committee acknowledged that it was uncertain about the proper calibration of the IRB risk-weighting formulas. Accordingly, it did "not have enough information at the moment to assess the full impact of the proposal" (Basel Committee 2001a, paragraph 52). As would later become clear during a series of quantitative impact studies (QIS), the committee

---

34. See William McDonough, "Update on the Major Initiative to Revise the 1998 Capital Accord," remarks to the 4th Annual Supervision Conference of the British Bankers Association, June 19, 2000.

35. Indeed, the committee characterized its approach as "evolutionary," anticipating revisions of its rules as risk management techniques developed further. Thus, even with respect to matters it did address in CP-2, the committee raised the prospect of regular changes.

has never really solved the problem of predicting the impact of its proposals on required capital levels.

Thus, despite its length, CP-2 was less a fully articulated plan resembling a proposed regulation in US administrative law practice than, in the committee's words, "a starting point for additional dialogue" (Basel Committee 2001a, 53). While the committee used this language to refer only to the issue of calibrating the risk weights, it may as well have referred to the entire proposal. The gaps in CP-2 and numerous elements of the proposal that *were* included elicited another round of strong criticism—principally from banks but also from consultants and commentators. These complaints led to abrupt shifts of position by the committee on some fairly basic issues and a series of delays in completing the revised framework.

The delays and extensive revisions not only called into question the wisdom of the committee's approach but also gave each bank or group of banks in the member countries ample time to organize in pursuit of changes in the proposal that would be to their liking. The result was a series of ad hoc accommodations by the committee to a wide variety of demands for change. By releasing CP-1 and CP-2—two fundamentally incomplete proposals—the Basel Committee ensured that it would spend much of the Basel II process reacting to criticism and on the defensive. In a sense, the committee became captive to its own process, forging indomitably ahead in order to avoid the failure of an abandoned project but needing constantly to placate the banks' opposition if it was to make progress.

Although a proposal as detailed as CP-2 defies easy summary, its key elements are set forth in box 4.2. Notwithstanding the extensive disparagement of the CP-1 proposal, the basics of the "standardized" approach to capital requirements remained the same, though several modifications were made, most for the stated end of increasing risk sensitivity. Among the more important were the addition of a fourth 50 percent risk bucket for corporate exposures, a preferential risk weight for short-term exposures to other banks denominated in the local currency, and the possibility that a bank or corporation could have a lower risk weighting than the sovereign in its country of incorporation. In response to the criticism that lending to developing country sovereigns would be seriously affected by the absence of external credit ratings for most such countries, the committee specified that export credit agencies were a permissible source of credit scores for sovereign exposures.

The committee's key innovations in CP-2 were the IRB proposals, which envisioned two distinct approaches. Creation of the "foundational" internal ratings–based (F-IRB) approach responded to the wider-than-expected demand among banks in member countries for participation in an IRB approach. The A-IRB approach was assumed to be applicable only to a relative handful of big banks. Thus was established the second key structural feature of Basel II. The first was the three-pillar approach

Box 4.2   Changes proposed in the second consultative paper

Pillar 1: Minimum Capital Requirements

Standardized Approach

- addition of export credit agencies as source of ratings for sovereign risk
- adjustments to risk weight proposed in the first consultative paper (CP-1) (e.g., exposure to a bank may be rated as less risky than that bank's sovereign)
- wider range of collateral acceptable for credit risk mitigation

Internal Ratings–Based (IRB) Approach

- creation of two IRB approaches
- foundational approach uses banks' estimates of probability of default and supervisory parameters for exposure in the event of default, loss if default occurred, and maturity of the exposure in calculation of risk weights for each sovereign, bank, and corporate exposure
- advanced approach permits use of bank estimates of probability of default, exposure in the event of default, loss if default occurred, and maturity of the exposure
- capital requirements determined through supervisory formulas into which probability of default, exposure in the event of default, loss if default occurred, and maturity of the exposure are inputs
- separate treatment of retail exposures based on risk associated with distinct segments of retail lending

Asset Securitization

- both standardized and IRB approaches
- clarification of "clean break" requirement
- differentiated capital requirements for originating, investing, and sponsoring banks

Operational Risk

- basic indicator approach to calculate requirement using percentage of a single indicator (e.g., gross income)
- standardized approach to use different indicators and percentages for different business lines

(box continues on next page)

Box 4.2   Changes proposed in the second consultative paper
(continued)

- internal measurement approach to use combination of internally-developed data and supervisory factors

Pillar 2: Supervisory Review of Capital Adequacy

- elaboration of four principles from CP-1
- interest rate risk to be evaluated as part of supervisory review rather than subject to capital charge calculation

Pillar 3: Market Discipline

- elaboration of required disclosures for:
    - ◆ scope of application;
    - ◆ composition of capital;
    - ◆ risk exposure assessment and management processes; and
    - ◆ capital adequacy.
- distinctions between "core" and "supplementary" disclosures
- expectation of supervisory response to inadequate bank disclosures

Source: Basel Committee (2001b).

---

adopted in CP-1. Now CP-2 had introduced three separate methodologies for banks of varying risk management capabilities. This feature applied not just to the calculation of risk weights but also to other key elements of pillar 1.

The essence of the IRB approaches was that qualifying banks could use their own estimates of the probability of default of each of its exposures. Under the A-IRB approach, banks would also be able to use their own estimates of their exposure in the event of default, loss if default occurred, and maturity of the exposure. These values would be converted into risk weights through formulas devised by the supervisors. Separate formulas were provided for corporate, sovereign, and bank exposures. A somewhat different framework would apply to retail exposures.[36] The committee indicated that separate frameworks were also necessary for project finance and equity exposures but that it had not yet developed them.

---

36. Since banks do not customarily assign ratings to individual retail exposures, the committee chose to follow bank practice in allowing the grouping of exposures into categories, or "segments," based on similar risk characteristics.

To be eligible for an IRB approach, a bank would have to meet minimum requirements relating to its internal rating, credit assessment, and disclosure practices. To qualify for the A-IRB approach, a bank would have to meet additional requirements applicable to the calculation of exposure in the event of default, loss if default occurred, and maturity of the exposure. In proposing reduced capital requirements for credit risk mitigation techniques such as collateral and credit derivatives, the committee also set forth different methods, with the A-IRB approach again allowing the greatest use of internal assessments.

The committee provided special rules for calculating capital requirements for securitization exposures. Reflecting the concern that securitization was a form of regulatory arbitrage under Basel I, CP-2 mandated the deduction from capital of retained first-loss positions and similar credit enhancements. The capital required for other securitized holdings depended on whether the bank had originated the securities or was an investor in securitized assets of another issuer. Here again, the committee contemplated standardized, F-IRB, and A-IRB approaches. However, its securitization proposals for the IRB approaches were explicitly tentative and not fully developed.

While the committee had acquiesced to much of the criticism of CP-1, it held fast to its objective of introducing a capital charge for operational risk. Once again, though, CP-2 was more suggestive than fully elaborated. The committee proposed to parallel its three approaches to credit risk capital requirements with three approaches to operational risk. The *basic indicator approach* would link the charge to a "single indicator that serves as a proxy for the bank's overall risk exposure" (Basel Committee 2001a, paragraph 163). The committee suggested, but did not specify clearly, that gross income would be the relevant indicator. The *standardized approach* would also base the charge on an indicator that proxied for risk exposure, but here both the indicator and the percentage taken would vary by business line (e.g., corporate finance, retail banking). Finally, the *internal measurement approach* would permit a bank to use its own inputs to quantify the risk of operational losses in each of its business lines; the output would then be adjusted by a factor designated by the committee to yield the operational risk charge.

Notwithstanding the continued insistence of the committee that all three pillars were to be important regulatory tools, the disproportionate emphasis on pillar 1 had, if anything, increased in CP-2. The supervisory review process of pillar 2 was elaborated modestly from the CP-1 baseline through the articulation of four supervisory principles (box 4.3). The committee also issued guidelines for supervisory review of the minimum standards for IRB eligibility, supervisory transparency and accountability, and the review of interest rate risk. The last of these represented another accommodation by the Basel Committee to criticism from banks, which had argued in reaction to CP-1 that the variety of their methods for

---

Box 4.3   Key principles of supervisory review in the second consultative paper

Principle 1: Banks should have a process for assessing their overall capital in relation to their risk profile and a strategy for maintaining their capital levels.

Principle 2: Supervisors should review and evaluate banks' internal capital adequacy assessments and strategies, as well as their ability to monitor and ensure their compliance with regulatory capital ratios. Supervisors should take appropriate supervisory action if they are not satisfied with the results of this process.

Principle 3: Supervisors should expect banks to operate above the minimum regulatory capital ratios and should have the ability to require banks to hold capital in excess of the minimum.

Principle 4: Supervisors should seek to intervene at an early stage to prevent capital from falling below the minimum levels required to support the risk characteristics of a particular bank and should require rapid remedial action if capital is not maintained or restored.

Source: Basel Committee (2001b).

---

managing interest rate risk made it inappropriate for pillar 1 coverage. The implications of some of these guidelines were potentially far-reaching. For example, the CP-1 idea that banks should generally hold capital above the minimum required level was repeated. Another principle, seemingly echoing the US system of prompt corrective action, suggested that supervisors should intervene "at an early stage" to prevent capital from falling below regulatory minimum levels. Yet all of these guidelines seemed hortatory in nature and were generally addressed to supervisors, rather than banks.

The pillar 3 proposals in CP-2, on the other hand, built on an earlier committee paper to present a fairly detailed list of items to be disclosed by banks. The committee specified disclosures that it believed would facilitate the exercise of market discipline on risk-taking by banks. These requirements, divided into core and supplementary disclosures, were grouped into 10 topical areas (box 4.4). Substantially greater disclosure was recommended for qualifying banks that elected an IRB approach. Despite the detail it provided, the committee's expectations for implementation of pillar 3 were somewhat ambiguous. In particular, it noted that the legal authority of supervisors to require public disclosures by banks varied among member countries. Thus, although "some kind of enforcement response" was expected, that response might be indirect in some cases.

Box 4.4   Areas for public disclosure by banks in the second consultative paper

- Scope of application of capital accord within a banking group.
- Breakdown of bank's capital and supporting accounting procedures.
- Breakdown of credit risk exposures and description of credit risk management techniques.
- Identification and use of external credit assessment institutions (for banks using standardized approach).
- Internal ratings–based (IRB) methodology, coverage, and ex post performance of IRB methods, broken down for each portfolio (for banks using an IRB approach).
- Exposures covered by credit risk mitigation measures, process for managing collateral, and methods for assuring continued creditworthiness of guarantors and credit derivative counterparties.
- Methodology for calculating market risk capital requirements and, for banks using internal models approach, information about model, value-at-risk data, and backtesting.
- Operational risk methodology and exposure(s).
- Interest rate risk management technique and impact on earning and regulatory capital of rate shocks.
- Regulatory capital requirements for credit (including off-balance-sheet exposures), market, and operational risk; analysis of factors affecting capital adequacy; economic capital allocated to bank's transactions, products, customers, business lines, or organizational units, as appropriate.

Source: Pillar 3 (Market Discipline), supporting document appended to Basel Committee (2001b).

The committee asked for comments on CP-2 by May 31, 2001. More than 250 comments were received in this four-month period.[37] Even before that date, interested parties had spoken publicly, and privately to Basel Committee members, of their concerns. Many of the comments came from banks and associations representing banks or risk management officers, but comments were also received from other financial institutions, central banks and banking regulators around the world, international

---

37. Comments to CP-2 and CP-3 were all uploaded onto the Basel Committee website. Comments on CP-2 may be found at www.bis.org/bcbs/cacomments.htm (accessed May 15, 2008).

institutions, academics, think tanks, and credit rating agencies.[38] While it is obviously impossible to distill thousands of pages of comments into a fully representative synopsis of a few paragraphs, the most frequently recurring themes can be summarized as follows.

First, commenters speaking directly or indirectly on behalf of banks generally applauded the committee's embrace of IRB capital regulation, though quite a few continued to advocate faster movement toward the full use of internal models. Second, many academic or quasi-academic commenters expressed skepticism about the feasibility of the IRB approach to capital regulation, though the degree of skepticism varied considerably within this group. Third, while banks and others offered suggestions on a wide range of technical issues, a few provisions elicited criticism from a particularly high proportion of commenters. Among these were the proposal for a formulaic approach to a quantified capital charge for operational risk and the proposal to require credit risk capital charges for expected, as well as unexpected, losses.[39] Fourth, some commenters took issue with the risk-weighting formulas under the IRB approaches (and, in some cases, the standardized approach). Most frequently mentioned were the effects on firms in emerging markets and on small and medium-sized enterprises in the Basel Committee countries themselves. The committee's use of a "scaling factor" that multiplied by a factor of about 1.5 the probability of default value generated by the bank's internal system was also criticized. Fifth, many commenters noted that the CP-2 proposals were incomplete in important respects and thus they could not judge the committee's proposals as a whole. Sixth, many banks complained that the menu of disclosures proposed under pillar 3 would require banks to reveal much proprietary information and, in any case, would be needlessly expensive for the likely value to investors.

Seventh, and ultimately most important, many banks complained that regulatory capital would rise under the CP-2 proposals. The banks' conclusion, based on some quick number crunching, was borne out by the committee's second quantitative impact study (QIS). QIS-2 had been initiated in April 2001, a few months after release of the CP-2. The results, reported in November of that year (Basel Committee 2001c), revealed that regulatory capital levels would increase under each of the three CP-2 ap-

---

38. The very fact that certain entities submitted comments raised interesting questions. For example, the Federal Reserve Banks of Chicago and Richmond both sent letters to the Basel Committee, giving rise to the inference that the Board of Governors and the New York Fed had not fully involved the rest of the Federal Reserve System in developing their Basel Committee positions.

39. This proposal was particularly unwelcome to banks in the United States and other countries where the practice is to set aside reserves for expected losses. The banks argued that the CP-2 proposal would, in effect, require them to provision for expected losses twice—once in their reserves and once in their capital requirements.

Table 4.2 Results of second quantitative impact study change in capital requirements under second consultative paper proposals (percent)

	Standardized		Foundation IRB		Advanced IRB	
Group	Credit	Overall	Credit	Overall	Credit	Overall
G-10						
Group 1	6	18	14	24	−5	5
Group 2	1	13				
European Union						
Group 1	6	18	10	20	−1	9
Group 2	−1	11				
Other (non-G-10, non-EU)	5	17				

IRB = internal ratings–based

Notes: The second quantitative impact study (QIS-2) exercise involved 138 banks from 25 countries. Group 1 banks were diversified, internationally active banks. Group 2 banks were smaller or more specialized banks. Banks from Basel Committee member countries that were also European Union (EU) members were included in both the G-10 and EU categories in the reported results.

Source: Basel Committee (2001c).

proaches (see table 4.2 for a summary of the results).[40] For the A-IRB approach, the capital charge for credit risk alone would decline modestly, but the proposed new requirement for operational risk would result in increased overall regulatory capital. The overall percentage increases for the standardized approach were in the mid-teens. Most embarrassing for the Basel Committee, the overall percentage increases for the foundational IRB approach were even higher. Thus, under the CP-2 proposal, banks would have no incentive to shift from a standardized to the F-IRB approach.

As noted earlier, the committee's stated intentions were to maintain average regulatory capital levels unchanged from Basel I under the new standardized approach and to bring about a modest reduction from Basel I levels for banks adopting one of the IRB approaches. However, in light of the implications of the CP-2 methodologies for minimum capital levels, the committee now had a credibility problem. It did not seem to understand the effects of its own proposals. Far from being the "dream" for banks that Bill McDonough had promised, some banking executives, in the words of one, saw "themselves being railroaded into the new approach at a lot of cost."[41]

---

40. By the time the Basel Committee released the QIS-2 results, it had already decided to reduce the operational risk charge significantly. Thus, when the banks initially ran their numbers after release of the CP-2 proposals, they would have observed a substantially greater increase in capital requirements.

41. See John Willman, "Industry Backs Postponing New Rules on Amount of Capital Banks Must Hold," *Financial Times*, June 25, 2001.

The complaints about regulatory capital levels were in one sense a combined recapitulation of many of the banks' other complaints. The operational risk charges, inclusion of expected losses in the capital requirements, and specifics of the risk-weighting formulas all contributed to the required capital level. Similarly, a number of banks had objected to what they saw as arbitrary limitations on the degree to which credit risk could be mitigated, either directly through such devices as collateral or indirectly through portfolio diversification. In another sense, though, the banks' objection to the capital levels required by the CP-2 proposals was their *only* complaint. An increase in regulatory capital would, at least presumptively, entail foregone profits from the additional increment that could otherwise have been lent out. Hence any feature of CP-2 that boosted capital requirements was unwelcome. On the other hand, the banks were quite rationally prepared to accept regulatory features that they found arbitrary, costly, or even ill-conceived, so long as their capital requirements declined enough to make the changes on net profitable.

Process of Continuous Revision

The reception of CP-2 by bankers and other industry observers was no more positive than that accorded CP-1 a year-and-a-half earlier. Within a few months of the January 2001 release, the Basel Committee faced an unenviable situation. Its proposals, already lengthy and complex, were admittedly incomplete. Numerous technical features of the proposals were widely questioned. The impact of the proposals on minimum capital requirements appeared to be the opposite of what the committee had intended. Although US regulators had been the prime movers of a wholesale revision of the capital accord, they were internally divided. Soon there would be questions raised by elected officials in both Europe and the United States on the competitive implications for banks.

In May, influential groups of banks requested a delay in the revision of CP-2 in order to provide adequate time for the industry to react to the still inchoate proposals. In light of all these difficulties, it was unsurprising that the Basel Committee soon acknowledged that it could not keep the timetable announced in the CP-2. On June 25, the committee issued a press release announcing a delay of the final accord until 2002 and indicating a number of areas in which it intended to make changes in response to criticisms of the CP-2. This would not be the last delay. The next version of the committee's proposals would not be issued until April 2003 and, even then, would become known as the third consultative paper (CP-3) rather than the "final" version promised by the committee, which would not be issued until June 2004.

Delays and missed deadlines are common in international negotiations. Yet the three-and-a-half years between the issuance of CP-2 and release of the final revised framework were not characterized by the long periods of inactivity that usually attend such delays. Nor did the committee retreat from public view to work on its proposals in splendid isolation. On the contrary, it was now engaged in more or less constant negotiations, frequent revisions of its proposals, and nearly continuous dialogue with the banking industry. Between the June 2001 announcement and the release of CP-3, the committee issued no fewer than 10 substantive proposals on specific elements of the IRB approach (summarized in box 4.5). In truth, the committee's process appeared driven by its efforts to respond to the nearly constant barrage of objections to its proposals, including its failure to have adequately elaborated certain elements of the CP-2 package.

In many instances, it is not easy to determine if the committee's modifications in response to the many objections from banks reflected an enhanced technical understanding of matters not fully grasped in CP-2, on the one hand, or a tactical accommodation in the face of broad-based opposition, on the other (or some of both). For example, US banks with significant credit card operations had complained about the CP-2 proposals. In July 2002, the committee announced a series of changes in the treatment of retail exposures. The risk-weight curve for qualifying revolving exposures was changed in such a way as to "produce capital requirements materially below those previously proposed by the committee."[42] Risk weightings for other retail exposures and for residential mortgages were reduced. The former change was justified as an "effort to achieve greater risk sensitivity," the latter as "an effort to maintain consistency with likely changes in capital requirements under the retail IRB framework."

Whatever the motivations for any specific change, the cumulative effect of so many alterations was helpful neither to the committee's credibility nor to the coherence of its proposals. Whether the committee had such limited knowledge of risk-weighting procedures that it needed to be educated by the banks at every step, or it understood those procedures but was acquiescing to the demands placed before it, the pattern of regular and extensive changes could hardly produce confidence. Committee members seemed aware of the effects of their activities but were apparently unable to change course.[43]

The period between CP-2 and CP-3 also saw an increase in pressures on Basel Committee members from elected officials. The highest profile

---

42. See Bank for International Settlements, "Basel Committee Reaches Agreement on New Capital Accord Issues," press release, July 10, 2002.

43. In February 2002, two members of the Basel Committee were quoted, albeit anonymously, precisely to this effect. One observed that "[a]s soon as you develop an approach, it's not too long before you hear from the banks complaining about something. So you adjust—at the cost of a more complex calculation for everybody." Another was quoted as characterizing Basel II as the "great monster." See "The Good Tailors of Basel," *The Economist*, February 21, 2002.

Box 4.5   Proposals issued between the second and third consultative papers

Date	Proposal
July 2001	Modification of treatment of expected and unexpected losses.
August 2001	Proposal on internal ratings–based (IRB) treatment of equity exposures.
September 2001	Changes in credit risk mitigation techniques (including moving the "w" floor to pillar 2 and allowing netting among counterparties in repo-style transactions).
	Reduction in number of disclosures required under pillar 3 (market discipline).
	Changes and elaborations in operational risk proposal (including reduction in percentage of minimum capital to be required as operational risk charge, elaboration of an advanced management approach using banks' internal systems).
October 2001	Proposal on IRB treatment of securitizations.
	Proposal on IRB approach to specialized lending exposures.
July 2002	Major changes in previously announced proposals (including creation of new risk-weight curve for credit card exposures, more favorable risk weightings for exposures to small and medium-sized enterprises, elimination of floor capital requirement under an advanced management approach to operational risk, changes in floor capital requirements).
October 2002	Second set of proposals on treatment of asset securitizations.
February 2003	Guidelines for bank management of operational risk.

Source: Basel Committee.

example was Chancellor Gerhard Schröder's warning in the fall of 2001 that Germany would veto any European capital adequacy directive based on the CP-2 proposal. Behind this threat lay the familiar German concern with the risk weighting of exposures to small and medium-sized business.

Coincidentally (or, perhaps, not so coincidentally), the committee soon thereafter released the results of QIS-2, on the basis of which it began mooting ideas for a number of changes to CP-2, including the risk weightings for small and medium-sized business lending (Basel Committee 2001d). In July 2002, the committee announced modifications to its proposal that would reduce the risk weighting of such exposures.[44]

As the Basel process dragged on, legislators began to pay more attention and, inevitably, become more involved. Some German members of the European Parliament echoed Chancellor Schröder's concerns about the impact on small and medium-sized business. Several influential members of the US Congress communicated to US regulators their unease over various aspects of CP-2. Senator Richard Shelby (R-AL), chairman of the Senate Banking Committee, worried about the competitive effect on smaller banks that would not use an IRB approach, a concern that would later be echoed by his counterpart, Representative Michael Oxley (R-OH), chairman of the House Financial Services Committee.

Representative Oxley, along with members of his committee from both parties, also expressed concern about the proposals on operational risk and, more generally, the potential for competitive disadvantages for US banks. The former item arose from complaints by State Street Bank & Trust and Mellon Bank, which have very sizable processing, custodial, or investment management businesses relative to their conventional commercial banking operations. These banks stood to incur the significant new capital charges for operational risk while deriving little or no benefit from the reduced capital requirements for credit risk contemplated under Basel II.[45]

The committee released CP-3 (Basel Committee 2003a) in April 2003 and, less than a week later, the results of its third quantitative impact study, QIS-3 (Basel Committee 2003b, 2003c). Both documents incorporated major changes—previously announced by the committee—on retail exposures, small business lending, operational risk, credit risk mitigation, and asset securitization. Similarly, CP-3 included a number of technical, though in some cases significant, modifications to the pillar 1 rules that had first been set forth in the committee's October 2002 instructions to banks for completing the QIS-3 survey (Basel Committee 2002b). Thus, to a considerable extent, the results of QIS-3 were a test run of the CP-3 rules, even though the study had been conducted prior to the release of CP-3 itself.

---

44. Ibid., footnote 42.

45. See Steven G. Elliott, letter on behalf of Mellon Financial Corporation to Basel Committee on Banking Supervision, May 29, 2001; and David A. Spina, chairman and chief executive officer, Street Corporation, testimony before the US House of Representatives Financial Service Committee Subcommittee on Domestic Monetary Policy, Technology and Economic Growth, February 27, 2003.

These results suggested that the tide had turned in favor of banks that would adopt the A-IRB approach. Overall capital requirements were projected to be only about 2 percent lower for A-IRB banks. However, credit risk capital requirements were down about 14 percent; the net reduction of only 2 percent resulted from the capital charges for operational risk. Insofar as there was continuing pressure on the committee to provide A-IRB banks with more flexibility on operational risk, these banks could reasonably have expected even more favorable results as further changes were made. Moreover, in releasing the results, the committee indicated that its biggest area of uncertainty was credit risk mitigation, where many banks' data systems had not been able to produce good information on all the collateral that would have qualified to reduce capital requirements. Thus, in the committee's view, the QIS-3 results probably overstated capital requirements (Basel Committee 2003b).[46] In addition, some banking industry analysts thought that the different mix of assets in large US banks, compared with European and Japanese banks, would yield overall capital reductions of 10 to 15 percent.[47]

In the immediate aftermath of the CP-3 release, prospects for Basel II looked no better than previously. They may even have looked a bit worse. The comments on CP-3 filed with the committee were numerous, lengthy, and in many cases quite critical. Some recapitulated common complaints lodged after CP-2—the requirement for capital to be held against expected losses for which provisions had been taken, the reluctance of the committee to lower capital requirements for well-diversified portfolios, the specifics of the formulas for some types of exposures, and the cost of the entire undertaking for prospective A-IRB banks. But there were some new emphases as well.

The IIF, echoed by a number of other banking associations, identified the procyclicality of the proposals as a fundamental defect (Institute of International Finance 2003). As the IIF itself noted, all risk-weighted capital requirements are inherently procyclical, in that they require more capital to be held—and thus dampen new lending—as the credit circumstances of borrowers decline. This issue is discussed in detail in chapter 5. For present purposes, it suffices to note that this new emphasis by the banking groups was an adroit reformulation of earlier arguments, since they charged that the failure of the Basel Committee to incorporate in its formulas the mitigating effects of portfolio diversification exacerbated the procyclical character of the committee's proposals. The potential drag of procyclical banking regulation on expansionary monetary policy during a recession was of

---

46. Some representatives of the banking industry questioned whether more complete knowledge of bank collateral positions would ultimately reduce capital requirements (Institute of International Finance 2003).

47. See Rob Garver, "Basel Rules Seen Lowering Requirements Up to 15%," *American Banker*, May 6, 2003, 4.

obvious concern to central bankers on the committee, who were both banking supervisors and guardians of macroeconomic policy.

Beyond continued complaints from banks, the Basel process seemed in mid-2003 to be suffering from internal dissension as well. To some extent, disagreement arose from the different domestic circumstances of the European and US regulators. As they negotiated the international arrangement, European members of the Basel Committee were looking ahead to a revised European Union (EU) capital adequacy directive (CAD). Issues that were addressed in the Basel deliberations would, at least presumptively, not be reopened when the new CAD was drafted for approval by the council and the European Parliament. In addition, continental bank regulatory systems had traditionally relied less on the ad hoc supervisory interaction between banks and regulators characteristic of the US and UK systems and more on outside auditors to assess bank compliance with capital regulations. Thus, regulators from the continental European countries had a dual incentive to seek more, rather than less, detail in the Basel arrangement.

For their part, US regulators were feeling considerable pressure from banks and, increasingly, from members of Congress on such issues as capital requirements for expected losses, operational risk, and the proposed capital requirement for the unused portions of credit limits for credit cards. The business profiles of influential US banks and, in the case of expected losses, US practices of provisioning meant that these were important constituency issues for US regulators.[48] European regulators were also unhappy with US regulators for announcing in February 2003 their unilateral

---

48. Under the definition of capital created by Basel I, banks are permitted to count loan-loss reserves of up to 1.25 percent of risk-weighted assets as tier 2 capital. However, in order to qualify for tier 2 treatment, these reserves must not have been set against any particular exposures identified as impaired. Instead, they must have been "generally" provisioned—that is, set aside on the basis of past experience that losses of a certain magnitude could be expected in the bank's current portfolio (Basel Committee 1988, 16). Under CP-2, capital requirements would apply to an identifiable expected, as well as unexpected, loss from a particular exposure, even where the bank had set aside reserves to cover that expected loss. CP-2 indicated that the definition of capital would remain as under Basel I. Since provisioning for identified losses was not eligible for tier 2 capital treatment, banks that engaged in such provisioning would get no capital benefit. Unlike Basel I, however, where the capital charge for a loan was based solely on the category of borrower, under the IRB approaches of CP-2 the bank's capital charge against an impaired loan would increase, because the probability of default and/or loss given default would be increasing. Hence, in the view of many US banks (and Comptroller Hawke), CP-2 essentially required a double charge for the same expected loss. The Basel Committee was aware of this issue. However, it noted that, in many countries, provisioning was essentially limited to general provisioning, which was taken into account in the calculation of tier 2 capital. Hence it proposed calculating capital charges on the basis of expected as well as unexpected losses, with some complicated offsets for provisioning, particularly specific provisioning. The problem was that the United States was not like most countries, since regulatory and accounting practice required banks to provision for identifiable expected losses.

decision that the new Basel rules would apply only to the very largest US banks, [49] a decision that was also influenced heavily by domestic politics.[50]

To make matters more complicated, it appeared that US regulators themselves were far from united on the new proposals. Only two days after CP-2 was issued, a senior official of the Office of the Comptroller of the Currency had questioned publicly whether the degree of complexity contained in the proposal would be acceptable to banks or excessively burdensome for bank examiners. This was only the first of what would become periodic expressions of skepticism from the comptroller's office, including the comptroller himself.[51] Over time, it became clear that FDIC officials were also concerned about the direction in which the Basel Committee proposals were headed, particularly in their effects on required

---

49. While the Europeans were understandably disappointed, they should not have been completely surprised. In late 2000, before CP-2 had been formally issued but well after its direction had become clear to Basel Committee members, the US bank regulatory agencies issued an advance notice of proposed rule making in which they referred to the possibility of the new Basel agreement adopting an IRB approach and solicited views as to options for capital rules applicable to "noncomplex" institutions (US Department of Treasury et al. 2000).

50. The shifting policy of the US banking agencies with respect to the capital rules that would be applicable to the roughly 8500 non A-IRB financial institutions is one of the stronger pieces of evidence for the proposition that the agencies had not fully thought through their goals and strategy before embarking on Basel II. The 2003 announcements was apparently motivated by the conclusion that the expense of shifting from Basel I as modified by US practice to the standardized approach of Basel II was not worth the anticipated safety and soundness benefits. However, as it became clear that the regulatory capital requirements of the A-IRB banks would decline significantly, representatives of all the other banks complained that they would be unfairly disadvantaged in those business lines such as residential mortgages where there was competition between the largest banks and regional, or even community, banks. The regulators responded by proposing a "Basel IA" that would, among other things, reduce capital requirements for some exposures, such as mortgages. Then, as part of the 2007 compromise on A-IRB implementation, described later in this chapter, the agencies shifted from a "Basel IA" approach to an intention to propose a "standardized" approach.

51. Comptroller Hawke's skepticism was expressed especially often in the first half of 2003 through press interviews, speeches, and congressional appearances. Though he embraced the idea of a reform project, Hawke underscored his belief that the proposals were excessively complex and worried about the imprecision of forecasts as to how Basel would change capital requirements. He emphasized repeatedly that he would carefully consider all comments to proposed implementation of the eventual Basel II rules in the United States and would not hesitate, if necessary, to make changes in the method of US implementation. Stressing that Basel II would not be an agreement binding under international law, he implied, but did not explicitly say, that these changes would not necessarily be completely consistent with the Basel II agreement itself. See Charles Pretzlik, "US Regulator Questions Basel Timetable," *Financial Times,* June 17, 2003, 28. See also John D. Hawke, testimony before the Subcommittee on Domestic Monetary Policy, Technology and Economic Growth of the Committee on Financial Services, US House of Representatives, February 27, 2003; remarks to the Centre for the Study of Financial Innovation, London, March 13, 2003; testimony

capital levels.[52] There were even occasional hints that the bank supervisors within the Federal Reserve were less enthusiastic than the governors and staff economists who had been championing the Basel II process.

After influential members of the House Financial Services Committee introduced a bill to require the four banking agencies to develop a unified position on Basel issues (and giving the secretary of the treasury default authority to determine the US position), the regulators proclaimed during June 2003 hearings on this bill that they were working well together. But just a month later, in releasing their joint advanced notice of proposed rule making for implementation of Basel, Comptroller Hawke and FDIC Chairman Donald Powell released separate statements that called into question the very concept of the IRB approach.[53] These disagreements have flared and subsided with changes in the personnel leading the banking agencies and in the Basel proposals themselves. But they have never disappeared and, indeed, continue to the time of this writing to bedevil US implementation efforts.

Despite all these problems, prospects for the Basel II effort brightened considerably in the fall of 2003. Whether part of an intentional strategy to gain the big banks as a key ally, or as a result of a series of reactive changes, the Basel Committee was slowly winning over the large banks. The successive modifications led banks to see the possibility of significantly reduced capital requirements. Also, for quite independent reasons, some US and European regulators were becoming increasingly intent on producing a final revised framework and moving to implementation. As already mentioned, the Europeans needed to move forward on a new EU capital adequacy directive and were thus anxious to have a completed Basel II. Federal Reserve officials, while acknowledging that a good deal of refinement was still necessary for the A-IRB approach, had taken the position that the only way to learn enough to make these refinements was to implement the new rules. Finally, Bank of Spain Governor Jaime

---

before the Committee on Banking, Housing, and Urban Affairs, US Senate, June 18, 2003; and testimony before the Subcommittee on Financial Institutions and Consumer Credit of the Committee on Financial Services, US House of Representatives, June 19, 2003.

52. Documentary evidence of the disagreement, in the form of a memo by FDIC Chairman Donald Powell and a reply from Federal Reserve Board Vice Chair Roger Ferguson, was leaked to the press in June 2003. Powell expressed concern that the Basel II proposals would leave large banks insufficiently capitalized and create competitive disadvantage for small banks. He also complained that the Basel II process was being "rushed into place, with discussions of significant alternatives now virtually ruled out by the timeline and by the international collaborative nature of the project." Ferguson replied that the Basel process had been "transparent and consultative" and that it was time to "move on to the next step" in the international process. See Rob Garver, "Basel Proposal Prompts FDIC to Query Fed, OCC," *American Banker*, June 17, 2003, 1.

53. See Rob Garver, "Split Among US Regulators May Stall Basel II Capital Plan," *American Banker*, July 14, 2003, 1.

Caruana succeeded Bill McDonough as chair of the Basel Committee in May 2003, bringing with him a style of shuttle diplomacy that was well suited to mediating the bevy of disputes that hindered completion of an agreed-upon version of the new capital accord.

The watershed moment came at the October 2003 Basel Committee meeting. The fruits of Caruana's efforts were apparent in what became known as the "Madrid compromise." The committee announced a proposal to modify the requirement for capital to be held against expected losses, a major victory for US banks (and for Comptroller Hawke, who had championed their cause).[54] The committee also announced its intentions to eliminate the so-called "supervisory formula" for asset securitization that had so rankled the large banks,[55] revisit the treatment of credit card exposures, and modify certain credit risk mitigation techniques.[56] Caruana had successfully navigated around German objections that the United States was trying to reopen major negotiating issues so that US regulators could take home a major prize to their banks. The apparent quid pro quo had been that, despite misgivings with the timetable in some US quarters, a final revised framework would be completed by mid-2004. Hawke, for the first time, expressed optimism about prospects for the Basel process.[57]

In the succeeding months, the committee elaborated its changes on expected losses, securitization, and other issues (see box 4.6 for a summary of all changes between CP-3 and the final revised framework). In May 2004, the committee announced that it had resolved remaining issues—including changes to the formula for revolving retail exposures (credit cards)[58]—and that it would publish the text of the new framework in June.[59]

---

54. The compromise was that a bank would not be required to hold capital against expected losses from an exposure to the extent that it had taken provisions for those expected losses. If, however, the expected loss exceeded the actual provisions, the shortfall must be deducted equally from tier 1 and tier 2 capital. A provision exceeding the expected loss can be included in tier 2 capital. Because of this last feature, the loan loss reserves are no longer eligible for tier 2 capital treatment under the IRB approach (Basel Committee 2004a). The final revised framework limits the increase in tier 2 capital to 0.6 percent of risk-weighted assets.

55. The supervisory formula was a method for risk weighting unrated securitized exposures. As proposed in CP-3, it was, even by Basel II standards, incredibly complicated. In the end, the formula was not eliminated but modified. The change aligned the capital charge for these exposures more closely to banks' internal ratings (Basel Committee 2004b).

56. See Bank for International Settlements, "Basel II: Significant Progress on Major Issues," press release, October 11, 2003.

57. See Gary Silverman, "US Banks 'Should be Pleased' at Latest from Basel II," *Financial Times*, October 15, 2003, 15.

58. The compromise here involved fixing a specific, reasonably low, correlation number for potential losses attributable to the unused portions of credit lines.

59. See Bank for International Settlements, "Consensus Achieved on Basel II Proposals," press release, May 11, 2004.

Revised Framework

On June 26, 2004, the Basel Committee officially released Basel II, formally called "International Convergence of Capital Measurement and Capital Standards: A Revised Framework" (Basel Committee 2004c). Including appendices, the paper was 250 pages long. The revised framework incorporated the October 2003, January 2004, and May 2004 proposals, and made some additional changes—notably in the areas of credit risk mitigation and qualifying revolving retail exposures. For all the technical and political adjustments along the way, the stated aims of the committee echoed those voiced at the outset of the long Basel II process.

> The fundamental objective of the committee's work to revise the 1988 accord has been to develop a framework that would further strengthen the soundness and stability of the international banking system while maintaining sufficient consistency that capital adequacy regulation will not be a significant source of competitive inequality among internationally active banks. (Basel Committee 2004c, paragraph 4)

The committee added that it believed "the revised framework will promote the adoption of stronger risk management practices by the banking industry, and views this as one of its major benefits." This outcome, while in some sense a corollary of the safety and soundness aim, had not been emphasized by the committee as a whole when the Basel II process began, although Federal Reserve officials had embraced such a goal.[60]

So too, for all the modifications made in the preceding few years, the basic structure of the revised framework had not changed, including the three-pillar approach introduced in CP-1, the three alternative methodologies unveiled in CP-2, the inclusion of a capital requirement for operational risk, special rules for dealing with securitizations, and adjustments to take account of credit risk mitigation techniques (box 4.7 outlines the main elements of the revised framework). However, the legacy of years of compromise and adjustment is conspicuous, in the form of dozens of rules or standards on which discretion is granted national supervisors in implementing the revised framework into national law. To some degree, these items reflect the committee's awareness that various features of national banking law and practice may require somewhat different treatment in capital adequacy regulation.[61] They also reflect the concern expressed by then-Comptroller Hawke and others that the Basel II process was overspecifying its rules, particularly for the IRB methodologies. At the same time, though, the exercise of discretion on many of these rules will permit nontrivial divergences in national implementation, thereby calling into question the purported goal of removing capital regulation as a source of competitive inequality.[62]

---

60. Even after release of the revised framework, work continued—jointly with the International Organization of Securities Commissions—to align the new rules with the requirements for market risk, refine and expand recognition of the effects of guarantees, and provide a new way of modeling exposures to counterparty credit risk. This additional work was subsequently joined to the text of the 2004 document and is now available in a comprehensive version (Basel Committee 2006g).

61. A number of provisions granting national discretion actually grant discretion to apply more stringent criteria than set forth in the revised framework. As was the case under Basel I, and as is implicit in the concept of pillar 2, national supervisors will never be understood to have deviated from shared expectations by imposing stricter capital requirements on their banks. Thus, at first glance, this set of provisions is something of a puzzle. However, in many cases the Basel Committee members intending to apply such criteria may want them mentioned specifically in the revised framework.

62. An example should illustrate the point. As a result of the political accommodation with Germany, a favorable adjustment is made to the risk-weight formula for corporate exposures as applied to small and medium-sized enterprises. The revised framework stipulates that the determination of whether a corporation qualifies as a small or medium-sized enterprise is generally to be based on its annual sales. However, supervisors are permitted to allow banks to substitute total assets for total sales as the determinative threshold "when total sales are not a meaningful indicator of firm size" (Basel Committee 2004c, paragraph 274). The standardized approach also contains numerous opportunities for the exercise of national discretion, not least of which is that national supervisors are to make the determination whether an external credit assessment institution qualifies for use by its banks (Basel Committee 2004c, paragraph 90).

Box 4.7   Outline of revised framework (Basel II)

Pillar 1

Credit Risk

Standardized Approach

- addition of a 150 percent risk category to the 0, 20, 50, and 100 percent Basel I categories
- risk ratings may be based on evaluations of external credit assessment institutions; corporate exposures may thus be as low as 20 percent
- credit conversion factor approach retained for off-balance-sheet exposures; conversion factor for commitment with maturity under one year increased from 0 percent under Basel I to 20 percent
- addition of alternative, "comprehensive" method to Basel I approach for using collateral to reduce credit risk
- supervisory discretion to allow guarantees and credit derivatives to reduce capital requirements

Internal Ratings–Based Approaches

- exposures allocated to risk categories based on internal bank assessments of probability of default and—in the advanced internal ratings–based (IRB) approach—loss given default, exposure at default, and maturity
- probability of default, loss given default, exposure at default, and maturity used as inputs for risk-weighting functions provided in the revised framework
- separate functions for sovereign, bank, corporate, retail, and equity exposures
- corporate exposure function varies for project finance, object finance, commodities finance, income-producing real estate, and high-volatility commercial real estate
- retail exposure function varies for residential mortgage loans and revolving exposures (credit cards)
- expected losses dealt with through provisioning and adjustments to capital
- extensive requirements for IRB eligibility—e.g., rating system design, validation of internal estimates, disclosure requirements
- scaling factor to IRB capital requirement to be imposed in order to achieve aim of maintaining aggregate levels of capital

(box continues on next page)

Box 4.7 Outline of revised framework (Basel II) *(continued)*

Securitization Exposures

Standardized Approach

- external ratings used to risk-weight exposures
- deductions from capital generally required for unrated exposures
- originating banks required to deduct retained exposures below investment grade
- with exception of eligible liquidity facilities, off-balance-sheet exposures generally converted to credit equivalent at 100 percent
- special capital requirements for early amortization provisions

Internal Ratings–Based Approach

- for externally rated exposures, IRB banks must use ratings-based approach, similar to standardized approach but taking into account seniority and granularity of exposure
- unrated exposures generally risk weighted through highly complex supervisory formula that incorporates certain bank-supplied inputs
- bank may use internal assessment approach for exposures to an asset-based commercial paper program
- special capital requirements for early amortization provisions

Operational Risk

- basic indicator approach requires capital charge of 15 percent of bank's average annual gross income in preceding three years
- standardized approach requires capital charge of between 12 and 18 percent of bank's average annual gross income in preceding three years for each of eight lines of business
- advanced measurement approach requires capital charge equal to risk measure generated by bank's internal operational risk measurement system

Market Risk

- conforming changes to 1996 Market Risk Amendment to minimize arbitrage possibilities between assets held in banking book and those held in trading book

(box continues on next page)

Box 4.7   Outline of revised framework (Basel II) *(continued)*

Pillar 2

Four Principles for Supervisory Review

- bank process for assessing overall capital adequacy in light of its risk profile
- supervisory ability to monitor and enforce regulatory capital requirements
- supervisors should expect banks to operate above minimum regulatory capital levels and have ability to require banks to hold capital above minimum
- supervisors should seek to intervene at an early stage to prevent capital from falling below minimum levels and should require remedial action

Selected Specific Issues

- supervisors must take action to deal with "outlier" banks, defined as those whose capital could decline by more than 20 percent in response to an interest rate shock of 200 basis points
- supervisors should assess bank credit risk concentration and management
- supervisors should adapt to securitization innovations

Pillar 3

- banks should have a formal disclosure policy and internal controls to implement it
- specific disclosure requirements on scope of application of revised framework in the banking group, capital structure, capital adequacy, credit risk, credit risk mitigation, counterparty credit risk, securitization, market risk, operational risk, equities, and interest rate risk
- credit risk disclosure requirements include explanation and description of internal ratings system for portfolios subject to IRB approach

Source: Basel Committee (2004d).

The committee stated its intention that the revised framework be "available for implementation" as of the end of 2006. However, the "most advanced approaches" required another year of impact studies or "parallel calculations" and thus would not be available for implementation until the end of 2007. In fact, the pace of implementation was slower, particularly in the United States. The European Union moved forward relatively expeditiously and without major controversy. As previously noted, the negotiation of Basel II was understood within Europe as a prelude to a new capital adequacy directive. In October 2005, the European Union adopted a new directive that incorporated the Basel II rules without significant change. That directive, binding on the member states but not applicable directly to financial institutions, is now in the process of national implementation. As described in chapter 6, implementation elsewhere—including in numerous non–Basel Committee countries—is proceeding unevenly but is in general moving forward.

Implementation in the United States has been substantially more controversial. As with Basel I, the federal banking regulators maintain they can implement the internationally agreed-upon capital standards under preexisting statutory authority. Thus, there have been no efforts to seek congressional approval or implementation of Basel II. Because prudential bank regulation is rarely a matter of general public concern except in the wake of financial failures such as the savings and loan crisis in the 1980s, debate over Basel II was confined to banking interests, regulatory agencies, a relative handful of influential members of Congress, and a small group of academics and policy commentators. Even with this qualification, though, consideration of Basel II has still been more open and sustained than in most other countries, as is often the case with international arrangements in the United States. In part for this reason, the implications of Basel II for bank safety and soundness have been addressed to a greater extent than elsewhere. However, the jockeying for competitive position has, if anything, been more spirited in the United States. Particularly in light of the fundamental questions about financial regulation raised by the subprime crisis, it is too early to say if national competitive equality concerns will ultimately trump prudential regulatory concerns, but the political history of Basel II suggests the possibility is real.

As described earlier in this chapter and further elaborated in chapter 6, congressional and constituency pressures on the Federal Reserve and the other regulators during the negotiations were largely centered on potential competitive disadvantages for US banks—whether with respect to the effects of A-IRB requirements on the portfolios typically held by large US banks, the impact of operational risk requirements on large custodial banks, or the impact of reduced capital requirements for large banks on their smaller competitors. In the two years following the release of the revised framework, however, a mild backlash occurred. Senators Shelby and Paul Sarbanes (D-MD), the chair and ranking member of the Senate Banking Committee, respectively, held hearings in 2005 and 2006 during which they openly expressed concern about the impact of Basel II on the safety and soundness of American banks. Sheila Bair, the newly confirmed chair of the FDIC, struck a distinctly more cautious note than her counterparts at the Federal Reserve and the Office of the Comptroller of the Currency,[63]

---

63. John Dugan, who had succeeded Jerry Hawke as Comptroller in 2005, seemed generally more favorably disposed to Basel II.

even as all four bank regulatory agencies continued to profess they were working successfully together.

With substantial uncertainty concerning the actual effects of the A-IRB approach on capital levels (to be discussed in the next chapter), as well as some concern with specific features of the pillar 1 rules, the strongest proponents of the A-IRB approach were on the defensive again. But now the questions were coming from those who feared regulatory capital would be reduced too much, rather than too little. After prolonged delay, the four federal bank regulatory agencies finally issued their notice of proposed rule making. The agencies reiterated their position that A-IRB would be required of "core" banks, defined as those with consolidated assets of at least $250 billion or consolidated total on-balance-sheet foreign exposure of at least $10 billion. Other banks were to be allowed to "opt in" to the A-IRB approach if they meet the qualifications set forth in Basel II, as elaborated by the US agencies. The proposed regulation also modified the rules in the revised framework in ways that would effectively increase capital requirements (US Department of the Treasury Office of the Comptroller of the Currency et al. 2006a).[64] In addition, the agencies proposed three overall safeguards against a significant drop in capital requirements for A-IRB banks:

- a transition floor for each bank in its first three years under A-IRB of 95 percent, 90 percent, and then 85 percent of the amount of capital that would be required under "general" capital rules, in contrast to the Basel II floors of 90 percent and 80 percent of Basel I requirements during the first two transition years[65];

- a commitment to modify the A-IRB framework if the aggregate capital of banks covered by it declines by more than 10 percent; and

- retention of the leverage ratio requirement and prompt, corrective action requirements under US law.

In proposing these safeguards, the agencies invoked the original stated aim of the Basel Committee to maintain the overall level of risk-based capital requirements. The proposal, which obviously masked some tension among the bank regulatory agencies, produced a counter reaction from cer-

---

64. For example, the proposed rule contained a broader definition of "default" than was included in Basel II and did not allow the adjustment successfully inserted by the Germans that provided a lower capital requirement for lending to small and medium-sized businesses.

65. The reference to "general" capital rules is apparently intended to refer to the rules that will be applicable to US non-A-IRB banks as of the time the A-IRB approach is adopted by a bank. Today those rules would be existing capital rules. By the time of implementation, those rules may have been changed under the so-called Basel IA initiative of the federal banking agencies.

tain banking industry interests. They argued that the "nonconformity" of the proposed regulation with Basel II would place US banks at a significant competitive disadvantage relative to their European counterparts. Four large banks that would be mandatory A-IRB institutions suggested that the standardized approach of Basel II be an option for all US banks, presumably because the safeguards in the agency-proposed rule could limit their capital reductions to the point where they did not exceed the expense of implementing the A-IRB approach. This proposal, in turn, was anathema to the Federal Reserve, which reiterated the disutility of a standardized risk-weighted capital approach for large, complex banking institutions.

After the 2006 elections—which saw both the retirement of Senator Sarbanes and the shift of Senator Shelby from chair to ranking member of the Banking Committee—congressional pressure to maintain capital levels waned. A period of uncertainty followed, during which it was rumored that the Federal Reserve and the Office of the Comptroller of the Currency might issue their own regulations that would omit the proposed rule's safeguards. Just when it appeared that the traditional consensus-based action of the banking agencies on capital regulation might break down, Fed Chairman Ben Bernanke became more directly involved and helped forge a compromise, announced by the agencies in July 2007. The three years of transition floors would be retained, along with the leverage ratio and prompt corrective action (themselves statutory requirements). However, the 10 percent aggregated capital floor, which had always been the most controversial of the safeguards, was dropped in favor of a commitment to evaluate the framework after the second transition year, and to address any "material deficiencies" that might be identified.[66] The agencies further announced that they would issue a proposed rule providing all "noncore" banks with the option of electing the standardized approach of Basel II. In so doing, the agencies explicitly dropped the idea of a "Basel IA"[67] and implicitly reaffirmed that the largest US banks would be required to adopt the A-IRB approach.[68]

---

66. The agencies announced their agreement in the form of a press release, likely issued to quell speculation that the tradition of the four acting in unison on capital requirements had collapsed.

67. This was not, however, the end of efforts to develop an alternative to Basel I for US banks that would not adopt the A-IRB approach. In June 2008 the banking agencies issued for public comment a rule that would create a "standardized framework" for such banks. The Federal Reserve described the proposal as one that would "implement certain of the less-complex approaches for calculating risk-based capital requirements that are included in the international Basel II capital accord." Federal Reserve Press Release, June, 26, 2008. Reactions from many smaller banks were not favorable. Principal concerns included the relative complexity of the proposed new risk-bucket system and the addition of operational risk capital charges. The agencies indicated their intention to issue a final rule by mid-2009.

68. Even this apparent resolution was not without ambiguity. The staff memorandum to the FDIC board recommending adoption of the final rule implementing A-IRB indicated that

In November the agencies finally approved the text of a joint rule that reflected the July agreement (US Department of the Treasury Office of the Comptroller of the Currency et al. 2007). Early on, the comments of banking interests filed in response to the proposed rule had criticized each deviation from the Basel II text, large and small, as creating a competitive inequality for US banks. In the final rule, the agencies noted that complaints about competitive effects had been a pervasive theme in the comments. They accommodated the banks on a number of specifics, including withdrawing their proposal for a broader definition of default for wholesale exposures than is included in Basel II. But in other instances the agencies held firm, as in their continued refusal to permit US banks to apply the special function for small and medium-sized enterprises that had been successfully demanded by German supervisors in the negotiations.

The wariness among the banking agencies concerning Basel II's implementation in the United States is perhaps most evident in their awkwardly worded (and doubtless painstakingly negotiated) statement of intention on reviewing, and possibly modifying, operation of the A-IRB approach. During the transition years, the agencies will jointly issue annual reports on the effectiveness of the new framework. In addition, after the end of the second transition year, the agencies will publish a study "to determine if there are any material deficiencies." If this study finds there are material deficiencies, banks would not be permitted to "exit the third transitional floor period" before unspecified regulatory changes are made. However, as further evidence of the continuing difference in perspective among the agencies, the primary federal supervisor of a bank could disagree with the finding of material deficiency and authorize the bank to exit the transitional period if it provided a public report explaining its reasoning.[69]

---

the notice of proposed rule making to make the standardized approach an option for "certain" US banks would "pose a question in the Basel II standardized notice of proposed rule making whether core banking organizations should be allowed to adopt the standardized approach as an alternative." The Federal Reserve had vigorously opposed this idea earlier, and there is no reason to believe it has had a change of heart. The final joint rule is worded so as to preserve the position of both agencies: "The agencies have decided at this time to require large, internationally active US banks to use the most advanced approaches of the New Accord."

69. The agencies apparently expect that their disagreements of the past few years will not abate during the transitional period. Presumably an agency that concluded there was no material deficiency in the A-IRB system could simply withhold approval of the joint evaluation, thereby obviating the need to disagree with it and allow a bank to exit the transitional period. The agencies may anticipate that they will need to compromise in order to issue the evaluation. The Federal Reserve Board and Office of the Comptroller of the Currency nonetheless will preserve their ability (which is legally unimpaired in any case) to let banks exit the transitional period and thus allow their capital to drop below 80 percent of the levels that would be required under the rules then applicable to non-A-IRB banks in the United States—presumably some form of the standardized approach.

Responding to the Subprime Crisis

Even as US regulatory agencies were struggling to reach consensus on an implementation plan, and before Basel II was up and running anywhere, dramatic developments in financial markets raised questions as to both the soundness of the A-IRB approach and the wisdom of supervisors having spent so much of the preceding decade focused on it. The catalyst was the subprime crisis that erupted in the summer of 2007 and, as of this writing in the spring of 2008, has yet to fully play out. The supervisory response has been somewhat schizophrenic: a general though not universal reaffirmation of the importance of implementing Basel II, along with proposals for some significant changes in response to the revealed flaws of the revised framework.

Problems in the market for securitized subprime mortgages became apparent early in 2007, when spreads on various structured products widened substantially, a seemingly lagged response to two years of increasing delinquencies on the underlying subprime mortgages (Borio 2008, 5). After a brief rebound, market repricing took hold with a vengeance in the early summer. Spreads shot upwards precipitously on most securities backed by home equity loans, including many that had been highly rated by external rating agencies and that were now downgraded en masse. Delinquency rates for subprime mortgages continued their upward trend. Many off-balance-sheet entities created by financial institutions to transfer risk were having difficulties rolling over their issues of commercial paper, because the institutional investors that buy this paper had realized they could no longer rely on the quality of the underlying mortgage-based assets. The off-balance-sheet entities—both conduits and the now-infamous structured investment vehicles—were thus forced to call upon the backup liquidity facilities provided by the sponsoring financial institution.

By late July 2007, the impact of these developments on banks was dramatically illustrated when IKB, a German bank, was unable to provide adequate support to one of its sponsored funding vehicles and had to be rescued by its principal shareholder and a consortium of other banks.[70] Though IKB was a relatively small bank, its difficulties were not dissimilar to those experienced by much larger banks on both sides of the Atlantic. A number of hedge funds and large nonbank mortgage companies also experienced severe difficulties. The spread of liquidity problems and continued credit deterioration in the underlying mortgage assets soon developed into something approaching a systemic liquidity crisis. In August LIBOR rates spiked suddenly. Banks had become increasingly unwilling to lend to one another, both because of concerns about the condition of potential counterparties afflicted with falling asset values and because they were

---

70. See "Sold Down the River Rhine," *The Economist*, August 9, 2007, 32.

focused on strengthening their own liquidity positions. In September a British bank—Northern Rock—suffered a deposit run and had to receive emergency assistance from the Bank of England.

The ensuing months saw a cascade of adverse developments that reinforced one another. Throughout the fall and winter, large US and European banks that had sponsored off-balance-sheet entities or dealt substantially in various forms of securitized mortgage assets took a series of write-downs. Following a stillborn effort by three large banks—encouraged by the Bush administration—to create an $80 billion fund to purchase assets from structured investment vehicles in order to relieve the liquidity crunch, a number of banking organizations brought tens of billions of dollars of structured investment vehicle assets back onto their balance sheets in the fall. The fact that at least one of these institutions, Citigroup, had no contractual obligation to do so suggested that *no* capital requirements would have captured the risks that had been effectively assumed.[71] Capital ratios of banks and bank holding companies dropped, and a number of banks sought large injections of new equity from sovereign wealth funds and other sources of readily available capital. Credit problems spread to other forms of securitized assets, while credit markets remained somewhere between impaired and frozen.

At first glance, the origins and severity of the subprime crisis seem to reflect very badly on Basel II. After all, three of the prominent features of the revised framework were reliance on external rating agencies, use of internal risk assessments, and lower capital requirements for residential mortgages. Yet defaults on mortgages were at the center of the crisis, credit models had clearly failed to capture the risks embedded in the securitized assets, and the rating agencies had seemed—as in the Asian financial crisis a decade before—to be behind the curve.[72] The origins of the subprime crisis—from the so-called "originate-to-distribute" model of mortgage lending to the serious liquidity problems of financial institu-

---

71. The motivation for Citigroup's action was understood by market actors to be grounded in reputational considerations. If Citigroup did not stand behind an entity that it had created, its customers might become more reluctant to involve themselves in future Citigroup ventures. Appropriately enough, Citigroup's response in late 2007 had been anticipated 20 years earlier by its then-chairman, Walter Wriston, in testimony before the Senate Banking Committee: "[I]t is unconceivable that any major bank would walk away from any subsidiary of its holding company. If your name is on the door, all of your capital and assets are going to be behind it in the real world. Lawyers can say you have separation, but the marketplace . . . would not see it that way" (US Senate 1987, 9).

72. In the spring of 2008, reports surfaced to the effect that Moody's own computer modeling had incorrectly assigned higher-than-warranted ratings to various forms of structured debt instruments. See Sam Jones, Gillian Tett, and Paul J. Davies, "Moody's Error Gave Top Ratings to Debt Products," *Financial Times*, May 21, 2008, 1. If further inquiry bears out these reports, the incident will at once capture the potential dangers of excessive reliance both on modeling and on external rating agencies in setting regulatory capital.

tions—led some to resurrect the criticism that the Basel II exercise had commanded far too much of the Basel Committee's attention in the preceding decade, at the expense of other important supervisory challenges.

Defenders of Basel II countered that, had the revised framework been in place, banks would have been required to set aside capital against the risks entailed in their credit enhancements for their off-balance-sheet entities, whereas Basel I did not require any capital set-asides for commitments of less than a year's duration. They also underscored the core aim of Basel II to provide greater risk sensitivity. Finally, they suggested that Basel II's emphasis on better risk management and stress-testing might have placed banks in a stronger position.[73] The first point was somewhat weakened by the fact that US regulators had unilaterally instituted capital requirements for credit enhancements in 2005, well before the subprime crisis. The last two points undoubtedly had merit but did not really counter the criticism concerning models, rating agencies, and the lowering of capital requirements for mortgages.

Even as strains on banks from the subprime crisis were becoming evident in the spring and summer of 2007, regulators from Basel Committee countries generally gave no indication that events counseled a reconsideration of Basel II. On the contrary, the emphasis in public statements was on the need to move forward with implementation.[74] As losses mounted and strains became a full-blown crisis, however, serious questions about the adequacy of regulatory systems for commercial banking and other large financial institutions were being asked by knowledgeable people both in and out of the official sector. At their October 2007 meeting, the G-7 finance ministers and central bank governors instructed the Financial Stability Forum (FSF)—an umbrella group of national and international financial authorities that includes the Basel Committee—"to undertake an analysis of the causes and weaknesses that have produced the turmoil and to set out recommendations for increasing the resilience of markets and institutions going forward" (Financial Stability Forum 2008, 1) In April 2008, the FSF released its report and recommendations, which included proposed changes to Basel II. A week later, the Basel Committee echoed the FSF in its own press release.[75]

---

73. See "Special Report on the World Economy: On Credit Watch," *The Economist*, October 20, 2007, 94.

74. See Randall S. Kroszner, "Basel II Implementation in the United States," speech at the New York Bankers Association Annual Visit, Washington, July 12, 2007; see also Nout Wellink, "Basel II and Financial Institution Resiliency," remarks at the Risk Capital 2007 Conference, Paris, June 27, 2007. Most regulators avoided saying much of anything about Basel II during this period. At least one used the developing problems to highlight preexisting skepticism about the new regime. See Sheila Bair, remarks at the Risk Management and Allocation Conference, Paris, June 25, 2007.

75. Bank for International Settlements, "Basel Committee Announces Steps to Strengthen the Resilience of the Banking System," press release, April 16, 2008.

Box 4.8   Proposed changes to Basel II following the subprime crisis

Pillar 1

■ higher capital requirements for complex structured credit products "which have produced the majority of losses during the recent market turbulence"
■ strengthened capital treatment of liquidity facilities extended in support of off-balance-sheet entities
■ strengthened capital requirements for assets held in the trading book (in cooperation with the International Organization of Securities Commissions)
■ monitoring of Basel II minimum requirements and capital buffers over the credit cycle in order to determine if further measures were needed "to help ensure . . . a sound capital framework for addressing banks' evolving and complex risk profiles"

Pillar 2

■ new guidance on risk management practices, including management of firmwide risks, stress testing, capital planning, off-balance-sheet exposures, and associated reputational risks; management of risks relating to securitization; and supervisory assessment of banks' valuation practices

Pillar 3

■ enhanced disclosures relating to complex securitizations, asset-backed commercial paper conduits, and the sponsorship of off-balance-sheet entities

Other

■ sound practice standards for the management of liquidity risks
■ supervisory guidance for assessing banks' valuation practices

Source: See footnote 75.

The intended changes, summarized in box 4.8, were obviously directed at the most immediate culprits in the subprime crisis—securitizations and exposures to off-balance-sheet entities. In one sense, the committee had proposed the minimum number of adjustments while still appearing responsive. The most immediate attention was directed toward liquidity management, a response essentially compelled by the circumstances of the crisis, in which liquidity problems had played such a prominent role.[76] This acceleration of the committee's activities on liquidity risks could be read as an implicit acknowledgement that it had erred in deferring major work on this subject until Basel II was completed. Still, the committee evidenced no reconsideration of the risks associated with residential mortgages themselves (as opposed to securitizations of those mortgages) or disquiet with the role of external rating agencies in Basel II, much less with the core reliance of the IRB approaches on internal risk models.

Conclusion

Robert Putnam's (1988) well-known idea that the politics of international negotiations are often best understood as a "two-level game" in which domestic and international politics are entangled is a useful heuristic device in assessing the Basel II process. Kapstein (2006) models patterns of international cooperation among financial supervisors by inserting into the two-level game the privately generated demands for a level playing field and the publicly generated demands for a stable international financial environment. While Kapstein focuses more on the substantive merits of Basel II than on the strategic setting within which the agreement was forged, the review of Basel II history in this chapter can also be filtered through the Putnam metaphor to reveal factors that helped shape those substantive outcomes.

The principal conclusion that emerges from this review is that the Basel II process was launched without an adequately developed set of goals. The regulators participating in the Basel Committee set out to deal with the problems created by Basel I but, as soon became clear, they had little idea of where they were headed. Indeed, the international process was being used by the Federal Reserve to overcome the resistance of other US bank supervisors to the use of internal models, rather than to advance a well-developed capital requirements model. There was thus no shared US negotiating position or substantive goal. As a result, the various national participants could not know what Putnam characterizes as the "win-sets" of negotiators—the set of possible international outcomes that are politically viable at home.

---

76. The committee had already issued a February 2008 paper on liquidity risk that reviewed recent developments that had revealed the inadequacy of banks' systems for managing this risk and surveyed relevant existing supervisory regimes (Basel Committee 2008a). In June 2008, the committee issued a consultative draft (Basel Committee 2008b) that overhauled the guidance it had previously issued in 2000. The new guidance was built around 17 principles. Most were directed toward sound risk management practices for banks, though a few were directed at supervisors. The committee did not propose any quantitative liquidity requirements.

In the United States, moreover, Federal Reserve officials appear to have misjudged—or at least taken insufficient account of—the domestic political economy of capital regulation. It appears that they were so focused on converting other regulators—both in the United States and other Basel Committee countries—to some variant of an internal models approach that they never devised a domestic political strategy to deal with constituent interests and pressures. In the absence of the banks' need for government assistance, as had occurred prior to the negotiation of Basel I, there was no political momentum from external sources such as Congress for revamped capital regulation. The features of the Basel II process resembling trade negotiations accordingly took on increased prominence, as banks and at times their allies in elected office pressured regulators for increased competitive advantage, with little regard for prudential considerations. The influence of the large financial institutions was strengthened further as it became apparent that the committee had insufficient expertise to develop the A-IRB approach on its own and thus relied on the banks to provide much technical input into the process.

Though harder to document, a possible additional factor was that, once publicly committed to the Basel II process, its principals were loath to abandon it, even as they lost control of the exercise that was becoming extraordinarily complex and being buffeted by domestic political forces. The declaration by former US Trade Representative Carla Hills that "no agreement is better than a bad agreement" has become something of a mantra for trade negotiators trapped in difficult negotiations, presumably intended to reassure domestic constituencies that their interests will not be sacrificed in an effort to maintain international harmony. In fact, Ambassador Hills may be one the few trade negotiators to have actually lived by her oft-echoed declaration. Negotiators more frequently appear to regard an inability to reach agreement as failure and thus are more likely to conclude an agreement and then defend it as best they can. This tendency is doubtless due in part to their personal interests, since negotiators who do not negotiate agreements have few accomplishments to which they can point at the end of their tenure in office. Yet, just as domestic interests fear, a troubled negotiation may also be brought to a "successful" conclusion because of concerns that collapse of the effort will have negative effects on existing patterns of cooperation.

Whatever their reasons, the principals in the Basel II negotiations doggedly continued their effort, even if that meant repeatedly accommodating the demands of financial institutions and individual Basel Committee countries. The next chapter evaluates the results of those negotiations and, given this background, not surprisingly finds serious flaws in Basel II. While it is, of course, impossible to say whether the product of a new Basel Committee effort on capital regulation would have been substantially improved by a more extended period of study and consultation in a nonnegotiating context, it is reasonable at least to conclude that the way in which the Basel II process was launched and conducted increased the chances of a suboptimal outcome.

A final point is that the revised framework was not the last word on the Basel II exercise. This is one of the respects in which that exercise resembles a domestic regulatory process more than a trade negotiation. Release of the revised framework may have signified an end to major changes, and the text itself technically has not been changed. Still, the Basel Committee issued no fewer than eight papers elaborating or interpreting the revised framework between July 2004 and August 2006.[77] Indeed, at the time the revised framework was released, Basel Committee Chair Jaime Caruana indicated that Basel II will, in response to technological developments, continue to change even after it takes effect. As detailed in the preceding section, the 2007–08 subprime crisis prompted reconsideration of significant elements of Basel II even before it had been fully implemented. Unlike Basel I, which was amended a handful of times over its first decade, Basel II may be subject to nearly continuous revision. This prospect raises the question whether that process will be a fundamentally technical one or whether it will present repeated occasions for the reassertion of nationally grounded interests.

The current situation in the United States does not suggest an obvious answer to this question. Following release of the revised framework, there was a temporary rebalancing of the political and institutional forces affecting capital regulation in the United States. The result was an extended domestic debate and a partial retreat from a commitment to the A-IRB approach. The relative weights of competitive equality and prudential concerns shifted back and forth several times, a phenomenon perhaps made possible by the absence of general political interest in the subject. As of this writing, the domestic politics of capital regulation in the United States had not found an equilibrium point. While the aftermath of the subprime crisis may give an advantage to prudential considerations, experience suggests that this weight will rather quickly be removed from the scales once the crisis has passed.

---

77. Most of these papers have been in the form of guidance in the interpretation or implementation of the revised framework (Basel Committee 2004e, 2005a, 2005b, 2005c, 2005d, 2006a, 2006b). One was a more significant effort to deal with potential "double default" situations involving exposures arising from trading activities (Basel Committee 2005e).

5

Assessing Basel II as a Regulatory Model

The objective and outcome of the Basel II exercise was to produce the rules by which minimum capital requirements would be set under domestic bank regulatory policy in each Basel Committee country. This chapter assesses the effectiveness and efficiency of these rules as a model for domestic capital regulation. The focus is on the advanced internal ratings–based (A-IRB) approach, the fundamental innovation of Basel II that breaks with the Basel I method for setting capital requirements and that will be adopted by most large multinational banks. The chapter first examines the degree to which Basel II can be expected to lead to the improvements in capital regulation touted by its proponents: greater risk sensitivity of minimum capital requirements, the generation of a common "language" to assist supervisors and market actors in their evaluation of banks, and enhanced risk management in A-IRB banks. Next, two possible negative effects are considered—an amplification of the procyclicality inherent in all capital regulation and the distortion of competition between A-IRB banks and non-A-IRB banks.

The picture that emerges from this examination is at best a mixed one. There are good reasons to doubt the benefits of Basel II as a domestic regulatory model. The grounds for these doubts arise even at the conceptual level; they are considerably stronger when one takes into account the administrative and institutional factors that will shape the A-IRB approach in practice. Of course, the utter absence of experience with an A-IRB approach lends a speculative character to all arguments about its merits. Indeed, the various transition safeguards are justified by fears that the leap of faith by regulators in adopting A-IRB could take them over a cliff. Still, the analysis in this chapter—standing alone—cannot provide a final answer on the policy desirability of Basel II, even though it should engender considerable skepticism over the viability of this regulatory model. Two additional steps will be needed to complete this evaluation.

First, an assessment of the international impact of Basel II is required. Even though this arrangement may not produce optimal prudential regulation in all countries or even in any one country, it may improve the safety and soundness of domestic banking systems by creating a more stable international banking system. Consideration of this possible trade-off will come in chapter 6, which examines the merits of Basel II as a specifically international arrangement. However, at this juncture we can note that the further a regulatory model strays from the optimal, the more offsetting international benefits would be required to make that arrangement a desirable one.

Second, regulatory models obviously cannot be judged in isolation. The ultimate question pertaining to any model will always be "compared to what?" While this chapter does, to some degree, use the existing Basel I model as a baseline for judging the A-IRB approach, a direct comparison of the merits of Basel I, Basel II, and other possible alternatives is left to chapter 7.

A related point is that a proponent of an IRB approach might respond to some of the criticisms of Basel II made in this chapter by asserting that the problems lie not in the concept of an IRB capital regulation model but in its specific embodiment in Basel II. Such a proponent might suggest improvements to remedy the particular infirmities of the Basel II version.[1] Since the merits of an IRB approach are of considerable importance, the analysis in this chapter straddles somewhat the broader concept and the particular Basel II version.[2] Ultimately, though, an assessment of the Basel II process must focus on the substance of the revised framework. So, for example, the argument that the Basel Committee might eventually embrace a full model approach cannot offset criticisms of the revised framework, which is intended to be the basis for capital regulation indefinitely. The very reason for the hybrid methodology is that the Basel Committee believes itself unable, on the basis of current knowledge and practice, to fashion and adopt a full model approach. There is neither a timetable for

---

1. Indeed, Basel II itself has been something of a moving target. The lengthy proposal was substantially overhauled several times during the nearly six years of negotiation. Even since the revised framework was issued in June 2004, the Basel Committee has continued to issue supplemental guidance on its implementation. Some Basel Committee participants have even suggested that Basel II might prove to be a transitional regulatory standard and that qualifying banks will eventually be permitted to use a so-called full model approach to calculating risk-weighted assets.

2. Although this chapter implicitly considers the appropriateness of an A-IRB approach as a model for US banking regulation, much of the analysis would be relevant to its application in any Basel Committee country.

reaching this endpoint nor a well-articulated statement of what the endpoint would look like.

Additionally, it should be noted that *any* process for generating and implementing a regulatory model—whether purely domestic or international—will be shaped by a particular array of political and institutional interests. For example, as suggested in the preceding chapter, the dynamic of the Basel II process may have been such as to place downward pressure on the stringency of the A-IRB rules. Thus, while a proponent of an IRB approach might legitimately claim that a different set of choices could have yielded a better regulatory model, it seems unlikely that any idealized version would ever be implemented. Moreover, of course, Basel II is the only actual case of an IRB approach we have to consider.

Before turning to this analysis, though, it is necessary to ask the preliminary question whether, or at least how much, capital requirements matter.

Do Regulatory Capital Requirements Matter?

The pillar 1 rules explicitly set requirements for *minimum* capital levels. Suppose that other domestic bank regulations or market forces require higher levels of capital than would be mandated by Basel II alone? In this eventuality, the practical impact of the new arrangement will be limited, whatever the intentions of the Basel Committee and the peculiarities of the A-IRB approach. The possibility that market forces will constrain capital reductions under Basel II was suggested by comments filed on the third consultative paper (CP-3) by Standard & Poor's (2003). Surveying the results of the third quantitative impact study (QIS-3), S&P expressed skepticism concerning the accuracy of the probability of default ratings by the participating banks, which the rating agency suspected of being generally too favorable. Further, S&P questioned some important premises behind the CP-3 formulas, such as the assumption that higher-risk corporate borrowers are less correlated to systemic factors affecting an entire loan portfolio. Of course, in light of subsequent changes, the specifics of the CP-3 formulas are no longer directly relevant. What is interesting for present purposes is S&P's comment that "banks that substantially reduce their capital on the basis of the accord, as a result of metrics with which Standard & Poor's does not agree, could be downgraded." To the extent that S&P, as an external rating agency, can be regarded as a surrogate for bank investors and counterparties, these comments could have significant implications for the practical effects of Basel II. If market actors demand higher levels of capital than are required by Basel II, then the impact of the new arrangement will be more limited than its terms might suggest.

Do market demands lead banks to hold capital well in excess of minimum regulatory requirements? Experience under Basel I clearly reveals that banks in Basel Committee countries have generally maintained risk-weighted capital levels significantly above the 8 percent minimum. Since maintaining higher capital levels imposes costs on banks, this is a phenomenon in need of explanation. The two reasons most frequently suggested are market demands and self-imposition of a buffer to assure regulatory compliance in the face of unexpected strains on assets.

The evidence that banks, including the very largest banks, hold capital well above the regulatory minimum is very strong. Using Bankscope data, Peura and Jokivuolle (2004) examined the capital levels of 128 large banks (defined as holding tier 1 capital in excess of 3 billion euros) from G-10 countries during 1997–2001. They found that the median risk-weighted capital ratio for all 128 banks was 11.2 percent during this five-year period, with regional averages ranging from 11.9 percent for US banks to 10.8 percent for European banks (Peura and Jokivuolle 2004).[3] Generally speaking, the largest banks—those most likely to use the A-IRB approach—hold lower amounts of capital than regional or community banks. Yet risk-based capital levels of even the 10 largest US banks have, for the last decade, nearly always been above not only the Basel I 8 percent requirement but also the US regulatory requirement of 10 percent for banks to be "well capitalized" and thus permitted to affiliate with a broad range of nonbank financial institutions.[4] In fact, in any given year, most of the 10 largest banks have had risk-weighted capital levels above 11 percent (appendix table 5A.1).

As suggested by the S&P comments, one possible explanation for banks holding capital in amounts 30 percent or more above regulatory minimums is that markets demand these levels. More precisely, economic capital requirements may exceed regulatory capital requirements for most banks most of the time, in the sense that a bank's maximum return can be realized only with higher capital levels. Counterparties and debt investors may demand very high external credit ratings that, in turn, are bestowed by credit rating agencies such as S&P only on banks with much higher capital levels than the regulatory minimum.[5] For counterparties in

---

3. The limitations of reported data are also apparent from the Peura and Jokivuolle data, which report that the median capital level of large Japanese banks over 1997–2001 was 10.9 percent. This rather healthy ratio does not accord with the contemporaneous, well-known travails of the Japanese banking system. The 10.9 percent figure, based in significant part on the information reported by banks themselves, likely reflects a combination of overvalued assets on bank balance sheets and an overly generous calculation of qualifying capital.

4. The Gramm-Leach-Bliley Act of 1999 permitted banks to affiliate with a broader range of nonbanking financial companies—such as those underwriting insurance—and removed restrictions on other affiliates of banks, such as securities underwriters. In order to take advantage of the new rules, however, the banks must be "well capitalized." The authors of some recent economic studies seem unaware that the 10 percent level is now meaningful under US law.

5. It is also possible that investors or counterparties will make their own assessment of a bank's capital position, though the time and expense involved make this unlikely in most cases, even where the other party would have adequate access to relevant information on the bank's assets.

certain transactions, such as swaps, these demands may be absolute, in the sense that they will simply not deal with banks that do not have the highest credit rating. For investors, these demands may be a manifestation of the usual risk/reward trade-off, whereby they are willing to receive a lower interest rate on their lending to a bank with larger amounts of capital. If this explanation is valid,[6] a reduction in regulatory capital minimums under Basel II could have little effect on actual capital levels, since large banks might conclude that the higher cost of their own borrowings, or the unwillingness of some counterparties to deal with them, might not be worth the extra lending flexibility provided by reduced capital requirements.

Another explanation for the pervasiveness of capital ratios substantially above regulatory minimums is that, in setting their capital levels, banks plan for the downside of business cycles and other negative contingencies. An economic or business shock that quickly depressed the value of a bank's assets (e.g., through above-average loan write-offs during a recession) could lead to a costly breach of regulatory requirements. As explained below, the consequences of falling below regulatory capital minimums can be quite serious. During an economic downturn, provisions for nonperforming loans and capital write-offs for defaulted loans may increase fairly quickly. Since capital may be difficult to increase in the short term, banks may be compelled to sell off assets with high risk weights in order to reduce the bank's total risk-weighted assets.[7] Lacking the originating bank's experience with the borrowers, potential purchasers of the loans may worry that the loans being sold are lemons. Banks would then be forced to sustain significant losses on these asset sales.

A good bit of theoretical research demonstrates the cost effectiveness of banks holding capital buffers above regulatory minimums to avoid forced dispositions of valued assets at distress prices.[8] The optimal size of this buffer is determined by factors such as the cost of recapitalization, the volatility of bank revenues, and the sanctions for noncompliance. Although the theoretical research has not been accompanied by what seems the logical adjunct of simply asking bank executives why they maintain the capital levels they do, there is some empirical support to complement the theoretical and commonsense foundations for this proposition. Milne (2002) points out that small banks that do not borrow on public markets also maintain

6. The UK Financial Services Authority has observed that capital practices by British banks are consistent with the market demand hypothesis (Richardson and Stephenson 2000).

7. For example, under Basel I rules, by selling off 100 percent risk-weighted loans and holding the receipts from those sales in US government securities, which are zero risk-weighted, the bank will reduce its capital requirements by 8 percent of the book value of the assets sold.

8. See, for example, Estrella (2001), Furfine (1999), Milne and Whalley (2001), Barrios and Blanco (2003), and Perua and Jokivuolle (2004).

higher capital levels than required by law.[9] A study responding to Milne counters that banks with capital ratios above the minimum but with external credit ratings below a certain level (presumably based in part on the fact that capital is not *enough* above minimum) have only small holdings of swap liabilities compared with the average for banks of a similar size (Jackson, Perraudin, and Saporta 2002). The authors infer that market access for these banks is limited. They also admit that it is difficult to distinguish the regulatory buffer and market discipline explanations empirically.[10]

It may be that both explanations are right. Purchasers of publicly traded debt, swap counterparties, and external rating agencies may well insist that a bank have capital ratios significantly higher than regulatory minimum levels, but not because they have some absolute level of capital in mind. Instead, they may simply want to see ratios well above the minimum or, perhaps, average levels, whatever those levels might be.[11] This explanation is somewhat undermined, though maybe not completely, by the S&P's comments, which set forth a principle for determining the requisite capital cushion—namely, that capital be sufficient to permit the continued operation of the bank, not just to satisfy all obligations should the bank be liquidated.

National banking laws or supervision may also impose capital requirements that set minimum levels above those determined under the A-IRB approach. US banking authorities require that a bank have tier 1 capital of at least 6 percent of risk-weighted assets and total capital of at least 10 percent of risk-weighted assets in order to be classified as "well capitalized." Significant bank activities, including the ability to affiliate with certain nonbanking financial institutions such as insurance underwriters and merchant bankers, are contingent upon the bank being well capitalized. British banking authorities set target capital ratios for banks on an individual basis

---

9. One effort to compare the results of some of the theoretical models with actual bank capital ratios suggests that bank capital ratios are higher than recapitalization costs would suggest they should be (Peura and Keppo 2006). Thus the phenomenon of high bank capital ratios under Basel I continues to elude a fully satisfactory explanation.

10. Ashcraft (2001) makes a provisional, but potentially weighty, empirical claim that the increase in bank capital ratios was not attributable to regulatory requirements. He finds that banks with low capital ratios tended to mean-revert before any changes in policy. The paper is, however, based on a limited sample and time frame.

11. In launching the Basel II process, William McDonough suggested something along these lines: "Banks also maintain high capital levels because the marketplace has learned the same lessons and demands those levels. But I don't think the framers of the accord realized the powerful influence their thinking would have on the techniques used by market analysts and rating agencies to evaluate bank financial condition. Their analyses often build on the Basel capital standard and its risk-weighting scheme and their expectations are generally that banks' actual capital ratios will exceed the Basel minimums." See William McDonough, "Issues for the Basel Accord," remarks at the Conference on Credit Risk Modeling and Regulatory Implications, London, September 22, 1998.

that are well above the regulatory minimum, and trigger ratios that are closer to, but still above, the Basel I minimum.[12] Both forms of national regulation help account for the higher capital ratios noted earlier, since the effective minimum regulatory level for "well-capitalized" US banks and most British banks will be above 8 percent. Pillar 2 of the revised framework establishes for all Basel Committee members the "principle" that supervisors "should expect banks to operate above the minimum regulatory capital ratios and should have the ability to require banks to hold capital in excess of the minimum" (Basel Committee 2006g, paragraph 757).

The US and UK regulatory policies should both lead to regulatory capital levels higher than the A-IRB approach minimum. Although the pillar 2 principle of an expectation of operation above minimum levels lacks specificity and a clear sense of obligation, it would by definition produce capital levels at about the A-IRB minimum were it to be faithfully implemented. However, each of these three policies contemplates that the additional increment of regulatory capital be added to a benchmark defined by the prevailing requirement for a risk-weighted capital ratio. Presumably, then, the amount of capital required under US and UK practice will decline in an amount roughly proportional to any decline in minimum capital requirement from Basel I to Basel II.

A more significant constraint on the effective decline in capital under Basel II formulas is found in another feature of US bank regulation. During the Basel II negotiations, the Federal Deposit Insurance Corporation (FDIC), which is responsible for overseeing federal capital requirements in state banks that are not members of the Federal Reserve System and has a broader interest in capital requirements because it insures all banks, released a study suggesting that Basel II was on a collision course with other elements of US law (FDIC 2003). Specifically, US law requires "prompt corrective action" whenever the capital of a bank falls below certain levels (12 USC. §1831o). Two distinct capital adequacy requirements must be met. First, risk-weighted capital must exceed certain specified levels (12 USC. §1831o(c) (2)). Second, the bank's simple *leverage ratio*—that is to say, qualifying tier I capital divided by total, nonweighted assets—must exceed certain specified levels (12 USC. §1831o(c) (1)).

Generally, this ratio must be at least 4 percent, though it must be at least 5 percent to meet the "well capitalized" requirement for banks owned by financial holding companies, a category that includes all of the top 20 US banks. The rationale for a separate simple leverage ratio requirement is that it is less subject to manipulation or mistake in the risk-weighting process, precisely because it is not adjusted based on estimates

---

12. As the terms imply, the "target" ratio is that which the UK Financial Services Authority believes the bank should aim for, and the "trigger" ratio is that whose breach will elicit a supervisory response of some sort. The latter is roughly analogous to the capital thresholds under US prompt corrective action rules.

of asset riskiness. Basel II does not include a simple leverage ratio requirement, and most countries do not impose one on their banks. The FDIC study anticipated, based on QIS-3 results, that the capital required by the A-IRB, risk-weighted approach could fall well below that which is required by the simple leverage ratio.

Following publication of the revised framework and analysis of the fourth quantitative impact study (QIS-4) results, the FDIC updated its study in an appendix to Chairman Donald Powell's November 2005 testimony. The FDIC used the QIS-4 results to calculate the risk-weighted capital levels that the 26 participating US banks would need to maintain in order to be "well capitalized" under the 6 percent tier 1 ratio requirement once A-IRB was in effect. Then it calculated the leverage ratio requirements for those same banks. It found that, with the levels of capital required under the A-IRB approach, 17 of the 26 banks would be undercapitalized to varying degrees on a leverage-ratio basis. Three of the banks would be "critically undercapitalized," a classification under US law that creates a presumption that the bank should be placed into receivership.[13]

The degree to which the leverage ratio is binding as a practical matter can be illustrated by examining the positions of the 10 largest US banks at the end of 2003, toward the end of the Basel II negotiations (table 5.1). The leverage ratios for all 10 were, as required, above the 5 percent minimum for the bank to be "well capitalized." Most banks have ratios well above that level. However, two banks were sufficiently close to the minimum to face a potentially binding effect, either from the literal application of the regulatory requirement or from market demands derivative from that requirement. Consider, for example, the position of JPMorgan Chase. With consolidated assets of $628.6 billion, the bank needed at least $31.4 billion in qualifying tier 1 capital to satisfy the 5 percent leverage ratio. At year-end 2003, JPMorgan Chase had $34.9 billion in qualifying tier 1 capital, yielding the leverage ratio of 5.57 percent indicated in table 5.1. Thus there was a $3.5 billion buffer. That $3.5 billion is the maximum by which JPMorgan Chase could reduce its capital, no matter how advantageous Basel II turned out to be for its risk-weighted ratio requirement. Accordingly, with the then-prevailing (Basel I) risk-based capital requirement of $34.7 billion (8 percent of the $434.2 billion in risk-weighted assets), there is an effective limit of about a 10 percent reduction in the required risk-based capital ratio (3.5/34.7).

Of course, the existing buffer over the 5 percent leverage ratio requirement may itself be necessary for either or both the reasons discussed earlier. Debt investors and counterparties may demand that the bank maintain this higher-than-minimum level. The bank itself may hesitate to

---

13. See appendix B to Donald Powell's prepared testimony on the "Development of the New Basel Capital Accords" before the Committee on Banking, Housing, and Urban Affairs, US Senate, November 10, 2005.

Table 5.1   Capital ratios for 10 largest US banks as of December 31, 2003

Bank	Consolidated assets (billions of dollars)	Leverage ratio (percent)	Risk-weighted assets (RWA) (billions of dollars)	Tier 1 RWA ratio (percent)	Total RWA ratio (percent)
JPMorgan Chase	628.6	5.57	434.2	8.05	10.43
Bank of America	617.9	6.88	481.2	8.73	11.31
Citibank	528.1	6.57	427.2	8.40	12.56
Wachovia	353.5	5.85	258.5	7.60	11.72
Bank One	256.8	7.97	166.2	10.13	13.71
Wells Fargo	250.5	6.24	202.3	7.57	11.24
Fleet	192.3	8.30	178.5	8.49	11.30
US Bank	189.1	6.31	156.6	6.60	10.84
Suntrust	124.4	7.35	112.2	7.92	10.85
HSBC Bank	92.9	6.22	62.0	8.99	11.82

Note: The figures for consolidated assets are subject to minor adjustments before calculation of leverage ratio.

Source: Call reports filed with Federal Financial Institutions Examination Council, Schedule RC-R.

reduce capital any further because it could lose its buffer against unexpected reversals that could otherwise take its capital below minimum regulatory levels and thereby force sales of desirable assets or trigger negative supervisory consequences.[14] Thus, assuming the leverage ratio requirement is retained in its present form, a bank in a position similar to that of JPMorgan Chase in 2003 may have even less room to reduce capital.

In short, whether directly or indirectly, the leverage ratio places a floor under the capital requirements for US banks no matter how much the A-IRB formula might permit risk-weighted capital ratios to decline. Although US banking agencies do have administrative discretion to reduce the simple leverage ratio requirements, at least down to the 2 percent statutory minimum, this is not the current stated intention of the federal supervisors. In their 2003 advance notice of proposed rule making, the agencies indicated they would retain the leverage ratio and prompt corrective action system in it present form. Significantly, they further "recognized that in some cases, under the proposed framework, the leverage ratio

---

14. At the least, these consequences would include increased scrutiny by the bank's federal banking supervisor. Failure to expeditiously raise capital levels above the "well capitalized" threshold could, in theory, result in removal of a holding company's status as a "financial holding company" and thus require divestiture of any nonbanking affiliates engaged in insurance underwriting, some forms of securities underwriting, merchant banking, and certain other activities.

would serve as the most binding regulatory capital constraint" (US Department of the Treasury Office of the Comptroller of the Currency et al. 2003, 45902). In their 2007 final rule implementing Basel II, the agencies confirmed that the current leverage and prompt corrective action requirements would remain in effect (US Department of the Treasury Office of the Comptroller of the Currency et al. 2006a, 55839).

Despite the apparent unanimity among the regulatory agencies, retention of the leverage ratio has been far from an uncontested position. The argument against it is that the bluntness of the leverage ratio is inconsistent with the risk-sensitive IRB approach. Susan Bies, then the Federal Reserve Board governor with principal responsibility for Basel II matters, stated publicly in March 2005 that "the leverage ratio down the road has got to disappear."[15] Her remark set off a minor maelstrom in bank regulatory circles, and Bies publicly backed off this position, joining the other regulatory agencies in endorsing retention of the leverage ratio at subsequent congressional hearings. Large US banks unsuccessfully targeted the leverage ratio (and the other safeguards against declining capital levels) for removal from the proposed agency rule implementing Basel II before it became final.[16]

Indeed, the attitude of large banks is a good source of evidence about the likely impact of Basel II. Since the emphasis of the Basel II process began to shift toward IRB approaches, many banks worried that the final product would impose enormous compliance costs in the form of required changes to credit risk models and risk management practices. While the results of QIS-3 may have cheered those banks for which significant declines in capital requirements were predicted, they must only have increased concern at the less fortunate banks whose capital requirements were predicted to stay roughly the same, much less at those banks whose capital charges would rise materially. There were, for example, reports that Deutsche Bank's required capital would increase by 20 percent.

As detailed in chapter 4, the direction of changes between release of QIS-3 and publication of the revised framework was largely toward reducing the capital charges yielded by the Basel II formulas. Many of these changes were in response to comments and complaints from banks and those who represent banking interests. The result has been a palpable shift in the prevailing attitude among banks. While recent attention to the potential for large declines in bank capital has apparently dissuaded banks from publicly celebrating anticipated capital declines, they were not so cautious earlier in the Basel II process. Citibank, for example, pub-

---

15. See Michele Heller and Todd Davenport, "Congressional Pressure for Consensus on Basel II," *American Banker*, March 15, 2005, 4.

16. See Steven Sloan, "Four Big Banks Detail Basel Objections," *American Banker*, September 26, 2006, 1.

licly stated that its capital requirements would decline by $5 billion under Basel II, a figure that would translate into a decline in minimum capital of approximately 15 percent,[17] coincidentally a percentage decline identical to that projected by QIS-4 for aggregate capital for US banks.[18]

The dynamic of the Basel II negotiating process described in chapter 4 made it likely that most large banks would welcome the final product. That indeed seems to be the case. Following publication of the revised framework, efforts of large US banks shifted to resisting the various safeguards proposed by the banking agencies to guard against significant capital declines once Basel II is implemented. Even though adequate empirical work may be lacking, it seems reasonable to conclude that large banks would acquiesce in the A-IRB approach only if they anticipated sizable net benefits from reduced capital requirements less the costs of qualifying and maintaining the requisite internal rating systems.[19] It is thus unlikely that banks anticipate that market considerations will prevent them from realizing these capital reductions. Their plea that the leverage ratio be eliminated, in turn, suggests that it would require higher levels of capital than under the A-IRB approach.

In sum, neither market forces nor complementary national regulation can be confidently expected to maintain capital levels at present levels once the A-IRB approach is implemented. Although there is some uncertainty on the point, market actors may judge bank capital positions based on the

---

17. This calculation is based on a statement by the chief financial officer of Citigroup that it is $15 billion "overcapitalized" and, under Basel II, would be $20 billion "overcapitalized." See Matthias Rieker, "Global Markets Strength Earns Citigroup Upgrade," *American Banker*, March 30, 2004, 18. Although the news report of this statement was unclear as to whether this figure refers to the holding company or Citibank itself, the $15 billion number comports with the amount of capital Citibank held above the Basel I 8 percent requirement, as computed from its call reports filed at the end of 2003. Given Citibank's risk-weighted assets, the 8 percent threshold would require approximately $34 billion in qualifying capital. Thus, the anticipated $5 billion reduction would translate into an approximately 15 percent decline in Citibank's minimum capital levels. (Actually, in order to remain a financial holding company, Citigroup would need to assure that Citibank meets the 10 percent risk-weighted capital level, but this fact does not affect the impact of the shift from Basel I to Basel II.) Citibank's estimate of its position under Basel II preceded the May 2004 Basel Committee decision to impose a scaling factor on A-IRB capital ratios.

18. The banks' benchmark was well summed up by the senior risk manager at a major US bank, who was quoted at about the time CP-3 was released as expecting a quid pro quo: "If we're going to implement Basel II, we want to have lower capital" (Buerkle 2003, 32).

19. While it is possible that large banks contemplating a significant decrease in their capital requirements might become even more enthusiastic about Basel II if it promised to raise their competitors' costs, the domestic political dynamic around Basel II does not seem to have included significant overt efforts by banks to disadvantage their competitors, as opposed to seeking advantages for themselves. This dynamic is consistent with a general tendency to relax capital requirements as the Basel II process progresses.

degree to which they exceed existing minimum regulatory requirements as much or more as on the basis of an independent calculation of the actual bank capital levels that will justify certain ratings, interest rates, or counterparty positions. As to other forms of national regulation, there is no basis whatever for knowing whether, or how, the pillar 2 principle of higher-than-minimum-capital expectations will be realized. Most national regulation that mandates higher capital levels builds off the minimum risk-weighted requirements. Where there is a capital requirement unrelated to the prevailing risk-weighted determination, notably the US leverage ratio requirement, it appears conceptually at odds with the A-IRB model.

Potential Benefits of the Advanced Internal Ratings–Based Model

A shift toward a regulatory model based on banks' internal credit risk models holds the prospect for significant improvement in capital regulation, which in turn could enhance bank safety and soundness. Most importantly, this regulatory approach could align capital requirements for credit exposures much more closely with the actual risks entailed by those exposures. The greater part of this chapter addresses the central issue of whether the promise of greater risk sensitivity of capital requirements will be realized. Supervisors associated with the Basel Committee have identified two additional benefits that are in some sense derivative of this key claim for an improvement in bank safety and soundness. First, they anticipate that the implementation of A-IRB will facilitate monitoring of large, internationally active banks through creation of a "common language" of risk. This reasoning obviously applies to supervisors, since they should be better equipped to understand the risk profiles of foreign banks operating in their countries. But proponents have also touted the benefits of a common language, as complemented by Basel II's disclosure requirements, for investors and other bank counterparties. They have, accordingly, argued that Basel II will foster more effective market discipline on bank activities and performance. Second, supervisors contend that the unfolding of the Basel II process itself has encouraged banks to improve their own risk management processes.

Greater Risk Sensitivity

The internal ratings approach to setting capital requirements looks to the bank's own estimate of the credit risk entailed by particular claims, rather than to a fixed risk category determined by the generic type of borrower (government, bank, corporation, etc.). This core feature of an IRB approach responds directly to the major criticism of Basel I. The upshot should be that capital requirements are better calibrated to the actual risk entailed in a credit exposure and that the scope for regulatory arbitrage has been reduced. The credit risk estimate will generally be computed based on financial information specific to the borrower (e.g., cash flow, liquid assets, net worth) and experience with the borrower.[20] Extensions of credit may be rated solely on the basis of certain formulas used in the credit risk model. (These formulas are used to calculate probability of default; for example, they are distinct from the formulas used to derive the risk weighting of the claim once the probability of default and other inputs have been generated.) However, human judgment may also be brought to bear where large extensions of credit are under consideration, or where there are important business reasons other than those routinely fed into the risk model. Because large banks generally use seven or more risk categories, the risk presented by a particular claim would not only be determined by reference to the actual financial position of the borrower but would also be more precisely calibrated than under Basel I.

This new regulatory paradigm builds on the practice of large banks in generating their own credit risk estimates for internal risk management purposes. Of course, the detailed requirements of Basel II will require banks to use metrics established by supervisors, which will be different from those used in bank models solely for internal purposes. Still, an important assumption of this regulatory approach is that banks themselves possess a comparative advantage over supervisors in terms of the resources, expertise, and experience necessary for sophisticated assessment of credit risks. Moreover, if the Basel Committee were eventually to move toward using not just a bank's internal ratings, but its actual credit model, then this comparative advantage in risk sensitivity over Basel I should be even greater.

As discussed in chapter 3, the extent to which banks are intentionally arbitraging credit risks within the Basel I framework has not been established with any precision. But there is little question that, whatever the intentions of bank managers, the bluntness of the Basel I rules means that regulatory capital requirements are not well correlated with the actual risks presented by a bank's portfolio of credit exposures. Until the subprime crisis, the record of major bank stability under the Basel I rules was a very good one. However, while the significance of the Basel I capital rules in contributing to the crisis will likely be definitively established only after considerable study and debate, it is certainly possible that the relative risk insensitivity of the 1988 rules played a significant role. Moreover, the disincentive of banks to assume certain exposures because of

---

20. Retail exposures will be weighted based on portfolio characteristics, rather than risk ratings of individual borrowers.

Basel I rules that penalize a creditworthy borrower creates an opportunity cost—admittedly hard to quantify—to the economy as a whole.[21]

In theory, then, greater risk sensitivity in capital requirements should be a major advance in bank regulation. The key policy question is whether it is likely that these theoretical benefits will be realized in practice. More precisely, the question is whether, in both conceptual and practical terms, an IRB approach to capital regulation is likely to realize these benefits. The nature of credit risk modeling, the difficulties encountered by regulators in calibrating these models, and the challenges posed by an IRB approach for supervision and monitoring combine to raise substantial doubt that this question will be answered affirmatively.

Reliability of Credit Risk Models

Issues pertaining to the reliability of credit risk modeling go to the heart of the entire A-IRB approach and thus, fundamentally, to the direction that Basel II has established for financial regulation. One concern is that the current state of the art does not support the reliance to be placed on these models for purposes of calculating regulatory capital levels. Sharing this concern, the Basel Committee has in effect created its own model, with certain standardizing assumptions. The committee seems convinced that any approach to capital regulation that builds on a bank's own risk systems can only be worked out satisfactorily through its actual implementation, while many of the committee's critics doubt that credit risk modeling (or the intermediate approach of Basel II, using the banks' internal ratings) will ever be viable as a basis for capital regulation. In any case, the committee's creation of its own model leads to a second concern—that the extensive, standardizing detail of the A-IRB model is at odds with the rationale of more closely grounding regulatory capital requirements in the most sophisticated and accurate risk assessment techniques. There is thus a risk that the A-IRB approach will yield the worst of both worlds— that is, the assumptions and limitations of the model will prove ill-founded, particularly in moments of stress, while not taking advantage of the sophistication and customization that large banks seek in their own risk management systems.

Basel II's embrace of credit risk modeling followed on the Basel Committee's 1996 amendment to Basel I, which prescribes value-at-risk (VaR) modeling to calculate the market risk attributable to securities on the trad-

---

21. Of course, the Basel I rules are problematic for reasons beyond the insensitivity of the applicable risk categories. Two important examples are the failures to take due account of credit risk mitigation and of the risks that may be associated with retained interests or obligations in securitizations. Improvements in these features of Basel I are possible without a basic shift in the basis for calculating risk; indeed, the standardized approach of Basel I addresses these problems.

ing books of banks. For US commercial banks, at least, the trading book was traditionally relatively insignificant compared with the banking book, in part because of legal restrictions on bank ownership of equities. But VaR risk management is quite common among nonbank financial entities that engage in significant trading activity. Notwithstanding the widespread use of the technique for both business and regulatory purposes, the reliability of VaR modeling for market risk is still questioned on both theoretical and empirical grounds (Alexander and Baptista 2006, Herring and Schuermann 2005). These questions have become more pointed in the wake of the 2007 disruption in the market for securitized mortgages and other forms of securitized loans. Indeed, as noted in the previous chapter, one response of the Basel Committee to the subprime crisis was to announce its intention to strengthen capital requirements for assets held on the trading book. Still, the state of the art of VaR market risk modeling is, by any measure, substantially more advanced than for credit risk modeling. Credit risk modeling, which includes calculation of risk ratings, is a relatively new undertaking, at least in its comprehensive form.[22] There are numerous important questions about its reliability.

First, any model is obviously only as good as its assumptions and inputs. If the credit risk parameters supplied by banks are unreliable, even a well-constructed model will give a misleading picture of actual risk. In the vernacular of risk managers, "garbage in, garbage out." One difficulty is the potential for intentional distortion of model inputs, which is discussed below. Even assuming good faith on the part of the banks, the relative dearth of useful historical data is cause for concern. There is generally less than a decade of historical data available on the basis of which to generate the values incorporated into the model. Importantly, most models are operating with data that do not reflect an entire business cycle (Jackson 2006). Each time a bank introduces an innovative or complex credit exposure, there will by definition be no historical data for use in the model. Risk managers will thus have to extrapolate from experience with existing credit products, which may or may not be sufficiently close in salient characteristics to approximate the credit risk associated with the new product. These concerns are not purely hypothetical, of course. The disaster that can befall firms when markets move in new ways, exemplified by the implosion of Long-Term Capital Management in 1998, has again been impressed upon market actors by the fallout from the collapse of markets for securitized subprime mortgages in 2007. While the losses in question were dominantly trading rather than banking losses in both instances, the origins of the subprime debacle lay in actual and anticipated

---

22. A snapshot of the state of the art is provided in Martin (2003). A more complete explanation of key issues in the construction and use of credit models is included in Saidenberg and Schuermann (2004).

jumps in defaults by homeowners—in other words, credit risk. There were no useful data to input into models, because there had never been so much subprime lending before.

Second, a related difficulty is that it is considerably more difficult to backtest credit risk models than market risk models.[23] While the prices of traded securities change daily, defaults are relatively unusual events and tend to occur in clusters because of adverse macroeconomic conditions. Because there had been no serious recession during the period in which data used for development of Basel II had been gathered, there was little opportunity to stress test the models, a serious concern unless one believes heroically that severe recessions are a thing of the past. Remarkably, six months *after* the Basel Committee issued the revised framework, another committee housed within the Bank for International Settlements issued a report that the state of the art for stress testing involving loan portfolios badly lagged that for market risks (Committee on the Global Financial System 2005).

Third, although progress has been made in recent years, credit risk models have not yet fully captured correlations among the various relevant variables. For example, the designers of credit risk models have not yet determined how to determine reliably when the same circumstances that increase the probability of default also lead a borrower to draw down its existing lines of credit and diminish the value of the collateral securing the loan.

Fourth, as mentioned earlier, the extreme value tails of banks' credit risk models bear substantially more serious policy implications than those of market risk modeling, at least as it applies to commercial banks.[24] It is difficult to be comfortable in an environment in which a 500-year flood comes once a decade.[25]

---

23. "Backtesting" refers to a process of ex post validation of a model by comparing its predictions of anticipated losses with actual experience. The difficulties are discussed in Lopez and Saidenberg (2000).

24. Even within well-established and highly liquid trading markets, the number of extreme events seems to be significantly higher than standard distribution analysis suggests. For example, the standard distribution of the S&P 500 daily return would suggest that an outlier change of five sigmas should occur only about once every 10,000 years. But the data from 1929 to 2003 reveal about 30 such events (Daníelsson 2003). For this reason, Daníelsson et al. (2001) have suggested turning to extreme value theory, which seeks to capture the risk in the tails of probability distribution functions. But if VaR-type credit risk modeling is not fully matured, extreme value theory is only in its infancy and thus cannot be considered a viable near-term basis for regulatory requirements. For a caution on using extreme value theory, see Lucas et al. (2002).

25. Rebonato (2007, 252) argues that a 99.9th percentile, one-year risk calculation is a "meaningless concept" because, among other things, there are simply too few relevant observations in the data set forming the basis for the calculation of a once-in-a-thousand-year event.

Fifth, models do not reflect the fact that risk can be endogenous in some circumstances. The conventional assumption that the uncertainty of asset values results from exogenous causes seems to hold in normal times. But this assumption is misplaced during times of stress. Numerous analysts have argued that, when widely adopted, VaR models for evaluating market risk create a kind of negative feedback loop that makes the sources of risk partly endogenous.[26] That is, where market actors are using similar models, an initial decline in market price of an asset can prompt many of these actors more or less simultaneously to sell their holdings of this asset in order to minimize their losses or improve their capital position. But sales by a significant number of actors will drive the price of the asset down further, possibly prompting another round of sell-offs. This self-reinforcing dynamic can magnify volatility and thus, on net, increase risk.[27] Credit risk models may have an analogous, though less dramatic, effect. As the creditworthiness of a particular type of asset declines, the internal risk rating of exposures associated with such assets will also deteriorate, requiring additional capital set-asides. Similar models in different banks could then provide a shared incentive to dispose of those assets in order to protect their capital ratios. As with the trading risk situation, the result could be a glut of similar assets on the market, driving down the price and thus placing the banks in a less favorable position. The circumstances that would drive significant numbers of banks simultaneously to attempt to sell off portions of their loan portfolios may occur precisely when capital ratios are already declining toward regulatory minimums.[28]

The Federal Reserve Board, which was consistently among the most enthusiastic proponent of the A-IRB approach among the Basel supervisors, acknowledged during the Basel II process that even the credit risk models used at the largest banks have not "attained the sophistication and robustness" that would be necessary to rely on them for regulatory purposes.[29] It is for this reason that the A-IRB approach is based not on the use of bank credit models as such but on the use of banks' internal credit ratings, which are used as inputs into what is in effect a common credit risk model created by the committee itself. Banks may qualify for

---

26. See Daníelsson, Shin, and Zigrand (2004); Basak and Shapiro (2001); and Morris and Shin (1999). An illuminating first-person narrative of experiences with such negative feedback loops is provided by Bookstaber (2007).

27. Daníelsson, Shin, and Zigrand (2004) point out the similarities between this dynamic and the observed impact of such practices as portfolio insurance and dynamic hedging techniques.

28. For an application to credit risk models, see Daníelsson et al. (2001) and Blum (1999).

29. See Roger W. Ferguson, Jr., remarks at the ICBI Risk Management 2003 Conference, Geneva, December 2, 2003.

the A-IRB approach only after they have adopted best-practice operational requirements, although—as one commentator has observed—there may not be sufficient history to determine if best practices are good enough. In any case, each of the five questions on the use of credit risk models applies to a greater or lesser extent to this hybrid approach.

The committee's decision to create its own model raises a second set of concerns about the new regulatory regime. There is an inconsistency, at least at a conceptual level, between the Basel II proposal and the principle that supposedly informs the development of a regulatory paradigm based on internal bank models—that credit risk will be more accurately measured if capital requirements are aligned with the sophisticated risk assessment and management techniques available to financial institutions. The Basel Committee believes that it must specify rules because credit risk models are not sufficiently reliable, but each specification for a particular element of the risk assessment and management process is an actual or potential departure from state-of-the-art internal risk evaluation.

Many assumptions embedded in the Basel II formulas have been questioned by economists during and after negotiation of the revised framework.[30] For example, the correlation factors embedded in the Basel II formulas assume that assets with higher probabilities of default are likely to be more idiosyncratic in the factors affecting them and thus less influenced by economywide factors. Yet an analysis by FitchRatings revealed that the correlation factors in the revised framework—while generally and appropriately grounded in conservative assumptions—diverged from empirically derived correlations for certain asset classes. In these classes, correlations increased as a function of probability of default, a result directly contrary to the Basel II assumptions (FitchRatings 2008). The same study predicted that the correlations found during the subprime crisis will exceed those derived from longer-term data.

Similarly, an implicit assumption of major importance lies behind the apparent expectation of the revised framework that probability of default and loss given default will be calculated independently of one another and then inserted into the applicable formulas. In fact, both theoretical and empirical work suggests that the value of collateral is inversely related to the probability of default on the underlying loan (Thomas and Wang 2005). Other contestable assumptions in the Basel II formulas include the presumed greater need for maturity adjustments for high-quality exposures on the ground they are more likely to deteriorate than are exposures whose initial quality is lower and the relatively greater impor-

---

30. These criticisms are reviewed and supplemented in Kupiec (2006), Thomas and Wang (2005), and Crouhy, Galai, and Mark (2005).

tance of idiosyncratic risk factors in loans to small and medium-sized enterprises than in loans to large businesses.[31]

The committee's own credit risk model thus includes numerous simplifying departures from existing credit risk models that reflect the current state of the art. The development and use of this model raises a broader problem, one that potentially undermines the very intention of the committee to draw on the expertise of the largest and, presumptively, most sophisticated banks. If, as with the risk-weighting formulas, the committee imposes rules because it believes even the best models to be insufficiently tested, then it will have substituted its own judgment for that of the most sophisticated market actors. Even if it imposes a rule that reflects current best practice, it is making a judgment that the practice is best for all banks. The rule may also quickly become yesterday's best practice, since models may evolve rapidly based on experience and technical advances.[32] In either event, the regulators are substituting their own judgment for that of the risk managers themselves. There are certainly times when regulators *should* substitute their judgment for that of the entities they regulate. But, with respect to the Basel II proposal, this inclination is at odds with the stated rationale for the new paradigm. It also creates new possibilities for regulatory arbitrage, as banks again see a divergence between their experience with actual credit risk and credit risk as defined for regulatory purposes.[33]

Two examples illustrate this point. First, the revised framework includes detailed specifications of the circumstances under which collateral will be recognized as reducing credit risk. Unlike risk-weighting formulas, the collateral practices of major banks seem relatively well developed and robust. It appears as though the desire for uniformity has, in this instance, trumped the customized risk management techniques of banks themselves. Second, it has been widely observed that the approach mandated in Basel II has already been superseded by the most sophisticated risk management techniques of large banks. In particular, some large

---

31. This assumption was questioned by the US banking agencies in their advance notice of proposed rule making (US Department of the Treasury Office of the Comptroller of the Currency et al. 2003, 45, 914). However, this special formula for small and medium-sized enterprises, which was of great importance to Germany, was not changed in the final version of the revised framework.

32. The possibility that rules are imposed because the committee fears banks will game the system is discussed in the next section. This response is also inconsistent with the regulatory principle behind Basel II.

33. The possibility is nicely illustrated by Kaltofin, Paul, and Stein (2006), who explain how banks can segment their retail credit exposures to reduce their capital requirements under Basel II. They identify both how this can be done in accordance with the actual risks presented by the retail portfolios and how the discretion required in implementation opens up the possibility that "actions will be hidden from view by banks" (Kaltofin, Paul, and Stein 2006, 21).

banks argue that portfolio composition factors have now been successfully incorporated into their credit risk models. That is, the more advanced models recognize that the credit risk associated with the bank's assets as a whole is not the simple sum of the risks attached to each individual asset. Just as overall market risk may be reduced through portfolio diversification, so overall credit risk may be reduced or increased by certain compositions of banking book assets.

In failing to take account of portfolio correlation in credit risk models, Basel II is arguably departing from its stated aim of aligning actual risk and regulatory capital more closely. The US banking agencies responded to this criticism with a defense of the portfolio-invariant character of the A-IRB formulas (US Department of the Treasury Office of the Comptroller of the Currency et al. 2003, 45, 910–45, 911). Again, though, the agencies essentially declared that the experience of a particular bank, based on defensible modeling practice, is irrelevant for regulatory purposes. Moreover, many observers continue to question exclusion of this factor from the A-IRB model. Although banks have presumably argued for its inclusion in the expectation that it will reduce capital requirements still further, independent analysts such as Fitch raise the opposite concern—that concentration of a bank's credit portfolio in particular geographic markets may imply a higher correlation among those assets than assumed in Basel II, with a consequent understatement of appropriate minimum capital needs (FitchRatings 2004). A recent study by a task force of the Basel Committee itself concluded that there may be a significant impact on required capital of credit risk concentration, particularly sector concentration, which the task force defined to include both geographic and industry exposures (Basel Committee 2006e). The assumption in the A-IRB model that there is only a single systematic risk factor is not valid where there are significant imbalances in geographic and industry exposures, particularly where relevant geographic and industry risk factors are correlated with one another.

A glaring example that illustrates the Hobson's choice confronted by the Basel Committee in devising the A-IRB approach is the regimen applicable to securitization exposures. Some of these rules rely heavily on ratings provided by external agencies such as Moody's, Standard & Poor's, or Fitch, even for banks using an internal ratings approach. Thus the revised framework requires use of external ratings for any securitization exposure that is rated, or where a rating can be "inferred" based on the relationship between an unrated and rated exposure (Basel Committee 2006g, paragraph 609) Where a bank has an exposure—such as a liquidity facility or a credit enhancement—to a securitization entity issuing asset-backed commercial paper, the bank may use its internal assessments of risk, though even here the bank's ratings must be "mapped" to the external agency's ratings, which continue to apply to the commercial paper itself (Basel Committee 2006g, paragraph 619).

The related turmoil in both the commercial paper and securitized mortgage markets during the summer of 2007 suggests the inadequacy of either alternative. The external ratings of securitized mortgages proved grossly misleading. The internal assessments of risk exposure to conduits and other special-purpose securitization vehicles are of course not public, but the losses suffered throughout the industry suggest that those assessments fell well short of identifying the actual risks involved. The securitization example may be an indication that neither banks' internal risk assessment nor an external rating is reliable enough to serve as the foundation of a capital regulation system.[34] It thus raises questions about the entire Basel II enterprise.

As earlier noted, various Basel Committee officials have suggested that Basel II will eventually move toward acceptance of a full model approach, which would presumably incorporate portfolio risk diversification factors and any future improvements. A transitional regulatory method may be necessary as a practical matter, insofar as supervisors will want experience with the limited model approach before permitting even less well-established enhancements. One can argue, though, that the transitional arrangement is itself too much a shot in the dark, given the uncertainties just recounted. Basel II proponents might offer two rejoinders to this argument: First, there may never be enough certainty about the operation of an A-IRB approach until it is actually put into practice; and second, whatever the deficiencies of current credit risk modeling, it surely is an improvement on the blunt risk-weighting rules of Basel I.

There is obviously merit to these points. Still, these responses do not answer the key questions of whether the improvements in risk sensitivity of capital ratios to be gained by Basel II are worth the cost and likely to be realized in practice. Complex as the current proposal is, it entails many simplifying assumptions that do not comport with the actual practice of large banks using their own credit risk models. The vigorous and ongoing debate over credit risk modeling, particularly its difficulty in capturing the extreme tail events that are most worrisome in banking systems, suggests that a complete transition to a paradigm based on sophisticated industry practices is at best a good ways off and possibly something that will never be attained. Before reaching conclusions on the utility of the A-IRB model, however, it is important to examine in more detail the likely effects in practice of the specific Basel II rules.

---

34. There are numerous other problems engendered by use of either internal, bank-generated, or external agency ratings. One good example of the latter is the potential for "ratings shopping" by banks or their customers. Because the major rating agencies apply different technical criteria in assessing companies (or securitizations), an issuer may be able to modify certain features in order to qualify for the requisite level of rating from one agency, thereby qualifying for more favorable capital treatment, even though the underlying creditworthiness of the issue is sufficiently debatable not to earn a similar rating from other external agencies.

Impact on Capital Levels

The starting point for examining the impact of the specific A-IRB approach of Basel II is determining how capital requirements will actually change with its implementation. A dramatic decrease would raise concerns as to whether the relatively untested IRB approach to capital adequacy was reasonably safeguarding the international financial system. On the other hand, if bottom-line capital requirements were to change little after Basel II, one might question whether the entire costly enterprise was worth undertaking. As it turns out, the seemingly basic question of how much impact the A-IRB approach would have on capital levels was actually quite difficult to answer during the negotiations. The uncertainty on this point not only calls into question the degree to which the Basel Committee understood the implications of its proposal. It also reveals considerable ambiguity in the regulatory purpose to be served by the pillar 1 capital adequacy requirements.

Uncertainty exists as to both the effect of the risk-weighting formulas on capital levels and the intentions of the Basel Committee in setting those formulas. As to intentions, the committee has identified two objectives—leaving minimum capital requirements "broadly unchanged" and offering an incentive for banks to adopt the IRB approaches.[35] The committee has not elaborated on how these potentially conflicting goals are to be reconciled. Obviously, the most potent incentive for banks to adopt A-IRB is a reduction in capital requirements that permits an increase in lending whose profitability more than compensates for the incremental costs of the A-IRB approach. Since those costs are significant and front-loaded, the necessary reduction in capital requirements may have to be significant to create an adequate incentive.

The emphasis on one or the other of these two intentions has differed in official statements made at different times and, it would seem, in some statements made at the same time by different officials. In its first consultative paper (CP-1) issued in June 1999, the Basel Committee stated unambiguously that "the new framework should at least maintain the overall level of capital currently in the banking system" (Basel Committee 1999b, paragraph 10). In an "explanatory note" accompanying release of its second consultative paper (CP-2) in January 2001, the Basel Committee said that its goal remained unchanged, but stated it in rather different terms—"to neither raise nor lower the aggregate regulatory capital . . . for internationally active banks using the standardized approach." For banks using the IRB approach, the committee said its "ultimate goal is to ensure that the regulatory capital requirement is sufficient to address underlying risks and contains incentives for banks to migrate from the standardized

---

35. The committee has juxtaposed these two aims in several of its pronouncements. See, for example, Basel Committee (2003c); and Bank for International Settlements, "Consensus Achieved on Basel II Proposals," press release, May 11, 2004.

approach to this IRB approach" (Basel Committee 2001e, 5). While this shift in emphasis might have seemed quite natural given that the IRB approach had moved from a mere concept in CP-1 to a proposal in CP-2, the committee changed once again in 2002. In explaining its efforts at assessing the impact of the IRB proposal, the committee referred to its "goal of neither significantly decreasing nor increasing the aggregate level of regulatory capital in the banking system."[36] Insofar as this statement dealt with the IRB approach, the omission of any reference to the differentiation between standardized and IRB approaches in CP-2 appears significant. The formulation was again modified and eventually articulated in the revised framework as "to broadly maintain the aggregate level of [minimum capital] requirements, while also providing incentives to adopt the more advanced risk-sensitive approaches of the revised framework" (Basel Committee 2004c, paragraph 15).

The variation in formulations of the basic goal by the committee is reflected in the disparate statements of US banking supervisors. Again, at first glance agency positions appear both simple and uniform. The joint-agency "Advanced Notice of Proposed Rulemaking" issued in August 2003 states unequivocally that the "agencies do not expect the implementation of the new accord to result in a significant decrease in aggregate capital requirements for the US banking system" (US Department of the Treasury Office of the Comptroller of the Currency et al. 2003, 459010). The proposed rule issued in 2006 quoted this language, asserted its consistency with the committee's formulation as just quoted from the revised framework, and restated the commitment of the four federal banking agencies to these objectives (US Department of the Treasury Office of the Comptroller of the Currency et al. 2006a, 55839). Likewise, the final rule affirmed "the agencies' intention to avoid a material reduction in overall risk-based capital requirements under the advanced approaches" (US Department of Treasury et al. 2007, 69295). However, as described in chapter 4, this final rule was itself a careful compromise among the banking agencies, reflecting the concerns of some that the A-IRB approach would in fact lead to significantly reduced capital requirements.

The tension between the Basel II objectives was evidenced in the differing emphases struck by the US banking agencies during the negotiations. Perhaps the most visible example was during a congressional hearing in June 2003, at the very time the "Advanced Notice of Proposed Rulemaking" was being drafted, Fed Vice-Chairman Roger Ferguson, who had assumed the Fed's leadership role on Basel after William McDonough resigned, argued that it made little sense to implement a more risk-sensitive framework just to end up with Basel I capital levels. He

---

36. Basel Committee on Banking Supervision, "Basel Committee Reaches Agreement on New Capital Accord Issues," press release, July 10, 2002.

concluded that "some modest reduction in the minimum regulatory capital for sound, well managed banks could be tolerable if it is consistent with improved risk management." He added that "if the evidence suggested that capital were declining too much, the Federal Reserve Board would insist that Basel II be adjusted or recalibrated," though he did not specify the standard for judging whether capital declined "too much."[37] Comptroller John D. Hawke, testifying immediately after Ferguson, offered a quite different perspective. His overall tone was one of caution, even skepticism, about the Basel II approach. With respect to the impact on overall capital amounts, he stated unequivocally that the "first objective of the Basel Committee in embarking on the Basel II effort was to calibrate minimum capital requirements to bring about a level of capital equal to the global requirements of the present Basel Accord."[38]

The differences in Basel Committee and US banking agency statements might be dismissed as matters of nuance were the *actual*, as opposed to *intended*, impact of Basel II becoming clear. But the test runs of the Basel II formulas—the quantitative impact studies—raised as many questions as they have answered. The three more recent studies—QIS-3 (2003), QIS-4 (2005), and QIS-5 (2006)—together reveal that the Basel Committee supervisors cannot say with any credibility what minimum capital levels will be generated by the A-IRB model once it is implemented.

QIS-3 collected data from 74 banks, most though not all from Basel Committee countries (Basel Committee 2003b).[39] These banks used their internal ratings as the relevant variables in the risk-weighting formulas proposed by the committee. The results are now essentially meaningless as predictors of Basel II capital levels, because CP-3 and the final version of the framework made such extensive changes in the A-IRB formulas. Nonetheless, some of the experience with QIS-3 did raise an issue of continuing interest.

The results showed wide dispersion in the effects of the A-IRB approach on minimum capital requirements of individual banks, with increases of up to 46 percent and decreases of as much as 36 percent (Basel Committee 2003d). The breadth of this dispersion surprised many, even though everyone had expected some effects along these lines. Still, the

---

37. See Roger W. Ferguson, Jr., 2003, testimony before the Subcommittee on Financial Institutions and Consumer Credit of the Committee on Financial Services, US House of Representatives, June 19, 2003.

38. See John D. Hawke, testimony before the Subcommittee on Financial Institutions and Consumer Credit of the Committee on Financial Services, US House of Representatives, June 19, 2003.

39. Fifty-seven of these banks were from Basel Committee countries. Although many results were aggregated, presumably in order to protect the information of individual banks, it seems likely that most of the banks running A-IRB simulations were among those designated in the study as "group 1" banks, meaning those with assets in excess of 3 billion euros.

weighted average change was reassuring—a decline of only 2 percent. However, closer inspection revealed a different picture. Although the *total* capital requirement for banks testing the A-IRB approach would have declined by only 2 percent, the capital requirement for credit risk alone would have declined by 13 percent.[40] The percentage point differential was attributable to the capital charge for operational risk. As noted in chapter 4, Basel II is, for the first time,[41] imposing a capital charge for operational risk, with three variants roughly parallel to the three variants for credit risk. The convenient compensatory role played by operational risk made some wonder whether the operational risk standard would end up being a kind of wild card to ensure that overall capital levels did not fall excessively. This potential wild card role for the operational risk requirement was largely foreclosed by the subsequent development of the advanced measurement approach (AMA), which is generally available to the very banks that will be using A-IRB. The AMA reduced the anticipated operational risk capital requirement for at least some, and probably most, of these banks.

The QIS-3 results and the subsequent changes in A-IRB formulas that would lead to lower capital levels prompted the Basel Committee to take additional steps to deal with the uncertainty regarding the minimum capital requirements associated with Basel II. First, CP-3 created a floor for a bank's capital requirements in the first and second years of the A-IRB regime of 90 percent and 80 percent of Basel I levels, respectively. It said nothing about the intended impact of Basel II on capital levels thereafter. Second, in its May 2004 release announcing consensus on the major outstanding issues, the committee reiterated its two objectives and essentially

---

40. The QIS-3 results showed a 17 percent reduction in minimum credit risk capital requirements at US banks, a figure that the FDIC (2003) believes to reflect more rigorous credit loss assumptions than historical experience would suggest. The latter point is potentially at odds with the conclusion of Standard and Poor's (2003) that participating banks used too *generous* a set of credit loss assumptions. These observations could be consistent if non-US banks used particularly generous credit risk assumptions. Additional information on the impact on US bank capital levels is provided in the "Advance Notice of Proposed Rulemaking" issued by the US banking agencies, which provided information on the changes in capital requirements determined during QIS-3 for 20 large US banks. Required capital for corporate exposures would decline 26 percent (as opposed to a 14 percent decline for all the banks included in the A-IRB part of QIS-3); for small and medium-sized enterprise corporate exposures, it would decline 39 percent (compared with a 3 percent decline for all banks); for residential mortgages, it would decline 56 percent (compared with a 58 percent decline for all banks); for nonmortgage retail exposures, it would decline 25 percent (compared with a 41 percent decline for all banks); and for revolving retail exposures, it would increase 16 percent (compared with an 8 percent increase for all banks).

41. Basel Committee documents have stated that a charge for operational risk was "implicit" in Basel I. In fact, the 1988 accord does not refer at all to operational risk, even in passing. Insofar as it stated that it was directed "mainly" at capital risk, the committee's current characterization is arguable but no more than that.

admitted that it was uncertain as to the impact of its proposed pillar 1 rules on capital levels. Accordingly, the committee indicated that it was "prepared to take actions necessary to address the situation"—specifically, by introducing a "scaling factor" that would, in a single step at the end of the capital calculation process, adjust capital requirements. Thus, in place of the now-unavailable wild card of capital requirements for operational risk, the committee substituted the deus ex machina of an apparently arbitrary scaling factor. While the committee specified its "current best estimate" of the scaling factor, it did not explain the criterion for selection of that factor (e.g., maintaining capital at the 90 percent floor already set for the first year of A-IRB). Nor did it say whether a scaling factor would be a temporary or indefinite feature of the A-IRB approach.

Evaluations since the revised framework was issued have not resolved the uncertainty over the effects of the A-IRB model on minimum capital levels. QIS-4 was undertaken on a limited basis in the United States, Germany, and South Africa beginning in 2004. Then, beginning in 2005, QIS-5 was undertaken using data from banks in all Basel Committee countries except the United States, as well as in 19 noncommittee countries.[42] Although the Basel Committee aggregated the QIS-4 and QIS-5 results as best it could, much of the US data was not technically compatible with the QIS-5 approach and thus was not included in a number of the analyses. Fortunately, the US results from QIS-4 have been separately reported by the four federal banking agencies (US Department of the Treasury Office of the Comptroller of the Currency et al. 2006c).

The QIS-5 results for large banks under A-IRB showed a 7.1 percent decline in required minimum capital from Basel I levels. Tier 1 capital requirements would decline even further, by 11 percent.[43] This figure, as in the QIS-3 results, included capital requirements for operational as well as credit risk (although, as would have been expected in light of the availability of the AMA approach to operational risk, the contribution of operational risk requirements had declined). In addition, this figure reflected application of the 1.06 scaling factor. Without the scaling factor, then, the decline in minimum capital levels would have been 12.4 percent, a substantially larger decline than found by QIS-3.

---

42. The combined QIS-4 and QIS-5 effort included data from 356 banks, of which 56 were large (tier 1 capital of over 3 billion euros), diversified, internationally active banks of the type most likely to operate under the A-IRB approach. A total of 84 banks, including some smaller Basel Committee country banks and 10 banks from noncommittee countries, ran data under the A-IRB approach (Basel Committee 2006d). The discussion of the consolidated results in the text focuses on the 56 "group 1" banks from Basel Committee countries.

43. This result is related to the fact that Basel II makes two changes that adjust the numerators in the tier 1 and total capital ratios differentially: first, the direct deduction of certain exposure types, and second, a new approach for determining the amount of reserves eligible for inclusion in tier 1 and tier 2 capital, based on the relationship of reserves to a bank's expected losses.

Because the QIS-4 protocol was developed prior to the issuance of the revised framework, it does not include the scaling factor and certain other late changes to the A-IRB approach. Thus, the relevant point of comparison of the finding that the aggregate minimum risk-based capital of the 26 US banks would fall 15.5 percent is with the 12.4 percent unscaled figure for the QIS-5 group 1 banks. As with the results for QIS-5 banks as a whole, the US QIS-4 results showed a greater drop in tier 1 capital requirements, by 22 percent in the aggregate. The median drops in total capital and tier 1 capital requirements were 26 percent and 31 percent, respectively.

The reductions in capital levels generated under QIS-4 appeared to surprise US banking authorities. Citing the need for more time "to better assess" the QIS-4 results, in April 2005 they delayed their planned notice of proposed rule making on Basel II implementation.[44] Disconcerting as it may be to realize that, even after agreement on the revised framework, the supervisors still did not know what they would find when the A-IRB method was tested, the dip in absolute capital levels may be less troubling than the dispersion in results among banks. The QIS-4 results revealed variations of 30 or more percentage points in the reductions in capital requirements associated with similar portfolios. It seems highly unlikely that the actual risk associated with sizable portfolios of, for example, home mortgages held by large banks vary to that extent. This intuition is reinforced by the disclosure of large variations in the risk weights assigned by participating banks to identical specific exposures.[45]

Representatives of a number of the banks participating in the QIS-4 study suggested that the predicted declines in capital requirements were misleading, in significant part because the data used for QIS-4 were generated at the most favorable point of the business cycle, when credit risk appears at its lowest. This observation raises the issue of the potentially undesirable procyclicality of the A-IRB approach, to be discussed below. The banks also pointed out that the agencies did not provide detailed guidance on a number of important methodological points, and thus the QIS-4

---

44. See "Banking Agencies to Perform Additional Analysis Before Issuing Notice of Proposed Rulemaking Related to Basel II," Joint Press Release FDIC-PR-37-2005 of the Board of Governors of the Federal Reserve System, Federal Deposit Insurance Corporation, Office of the Comptroller of the Currency, and the Office of Thrift Supervision, April 29, 2005.

45. Examples were provided in testimony given by Donald Powell, then chairman of the FDIC. Using the results of one reporting institution for a sample of large corporate credits that had identical lending relationships with many of the participating banks, other banks reported minimum capital requirements for the identical credits from 30 percent below to 190 percent above those of the benchmark bank. For representative mortgage products, the participating banks reported risk weights from 5 to 80 percent on identical exposures. See Donald Powell, prepared testimony on the "Development of the New Basel Capital Accords" before the Committee on Banking, Housing, and Urban Affairs, US Senate, November 10, 2005.

results may not accord with those that would follow actual implementation. In a sense, the banks' suggestions reinforced doubts that anyone actually knows what the effect of Basel II would be. While the reactions of supervisors to the various QIS results varied, most coalesced around the position that the only way to resolve the uncertainty surrounding the operation of the A-IRB approach was to forge ahead with implementation. There is surely reason to believe that further work by both banks and supervisors will eliminate some of the anomalies discovered in the QIS processes. The point remains, however, that Basel Committee countries have already embarked on implementation, with no assurance that the supervisors understand the impact on aggregate or individual bank capital requirements of the regulatory model they are about to impose.

The picture that emerges from all this is not a reassuring one. The Basel supervisors say they do not want significant declines in capital requirements, other than a modest amount to serve as an incentive to adopt the IRB approach. Yet they are moving ahead with a regulatory model that would—but for transition floors, scaling factors, and other instruments outside of the model itself—apparently lead to substantial capital reductions. Because they claim not to intend these reductions, they do not provide a reasoned argument for why lower regulatory capital levels are desirable. Yet the large banks that would operate under the A-IRB approach clearly anticipate that these regulatory capital declines would be the result of the model's implementation. The supervisors have yet to demonstrate their own mastery of the rules they have created, so that they will at least know what the effects of the A-IRB approach on minimum capital levels will be. Yet they insist that they must move forward with implementation of the model, because that is the only way they can determine what they have actually wrought. All in all, despite the years of work on Basel II, the record is remarkably incomplete as a foundation for making a fundamental change in safety and soundness regulation in the Basel Committee countries and throughout the world.

Difficulties in Implementation and Monitoring

The preceding sections have shown how the theoretical promise of an internal ratings approach in aligning capital requirements more closely to bank risk must be qualified both by limitations in the state of the art of credit risk modeling and by the problems created when the regulators are, in effect, constructing the credit risk model. The earlier discussion of the surprising QIS results gave a taste of the broader administrative and institutional problems that will be encountered as an A-IRB paradigm is put into practice. There are four areas of concern: compliance costs for banks; the supervisory challenge in designing and evaluating credit risk models; the supervisory challenge in monitoring bank operation of the Basel II risk assessment process; and difficulties in holding supervisors themselves accountable for their oversight of the capital adequacy regime.

Compliance with the A-IRB approach will be very expensive. Models and compliance systems must conform to the specific Basel Committee standards for this capital calculation method. At least five years of reliable historical data must be generated as the basis for risk ratings, and a bank must have been using a rating system based on this data for at least three years before being qualified by supervisors to use the A-IRB method. Once a conforming system is running, there are ongoing requirements for testing, data retention, and other validating procedures.

It is difficult to pin down exactly how much large banks must spend to put a qualifying A-IRB system in place. Although bank spending on regulatory compliance has been increasing steadily in recent years, Basel II is not the only major new requirement. Sarbanes-Oxley, the Bank Secrecy Act, and corporate governance scandals have also required increased investment in compliance. A study by Datamonitor, a British market analysis firm, estimated that banks likely to be covered by the A-IRB approach spent approximately $2 billion in 2004 and another $2 billion in 2005 in preparations. An October 2007 report by Aite, an American consulting firm, estimated that US banks alone would spend about $800 million in 2007 and predicted that this spending would rise to more than $1 billion in 2009 (Aite Consulting Group 2007).

While these amounts are large in absolute terms, they appear substantially more manageable when one considers the total assets of globally active banks from Basel Committee countries. Early estimates of $50 million to $100 million—which are in the range of 1 percent of assets for large banks—have been projected for individual bank startup costs. PriceWaterhouseCoopers, on commission from the UK Financial Services Authority, estimated that large British banks would on average spend 59 million pounds on implementing the new credit risk system, and 91 million pounds for Basel II as a whole (PriceWaterhouseCoopers 2005). Even with data provided by banks and the UK Financial Services Authority, the firm could not derive a reliable estimate for ongoing compliance costs. The US banking agencies polled the banks participating in QIS-4 and found that the banks' estimates of initial implementation costs were lower—approximately $42 million per institution (US Department of the Treasury Office of the Comptroller of the Currency et al. 2006a, 55907).[46]

Of course, cost alone tells us little. If there are significant economic gains because credit is being more efficiently allocated or because large

---

46. The responding banks told the agencies that they would have spent approximately 45 percent of this sum on risk management even without Basel II. Thus the agencies conclude that the incremental compliance costs are just over half the $46 million figure. This contrasts with the PriceWaterhouseCoopers study, which found that about 80 percent of the Basel II costs would be incremental expenditures.

banks are sounder, even these large startup costs will seem a bargain. But the banks that are spending the resources on compliance may not, understandably, be satisfied with an evaluation of net social costs and benefits. As one senior risk officer at a major US bank has said, "there's a sense of quid pro quo. If we're going to implement Basel, we want to have lower capital" (quoted in Buerkle 2003). If the large banks get sizable regulatory capital reductions, the expenditure of tens of millions of dollars will, for them at least, be worth the price.

In a well-functioning administrative process, the total social costs of a particular regulatory approach should be weighed against the total social benefits. Where the former exceed the latter, then the approach should be implemented if it is politically feasible to do so. Indeed, the excess of social benefits over costs is a kind of surplus that can be distributed among relevant parties based on political strength or appeal (so long as the redistribution does not render the surplus negative). But here it appears that the desire of the Federal Reserve Board and some other Basel Committee members for a new arrangement and the insistence of banks that they receive a quid pro quo are the constants in the current political economy equation. Thus, capital levels, the major remaining variable, are subject to downward pressure, perhaps even below the point at which social benefits exceed costs. It would be difficult to establish that this equation in fact describes developments during the Basel II process. Yet the repeated adjustments to the Basel II proposals that reduced expected capital requirements give grounds for concern.

The second area of concern is one of supervisory expertise. With the risk ratings generated by banks' internal models poised to play a central role in capital regulation, supervisory oversight of the construction and adoption of the models becomes central to the regulatory system. Prior to the reorientation of the Basel II process following the scrapping of the 1999 proposals, banking supervisory agencies in the United States and elsewhere had relatively little expertise with credit risk models. It is fair to say that only a small proportion of banking examiners are trained to evaluate credit risk models. Supervisory agencies have, of course, acquired financial model expertise in the course of working on Basel II. But a modest number of financial economists in the research or policy groups of the agencies will hardly be adequate for the task of supervising A-IRB banks once Basel II takes effect. In the United States, the agencies are assembling special teams of experts to evaluate the internal models of A-IRB banks. The plan is for this special group to move around the country as needed for examination of the A-IRB banks.

How successful this mode of oversight will be remains to be seen. Three potential problems are already apparent. First, the teams are being assembled on the assumption that a limited number of banks will be applying A-IRB. Should the advantages (in lower capital requirements) of A-IRB become apparent quickly, 10 to 30 additional banks may rather quickly attempt to qualify. At that point, the special teams will almost surely be stretched beyond their limit.

Second, the kind of expertise at issue here is much in demand throughout the financial services industry. The pay differential between government and private firms is very significant. Thus, the agencies may have some difficulty finding enough top-flight financial model experts with sufficient public service commitment that they will forego the higher salaries available in the regulated firms. If experience in other regulatory contexts is any indication, an even greater problem may be the early departures of those who have worked in a specialized regulatory area, as private firms snatch up government experts with inside regulatory experience.

Third, even a technically competent and experienced team of examiners may simply not be able to supervise an A-IRB bank without effectively ceding a good bit of discretion to the banks themselves. Telling in this regard is the published account of a manager from a large British bank, who describes his expectation of a decline in regulatory capital and his bank's consideration of how best to take advantage of this new regime. He goes on to recount how his bank "invested considerable effort in liaising with regulators," a process that "proved enormously valuable not only in obtaining guidance on interpretation but also in being able to shape the regulator's views on practical implementation issues" (Wilson 2004, 303).

Closely related to the supervisory challenge in evaluating and supplementing models is the need for ongoing monitoring of the banks' derivation of risk ratings. There are two distinct dangers. One is the possibility that the bank's employees or consultants will err in accumulating and analyzing the data that serves as the basis for the inputs (probability of default, loss given default, exposure at default, and maturity) to be plugged into the Basel II risk-weight formulas. These mistakes may be difficult for the nonexpert to spot, since they may involve the finance theory behind the models, as opposed to simple ministerial errors. They may also be difficult to identify because significant differences in risk weightings may be the result of discrete mistakes well up the computational line in classification or in an intermediate formula. The revised framework issued in June 2004 is 250 pages long,[47] much of which deals with the technical aspects of the formulas to be used in the various risk-weighting approaches. This "mind-numbing complexity" of the A-IRB approach, as former Comptroller of the Currency Hawke described it,[48] creates an extremely difficult supervisory job.

---

47. The "comprehensive" version of the revised framework released in June 2006 is about 100 pages longer than the June 2004 release. It incorporates the July 2005 guidance on the application of Basel II to trading activities and the treatment of double-default effects, the 1996 market risk amendment, and the portions of Basel I that were not revised in the Basel II process.

48. See John D. Hawke, remarks to the American Academy in Berlin, December 15, 2003.

The other danger is that the centrality of the bank's risk management model to its capital requirements will create an incentive to manipulate the values of the relevant parameters so as to lower the banks' capital requirements. This manipulation need not be outright misrepresentation. Bank officials could, for instance, make aggressively favorable, though still arguable, assumptions in developing their model. As the analytic aftermath of the QIS-4 process shows, the bank supervisory agencies themselves may not agree on what lies behind unexpected results. The consensus agency statements on QIS-4 suggested that the capital requirements derived from the exercise may have been unusually low because the study was conducted in relatively benign economic conditions and most institutions failed to properly incorporate downturn conditions into their loss-given-default estimates (US Department of the Treasury Office of the Comptroller of the Currency et al. 2006c). However, an FDIC staff analysis included as an appendix to congressional testimony by then-Chairman Powell rejected these hypotheses. The analysis noted that the estimates of loss experience reported by banks in QIS-4 far exceeded any losses actually experienced by banks since 1992. Powell pointedly concluded: "The FDIC applauds conservatism by banks in computing their risk-based capital requirements. However, just as banks can hold more capital than regulatory minimums, they can make QIS-4 assumptions that are more conservative than what the Basel II framework would require and hence far overstate the minimum capital that would be required if the framework were up and running."[49]

The Basel Committee recognized this danger early in its development of the IRB approaches and included in the CP-2 quite detailed specifications of the role that the risk inputs used for regulatory purposes must play in a bank's business operations. The final version of the revised framework retained a requirement that the internal ratings "play an essential role in the credit approval, risk management, internal capital allocation and corporate governance functions of banks" (Basel Committee 2006g, paragraph 444). Rating systems "designed and implemented exclusively for the purpose of qualifying for the IRB approach and used only to provide IRB inputs are not acceptable." However, as the Basel Committee itself acknowledged, the revised framework set forth this obligation as a principle, rather than in "prescriptive language" (Basel Committee 2006f). The committee's guidance emphasized the need for flexibility and the exercise of "considerable judgment" by supervisors in deciding whether the IRB "use test" has been satisfied. Thus, one wonders whether, in the end, banks may be able to maintain a different set of books for regulatory pur-

---

49. See appendix B to Powell's prepared testimony on the "Development of the New Basel Capital Accords" before the Committee on Banking, Housing, and Urban Affairs, US Senate, November 10, 2005.

poses than for most of their own business purposes, thereby reopening possibilities for bank manipulation of their own capital requirements.

The final institutional concern is that implementation of an IRB approach to capital adequacy regulation will increase the difficulty of holding supervisors accountable for their actions (or inaction). The problem of asymmetric information, pervasive in financial markets, extends to bank supervision. As noted earlier, financial institutions are among the most opaque of publicly traded firms. Relative to most other kinds of firms, the quality of a bank's assets is both more important and more difficult for outsiders to assess. Although the limited resources of examiners may leave them with less knowledge of a bank's assets than would be necessary to assess its condition accurately, they are privy to considerable information unavailable to investors, congressional oversight committees, academics, and other outsiders. It is thus difficult for these groups to judge the performance of bank supervisors. The 1980s savings and loan crisis revealed the potential damage to the financial system from "regulatory forbearance," whereby supervisors aware of a financial institution's precarious condition refrain from closing the institution or taking other robust remedial action in hopes that things will improve with time. The same opaqueness makes simple regulatory incompetence—an unawareness of problems, rather than a decision not to act after recognizing problems—difficult to identify.[50]

In an effort to discourage regulatory forbearance following the savings and loan debacle, Congress enacted legislation requiring prompt corrective action by supervisors whenever bank capital levels fall below the Basel I (and applicable simple leverage ratio) minimums (12 USC. §1831o). Progressively tougher action is required as bank capital falls below other thresholds. Although the prompt corrective action provisions are not in any strong sense enforceable by courts or other agents, they do establish expectations for supervisory action that will be applied ex post when a bank fails. The statute requires an investigation by the Inspector General (an office independent of the agency hierarchy) of a federal banking agency with supervisory responsibility for a bank whose failure results in a loss to the federal deposit insurance fund (12 USC. §1831o(k)). Congressional hearings tend to follow in any case in which supervisory ineptitude or bad judgment is suspected.

Capital adequacy ratios under Basel I have been far from foolproof indicators of looming bank difficulties. Since an asset remains at book value until management makes the unusual and significant decision to set aside reserves for possible losses or to write off the asset completely, a capital

---

50. Of course, the same information asymmetry would make outside detection of excessively stringent bank supervision harder. However, in such an eventuality bank management would have knowledge of the supervisory excess and an incentive to bring that excess to the attention of others—the examiners' superiors in Washington or sympathetic members of Congress, for example.

ratio can appear quite reassuring only weeks before serious difficulties develop for a bank. In this sense, the A-IRB approach promises some improvement in the external monitoring of banks. The more accurate assignment of an initial probability of default should make the capital ratio a more meaningful indicator of the quality of a bank's assets. The regular reassessment of probability of default generated by credit risk models could provide earlier indications of potential trouble for classes of a bank's assets. Thus, capital ratios should be less misleading than under Basel I. However, as noted earlier, the very complexity of the A-IRB approach gives banks more opportunities to manipulate, or make mistakes during, calculation of their capital ratios. The potential difficulties of supervisors in detecting such problems have also already been mentioned. Similar difficulties will make evaluation of supervisory performance more difficult. A post-insolvency inquiry into supervisory performance, for example, will have a harder time detecting forbearance. Under Basel I, a capital ratio is, precisely because of its relative bluntness and simplicity, more straightforward to determine. But under the A-IRB model, it may be extremely difficult for an independent entity such as the Government Accountability Office to reconstruct the series of decisions and judgments that went into the creation and supervisory assessment of the credit risk model.

Common Language for Credit Risk

Basel Committee officials have stated that the A-IRB regulatory model "will allow banks, supervisors and markets to communicate about risks with a common language" (Himino 2004, 41). The idea is that Basel II has created a standardized approach to quantitative risk measurement, which looks to the potential for future developments as well as reflecting the impact of past occurrences. This potential benefit is, of course, substantially dependent on the success of the A-IRB approach in steering banks to an accurate assessment of the risks posed by their credit exposures. Assuming success in this effort, a common language or risk could enhance bank safety and soundness both directly and indirectly.

A common language could be a useful supervisory tool even if Basel II does not achieve socially optimal regulatory capital levels, since its methodology could still reveal the relative soundness of internationally active banks and thus help to identify problem banks. Even though supervisors today presumably have access to banks' internal information pertaining to credit risk, that information may be difficult to compare across banks. The standardized Basel II categories and formulas could provide the basis for making these comparisons. This standardized information may be particularly important for bank agencies' assessment of foreign banks operating in their countries and for cooperative supervisory activities by agencies from multiple countries.

A common language of risk may also increase relevant information available to market actors—both investors in, and counterparties with, banks. The increased information flow may, in turn, indirectly contribute to bank safety and soundness in several ways. Like the data provided under securities laws, a common template for credit risk information may enable investors to evaluate the performance and prospects of banks more thoroughly and efficiently. In that event, the cost of capital for sounder banks should decline relative to that for banks whose exposures and capital positions are more troubling.[51] Conceivably, investors might even take action within corporate governance mechanisms to change management practices they find unduly risky.[52]

Before considering how likely these benefits are to be realized, it is worth pausing to consider why any form of government action is necessary in the first place—whether it be the creation of information templates for voluntary use or mandatory disclosure. The starting point for this explanation is that financial institutions appear to be among the most opaque of firms, as suggested by the finding that bond rating agencies diverge more in their ratings of banks and insurance companies than for any other kind of company (Morgan 2002). Although one might think well-capitalized banks have an incentive to reveal information that would reassure investors, there may be both collective action and internal incentive hurdles to this outcome.

As to collective action, banks obviously do reveal some relevant information but in a form that is not compatible with similar information published by other banks. No bank has the incentive to conform its information on its credit risk assessments, for example, to the methods used by other banks. A bank may also fear that disclosure of certain information would advantage its competitors sufficiently that its profits would be reduced more than any decrease in its cost of nondeposit borrowing. There may also be internal disincentives to information disclosure and dissemination. Bank management may be inclined to reveal only favorable information. Bank employees in trading, lending, or other operating units may not want their own management to have complete information, much less bank investors and counterparties. If their compensation is based on the imputed profitability of their own divisions, or even if they simply wish

---

51. One Federal Reserve official closely involved in the development of Basel II suggested that the common language will also benefit bank counterparties, and thus banks as well. Hendricks (2004) argued that the common tools and vocabulary created by Basel II would, by overcoming a collective action problem impeding development of a common measure of risk, significantly advance the development of more liquid markets for the trading of credit risk.

52. The potential for more robust forms of market discipline over banks is explored more thoroughly in chapter 7.

to avoid increased scrutiny from senior management, they have an incentive to mask losses or risks.

Thus, there may be good reasons for supervisors both to create a common framework for sophisticated credit risk assessment and to require public disclosure of some of the information generated by that framework. Basel Committee officials believe that the IRB approaches of pillar 1 create the appropriate framework and that the disclosures required by pillar 3 assure that this framework is properly disseminated. However, there is disagreement as to the likely effectiveness of these disclosure requirements in facilitating market discipline.

Herring (2005, 283–84) characterizes the pillar 3 approach as "feeble," for three reasons. First, he criticizes its omission "of considerable risk related data such as foreign/domestic currency breakdowns of assets and liabilities." Second, he suggests that banks are given so many rules and implementation choices under the A-IRB model that, even with disclosure of all relevant underlying data, capital ratios across banks will not really be comparable. This point is an implicit rebuttal to the potential benefit of Basel II in creating a common language about bank risk, whether for supervisors or market actors.[53] Third, Herring doubts that disclosure can produce real market discipline because of the belief in markets that more than 400 internationally active banks have an "extremely high" or "high" probability of receiving external support. Thus, the incentives of market participants to exercise discipline over banks are limited.

A different view emerges from the analysis of Basel II by FitchRatings (2004, 15), which characterizes the disclosure requirements as "robust." Even this upbeat assessment is qualified, however, by acknowledgement of the different approaches to risk management that lie behind the capital numbers. Moreover, the FitchRatings report does identify some issues concerning which disclosure is not explicitly required under Basel II, such as a bank's evaluation of stress scenarios and its management of capital levels based on that evaluation. Standard and Poor's appears not to share Fitch's endorsement, insofar as it has released a detailed set of recommendations for bank disclosures that goes well beyond what is required by Basel II (Standard & Poor's RatingsDirect 2007).[54]

---

53. When CP-3 was released in 2003, an official of the Risk Management Association questioned the utility of the requirement that banks disclose the percentage of their credits falling into each probability of default category, on the grounds that banks will use different methods to arrive at their probability of default decisions. See Rob Garver, "Basel II's Other Issue: Disclosure," *American Banker*, May 5, 2003, 1. However, as reflected in Herring's critique, that observation could apply to virtually all the disclosures required under pillar 3.

54. While indicating that the information required under pillar 3 would, "if consistent, risk focused, and sufficiently detailed," promote greater market discipline, S&P identified "best practice" with respect to disclosure that goes beyond pillar 3 requirements. Notably, S&P's additional items in the area of credit risk center around the very kinds of quantitative

As noted in chapter 4, the requirements are sufficiently unelaborated that we must wait for experience with actual disclosures to determine the real, rather than intended, scope of disclosure. Insofar as the banks successfully beat back some forms of disclosures proposed in CP-3, despite the importance attached to them by regulators,[55] there is some basis for skepticism that national regulators will lend a strong interpretation to the pillar 3 requirements. The relative lack of attention to pillar 3 is replicated in the proposed rule issued by the US banking agencies, which largely track the lists of required disclosures included in Basel II itself.

Incentive to Improve Risk Management

A third potential benefit of the A-IRB model is that it serves as an incentive for banks to adopt sophisticated risk management techniques. Supervisors were concerned that the senior management of commercial banks no longer understood the risks being assumed in many parts of their firms' increasingly complex business, a concern more than borne out by the subprime crisis. Gone were the days when a bank CEO had a hands-on sense of the risks entailed in even a large bank's significant operations—mortgage, consumer, corporate, etc. With the growth in off-balance-sheet activities, the explosion in creative securitization and other financial innovations, and the erosion of barriers between commercial banking and other financial activities, even the most diligent senior management was inevitably unaware of the nature and scope of at least some significant risks.

Of course, even without a regulatory inducement, the large banks had developed or adopted the internal credit risk models that they pushed on the Basel Committee in the early stages of the Basel II process. Senior management touted their investments in sophisticated risk management techniques. Yet when working-level people from the supervisory agencies met with their counterparts in the risk management divisions of the large banks, they were surprised at what they learned. While attention was surely being paid to new risk management techniques, progress toward implementing them was considerably less than had been advertised.

---

information that banks reportedly resisted having included in pillar 3. For example, S&P identifies the "amount of exposures at default, before and after risk mitigation, with a breakdown per risk bucket, the weighted average loss given default, and the associated regulatory capital requirements" (Standard & Poor's RatingsDirect 2007, 3).

55. For example, the CP-3 proposed requirement for disclosure of the percentage of credits falling into each probability of default category (Basel Committee 2003a, paragraph 775), mentioned in the preceding footnote, was strongly and successfully resisted by the banks. It does not appear in the final revised framework. Some supervisors contend that this is a particularly useful piece of data for investors because, even if the basis for ratings may differ among banks, it is the sort of information that would give informed observers of the industry a window into the bank's overall risk profile.

At first glance, the account of bank sluggishness in adopting sophisticated risk management systems may seem surprising. After all, a bank with a sound and profitable franchise should have had strong business incentives to take the steps necessary to preserve that franchise. Part of the explanation may lie in the simple fact that senior management is usually beset with problems of an immediate nature, where some influential actor or constituency is demanding action. In these circumstances, the medium-term imperative of improving risk management systems can easily slip from a list of management priorities. Also, of course, every organization faces competing demands for funds; the creation of a trading unit to participate in a new, high-return activity can easily win out over the investment of tens of millions of dollars or euros in upgrading risk management capabilities. As noted earlier, there is a divergence between the interests of the bank as a whole and the interests of its employees. The managers of operating divisions may not *want* their risks to be accurately assessed and managed. If their compensation is tied to their divisions' revenues or imputed profitability, they will have an incentive to engage in higher-risk, higher-return lending. In these circumstances, the risk manager is a decidedly unwelcome intruder.

This background helps explain what might otherwise have seemed an unusual statement in 2003 by Roger Ferguson, then vice-chairman of the Federal Reserve Board, to the effect that "Basel II, at least in its advanced form, is as much a proposal for strengthening risk management as it is a proposal for improving capital standards."[56] The Basel Committee became, in effect, an ally of risk managers within the large banks. By setting in motion a revision of capital standards that depended on implementation of a validated internal model and associated risk management systems, the committee gave risk managers strong arguments for more resources and priority within their own financial institutions. Indeed, staff of supervisory agencies reported privately that they had been told by some bank risk managers that it was important to keep setting deadlines for progress in order to keep the pressure on.

Significant anecdotal information suggests that the anticipation of Basel II requirements has indeed been an important factor in the acceleration of bank investment in credit risk management and risk exposure systems.[57] The aim of prompting improvements in bank risk management

---

56. See Roger W. Ferguson, Jr., remarks at the ICBI Risk Management 2003 Conference, Geneva, December 2, 2003.

57. A nonscientific survey of financial services companies by Ernst and Young found that more than 60 percent of the respondents said that Basel II was either a primary or significant driver of their recent investment. Of course, the usual caveats about self-selection of respondents to such surveys fully apply. The results of the survey are summarized in Peter Davis and Jorg Behrens, "Commercial Bankers See the Bright Side of Basel II," *American Banker*, April 2, 2004, 11. In the intervening years, following publication of the revised framework,

has taken its place alongside achieving better calibrated capital requirements in the standard justification for Basel II offered by central bankers and regulators.[58] Of course, the concomitant promise of lowered capital requirements for banks qualifying for the A-IRB approach provided an incentive that was presumably agreeable to bank management. As recounted in the previous chapter, the carrot appears to have grown ever larger during the Basel II process, while the stick remained the same size. Mindful of this trend and other criticisms of the A-IRB approach, some observers suggested only half-facetiously that the aim of Basel II to get banks to spend more on risk management had been achieved, and thus there was no need to implement the revised framework.

In sum, Basel II has generated increased attention to understanding bank risks and to techniques for managing them—at least among supervisors and senior bank management. With that attention has come increased investment in risk management systems. These developments are clear benefits flowing from the Basel II process. It is much less clear whether these benefits are worth the reduced levels of regulatory capital that will be required for many banks under the revised framework and the complexity inherent in the A-IRB approach. Nor is it clear whether such reductions are necessary to encourage a process of continual risk management improvement.

Potential Negative Effects of the Advanced Internal Ratings–Based Model

In addition to questions about the effectiveness of the A-IRB model in achieving its promised benefits, interested parties and commentators have identified two potentially significant drawbacks—exacerbation of the inherently procyclical effects of capital regulation and competitive disadvantaging of non-IRB banks. The former is, of course, not intended by the committee. While the committee did not set out to advantage one group of banks over another, the very fact that it has devised three different methods of capital regulation opens that possibility. In any case, there is disagreement over the likely magnitude of both these effects. Moreover, because the criticisms were raised early in the Basel II process, the

---

bank investments in risk management have presumably been driven by the need to prepare for the Basel II transition. The state of such preparation is generally regarded as somewhat slower than anticipated. The absence of certain relevant categories of data from recent trial runs of the Basel II standards in QIS-4 and QIS-5 lend credence to the inference that banks are not yet prepared to implement the A-IRB approach.

58. See Malcolm D. Knight, "Global Banking: Paradigm Shift—Managing Transition," speech to the Federation of Indian Chambers of Commerce and Industry—Indian Banks' Association Conference, Mumbai, September 12, 2007.

committee was able to respond so as to mitigate—though not eliminate—these unintended but foreseeable consequences of an IRB approach.

Macroeconomic Consequences

The Basel II model has prompted considerable academic discussion of whether it will exacerbate the procyclical effects induced by capital adequacy regulation. Chapter 3 explained why capital adequacy requirements have long been suspected of increasing the procyclical tendencies that are inevitable in lending patterns. There has been an extended debate as to whether Basel I itself had such an effect, particularly in amplifying the severity of the 1990–91 recession that followed close on the heels of Basel I implementation. As noted earlier, capital requirements such as those of Basel I appear to have a measurable effect on certain categories of borrowers, but the extent of macroeconomic effects remains uncertain.

The worry about Basel II is that three features of the A-IRB approach may lead to more pronounced procyclical impacts.[59] First, the very use of internal models is intended to lead to greater sensitivity to changes in the credit risk of a bank's assets. The models required by A-IRB look out one year to determine the probability of default on a loan. The revised framework specifies that ratings be updated at least annually, with more frequent assessments for higher-risk borrowers or when relevant new information is received.[60] During a recession, ratings will reflect the increased probability of default in that relatively short time frame and thus lead to higher capital charges. This contrasts with both Basel I, which assigns a loan to a risk bucket and makes no further adjustment unless a significant adverse judgment or event occurs, and with the standardized approach of Basel II, which uses external credit agency ratings. The latter are assigned with some attention to the creditworthiness of the firm through an entire business cycle and thus are less sensitive to macroeconomic variations (although at the cost of being necessarily less sensitive to actual risk at any given moment).

A second concern is that the inclusion of loss given default as a key parameter may have an amplification effect, both because the condition of a defaulting borrower may be more dire during a recession and because the

---

59. Goodhart, Hofmann, and Segoviano (2004) place Basel II in historical perspective in arguing that banking sector liberalization and capital adequacy requirements have already increased the procylicality of bank lending and that Basel II will considerably accentuate these trends.

60. Basel Committee (2004c, paragraph 425). In their initial joint advance notice of proposed rule-making on Basel II, US banking agencies also mandated that banks have a policy that requires a dynamic ratings approval ensuring that obligor and loss severity ratings reflect current information (US Department of the Treasury Office of the Comptroller of the Currency et al. 2003, 45, 956).

value of collateral may have diminished owing to a general decline in the prices of certain assets. If internal models reflect an expectation that losses during economic downturns will not only occur more frequently but will be on average larger,[61] the result would be still greater capital charges.[62] Third, the disclosure requirements under pillar 3, modest though they may be, could themselves affect bank behavior, as management considers the impact on investors and counterparties of information about deteriorating capital ratios. Cumulatively, these factors might increase capital charges sufficiently that, when combined with reductions in capital caused by actual losses, capital ratios will decline close to (or, conceivably, below) the regulatory minimum. Bank management would then be constrained from lending even to some borrowers that appeared creditworthy.

The scenario just hypothesized should not be misunderstood to reflect unanimity that Basel II will appreciably increase the procyclicality of capital requirements. While Estrella (2004); Goodhart, Hofmann, and Segoviano (2004); Kashyap and Stein (2004); Pennacchi (2005); and Persaud (2008) all find reasons to believe that procyclicality may be considerably exacerbated, Gordy and Howells (2006) and Saurina (2008) are skeptical that Basel II will have significant marginal procyclical effects. Allen and Saunders (2004), though concluding that credit risk models are likely to have a procyclical bias, hypothesize that this effect may be offset to some degree at large financial institutions by the countercyclical bias of market risk models. Policymakers have also argued that, by inducing banks to have better risk assessment management systems, Basel II will have a dampening effect on the naturally procyclical behavior of banks.[63]

---

61. In questioning whether the loss-given-default parameter will exacerbate procyclicality, Gordy and Howells (2006) cite two studies noting the tendency of banks to improve their collateral position on troubled loans. If these findings were generalized, they would suggest that the loss given default might decrease as probability of default increases, rather than the two variables moving in the same direction. However, a review of the literature by Allen and Saunders (2004) casts doubt on whether this is the case. They find a "growing consensus" that loss given defaults are correlated with probability of defaults, such that losses tend to increase as defaults do. Whether that consensus is well founded is another question—a more prudent position might be that the data are sufficient to draw only tentative conclusions.

62. The revised framework suggests that loss-given-default values will be calculated based on something approaching a through-the-business-cycle basis and thus be less susceptible to procyclical fluctuation (Basel Committee 2004c, paragraphs 472–473). However, adjustments to loss given default are clearly contemplated (Basel Committee 2004c, at paragraphs 485–487); depending on how these adjustments are made by banks, they could effectively weight recent experience more heavily. Here, as with so many things in Basel II, the outcome will depend on a combination of bank discretion and supervisory oversight.

63. See Saurina (2008); see also Jaime Caruana, "Basel II—A New Approach to Banking Supervision," remarks at the Fourth Annual International Seminar on Policy Challenges for the Financial Sector, Washington, June 1, 2004; and José Viñals, "Procyclicality of the Financial System and Regulation," speech at the Conference on Managing Procyclicality of the Financial System, Hong Kong, November 22, 2004.

Furthermore, in response to questions about procyclicality effects following the Basel Committee's new emphasis in CP-2 on the internal models approaches, the committee made several changes that were included in CP-3 and, ultimately, the revised framework.[64] Most importantly, the risk-weighting formulas were modified with an eye to procyclicality concerns. The asset correlation parameters decline with increases in probability of default, thereby reducing the speed with which capital requirements increase as the probability of default rises. Flattening the curve in this way should mitigate procyclicality effects. Second, Basel II includes as one of the many requirements to qualify for an IRB approach that a bank have sound stress-testing processes in place that, among other things, consider the impact of "economic or industry downturns" (Basel Committee 2006g, paragraph 434). In pillar 2, supervisors are enjoined to determine the capital level of each bank with an eye to external risk factors "such as business cycle effects and the macroeconomic environment" (Basel Committee 2006g, paragraph 752). The implication is that, in implementing the pillar 2 principle that supervisors should expect banks to generally operate above minimum capital levels, these supervisors will require additional capital where indicated by the results of these stress tests.[65] A third change, emphasized by policymakers such as Jaime Caruana,[66] was to prod—though not exactly require—banks to use a longer-term horizon in assigning risk ratings, so as to take into account the effects of economic downturns on creditworthiness.[67] That is, the committee has tried to incorporate into the IRB approaches an element of the through-the-cycle ratings practice reflected in the standardized approach because it relies on ratings from external agencies.

Of course, these changes are not without costs of their own. Flattening the risk curve makes capital requirements less sensitive to the actual risk assumed by a bank in extending credit at a particular point in time and

---

64. To investigate this issue, the Bank for International Settlements (BIS) convened a conference in March 2002 on "Changes in Risk Through Time." The conference included central bankers, supervisors, academics, and market participants. It prompted several BIS studies such as Allen and Saunders (2003) and Amato and Furfine (2003), led to some of the recent published academic work on this question, and influenced the modifications in the IRB approaches described in the text.

65. The UK Financial Services Authority (2006) has proposed an approach for doing just that in appropriate circumstances.

66. See Jaime Caruana, "Monetary Policy and Basel II," speech at the 33rd Economics Conference, Vienna, May 13, 2005.

67. Paragraphs 414–416 of the revised framework state that "banks are expected to use a longer term horizon in assigning ratings" and give several alternative methods for banks to do so (Basel Committee 2006g). The extent to which this expectation is implemented is clearly a matter of national supervisory discretion. The committee had considered requiring through-the-cycle ratings but, prior to publication of the revised framework, softened this obligation.

thereby widens the gap between economic and regulatory capital. That is, experience tends to show that default correlation *increases* as the probability of default increases.[68] Using the results of bank stress-testing to raise capital requirements again lodges considerable importance in a process that has never been tested by a serious economic downturn. Gordy and Howells (2006) argue that through-the-business-cycle ratings destroy the cross-temporal comparability of the IRB capital requirement and, accordingly, prevent market participants from inferring changes in bank portfolio risks from capital ratios.

Disagreement as to the macroeconomic effects of capital ratio changes underscores the degree to which the A-IRB approach will be a real-world experiment whose consequences are uncertain. A staff paper for the UK Financial Services Authority (2004) concluded that the "worryingly high" degree of volatility inherent in the pillar 1 requirements will be reduced by a combination of rating approaches that produce less cyclical estimates of probability of default and loss given default and the fact that some parts of bank portfolios are likely to be considerably less procyclical. On the other hand, the staff paper acknowledged that the problem was potentially a very serious one, in part because banks themselves seem generally unable to measure the impact in their own ratings systems. Later, even as the UK Financial Services Authority issued a proposal on additional capital charges as a buffer against cyclical downturns, it noted that the debate over potential macroeconomic effects of Basel II remains "lively and unresolved" (UK Financial Services Authority 2006, 84). More light could be shed on the issue by supervisory simulation of how Basel II would have affected capital requirements had it been in place in 2007, as the subprime mortgage crisis hit, and thereafter, as economic growth slowed, particularly in the United States.

The fact that there is debate over the procyclicality issue is modestly reassuring. Although the strengthening of procyclical effects by Basel II would be an unintended consequence of a regulatory change, at least it would not be an unanticipated one. A key question is whether the procyclicality question is best understood as another example of the trade-off between prudential concerns and economic growth concerns that is implicated in capital requirements more generally. If so, the procyclicality concern resembles many issues that arise in economic regulation, where the optimal trade-off between two social desiderata is difficult to determine with any precision. On the other hand, events leading up to the subprime crisis raise the possibility that the amplification of procyclicality effects in the A-IRB approach in itself poses a problem for prudential policy, quite apart from macroeconomic concerns. If, for example, the relatively small

---

68. Evidence for this proposition applied to retail lending is found in several papers included in a special issue of the *Journal of Banking and Finance*—Allen, DeLong, and Saunders (2004); Cowan and Cowan (2004); and Deitsch and Petey (2004).

risk associated with residential mortgages in a prolonged rising housing market results in low capital requirements for mortgages written over a number of years (and securities backed by such mortgages), then a sudden and sustained downturn in the market may not provide banks sufficient time to build capital in response to the substantially increased riskiness of their mortgage assets.

Supervisors will be watching the procyclicality effects of Basel II as the new regime is implemented. The Basel Committee has charged one of its subgroups with sharing information on the impact of cyclicality on capital requirements[69] and, as part of the supervisory response to the subprime crisis, has indicated it will analyze the data that becomes available by the end of 2008 to determine if further calibration is needed (Financial Stability Forum 2008, 15). In fact, there has already been considerable thought given to mechanisms that could mitigate procyclical effects without sacrificing too much risk sensitivity. One suggestion is to use a different risk curve formula for capital requirements depending on the state of the economy (Kashyap and Stein 2004). Thus, for example, a negative GDP growth rate would automatically reduce capital requirements, which would rise during periods of robust GDP growth. Another, related idea is for an autoregressive rule that would directly smooth the output from the capital formula during a recession (Gordy and Howells 2006). A third suggestion is to rely more on risk-based deposit insurance premiums and less on capital requirements (Pennacchi 2005). A fourth is to use accounting rules to impose a countercyclical loan-loss provision (Jiménez and Saurina 2006).

These and other solutions are not without their own problems (e.g., the lag time before accurate indicators are available for applying a "recession" formula), but one can at least imagine solutions consistent with the basic paradigm. However, any such solution would at a minimum further complicate an already complicated set of capital rules. Additionally, as will be discussed in chapter 6, many of these possible modifications to the A-IRB approach seem ill-suited to the international features of Basel II.

Competitive Equality

As soon as the Basel Committee proposed three methods for calculating regulatory capital, the question immediately arose whether different classes of banks within a national regulatory system would be competitively advantaged (or disadvantaged). As the IRB approaches were progressively modified so as to lower capital requirements, smaller banks became increasingly concerned that they would be disadvantaged relative to

---

69. Benford and Nier (2007) describe the exercise initiated by the UK Financial Services Authority and the Bank of England to monitor changes in capital requirements associated with business-cycle fluctuations as Basel II is implemented by British banks.

banks using an IRB approach. Under Basel I, every bank must set aside the same amount of capital for a loan of a particular amount to a particular customer. Because the A-IRB approach requires less capital for many loans or classes of loans than required under Basel I and the standardized version of Basel II, the large banks using A-IRB will enjoy lower regulatory costs in making those loans.[70] Thus, for example, the capital requirements for many residential mortgages and for extensions of credit to many established commercial firms drop significantly under an A-IRB approach. Smaller banks that find it economically infeasible to spend the resources necessary to establish and qualify an internal model system of risk assessment fear their ability to compete on such products will be compromised.

Numerous consequences might ensue. First, and most obviously, non-A-IRB banks could suffer a drop in revenues and profits, as they are priced out of certain lines of business.

Second, non-IRB banks could become attractive takeover targets for A-IRB banks. The former could see their profitable business opportunities decline even as the latter enjoy increases in their unencumbered capital immediately following implementation of Basel II. QIS results to date suggest that the mere fact of acquisition by an A-IRB bank would significantly lower the capital requirements associated with a non-IRB bank's portfolio of assets, instantly making these assets more valuable in the hands on an A-IRB bank.[71] While a further decline in the number of banks in the United States seems inevitable,[72] it may not be desirable to promote this decline through regulatory factors unrelated to efficiency.

Third, non-IRB banks may adapt by taking on more high-risk assets. A larger concentration of low-quality assets in smaller banks need not inherently decrease the safety and soundness of those institutions. Adequate diversification within the higher-risk category and adequate premia to account for the higher credit risk would in theory contain any risk to bank solvency. Alternatively, the banks could accept greater degrees of

---

70. As discussed below, the situation is further complicated by the fact that the foundational IRB approach yields significantly different capital requirements for some portfolios than does the A-IRB approach. This complication will not apply in the United States, which will not permit its banks to elect the foundational approach.

71. In Europe, there have been suggestions that banks adopting an IRB approach may also find themselves takeover targets. The reasoning behind this suggestion is that banks with substantial amounts of business in areas where capital requirements will decline most— such as mortgages—will find themselves with increased capital buffers that they are not able to draw down quickly through profitable lending opportunities. Because supervisors may discourage distributions to shareholders that appear directly tied to reduced regulatory capital requirements, these banks may become attractive targets for banks that could quickly take advantage of the capital buffer through additional lending.

72. In the last 20 years, the number of community banks in the United States has been halved from 14,000 to 7,000, while the proportion of deposits held by the 10 largest banks has more than doubled, from 16 to 40 percent.

interest rate risk by using short-term deposits to fund fixed-rate mortgages. However, history is sobering on these points. The notorious savings and loans problems of the 1980s developed in an environment in which the institutions were taking on higher-risk assets and greater interest rate risk, at least partly in response to the higher costs they encountered following the deregulation of depositor interest rates. Quite apart from any conscious strategy based on moral hazard (or outright fraud) by managers of these institutions, experience in managing a riskier portfolio appears to have come more slowly than the shift in the portfolio itself.

Fourth, it is possible that higher-risk lending will migrate not to Basel I banks but outside the regulated banking sector entirely. This may or may not be an appropriate outcome from the perspective of bank safety and soundness alone, though recent events give grounds for concern. In any case, such migration could well exacerbate problems in other areas such as consumer protection, a possibility illustrated by the widespread abuses in subprime lending that substantially predated the 2007 crisis.

Fifth, some regional and community banks express concern that non-IRB banks will be regarded as "second tier" by relevant investors, external credit-rating agencies, and sophisticated customers.[73]

These theoretical possibilities raise two questions. First, how likely are they to be realized in a significant way? Second, would such effects on net be undesirable?

As to the likelihood of significant effects, only the first two mentioned above have been the object of empirical work. The last three are obviously very difficult to quantify, in part because much depends on the reactions of supervisors, other governmental authorities, and market actors. A shift to higher-risk assets and consumer problems associated with the migration of lending to unregulated sectors could be prevented or contained with appropriate government responses, though perhaps not until significant harm has already been done. The fifth concern—the potential for second-class status for non-IRB banks—seems particularly speculative. Even with respect to the first two effects, which are susceptible to some quantitative analysis, there has been relatively little empirical work to date, perhaps because the A-IRB formulas changed repeatedly during the Basel II process and, as evidenced by the QIS exercises, the effects of the final formulas have been difficult to pin down. Still, as a rough starting point, the QIS-5 study reinforces expectations that the three approaches could yield very different

---

73. There may also be competitive consequences among A-IRB banks. For example, a loan of the same terms and amount to the same customer could yield different risk weights depending on the model and experience ratings of two different A-IRB banks. This regulatory anomaly may need to be addressed in cases of syndicated loans, for example, and it may rankle IRB financial institutions. The QIS results discussed earlier revealed just such anomalies. Conceivably, though, a sufficiently refined IRB system might be able to limit pronounced, non-random competitive effects arising from the bank-specific character of A-IRB risk weighting.

capital requirements for similar portfolios (Basel Committee 2006d). For example, results for the large banks likely to adopt the A-IRB approach showed that they could hold nearly 20 percent less capital under the A-IRB model than would be required under the standardized approach.

The potential competitive inequities in most Basel Committee (and many noncommittee) countries are mitigated to some degree by the availability of the foundational internal ratings–based (F-IRB) approach. Mid-sized banks appear ready to adopt that approach in substantial numbers. Since the greater differences in capital requirements for certain classes of assets seem to be between the F-IRB and standardized approach, these banks can likely avoid too great a disadvantage with the largest banks in lending arenas in which they compete head-on. In the United States, where the only choice is between the A-IRB and a standardized approach, the competitive inequalities are potentially greater.

Such work as has been done on effects in the United States comes mostly from current or former researchers at the Federal Reserve Board.[74] The lending markets in which direct and significant competition between very large and smaller banks has been investigated are small and medium-sized enterprise lending and residential mortgage lending.[75] Berger (2006) concludes that smaller banks do not in general compete with very large banks for the same kinds of small and medium-sized enterprise lending but that larger non-A-IRB banks may indeed be disadvantaged vis-à-vis A-IRB banks.[76] This study finds that community banks tend to make loans to small and medium-sized enterprises based on

---

74. This fact in itself is interesting. It may result from the greater institutional incentives of the Fed to address these questions in light of current policy controversies, notwithstanding the difficulties in projecting effects with so many remaining uncertainties. Specifically, Executive Order 12866 requires federal agencies to prepare a regulatory impact analysis for "significant regulatory actions." The output from Fed researchers may also reflect their opportunity to gain access to the raw data in the QIS studies. Interestingly, there seems to have been significantly more research in Europe on the issue of differential capital treatment under the different Basel II methodologies. Most of that research has been directed at lending to small and medium-sized enterprises, rather than at mortgage lending, perhaps a reflection of the relatively lesser degree of importance of mortgage lending in many continental European countries relative to the United States. One recent paper attempts a cross-country comparison of the impact of Basel II on small and medium-sized enterprise lending in Australia, Italy, and the United States (Altman and Sabato 2005).

75. One study, also by Fed researchers, suggests that capital requirements for credit card lending could be *lower* under the standardized than under the A-IRB approach (Lang, Mester, and Vermilyea 2007). However, the study notes that few smaller banks do much credit card business. The difference could be significant for those regional banks that will use the standardized approach, although this advantage will likely be outweighed by the disadvantages in other forms of exposures.

76. Although the Berger paper on small and medium-sized enterprise credit markets was not published until 2006, an earlier version was released as a Federal Reserve Board working paper in 2004.

classic "relationship" criteria such as local information, familiarity with the firms' executives, and the like. On the other hand, larger banks that will not adopt the A-IRB approach rely principally on financial information for such lending, just as the A-IRB banks do.

There is direct competition among banks of all sizes for mortgage lending. Here, again with a very limited amount of work in hand, the evidence is mixed. Two papers come to somewhat different conclusions. Calem and Follain (2005) project that the differential between A-IRB banks and other banks in capital requirements for high-quality mortgages will translate into a cost advantage of approximately 10 basis points for the A-IRB banks. They predict on this basis that A-IRB banks will gain between $116 million and $279 million in annual profits, while other banks will lose between $655 million and $880 million (the negative sum character of this outcome being attributable to increased consumer surplus from the greater competition). Hancock et al. (2005) question whether a 10 basis point differential will matter much in the mortgage market, where rates customarily are quoted in increments of one-eighth of a percentage point, or 12.5 basis points. More importantly, they assert that the effective capital rate for much of the US mortgage market is already lower than Basel I levels because of the huge presence in that market of government-sponsored enterprises such as Fannie Mae, which have considerably lower capital requirements.[77]

Reviewing both studies, Flannery (2006) cautions against drawing any firm conclusions, particularly if the leverage ratio remains in place. He inclines toward the view that the cost advantage of A-IRB banks will have some effect on the market. He hypothesizes that smaller banks able to do so may respond by shifting their mortgage portfolios to include some less creditworthy but higher-yielding mortgages. Because Basel I standards apply the same capital charge to all residential mortgages, no matter what their creditworthiness, this strategy would allow the smaller banks to lower their effective capital requirement for mortgages. Flannery notes both that some smaller banks may not be able to make these sorts of loans successfully and that there are supervisory implications for banks that *can* rebalance their portfolios. He also finds that the government-sponsored enterprises are likely to be net losers when large banks adopt the A-IRB approach.[78]

---

77. Capital requirements for government-sponsored enterprises such as Fannie Mae will almost certainly increase in the wake of the subprime crisis and the remedial legislation passed by Congress in July 2008. However, they are currently so much lower than those of commercial banks that a gap is likely to remain.

78. Mortgage markets, including the role of the government-sponsored enterprises, will very likely look quite different after the subprime crisis is fully resolved than they did beforehand. These changes could themselves affect the relative importance of the factors discussed by the studies mentioned in the text.

As to the possibility that nonadopting banks will become takeover targets of A-IRB banks, a study by Federal Reserve Board staff concluded that the new capital standard was unlikely to accelerate the pace of bank takeovers (Hannon and Pilloff 2004). The authors note that capital regulation has rarely been cited as an incentive for bank acquisitions in the past and infer that it must not be considered significant by industry actors. Based on an examination of the acquisition propensities of highly capitalized banks in the past and the effects of binding leverage ratios imposed under the prompt corrective action legislation, they find no statistically significant correlation between capital standards and acquisitions. As noted by Flannery (2006), however, the Basel II delineation of fundamentally different capital standards for different banks is a substantially different circumstance than those studied by Hannon and Pilloff. Thus we are left much where we began—with intuitions but little hard evidence.

In the absence of convincing evidence pointing one way or the other on the ultimate question of whether smaller banks will be greatly disadvantaged in practice, it is reasonable to ask whether, if some of these effects on nonadopting banks do become apparent, they should be considered a serious problem with the A-IRB model. Competitive equality concerns have traditionally played an important role in US banking policy—as between state and national banks, banks and nonbanks, and US and foreign banks. Similar concerns exist in some other countries. In Germany, the impact of regulations on the *lander* banks is a matter of considerable political, as well as economic, importance. Of course, so long as there is a balkanized system of bank regulation, conditions of competition among different classes of banks can be made truly equal only by eliminating the discretion of chartering and supervisory authorities to modify their regulations independently of other authorities. The phenomenon of competition among chartering and supervisory authorities in the United States is well known, both between state and federal authorities and between the federal banking agencies.

With respect to regulatory differences that correlate with the size of banks today, there is something to be said for the proposition that certain differences are appropriate. A community bank and Citibank may both take insured deposits and make loans, but the similarity essentially ends there. While they may compete for deposits to some degree, their competition for assets—with the important exception of residential mortgages—is relatively circumscribed. They generally function in different product markets. Citibank's activities include foreign sovereign lending, large syndicated loans, writing swaps, and many other activities beyond the capability of even the best run and most profitable community bank.

There are regulatory differences as well. The failure of a very large bank would pose a threat of systemic effects. Smaller banks fail nearly every year, sometimes creating losses for the federal deposit insurance fund but no risk to the financial system. Because of systemic risk concerns and the enormous complexity of a money-center bank's operations, the federal banking agencies have developed special systems for supervising the biggest banks. The Federal Reserve Board has, in conjunction with other federal regulators, developed a program for supervising "large, complex banking organizations" (DeFerrari and Palmer 2001). The Office of the Comptroller of the Currency divides its supervisory operations into two lines, one for the 24 largest national banks and another for all other national banks. Among other things, teams of supervisors are essentially permanently on site at the largest banks, whereas smaller banks are examined on site only once a year. The FDIC has considered reforms that would bifurcate the federal deposit insurance system. Large banks' premiums would reflect systemic risk factors but not the costs of closing small banks, whereas smaller banks' premiums would reflect the closure costs but not systemic risk premia. Thus, in keeping with the general norm that equal treatment means treating similarly situated actors equally, it is not at all clear that banking law should avoid all differentiation between large and small banks.

It would be a misguided public policy that declined to adopt an effective regulatory model for the largest banks only because it was not appropriate for smaller banks. But, as US regulators have found, it is politically misguided to ignore the potential for significant differences in capital requirements associated with particular forms of lending. Furthermore, with respect to the anticipated large reductions in capital requirements for mortgages under the A-IRB approach, for example, smaller banks rightly point out that the stakes are not abstract notions of competitive equality but a very real competitive advantage in a particular lending market. As a matter of policy, it seems difficult to justify imposing significant regulatory disadvantages on smaller banks in markets where they otherwise *could* compete with larger institutions.

It is perhaps a testament to the influence of community banks in Congress that their potential competitive disadvantages were addressed by the federal banking agencies before they even tried to move forward with implementation of the A-IRB approach. They first proposed a so-called Basel IA for nonadopting banks that would, among other things, reduce capital requirements for residential mortgages (US Department of the Treasury Office of the Comptroller of the Currency et al. 2006b). In 2007 they dropped this plan in favor of developing a revised standardized approach, which will presumably include lowered risk weightings for a number of asset classes, in part to avoid too much asymmetry in capital requirements for similar portfolios. Thus, the most contentious competitive equality point raised in domestic implementation of Basel II may eventually be resolved but at the cost of lowering the capital requirements for all banks, not just the A-IRB banks. This is one example of the downward pressure on regulatory capital levels in general that has been created by the Basel II process.

Conclusion

Two core aims of Basel II are unqualifiedly desirable: to align capital requirements more closely with the risks actually assumed by banks, and to continuously prompt banks to adopt the best-available risk management practices. However, the potential of the Basel II A-IRB proposal to achieve those aims is questionable. This approach entails a major change in the method for calculating capital requirements for the most systemically important banks. Yet the impact of this change on actual capital levels is not understood. Moreover, while most supervisors seem accepting of at least moderate declines in A-IRB bank capital levels, they have provided no analysis of why they believe current bank capital levels to be unnecessarily high.

Of equal concern, the A-IRB model is at the same time enormously complex, full of opportunities for bank and national supervisory discretion and only indirectly related to the state-of-the-art risk evaluation and management systems actually used by banks for business purposes. The latter feature may present an opportunity for a different form of regulatory arbitrage—one based on shaping the IRB process for regulatory purposes. Thus, there seems a disconcerting possibility that the Basel II approach has given us the worst of both worlds—a highly complicated and impenetrable process (except perhaps for a handful of people in the banks and regulatory agencies) for calculating capital but one that nonetheless fails to achieve high levels of actual risk sensitivity. Finally, the entire process raises serious problems of practical administration that must be overcome if the putative benefits of the A-IRB approach are to be realized. Financial innovations and experience with existing forms of exposure will require frequent parameter adjustment. The tasks of monitoring banks and supervisors are difficult enough in the unusually opaque world of financial intermediaries. The A-IRB model elevates these problems of technical adjustment, bank compliance, and supervisory accountability to new levels.

Basel Committee officials often respond to criticisms of Basel II by asserting that the pillar 1 capital calculations are only a part of the overall regulatory model. They point to the pillar 2 emphasis on supervision of bank risk management systems and, less frequently, to the pillar 3 disclosure requirements. One can agree that both these emphases are desirable without accepting the conclusion that the A-IRB approach as a whole is an appropriate regulatory model. Indeed, not only are the capital rules important in themselves, but the overwhelming amount of attention devoted to them in the last decade may have come at the expense of developing more innovative supervisory methods and market disciplines.

Ultimately, the most optimistic appraisal of the approach may be that it rests on an expectation that bank regulators will successfully adapt their supervisory techniques to make workable a scheme that is at once complex, ambiguous, and opaque. Whether that expectation is reasonable enough to justify what is in many respects a leap into the regulatory unknown is questionable. Given the emphasis on national competitive advantage that emerged during the Basel II negotiations, it is at least uncertain whether supervisors could—in normal times—muster the will and political insulation that would be necessary to vigorously exercise the supervisory authority referenced in pillars 2 and 3. The subprime crisis will, in the near term, likely create the conditions for strong supervisory action. As with the Latin American debt crisis that gave rise to Basel I and the savings and loan crisis that gave rise to prompt and corrective action requirements of US law, this most recent financial crisis will for a time give supervisors the political backing necessary to take strong positions on prudential issues. But, precisely because Basel II relies so heavily on continuous supervision rather than more traditional rule enforcement, the eventual dissipation of a sense of crisis could—unlike the earlier events—effectively preclude any lasting regulatory effect.

In sum, as a domestic regulatory model, the A-IRB approach as it emerged from the Basel II process may create as many problems as it solves. But to end this chapter where it began, this skepticism is only a partial rejoinder to the Basel Committee's conclusion that, on balance, Basel II is the best practically available approach to bank regulation. The next chapter addresses its merits as a critical part of an international arrangement, and the following chapter considers whether there is a more attractive alternative regulatory model.

Appendix 5A

Table 5A.1   Risk-weighted capital (RWC) ratios of 10 largest US banks, 1992–2006

1992

Bank	Ratio
Citibank	9.37
Bank of America	10.83
Chemical Bank	10.67
Morgan Guaranty	12.68
Chase Manhattan	10.66
Bankers Trust	12.29
Wells Fargo	11.03
Home Savings of America	12.99
Bank of New York	11.39
Great Western Bank	10.54

1993

Bank	Ratio
Citibank	11.13
Bank of America	11.89
Chemical Bank	12.48
Morgan Guaranty + A25	11.85
Chase Manhattan	12.24
Bankers Trust	13.47
Wells Fargo	14.14
Home Savings of America	12.52
PNC Bank	10.91
NationsBank of Texas	8.82

1994

Bank	Ratio
Citibank	12.68
Bank of America	11.75
Chemical Bank	11.86
Morgan Guaranty Trust	12.78
Chase Manhattan	12.23
Bankers Trust	13.31
Home Savings of America	12.17
Wells Fargo	12.70
PNC Bank	10.63
First National Bank of Chicago	12.51

1995

Bank	Ratio
Citibank	12.24
Bank of America	11.28
Chemical Bank	11.49
Morgan Guaranty Trust	11.24
Chase Manhattan	11.74
NationsBank	10.20
Bankers Trust	13.21
Home Savings of America	12.42
First National Bank of Chicago	11.28
Wells Fargo	13.27

1996

Bank	Ratio
Chase Manhattan	11.36
Citibank	12.12
Bank of America	10.98
Morgan Guaranty Trust	11.72
Wells Fargo	11.72
Bankers Trust	13.25
NationsBank	10.41
PNC Bank	10.39
Bank of New York	10.26
First National Bank of Chicago	11.18

1997

Bank	Ratio
Chase Manhattan	10.75
Citibank	12.18
Bank of America	11.30
NationsBank	10.98
Morgan Guaranty Trust	10.91
First Union	10.20
Bankers Trust	12.36
Wells Fargo	11.18
PNC Bank	10.55
Keybank	11.00

(table continues next page)

Appendix 5A

Table 5A.1 Risk-weighted capital (RWC) ratios of 10 largest US banks, 1992–2006 *(continued)*

1998		1999	
Bank	**Ratio**	**Bank**	**Ratio**
NationsBank	10.27	Bank of America	10.90
Citibank	12.60	Chase Manhattan	11.04
Chase Manhattan	11.28	Citibank	12.35
Bank of America	10.81	First Union	10.22
First Union	10.43	Morgan Guaranty Trust	12.17
Morgan Guaranty Trust	12.14	Washington Mutual	11.15
Washington Mutual	12.11	Wells Fargo	11.22
Bankers Trust	13.38	Bank One	11.48
Wells Fargo	11.20	Fleet	10.38
Fleet	10.84	HSBC	18.08

2000		2001	
Bank	**Ratio**	**Bank**	**Ratio**
Bank of America	10.85	Bank of America	12.55
Citibank	12.66	JPMorgan Chase	11.20
Chase Manhattan	10.88	Citibank	13.60
First Union	10.73	First Union	11.68
Morgan Guaranty Trust	12.31	Washington Mutual	10.93
Fleet	11.49	Fleet	10.57
Washington Mutual	11.36	U.S. Bank	12.65
Wells Fargo	11.94	Bank One	12.65
Bank One	11.14	Wells Fargo	11.79
SunTrust	10.77	SunTrust	11.00

2002		2003	
Bank	**Ratio**	**Bank**	**Ratio**
JPMorgan Chase	11.12	JPMorgan Chase	10.43
Bank of America	11.33	Bank of America	11.31
Citibank	12.58	Citibank	12.56
Wachovia	11.80	Wachovia	11.72
Washington Mutual	11.37	Bank One	13.71
Bank One	13.45	Wells Fargo	11.24
Wells Fargo	11.42	Fleet	11.30
Fleet	11.29	U.S. Bank	10.84
U.S. Bank	10.81	SunTrust	10.85
SunTrust	10.91	HSBC	11.82

Appendix 5A

Table 5A.1   Risk-weighted capital (RWC) ratios of 10 largest US banks, 1992–2006 *(continued)*

2004		2005	
Bank	**Ratio**	**Bank**	**Ratio**
JPMorgan Chase	10.27	Bank of America	10.90
Bank of America	12.60	JPMorgan Chase	11.04
Citibank	11.28	Citibank	12.35
Wachovia	10.81	Wachovia	10.22
Wells Fargo	10.43	Wells Fargo	12.17
Fleet	12.14	U.S. Bank	11.15
U.S. Bank	12.11	SunTrust	11.22
HSBC	13.38	HSBC	11.48
SunTrust	11.20	Keybank	10.38
Bank of New York	10.84	State Street	18.08

2006	
Bank	**Ratio**
Bank of America	10.85
JPMorgan Chase	12.66
Citibank	10.88
Wachovia	10.73
Wells Fargo	12.31
U.S. Bank	11.49
SunTrust	11.36
HSBC	11.94
FIA Card Services	11.14
Regions Bank	10.77

Source: Call reports filed with the Federal Financial Institutions Examination Council, Schedule RC-R.

6

Basel II as an International Arrangement

The preceding chapter raised significant questions as to whether the advanced internal ratings–based (A-IRB) approach of Basel II is a suitable model for domestic banking regulation. This analysis, though indispensable to determining whether Basel II is an advisable policy innovation, cannot end the inquiry. Basel II is, after all, an *international* arrangement, the product of an international committee of bank supervisors whose very existence evidences the belief that some degree of coordination on bank regulation is necessary. Thus, the ultimate assessment of Basel II also depends on whether it is likely to achieve valuable international cooperation. This chapter explores the relationship between the international arrangement and the Basel II regulatory paradigm to be implemented in domestic laws.

Described as an international arrangement rather than as the domestic regulatory model created by that arrangement, Basel II is a harmonized set of capital adequacy and supervisory requirements that, at least with respect to the IRB approaches, were developed more or less from scratch through international negotiations. These harmonized requirements, which are both detailed and complex, are to be overseen within a fairly informal institution composed of national banking supervisors. Basel I was also a harmonized set of capital adequacy requirements—albeit a considerably simpler one—overseen within the informal setting of the Basel Committee. Unlike Basel II, however, it did not include any explicit expectations as to how national officials would go about implementing the capital requirements for banks. That is, it laid down only the substantive rules that should be made binding on banks at the national level, not a particular approach to supervision. Moreover, the starting point for its negotiation was the bilateral US-UK understanding, which itself was based on notions of risk-weighted capital requirements that had been evolving for some time in a number of countries.

The potential benefits of the Basel approach to an international harmonization of capital requirements (again, with a special emphasis on the IRB methods) may be grouped into four categories.[1] First, shared capital rules may provide reassurance to each country that banks in other countries are sufficiently sound that they are unlikely to create significant counterparty risks for the country's own banks, or even trigger an international financial crisis. This potential benefit, shared by Basel I and Basel II, is most obvious as it applies to large, internationally active banks of the Basel Committee member countries themselves. To the degree that sensible harmonized standards are emulated by nonmember countries, two further benefits could ensue—increased assurances of soundness of large, internationally active banks from nonmember countries and decreased risk of emerging market financial crises triggered by a domestic banking crisis.

Second, capital harmonization may make conditions of competition among banks from different countries more equal. As discussed in chapters 3 and 4, this has been a strong motivating factor for both Basel I and Basel II.

Third, harmonized rules, standards, and supervisory procedures may facilitate consistency and efficacy of supervisory treatment for multinational banks. This enhanced international supervisory cooperation may derive in part from an international parallel to the domestic benefits of a "common language" for bank risk positions, a subject that has assumed greater importance to supervisors based on their experiences under Basel I.

Fourth, harmonization may yield direct benefits for nongovernmental actors. Multinational banks subject to supervision in multiple countries may find their regulatory burdens substantially reduced if a single set of capital requirements applies to all their subsidiaries and branches. The trading of credit risk and the scrutiny of banks by investors may be facilitated by the same common language developed for supervisory purposes. These kinds of effects may also be indirectly beneficial for safety and soundness goals.

---

1. The committee's statement of objectives in the first consultative paper included continued promotion of safety and soundness of the financial system, enhancement of competitive equality, a more comprehensive approach to risk (the "three-pillar" approach), and combining a focus on internationally active banks with the development of principles applicable to all banks (Basel Committee 1999b). With the shift in emphasis toward IRB approaches, the committee explicitly added increased risk sensitivity to its list of aims (Basel Committee 2002a), although this overall aim had obviously informed the Basel II project from the outset. Finally, as already noted, the committee has indicated its intentions to maintain aggregate capital levels at roughly current levels and provide an incentive for banks to adopt the IRB approaches. The aims of a more comprehensive approach to risk and increased risk sensitivity are, in fact, specific objectives in pursuit of the overall aim of increased safety and soundness.

Every effort to standardize regulation internationally raises the question of whether the harmonized regulation is appropriate for all countries. This is a particularly salient question with respect to Basel II, which attempts to harmonize rules at a level of detail greater than in any previous international effort in any regulatory area. The relevant inquiry consists of two parts. First, how effective is Basel II likely to be in achieving the desired benefits from harmonized banking regulation? Second, will these gains from harmonization outweigh the costs of accepting uniform international standards in place of a regulatory regime customized for national circumstances and preferences and administered more or less autonomously? The remainder of this chapter examines the relative importance of each of the potential gains from international cooperation and the likelihood that Basel II will in fact achieve these gains.

Like the previous chapter, this one is largely predictive, since policy decisions are by definition forward-looking. Indeed, because Basel is such a novel international arrangement, experience with existing arrangements is only obliquely instructive. We must rely on what we do know—the current state of banking regulation, the capabilities and political constraints of supervisors, the institutional features of the Basel Committee, and the history of the negotiations—in projecting the impact of Basel II. For all its elusiveness, though, this exercise is essential to answering the question of whether Basel II is well advised. The very novelty of Basel II also makes it an experiment of considerable interest in addressing challenges in regulating other forms of international economic activity or considering alternatives to trade agreements as mechanisms for reducing barriers to international trade and investment.

Safety and Soundness

As noted in previous chapters, enhancing the safety and soundness of internationally active banks has been a stated aim of the Basel Committee in both Basel I and Basel II. The idea is that the failure of one significant bank could, in an internationally integrated banking environment, create problems for banks from other countries. In an extreme case, a systemic crisis could develop. Indeed, the Basel Committee was itself formed by national supervisors in response to international financial tremors following the failures of the New York–based Franklin National Bank and the Cologne-based Herstatt Bank in 1974.

As a preliminary matter, it is interesting to note that neither in Basel I nor in its work on Basel II has the committee ever specified the precise safety and soundness objective of capital regulation. The absence of a stated rationale for capital regulation is not simply a matter of academic interest. As explained in chapter 2, different views on the incentives of banks, the effects of safety nets, and the rationales for bank regulation can yield rather different paradigms for capital requirements. Lacking any such statement, one is left to infer the theoretical underpinnings of Basel II from the revised framework itself.

Regulatory imposition of capital ratios can be justified as a device to force banks to hold the capital that markets would require in the absence of the government safety net, a protection against the systemic problems that could result from bank failure, or both. The A-IRB approach in pillar 1 appears to reflect the first of these justifications. It calls for construction of a probability density function of possible losses that could be expected to occur over a given time period. It then specifies the particular level of capital that will lower the probability of insolvency to a confidence level of 99.9 percent. This is a high standard, to be sure. However, the US bank supervisory agencies have acknowledged that this nominal target likely overstates the confidence level actually achieved, because of the possibility of errors in calculating the input values and the omission of portfolio concentration considerations. In any case, by definition, this basis for calculating capital ratios does not protect against an "extreme tail event"— that is, an event producing losses that *do* render the bank insolvent even if it maintains capital levels prescribed by the model.

For most firms in most industries, the opportunity costs incurred in insuring against extreme tail events are sufficiently large as to render this practice economically misguided. In the commercial banking sector, however, extreme tail events are roughly congruent with systemic crises. Because of the close interrelationships of banks through interbank lending and the payments system, an extreme tail event at one bank may generate massive negative externalities for the economy as a whole. In light of these considerations, the December 2003 Federal Deposit Insurance Corporation (FDIC) staff study argued that "the capital banks should hold from a social welfare perspective would normally be expected to exceed the capital that the banker calculates to meet his own needs" (FDIC 2003). The possibility of financial crisis has led one commentator to suggest that there should be two prudential capital standards—one that seeks to protect taxpayers through a maximum expected loss rate per dollar of insured deposits and an additional insolvency probability rule for large banks whose failure would pose a systemic risk (Mingo 2000).

One might have thought that an international agreement on capital requirements would be most directly concerned with containing systemic risk that might threaten the global financial system. However, although the matter is not without some ambiguity, it appears that Basel II is not directed at systemic risk. Like its 1988 predecessor, Basel II establishes formulas for *minimum* capital ratios. As already mentioned, national regulatory policies provide for higher regulatory capital ratios for many banks, and the supervisory principles in pillar 2 specify that national supervisors "[s]hould expect banks to operate above the minimum regulatory capital ratios and should have the ability to require banks to hold capital in excess of the minimum"(Basel Committee 2006g, paragraph 757). The emphasis of the brief section on above-minimum capital is on "bank-specific uncertainties." The committee states that pillar 1 includes a buffer for "uncertainties surrounding the pillar 1 regime that affect the banking population as a whole." Since the capital ratio calculations in pillar 1 are grounded in a conventional credit risk–modeling technique, there does not appear to be a specific evaluation relevant to systemic risk. Of course, if capital ratios are set at levels higher than the protection of deposit insurance funds alone would require, then one might say that a buffer has been provided with an eye toward preventing systemic problems. However, this conclusion assumes that the systemic risk associated with a bank's operations is in some sense proportional to its credit risks.

Thus, the better, though not conclusive, reading of the revised framework is that it tracks the views of Alan Greenspan recounted in chapter 2. Containment of systemic risk is a task for central banks in their lender-of-last-resort function. But if systemic risk containment is excluded as an objective of Basel II, one is left with a bit of a puzzle. Despite the importance to national supervisors of the safety and soundness of their banks and the present centrality of capital regulation to safety and soundness, the role of an international agreement in promoting this end is not as obvious as it may seem. At first glance, one might think that an international agreement could contribute to the safety and soundness of a country's own banking system by requiring each participating country to adopt a superior bank regulatory paradigm. Implementation of such a paradigm should reduce to acceptable levels the risk of illiquidity or insolvency and, accordingly, contain risk to counterparty banks headquartered in other countries. However, the question that immediately arises is why, if this regulatory paradigm is a superior one, participating countries must form an international agreement to implement it. Unilateral adoption would presumably be in the interests of each country.

A more persuasive argument for harmonizing international capital standards, at least where the negative spillover effects associated with systemic risk are not front and center, rests on concerns that each national regulator has some incentive to adopt less rigorous capital standards than the home countries of banks with which its banks compete. Alternatively, a national regulator may adopt robust standards but then fail to enforce them vigorously. In either case, national governments arguably indirectly subsidize their banks' risk-taking (White 1994). Dell'Ariccia and Marquez (2006) offer a variation on this argument with their suggestion that high capital standards in one jurisdiction create a positive externality for other jurisdictions. Internationally active banks from the other jurisdictions enjoy increased returns not just from their ability to make more loans with the additional increment of usable capital but also because the constraints imposed on the banks in the strict jurisdiction may reduce supply for those marginal loans and thus increase the interest rate that the less constrained banks may charge. If this effect were significant, the higher profits would—ironically—make the banks with lower capital requirements *safer*. At the same time the higher capital standards in the stricter jurisdiction may make its banks safer and thus pose less of a counterparty risk to other internationally active banks.

While some of these effects may be questioned on both theoretical and practical grounds, the basic point is that there will be pressures on national supervisors to relax prudential regulation so as to provide a competitive advantage to their banks. One can easily envisage regulators currying favor with domestic banks to advance their own careers or, more likely, coming under pressure from legislators or elected members of a government to do so. These external pressures, which arise from the domestic political influence of banks, may seek international competitive advantage for domestic banks or simply regulatory forbearance for the benefit of existing management or owners of a bank. Of course, if other national regulators "meet the competition" by relaxing their own standards, then competitive advantage for any one country's banks will have been lost, but the international banking system will be left more fragile. An international agreement that each country impose specified minimum capital levels could help insulate national regulators from domestic pressures and thus avoid this form of—if not quite a race toward the bottom—a slide toward lower elevations.[2] The initiative for this solution to the collective action problem might come from nonsupervisors concerned with the competitive position of their country's banks, as was the case with Basel I. Alternatively, supervisors themselves might seek the international arrangement to reduce anticipated domestic pressures that would follow a "unilateral" change in capital regulation, as might have been the case in Basel II.

Understood in this way, the safety and soundness rationale for Basel II is closely related to the competitive equality rationale discussed below. From either perspective, the problem is that supervisors in other countries may relax their prudential regulation in response to pleas for competitive advantage (or equality) by, or on behalf of, their banks. Hence a good bit of the discussion that follows is also applicable to the competitive equality rationale for Basel II. One important difference, though, is that the safety and soundness perspective demands analysis of the desirability of the harmonized standard. Regulators could pursue competitive equality for their banks by using virtually any standard, as long as it has similar effects on

---

2. As described in the text, this rationale for an international harmonizing agreement assumes both that the optimal capital standard would have been produced by the domestic regulatory process in the absence of international competition and that the trade-off between banking system soundness and availability of capital to the economy is similar for each country. Even if these simplifying assumptions are relaxed, the basic point about the potential for competitive regulatory capital reductions remains valid.

banks from different countries, but their prudential goals require an assessment of how well the paradigm achieves those goals. In fact, there is some basis for believing that the safety and soundness motivation was eclipsed during the Basel II process by the competitive equality motivation.

The contribution of Basel II to the safety and soundness of a national banking system will derive principally, though not entirely, from its combined effects on bank regulation domestically and in other countries. Strictly speaking, these effects should be gauged through a comparison between the revised framework as a regulatory paradigm and the regulation each country would have enacted in the absence of this international arrangement. In circumstances where, before the international negotiation, each country had its own regulation in place, one could begin with at least a general idea of what the regulatory situation would have been without the agreement (though the possible downward pressures on regulation would need to by hypothesized). However, in the case of the A-IRB approach of Basel II, there *was* no comparable national regulation. The very fact that the A-IRB approach was developed by the Basel Committee more or less from scratch renders highly speculative any effort to compare this regulatory model with the systems that would have prevailed around the world in the absence of an international arrangement. Accordingly, the discussion here focuses directly on the utility of the Basel II A-IRB approach as the method of capital regulation.

Domestic Costs of Internationally Harmonized Regulation

Any undertaking to harmonize among many countries one element of domestic regulation entails certain costs that are, in practice, unavoidable. Most important among these costs is the inevitable divergence of the internationally harmonized standards from those that would be most appropriate to each country's industry structure, scheme of financial regulation, and political preferences. For example, we have already noted in the context of US law that the relative significance of risk-weighted capital requirements depends in part on whether other capital requirements such as leverage ratios are also imposed. Similarly, a highly risk-sensitive deposit insurance system would address some of the same moral hazard problems that capital requirements are meant to offset.

A related shortcoming of harmonized regulation is that it may limit the capacity of national officials to adjust their regulatory practice to national conditions. That is, in placing a floor under the stringency of each country's capital regulation, a negotiated set of regulations will foreclose variations that would be superior to the harmonized rules. Despite the many elements of Basel II left to national discretion, there are rigidities that could develop into significant drawbacks, particularly over time. It appears, for example, that the assumption embedded in the Basel II formulas that asset value correlations are uniform across countries is at least partially undermined by empirical studies (FitchRatings 2004, 2008). Moreover, as European Union Commissioner Frits Bolkestein has pointed out in the context of EU implementation of Basel II, competitive equality considerations affect the trade-off between flexibility and comparability (Ayadi and Ross 2003).

A good illustration of this limitation in the context of Basel II relates to the problem of procyclicality. Some of the more creative thoughts on how to ameliorate this problem would provide for the adjustment of capital requirements as macroeconomic conditions in a country change significantly (Kashyap and Stein 2004, Gordy and Howells 2006). However, to allow these deviations—particularly given the difficulty of formulating ex ante a formula that links capital requirements to macroeconomic conditions—would be essentially to allow different capital rules for banks depending on their national economic conditions. The difficulty in monitoring the extent of such deviations by national regulators is part of the larger problem of monitoring Basel II considered below. In addition, this kind of solution to the procyclicality concern raises the prospect of a bank in a recession-afflicted country having lower capital requirements and thus potentially being advantaged in international lending markets over its competitors from robust economies. The upshot would be a compromise, if not of the safety and soundness aims of Basel II, then surely the competitive equality aim.[3]

Another cost, as is often observed with respect to international arrangements of all sorts, is that it is very difficult to make incremental but significant changes. The substantially larger number of relevant actors and effective requirement of unanimity (or at least consensus) make amendment of an international agreement considerably more difficult to achieve than a purely domestic regulatory scheme. The final version of Basel II reflects two complicated sets of bargains: first, between national supervisors and domestic constituencies (banks, legislatures, etc.); and second, between national supervisors and their counterparts from other countries.[4] These compromises are themselves related—domestic political imperative in one country can lead to a negotiated change in the proposed international rules, which in turn can require a renegotiation of other

---

3. Kashyap and Stein (2004, 28–29) further suggest that, in the absence of an ex ante mechanism for reducing capital requirements during bad macroeconomic times, regulators will improvise ways to forbear, "with all the accompanying potential for various forms of regulatory moral hazard . . . [because] it will be left to regulators to relax the rule as they see fit—perhaps in a highly subjective case-by-case basis—without any previously imposed restraints." This insight draws attention to the Basel Committee's relative lack of monitoring capacities, discussed later in the text.

4. The failure of US regulatory agencies to obtain informal agreement of the Congress on the emerging Basel II proposals led directly first to the need to change directions during the negotiations and then, more seriously, to the difficulties encountered by the agencies in attempting to implement the revised framework once it was completed.

countries' domestic rapprochements.[5] Not only does this dynamic alter the substance of the final agreement, creating some of the incongruities described earlier, but it also makes the agreement more difficult to modify. Changing one rule may disrupt the equilibrium between the two levels of the arrangement and thereby necessitate a more extensive reworking. Some may fear that attempting even modest change may reopen issues that were difficult to resolve in the first place.

Thus, there is a good possibility that, to the extent the rules-based approach of Basel II takes hold, it will be resistant to change in important particulars. If so, national regulators will have two unattractive alternatives. One is to depart from Basel rules unilaterally, thereby risking an unraveling of the arrangement. The other is to accept the constricting effect of an arrangement that began as an unstable hybrid and becomes increasingly detached from the sophisticated risk management techniques that supposedly informed the governing paradigm. US regulators appear to have opted for both alternatives in the case of Basel I. Because it was far less detailed than Basel II, there was ample room for national supervisors to supplement credit risk capital ratio requirements without breaching provisions of Basel I.[6] At the same time, the failure of the United States, or any other country, to unilaterally discard the Basel I method that nearly everyone agreed was outmoded suggests there is something to the "stickiness" of international agreements.

In some circumstances this stickiness may be a useful check on precipitous constituency-driven changes that might otherwise occur in some countries. However, in the context of Basel II, this characteristic is likely to be counterproductive. The rapid evolution of risk assessment and management techniques, along with the considerable uncertainty as to how the A-IRB methodology will work in practice, renders this higher hurdle problematic. Although some committee officials profess the intention to regularly adjust Basel II to technological change, it seems unlikely that changes in risk-weight formulas or other parts of the capital adequacy calculation will appear purely technical to banks and other interested parties. Judging by the complaints of large US banks over the federal banking agencies' inclusion in their notice of proposed rule making of several provisions that were stricter than parallel rules in the revised framework, even unilateral "Basel-plus" measures will be more difficult to implement than under Basel I, perhaps excepting periods during and immediately after significant financial dislocations. Thus there is a strong possibility that modifications to the A-IRB methodology will lag significantly behind advances in risk assessment technologies.

---

5. This dynamic is an example of the "two-level game" famously conceptualized by Putnam (1988) and discussed in the conclusion of chapter 4.

6. For example, US banking regulators imposed capital requirements specific to derivatives and securitized assets, two important classes of assets only obliquely dealt with in Basel I.

Benefits of Harmonized Regulation Abroad

Chapter 5 discussed the significant shortcomings of Basel II as a regulatory model for the United States. In light of the protracted controversy over its domestic implementation, it is at least questionable whether, in the absence of an international arrangement, the domestic regulatory process in the United States would have produced the A-IRB approach. Of course, the rationale for international harmonization of capital adequacy requirements implies that the suboptimality of the harmonized requirements for domestic purposes may be more than outweighed by the beneficial effects of better capital regulation in other Basel Committee countries. If Basel II is effective in aligning regulatory capital more closely to actual risk, even incompletely, its enactment and effective implementation by the home countries of internationally active banks could advance safety and soundness goals.

As has been seen, it is not at all clear that US banking agencies are capable of adequately evaluating internal risk models and monitoring their operation, particularly if dozens of banks elect the A-IRB approach. These concerns exist despite the relative activism of US bank supervision, which relies on the exercise of substantial supervisory judgment in assessing bank operations. Every bank is subject to complete on-site inspection at least annually. The large banks for which US regulators have indicated the A-IRB would be mandatory have permanent on-site teams of examiners.

Doubts concerning the desirability of the Basel II internal model approach to capital regulation in the United States can only be stronger with respect to most other Basel Committee countries. Bank examination elsewhere is considerably less intense. A number of countries—including Italy, Japan, and the United Kingdom—do not require annual onsite examinations (Nolle 2003).[7] More tellingly, a calculation by Office of the Comptroller of the Currency staff showed that the ratio of banking assets to supervisory staff in the United States was nearly 50 percent smaller than in any other Basel Committee country, suggesting that the supervisory process elsewhere is less oriented toward the interstices of a bank's risk management systems.[8] In general, supervisors in other countries rely more on an examination of information submitted by banks and reviewed by

---

7. In Japan, on-site examinations are to be conducted every other year, and in Italy every five years. In the United Kingdom there is no regular on-site examination schedule; the UK Financial Services Authority may conduct them at its discretion.

8. The ratios ranged from $1.14 billion per supervisory staff member in the United States to $17.9 billion in Japan and $18.7 billion in Switzerland (Nolle 2003). Of course, these gross numbers are just that and are not adjusted for such factors as the relative size of banking institutions, the manner in which staff are deployed, and the relative effectiveness of other tools for regulation (e.g., external auditors). Still, the differences are striking.

auditors.[9] This approach comports reasonably well with Basel I and the standardized approach in Basel II. It seems quite incompatible with a regulatory paradigm that builds on banks' internal risk management systems, as opposed to a system of clearly delineated risk buckets and weights.

This concern about the capacities of national regulators, and about the ability of their peers to monitor their supervisory performance, is another manifestation of what seems a disproportionate emphasis in Basel II on the pillar 1 rules for minimum capital ratios. Although Basel II sets forth as one its key principles in the pillar 2 regimen that the supervisor "review and evaluate banks' internal capital adequacy assessments and strategies," it stipulates that supervisory review may be effected through "some combination of" five methods (Basel Committee 2006g, paragraph 746). Since on-site examination is included as but one item in this list, along with "off-site review" and "review of work done by external auditors," it is quite possible that on-site examinations will continue to play a minor supervisory role, even of A-IRB banks. Similar concerns obtain for use of the foundational IRB approach, because a bank's internal calculation of probability-of-default values is a central element in determining capital ratios.

Pillar 2 puts forth a set of expectations for national officials to meet, but in doing so it elides the substantial divergence in supervisory capacities and traditions. Thus, Basel II itself does little to directly accelerate the development of the supervisory expertise and practice that will be necessary to oversee a capital regime based on banks' internal models. It may be that, in implementing the arrangement, all the Basel Committee members will see the need for a change that amounts to a supervisory revolution in some countries. Indeed, anecdotal information indicates that Germany, in particular, is altering its mode of supervision as part of its A-IRB implementation, although some other countries are said to have changed very little to date. At best, a shift in supervisory cultures will be a gradual and uneven process. Moreover, there is little in Basel II itself beyond the fact of the impending A-IRB approach to make this hope for a supervisory version of a "big bang" more likely to be realized.[10]

The aim of enhancing the safety and soundness of all internationally active banks is a worthy one. Yet there is considerable doubt that this aim will be served by an approach based on a conceptually contestable

---

9. See, for example, the assessment of the German supervisory system in IMF (2003, paragraph 60).

10. An additional question about the efficacy of Basel II is whether *any* system of capital requirements is being adequately monitored by national supervisors. After reviewing the limited available record of capital enforcement in the United States, Wellons (2005, 323) found "a tendency of supervisors to identify certain problems but to fail to follow through." Since there is not even limited enforcement data published for some other countries, it is very difficult to evaluate how well enforced Basel I capital standards have been.

paradigm that poses significant implementation difficulties in the United States and sits uneasily with the entire supervisory culture elsewhere. The monitoring problems identified in the domestic regulatory context in chapter 5 are only magnified in an international arrangement. US authorities, instead of being reassured by the existence of Basel II requirements, will surely harbor doubts as to whether supervisors in other countries are able to monitor banks' capital calculations adequately. (Conversely, supervisors in other countries might reasonably harbor reciprocal doubts about US supervisory performance, particularly if dozens of banks adopt the A-IRB approach, and particularly in light of the supervisory failures revealed by the subprime crisis.)

Even if national supervisors are able to supervise adequately, their counterparts will have difficulty satisfying themselves of this fact. The highly particularized nature of each bank's model makes the bank harder to monitor by national regulators, the regulators less accountable to their governments and publics, and national regulators harder to monitor by their counterparts on the Basel Committee. The opaqueness and complexity inherent in the A-IRB approach will pose significant problems for effective monitoring under any circumstances, but these problems might have at least been mitigated through institutional oversight mechanisms of some sort. However, the revised accord itself does not create any such mechanisms. Midway through the Basel II negotiations, the committee did create an Accord Implementation Group (AIG), described in greater detail later in this chapter. As its name suggests, the focus of the AIG and its three subgroups has been on implementation challenges. It is possible that the AIG will over time assume a role in monitoring implementation, since there is no clear line between addressing shared implementation challenges and scrutinizing national supervisory implementation. But this is a possibility, not a stated intention of the Basel Committee. Indeed, throughout its history the committee has shied away from anything resembling a process to promote compliance with its products, perhaps because of its firm view that its products are not legally binding.

It is also possible that the Basel Committee countries will derive benefits from the effect of Basel II on bank regulation in noncommittee countries. The approximately 100 non–Basel countries that have adopted Basel I had a variety of reasons for doing so. Noncommittee members of the European Union were bound by the Capital Adequacy Directive implementing Basel I. Many developing countries were urged by the International Monetary Fund (IMF) or World Bank to adopt both the Basel Committee core principles and the capital accord. Countries wanted to demonstrate to markets, foreign counterparties, and foreign supervisors that their banks are subject to the same capital requirements as G-10 country banks. These and similar motivations are also at work in the context of Basel II. Indeed, while the committee did not appear in 1988 to anticipate the extent to which its capital framework would be globally adopted, during the Basel II exercise it explicitly addressed the applicability of the new framework to other countries (Basel Committee 2004d).[11] The Financial Stability Institute (2006) has reported that 82 non–Basel Committee countries intend to implement Basel II in one form or another.[12]

One benefit potentially accruing to Basel Committee countries from broader application of Basel II is the extension of the same safety and soundness effects to be obtained from adoption by the G-10 themselves—reduced risk that banks from other countries that are counterparties to their own banks will transmit banking problems internationally (as well as the associated competitive equality effects). Even where a country's banks are not highly active internationally, their increased stability would help the G-10 countries avoid the potential foreign and economic policy reversals that could result from a foreign banking crisis.

Despite these possible benefits, there is reason to doubt they will be extensive. In fact, there is some reason to believe that, with respect to some developing countries, adoption of Basel II might reduce rather than increase the safety and soundness of their banking systems. The questions raised earlier about the appropriateness of Basel II for Basel Committee country banks are more serious even for noncommittee countries with reasonably advanced banking systems and regulatory capacities. Without even the imperfect monitoring opportunities afforded within the Basel Committee, oversight of a country's implementation of the revised capital adequacy framework will be limited to other international institutions,[13] rating agencies, and markets. Although these actors may be able to provide some useful monitoring of fairly straightforward capital rules, such as those contained in the standardized approach, it is unlikely that they could penetrate the process by which an A-IRB approach would be validated and operated.

The benefits of widespread nominal adoption of Basel II become even more clouded in the context of many emerging market and developing countries. Even the standardized approach was developed by the Basel

---

11. See also Jaime Caruana, "Overview of Basel II and its reflections on Financial Stability," remarks to the International Conference on Financial Stability and Implications of Basel II, Istanbul, May 16, 2005.

12. According to the results of a survey conducted by the Financial Stability Institute (2006), were the then-prevailing plans of these countries to be realized, more banking assets in those countries would be covered by the foundational IRB approach than by the standardized approach. Although only about 15 percent of banking assets in those countries would be covered by the A-IRB approach, there is considerable regional variation in regulatory intentions. In Latin America, for example, regulators report their intention to bring nearly a third of banking assets under the A-IRB approach in the next decade.

13. The most important of these is the IMF, which now regularly comments on financial regulation as part of its periodic reviews of its member states. However, the IMF does not pretend to conduct the kind of inquiry that would be necessary to monitor the thoroughness with which capital adequacy rules—particularly complicated ones—are implemented.

Committee with reference to banks from the G-10 countries. Powell (2004) identifies several provisions within the standardized approach that do not reflect the characteristics of banks in developing countries. For example, the basic indicator approach for operational risk requires a capital set-aside of 15 percent of gross income. As Powell points out, however, gross income for developing-country banks tends to be higher than in roughly comparable banks from Basel Committee countries. At a more basic level, Powell questions whether the standardized approach is an improvement over Basel I for many developing countries, where external ratings are simply not applicable to most lending. The reduced risk weighting of mortgages thought appropriate for most developed countries is questionable in the legal environments of many developing countries.

In a later study, Majnoni and Powell (2006) suggest that the IRB curves, based as they are on the credit portfolios of Basel Committee country banks, are probably calibrated incorrectly for most developing countries. The factors noted by Powell in his earlier paper are relevant to this conclusion. In addition, though, because the correlations among default risks are typically higher in an emerging market or developing economy than in a developed economy, the authors find that the formulas will not yield the same level of protection in the former as in the latter.

The point that the Basel II approaches may be poor fits for bank regulatory systems in much of the world is underscored in a paper by Bank for International Settlements staff examining implementation of Basel II in Asia. Hohl, McGuire, and Remolona (2006) report that Asian countries are eager to adopt and quickly implement Basel II. This impulse arises in part from an aim shared with the Basel Committee regulators—that is, the expectation that Basel II will drive advances in bank risk management. But it also arises in part from political pressures to give banks in those countries the same advantages of reduced capital requirements that are expected in Basel Committee countries. Based on their understanding of bank and regulatory behavior, the authors question the efficacy of relying on pillar 2 to deal with systemic and other risks. Historical patterns of herding in lending practices make systemic risk more endogenous than in European countries, for example, a tendency exacerbated by the usual procyclicality of capital flows into the region. The authors cite the relative passivity of many bank regulators in these countries as a reason to doubt that supervisors will force banks to assess and respond to systemic risks on their own.[14]

---

14. Indirect support for some of these concerns may, ironically, be found in a speech by Y.K. Choi, the deputy chief executive of the Hong Kong Monetary Authority, who points out that many Asian banks lack the internal resources necessary to develop and validate a rating system and that Asian supervisors are even less prepared than their G-10 counterparts to oversee implementation of the IRB approach. See Y.K. Choi, "Basel II Implementation in Asia," introductory remarks at the BCBS/FSI/EMEAP, Hong Kong, October 17, 2007.

Barth, Caprio, and Levine (2006) broaden the critique of the appropriateness of Basel II approaches worldwide into a suggestion that the emphases in Basel II may actually be counterproductive in many countries. Drawing on an extensive World Bank database of bank regulatory practices in more than 150 countries, they note the absence of robust evidence linking higher capital standards to greater bank stability, thus raising questions about the utility of pillar 1 in many national banking systems. They criticize more directly the application of pillar 2 in many countries. That may seem surprising on its face, since pillar 2 can be summarized as counseling strengthened official supervision. But they argue that, outside of countries with well-developed political systems of checks and balances, increased supervisory powers will tend to impede the flow of funds to creditworthy firms and lead to greater corruption in bank lending (Barth, Caprio, and Levine 2006, 311). Instead, they argue, bank regulation in many developing countries should be *more* reliant on market discipline than in countries with established and accountable administrative traditions and capacities.[15] This argument, if borne out by additional research and analysis, would call into serious question the benefits of applying Basel II in a considerable portion of the world.

Competitive Equality

Despite the origins of Basel I in a drive for competitive equality by US and UK regulators and the extent of subsequent attention to the issue, the relationship between capital requirements and competitiveness is not well understood. On the one hand, it is axiomatic that every additional dollar added to a capital buffer entails a foregone opportunity to lend that dollar and earn interest on it. Thus, the higher capital holdings restrict the bank's revenue-producing activities. Also, as suggested in the preceding section, lower capital requirements in one country may allow internationally active banks in that country to earn supracompetitive returns relative to banks subject to more stringent capital requirements. On the other hand, as was frequently pointed out during the debate on Basel II implementation in the United States, in the decade preceding issuance of the revised framework, US banks were among the best capitalized and most profitable in the

---

15. The Barth, Caprio, and Levine argument is supported by a study of the utility of the Basel Core Principles for Effective Banking Supervision in developing countries. Demirgüç Kunt, Detragiache, and Tressel (2006) find that countries that require regular and accurate reports of their financial data to regulators and market participants have sounder banks. They recommend, accordingly, that priority in implementing the core principles be given to their information provisions. Implicitly, this recommendation downgrades the importance of what has been termed the "supervisory model" of bank regulation, which calls for extensive, iterative, non-rule-based involvement by supervisors in bank practices.

world. One reason may be that higher capital levels signal strength to counterparties, which consequently may be willing to extend funds to the bank at a lower risk premium. Higher regulatory capital requirements may similarly signal to counterparties that a bank's supervisors are more likely to prevent the bank from encountering liquidity or solvency problems.

In short, the effects of higher or lower capital requirements on bank profitability likely depend on a variety of circumstance-specific factors. Naturally, if one country significantly reduces capital requirements while holding constant all other relevant factors, including the safety net that bank counterparties and investors believe the government maintains, then that country's banks will gain a competitive advantage relative to the status quo ante. This is one reason why the prospect that the IRB approaches may significantly lower capital requirements has prompted non–Basel Committee countries to adopt Basel II and why large US banks were so concerned when the implementation process in the United States fell so far behind that in the European Union. But the probability of this outcome says nothing about the degree to which equalizing capital regulation rules will equalize the ultimate competitive positions of banks from different countries. Here, perhaps, the most that can be determined is the relative effect of different capital regimes.

It is difficult to make the case that Basel II will, on the whole, further the goal of competitive equality to a greater degree than Basel I. In itself, this fact is not a criticism of Basel II. If the impact on competitive equality is roughly, or arguably, about the same under the two capital regulation regimes, then the Basel Committee supervisors will have protected their political flanks and freed themselves to reap whatever rewards Basel II may yield on effective prudential regulation and international regulatory cooperation. The problem is that the structure and dynamic of Basel II have themselves provoked sustained attention to the competitive implications of, and opportunities presented by, the new rules. The resulting pressures on national regulators to promote the competitive positions of their own banks may undermine to some degree whatever prudential and cooperative benefits might otherwise be realized.

As noted in chapter 3, efforts to isolate the effects that Basel I has actually had on competitive equality have at best been inconclusive (Jackson et al. 1999). Scott and Iwahara (1994), though making a good case for skepticism that much leveling had been achieved by Basel I, argue more through inference from existing information than from data directly examining the effects of the international arrangement. Still, their arguments should give pause to those who would place too much emphasis on the competitive equality effects of international capital standards.

Recall that the shared US and UK aim in Basel I was to counteract the generous de facto safety nets provided by the Japanese and French governments, which led investors and counterparties to be comfortable with lower levels of capital in those nations' banks. Yet the maintenance of unusually tight safety nets could lower the capital costs of banks by providing this additional assurance, even if the amounts of capital held by banks with similar assets were effectively equalized. In that case, a competitive advantage would persist. Moreover, national differences in tax or accounting systems could confer significant competitive advantage even if the cost of bank capital were roughly equalized. Finally, national supervisory discretion under Basel I created opportunities for regulatory forbearance in pursuit of national competitive advantage.

In an interesting, though hardly dispositive, study of the impact of national factors other than banking regulation on banks' competitive positions, Zimmer and McCauley (1991) found that there was indeed considerable divergence in the cost of equity for banks in six mature economies (Canada, Germany, Japan, Switzerland, the United Kingdom, and the United States). However, this divergence seemed generally to parallel the significant differences in the cost of equity capital for all firms within those countries. Obviously, this was just one study and, at that, a study predating implementation of Basel I. Still, it does suggest that other national characteristics, including home country investment bias, may outweigh the stringency of capital requirements in determining a bank's cost of capital.

In sum, it is difficult to get beyond informed guesses as to how much Basel I has leveled conditions of competition among banks in different countries, much less to determine how Basel II would fare on this point. As noted above, though, if the effect cannot be gauged in absolute terms, one can at least ask whether Basel II is likely to increase the leveling effect of capital standards relative to Basel I. Here again the picture is murky. There are some reasons to believe that the new rules will make competitive conditions more equal but also significant reasons to believe that they will not.

One reason to believe that international harmonization of capital standards could play a more important role in leveling the competitive playing field rests on the possibility that other determinants of a bank's cost of capital may have become less internationally divergent than in the late 1980s. For example, since home country bias among investors is widely believed to have diminished (though by no means disappeared) over the past 20 years, a contemporary version of the Zimmer and Mc-Cauley study would presumably reveal smaller national differences in the cost of equity capital for all firms. Were longstanding efforts to develop accepted international accounting standards to succeed, another source of national difference might decline in importance. However, there has been no apparent convergence in other bank regulatory requirements or tax policy during the intervening period. On the critical question of the effect of perceived government safety nets on bank counterparty behavior, there is little evidence of convergence among the Basel Committee countries.

Even if changes in private investment preferences and accounting policy have made divergent patterns of capital regulation a greater source of competitive inequality (and thus agreement on regulatory convergence a route to more competitive equality), these exogenous factors apply to the potential impact of *any* capital regulation. These secular changes do not give grounds for believing that Basel II will have a greater or lesser leveling effect than other specific capital rules. There *is* an argument that if it works as hoped, Basel II would lead to more efficient competition among banks—whatever their nationality—as banks' regulatory costs for holding particular assets more closely approximate their economic costs. The extensive detail of Basel II seems due in part to an effort by some national supervisors to achieve greater levels of competitive equality. But this effect on inter*bank* competition is essentially irrelevant to differences in *national* policies, such as the impact of extraordinary government safety nets or tax and accounting policies. Thus, unless there is some reason to believe that the convergence of regulatory and economic capital costs will have a disproportionately nation-specific impact, this convergence will do little to level the competitive playing field internationally.

Despite its attention to detail, significant national differences affecting capital ratio determinations are inherent in the A-IRB approach. For example, the definition of "default," which is obviously crucial to a calculation of the probability of default, varies significantly among Basel Committee countries. Accounting definitions of general reserves and usual bank practices with respect to recognition of loan impairment also vary across countries.[16] More generally, the dozens of issues left to national supervisory discretion by the revised framework mean that, even in formal terms, significantly different capital "rules" may be applied to banks in different countries.[17] In addition, ambiguous or incomplete provisions will require guidance to banks from national supervisors, creating another source of difference in the rules. One notable example cited by Jackson (2006) arises from the fact that banks have only a few years of data for many of the models that they will be using to calculate their internal ratings. Thus, statistical inferences to be drawn from this data will be of limited reliability, increasing the need for judgment by both banks and supervisors as to whether the outputs generated by models constructed with limited data are actually plausible.

---

16. The existence of these differences was one reason why the Basel Committee had proposed taking account of expected losses, as well as unexpected losses, in the risk-weighting formulas. As mentioned previously, the committee revised its proposal in October 2003 to exclude expected losses from the computation. As a result, the differences noted in the text may again be relevant. For a broader survey of differences in national banking regulation, see Barth, Caprio, and Nolle (2004).

17. The Basel Committee (2004d, 28–36) identifies more than 60 areas in which national discretion may be exercised.

It is, of course, impossible to say at the outset of the implementation process how significant national variance in interpretation will be for the levels of capital required by similarly situated banks. In many instances, these variations might be quite sensible for safety and soundness purposes, given the different financial and supervisory contexts in which banks based in different nations operate. In other words, some sacrifice of uniformity might be worth the gains for safety and soundness regulation. Indeed, variations in capital regulation may in theory compensate for differences in the actual or perceived safety net afforded banks by governments. However, the extent of national discretion and the opaque quality of the IRB calculations breed countless opportunities for the exercise of regulatory discretion in pursuit of national competitive advantage, as well as for sound prudential reasons.

Shirking or opportunism is possible under Basel I, of course. Supervisors may, for example, permit banks to maintain on their balance sheets at historic value assets that should be written off, with resulting charges to capital. Yet the very simplicity of the Basel I rules means that an outsider can generally derive a good part of an institution's capital requirement from the bank's own accounting statements. And even where supervisory neglect or forbearance allows misleading capital ratio reporting, the limited number of openings for distortion sometimes allows outsiders to see through the reported numbers. Few outside observers, much less other members of the Basel Committee, believed that Japanese banks were as well capitalized over the last decade as their reported ratios showed. As the Japanese banking crisis worsened and the Japanese economy stagnated, this forbearance looked progressively less like an effort to gain international competitive advantage and more like regulatory paralysis.

With an A-IRB approach in place, opportunistic forbearance will be harder to detect, certainly in noncrisis situations. It is useful to recall here the point made earlier in this chapter that a strong argument for a harmonized international capital standard is that it establishes a formal system of collective self-restraint by national bank supervisors. This argument is premised on the dual assumption that supervisors seek a policy outcome that protects the safety and soundness of their banks but that they are regularly subject to pressures, both internally and externally generated, to relax regulation for the competitive advantage of a country's banks. To be effective, then, the harmonized standard should limit the openings through which these pressures can be readily accommodated. For this reason, the substantial monitoring difficulties inherent in the A-IRB approach are also relevant to competitive equality effects. As noted earlier, domestic regulatory assessment of a bank's internal ratings will be a challenge to monitor even with access to relevant records. Detecting a failure by national regulators to correct a bank's flawed ratings will be more difficult still. The complexity and opaqueness of the A-IRB approach thus threaten to undermine one of the key roles of an international capital standard.

Neither the limited evaluation of the impact of Basel I on competitive equality nor the differences between Basel I and the A-IRB approach of Basel II suggest that the latter will be effective in leveling the terms of competition among internationally active banks. What the Basel II exercise *has* done is to provoke a debate on competitive equality that has, predictably, led to arguments that national regulators should not implement Basel-plus safety and soundness regulations because of their deleterious effects on the international competitive position of a country's banks.[18] In sum, rather than at least marginally promoting competitive equality, Basel II may undermine this end by fostering nationalistic opportunism. As this book is being completed, the Basel Committee supervisors have largely closed ranks in the face of serious questions about Basel II that have arisen in the wake of the subprime mortgage and securitization problems that poured forth in the summer of 2007. Once these problems are resolved, one can expect national competitive pressures to assume again the role they played in shaping Basel II itself.

Cooperative Supervision of Multinational Banks

Another potential benefit of the internationalization of capital standards in Basel II is the enhancement of supervisory cooperation among national bank regulators. Although obviously related to the overall aim of ensuring the safety and soundness of internationally active banks, increasing cooperation in the supervisory *process* is distinct from increasing cooperation through agreement on regulatory rules. The creation in 1974 of what is now known as the Basel Committee was motivated principally by the perceived need among national regulators for greater cooperation in the supervision of internationally active banks. For over a decade, efforts to close supervisory gaps between home country regulation of a bank and host country regulation of that bank's overseas establishments comprised

---

18. An example of this line of argument by large US banks comes from Jim Garnett in a statement on behalf of the Financial Services Roundtable to the Subcommittee on Financial Institutions and Consumer Credit of the Committee on Financial Services, US House of Representatives, September 14, 2006. For a sympathetic reaction from a regulator suggesting a willingness to trim these Basel-plus measures, see Ben S. Bernanke, "Bank Regulation and Supervision: Balancing Benefits and Costs," remarks before the Annual Convention of the American Bankers Association, Phoenix, Arizona, October 16, 2006. Notwithstanding the sympathetic hearing Chairman Bernanke was willing to give the banks, in the end he agreed to most of the Basel-plus measures included in the proposed rule making. Indeed, word-of-mouth reports circulating through the Washington grapevine suggested that he had played a key role in forging the July 2007 compromise among the regulatory agencies.

the principal work of the committee.[19] Those efforts remain an integral part of the committee's work today. In fact, prior to the Basel II process, many national supervisors who participated in Basel Committee meetings would probably have said that its most important function was to promote the exchange of views on common problems in supervising internationally active banks and, in the process, to build trust among national banking regulators.

Basel II, unlike the 1988 capital accord, tries to achieve a measure of harmonization in the supervisory process, as well as in substantive capital standards. To a considerable extent, this effort is necessitated by the substantive terms of the revised framework. The sheer complexity of an IRB approach poses technical and resource demands for each national regulatory agency. The opaqueness of the IRB process central to the establishment of minimum levels of regulatory capital requires close and competent supervision of each bank's risk assessment systems. Thus, the nature of national supervisory processes has become a matter of concern to the entire Basel Committee, precisely because those processes must be of high quality if the aims of pillar 1 are to be met. For this reason, pillar 2 of the revised framework sets forth the committee's expectations for supervisory oversight of the regulatory capital requirements of pillar 1 for credit and operational risk, including the validation of bank compliance with the minimum standards and disclosure requirements of the IRB methods. Pillar 2 also establishes expectations for supervisory review of risks not covered by the pillar 1 rules.[20]

---

19. The adverse effects of the failure of Bankhaus Herstatt on counterparty banks in the United States (and on foreign exchange markets more generally) underscored the potential dangers of these supervisory gaps. The first report of the new committee set out proposed guidelines for cooperation in the supervision of banks' foreign operations (Committee on Banking Regulation and Supervisory Practices 1975). These guidelines were formalized in what became known as the Basel Concordat (Committee on Banking Regulation and Supervisory Practices 1983b), which was later supplemented with guidelines on information sharing among regulators (Basel Committee 1990b). The failure of Bank of Commerce and Credit International revealed continued gaps in the supervision of international banks and, to some extent, a failure by Basel Committee members to abide by the terms of the existing guidelines. The result was a renewed commitment to cooperation, as the committee attempted to introduce a greater sense of obligation by specifying that certain of the existing guidelines were to be "reformulated as minimum standards . . . which G-10 supervisory authorities expect each other to observe" (Basel Committee 1992b).

20. The revised framework specifies (1) credit and operational risk that might not be captured under pillar 1 such as credit concentration, (2) risks not covered by pillar 1, such as interest rate and business risk, and (3) risks external to the bank, such as business-cycle effects (Basel Committee 2006g, paragraph 724). Thus, pillar 2 is used as a kind of catch-all to compensate for the limitations of the pillar 1 rules that arise either from an inability of the Basel Committee members to agree on an approach or to a judgment that supervisory discretion is preferable to a rule in dealing with a specific kind of risk. The relegation of interest rate risk to pillar 2 seems particularly unfortunate. A good case can be made that it can be more readily quantified than operational risk.

The IRB approaches of Basel II also compelled the committee to establish new forms of international cooperation among national supervisors. The relationship between home and host supervisors has been an enduring subject of Basel Committee activity, both because of concerns about regulatory gaps in overseeing multinational banks and because the countries in which such banks do business may have conflicting interests. Capital regulation under Basel I could have occasioned some conflicts of this sort, such as where a host country wants branches of foreign banks to maintain a certain level of capital, despite their not being separate corporate entities. While the 1983 Basel Concordat explicitly permitted this practice, the availability under Basel II of three acceptable methods for a bank's capital calculation raises the possibility of conflicting interests in a new form. For example, there may be circumstances where a large multinational bank adopts—on a consolidated basis and with home country approval—the A-IRB method but a host state wants the bank's local subsidiary to use the standardized method.[21]

Thus the call for international cooperation in pillar 2 (Basel Committee 2004d, paragraphs 780–783) is in the first instance a matter of dealing with complications created by the revised framework itself. But there may also be advantages derived from the increased attention to supervisory process and international cooperation foreseen under Basel II. There are three ways in which these efforts might enhance international cooperation so as to improve the effectiveness of international bank supervision:

- First, by extending upwards to the holding company level the requirement that capital standards be applied on a consolidated basis to internationally active banks, Basel II may fill an important regulatory gap.

- Second, Basel Committee officials have contended that the IRB approaches have created a common language by which advanced risk measurement standards are transformed into "truly workable and comprehensive standards" that enable supervisors to communicate about risks more effectively with banks and with one another (Himino 2004). This benefit, a byproduct of the broader Basel II goal of achieving greater convergence between bank risk and regulatory capital requirements, is an extension to the sphere of international

---

21. As Scott (2006) points out, this problem may be particularly acute for operational risk. The Basel Committee (2004d) suggests that "significant" subsidiaries within a holding company should calculate operational risk capital on a stand-alone basis. But since supervisors of subsidiaries not deemed "significant" may regard an allocated portion of the groupwide capital requirement as insufficient or inaccessible, they may not be comfortable with such an arrangement.

cooperation of the benefits of a common regulatory language considered in chapter 5.

■ Third, the extensive interaction among national banking supervisors required to refine the common language and to resolve issues raised by the consolidated application requirement may open and deepen channels of supervisory cooperation more generally. The result may be not only more effective cooperation in capital regulation but a kind of spillover benefit for the oversight of the activities and risks of internationally active banks other than credit risk.

The consolidated capital calculation requirement is explained by the committee as intended to eliminate "double gearing," some of which remained undetected despite the application of common capital rules in Basel I (Basel Committee 2006g, paragraph 21).[22] The consolidated application requirement furthers one aim of the Basel Concordat—ensuring that a bank's operations in multiple countries does not produce regulatory gaps. In this case the gap arises from the failure of regulators in different countries to realize that the same capital is being attributed to a bank in one country and an affiliated financial company in another country.

In Basel I, the committee had identified double gearing between a bank and its subsidiaries as a potential problem and thus had required that its minimum ratios be met at the *parent bank* level, consolidating the capital and liabilities of all bank subsidiaries. Basel II raises this requirement to the holding company level and specifies that banking subsidiaries should also meet capital standards on a stand-alone basis. In its first consultative paper, the committee explained this change as a response to the growth of complex bank ownership structures and the increasing expansion of banks into securities and insurance activities (Basel Committee, 1999b, 21) Although the committee did not give any examples of specific problems, it must surely have had in mind the situation of

---

22. The problem of "double gearing" is explained in a paper drafted by the Joint Forum on Financial Conglomerates (1999, 8), in which the Basel Committee participated: "Double gearing occurs whenever one entity holds regulatory capital issued by another entity within the same group and the issuer is allowed to count the capital in its own balance sheet. In that situation, external capital of the group is geared up twice; first by the parent, and then a second time by the dependant. Multiple gearing occurs when the dependant in the previous instance itself downstreams regulatory capital to a third-tier entity, and the parent's externally generated capital is geared up a third time. . . . The principal issue raised by double or multiple gearing is not the ownership structure as such (although some structures may also raise broader supervisory concerns), but the consequences of that structure for the assessment of a financial conglomerate's group-wide capital. When double or multiple gearing is present, assessments of group capital that are based on measures of solo capital are likely to overstate the external capital of the group."

Japanese banks, which cross-held notes and loans with friendly companies (Fukao 2003, 8).[23]

Uniform implementation of this extended consolidation requirement will be useful in plugging a potential gap in oversight of a banking firm's capital position. However, the consolidation requirement can apply, and double gearing can thereby be curbed, regardless of the nature of the underlying capital rules. US banking regulators imposed a similar consolidation requirement on bank holding companies under the Basel I capital rules. In fact, its application under Basel II will lead to new complications if, for example, some subsidiaries use the standardized version while others use an IRB version. The necessity for this sorting out is an example of the coordination problems that Basel II itself creates—a topic to be addressed later in this section.

As discussed in chapter 5, the putative utility of a common language for communicating about risk exposures depends on both the extent to which the language is truly "common" and the extent to which the elements of this language accurately signify the risks faced by a bank. The questions on both scores expressed in that earlier discussion are more serious in an international context. The numerous opportunities for the exercise of national regulatory discretion in implementing the A-IRB rules further limit the comparability not only of bank capital ratios but also of intermediate data such as the distribution of bank assets across probability-of-default categories. In addition, while one might assume a fair degree of consistency by regulators of any single nation in applying the mandatory elements of the A-IRB rules to its banks, there is little basis for assuming such consistency among the regulators of different nations. If one had to choose between regulation better tailored to the specific circumstances of a country's banking system and greater compatibility among reported capital ratios, the former may be the right choice. But that choice does limit the degree to which the capital ratios of A-IRB banks from different countries can be meaningfully compared.

Creation of a useful common regulatory language also depends on the creation of satisfactory mechanisms for exchanging information and on the range of incentives or disincentives affecting national supervisors. Thus, there is substantial overlap among the factors that will determine the benefits of a common supervisory language and those that will determine whether overall supervisory cooperation will become more effective as a result of Basel II.

---

23. The friendly companies in question were often insurance companies. Ironically, in light of this fairly well-documented instance of double gearing, Basel II does not require consolidated treatment of insurance company affiliates. Instead, it requires deductions of bank capital investments in those affiliates and supervisory development of a "group-wide perspective" to guard against double gearing (Basel Committee 2006g, paragraph 30). Given the complexity of the relationships of so many of these entities, this approach may well be sensible. However, it does allow for the continued possibility of some forms of double gearing.

The Basel Committee acknowledged there would be manifold impediments to smooth and harmonized implementation. In December 2001, well before the final revised framework had taken shape, the committee formed the AIG, which was "charged with fostering a significant measure of consistency in the way the new framework is implemented" (Basel Committee 2002a, paragraph 61). In October 2003, again before the revised framework was finalized, the committee published Basel II's "High-Level Principles for the Cross-Border Implementation of the New Accord," which specifically addressed the need for coordination arising from the requirement that the new rules be applied at each level of the banking group (Basel Committee 2003d). (The principles are set forth in box 6.1.) Subsequently, the committee issued more detailed guidance on the discrete topic of information sharing between the supervisors of home and host countries of internationally active banks (Basel Committee 2006b). The AIG currently has subgroups that focus on model validation, operational risk, and trading book activities.

The benefits of the extensive work on implementation—actual, planned, and potential—are difficult to evaluate. Considerable attention and coordination are needed to deal with the possibly differing preferences of home and host countries among the three different approaches for calculating minimum capital. Large international banks will presumably resist outcomes in which host country supervisors require higher capital levels for local subsidiaries than would be required under the A-IRB approach certified by home country supervisors. Even where a parent and all its subsidiaries use the A-IRB approach, for example, there will be a question as to what role host country supervisors will play in validation of the internal ratings model used by a bank. Thus, there is at least the possibility that contacts among supervisors become dominated by the technical challenges created by Basel II, to the subordination or exclusion of more general supervisory cooperation of the sort contemplated in the Basel Concordat.[24] In the worst case, disagreements over the interpretation and implementation of the A-IRB approach could undermine existing levels of trust and cooperation among national regulators.

Analysis of the incentives faced by national regulators also calls into question how effective exchanges of information and coordinated supervision will be. Bielicki and Bednarski (2006) note that a host supervisor of a foreign bank's subsidiary that is systemically important in its market, but only a small part of the bank's overall business, will have a different

---

24. An early example of this possibility is revealed in a speech by the chairman of the AIG, who noted that differences in the interpretation of key provisions of the A-IRB model—such as implementation of the downturn loss-given-default principles—are already becoming apparent and thus in need of discussion. See Nicholas Le Pan, "Basel II—Assessing Progress to Date and Next Steps," remarks at the 7th Annual Global Association of Risk Professionals, New York, February 28, 2006.

Box 6.1 High-level principles for Basel II implementation

Principle 1: The new accord will not change the legal responsibilities of national supervisors for the regulation of their domestic institutions or the arrangements for consolidated supervision already put in place by the Basel Committee on Banking Supervision.

Principle 2: The home country supervisor is responsible for oversight of the implementation of the new accord for a banking group on a consolidated basis.

Principle 3: Host country supervisors, particularly where banks operate in subsidiary form, have requirements that need to be understood and recognized.

Principle 4: There will need to be enhanced and pragmatic cooperation among supervisors with legitimate interests. The home country supervisor should lead this coordination effort.

Principle 5: Wherever possible, supervisors should avoid performing redundant and uncoordinated approval and validation work in order to reduce the implementation burden on the banks and conserve supervisory resources.

Principle 6: In implementing the new accord, supervisors should communicate the respective roles of home country and host country supervisors as clearly as possible to banking groups with significant cross-border operations in multiple jurisdictions. The home country supervisor would lead this coordination effort in cooperation with the host country supervisors.

Source: Basel Committee (2003d).

set of concerns than the bank's home supervisor. Specifically, they worry that the host supervisors will not have effective access to information on the bank's overall capital position so as to be able to identify nascent problems that might eventually endanger the subsidiary. One might add that, even if the subsidiary's problems are home grown, the capital allocated to that subsidiary may not reflect the bank's systemic importance. Kahn and Santos (2005, 2006) have hypothesized that, even within a single polity, the differences of interest among lenders of last resort, deposit insurers, and independent regulators may give these entities incentives not to share information fully. This possibility is presumably as great, or greater, when supervisors from different countries—with their interests in national competitiveness—are involved. Moreover, purely as a prudential matter, supervisors have a disincentive to disclose fully to their foreign counterparts information that suggests serious problems in a bank. Their quite rational fear is that their counterparts will quietly advise banks from *their* countries to reduce counterparty exposure to the troubled bank, potentially making that bank's problems a self-fulfilling prophecy.

Many such conflicts exist regardless of the degree of harmonization in national capital or other bank regulations. While the complexity engendered by Basel II may exacerbate these conflicts, or distract Basel Committee members from giving adequate attention to other common problems, the Basel II emphasis on supervisory process might have a happier outcome. It is possible that the concerted efforts to coordinate information flows and to achieve consistent treatment of a consolidated bank entity's various subsidiaries may serve as a catalyst for deeper, more effective supervisory cooperation generally.[25] As noted in chapter 3, the committee has never developed particularly robust institutional mechanisms for elaborating and monitoring the implementation of Basel I. The obvious need for ongoing work to assure the consistent implementation of Basel II may lead to more confidence on the part of national supervisors that their counterparts in other committee countries are committed to, and capable of, rigorous oversight of A-IRB banks. Although the opaque and individualized character of bank credit risk–rating systems will at best pose a monitoring problem, substantial advances in the international exchange of information may partially mitigate this problem. The AIG subgroups might over time play a tacit but effective role in monitoring the extent and quality of national implementation of the Basel II capital requirements. Far-reaching and successful cooperation on these issues might, in turn, lead to other cooperative measures to enhance supervision of international banking activities.

It is perhaps telling that even researchers in some Basel Committee member agencies have expressed a measure of skepticism that effective agreements on home/host issues will be put into practice by the committee (Jackson 2006, Santos 2006). The committee has given itself high marks for the progress of its various working groups, both in promoting consistent interpretation and implementation across jurisdictions and in

---

25. An early example of the potential for this dynamic is provided by the AIG's establishment of a monthly "clearinghouse" conference call to discuss on a more or less real-time basis experience with bank practices regarding downturn loss given default (LGD) for particularly sensitive portfolios like mortgages. As explained by the head of the AIG, this call will "allow supervisors to share experiences regarding LGDs in the applications they are considering, identify and discuss minor LGD implementation issues as they arise, identify any further LGD issues that other groups should address, and share information on what supervisors are telling banks about LGD issues." See Nicholas Le Pan, "Basel II—Assessing Progress to Date and Next Steps," remarks at the 7th Annual Global Association of Risk Professionals, New York, February 28, 2006.

coordinating home/host issues (Basel Committee 2007b). The committee also reports that it is tackling topics that were left out of the Basel II exercise, such as the definition of capital and the supervision of liquidity risk management. While self-reported progress and cooperation are more encouraging than indications of discord would be, it is surely too soon to evaluate whether the more ambitious plans for supervisory coordination in Basel II will ultimately lead to strong implementation at the national level and cooperative patterns at the international level. As proposed in chapter 8, however, some additional international institutional mechanisms could enhance chances that the quality of supervision of internationally active banks will be on net enhanced.

Indirect Benefits

Harmonization of national regulation will often reduce compliance costs of firms with operations in multiple countries. This outcome is obviously advantageous for the firms themselves. It can also be beneficial for society, so long as the net effectiveness of the regulation does not suffer—that is, the expenditure of fewer resources on compliance frees up more for productive activities. For international banks, this would mean more extensions of credit in the economy. Again at the margin, the reduction of the bank's total costs should boost its safety and soundness.

In the case of Basel II, however, these benefits seem unlikely to be realized, at least in the foreseeable future. On the contrary, the cost of compliance with capital standards will increase significantly. In the first place, of course, the IRB approaches will be substantially more expensive to develop, validate, and maintain than current Basel I standards (or the standardized version of Basel II). Moreover, the availability of multiple methods for calculating capital requirements, the opportunities for national supervisory discretion in implementation, and the sheer complexity of the A-IRB approach together suggest that compliance costs for internationally active banks will not be a source of savings.[26]

The evolution of a transparent common language regarding banks' capital positions would be useful to counterparties of, and investors in, large banking institutions. Not only might the disclosures required of banks increase the information about banks available to these other actors, but the standardization of disclosures might also help these actors evaluate the soundness of a bank relative to its international competitors, thereby providing another important data point for lending or investment

---

26. It is true that agreement on Basel II will keep costs lower than they would be were each country to develop its own incompatible requirements for IRB calculation of capital. But this is not much of a point in Basel II's favor.

decisions. However, for reasons previously discussed, the extent to which these putative benefits will be realized is quite uncertain.

Conclusion

The very origins of the Basel Committee underscore the need for international cooperation in the supervision of internationally active banks. Experience suggests that the cooperative arrangements maintained by the Basel Committee, including exchanges of information, could profitably be strengthened. But, as should now be clear, the nature of, and prospects for, international regulatory cooperation vary with the substantive regulatory model being engrafted in an international arrangement. Nout Wellink, president of the Netherlands Bank and current chair of the Basel Committee, has contended that "Basel II is as much about . . . long-term process, and the beneficial dialogue it has spurred between banks and supervisors, as it is about the more micro-level details of implementation."[27] Wellink's aspiration is consistent with a supple and efficient international process for understanding the risks assumed by internationally active banks and for supervising those banks effectively. However, it is to some degree belied by the Basel II process to date. The emphasis on negotiation over technical details with considerable financial impact, the tendency of national supervisors to negotiate on behalf of their national banks, and the complexity of the resulting A-IRB structure may not easily be transformed into the "flexible framework" foreseen by Wellink. In its own statements on implementation issues, the Basel Committee at times appears torn between flexibility and harmonization. For example, notwithstanding the enthusiasm of some committee officials for a common language, the committee has elsewhere noted that "consistency in implementation is best achieved not through developing top-down rules, but rather by tailoring implementation plans to the unique circumstances of each banking organization and its supervisors" (Basel Committee 2006c). The simultaneous achievement of consistency and customization will obviously create ongoing tension in the committee's work.

The assessment in chapter 5 of Basel II as a regulatory model found reason for doubt that it was either feasible or desirable. The consideration of Basel II as an international arrangement in this chapter suggests that salutary forms of international cooperation in banking supervision may not be well served by efforts to harmonize substantive capital regulation at this level of complexity. These international costs may have

---

27. See Nout Wellink, "Global Banking Supervision in a Changing Financial Environment," address at the 14th International Conference of Banking Supervisors, Mérida, Mexico, October 4, 2006.

been worth bearing in pursuit of an advantageous domestic regulatory paradigm. Conversely, the costs of a suboptimal domestic paradigm may have been worth sustaining in order to achieve big gains in international cooperation. Yet, except for the chance that the volume of cooperative contacts on Basel II will lead to a qualitative and beneficial change in supervisory oversight of international banks, it seems most likely that the substantive and international institutional drawbacks of Basel II will be mutually reinforcing.

7

Alternatives to Basel II

Chapter 5 revealed both potential benefits and significant problems associated with the advanced internal ratings–based (A-IRB) approach as a paradigm for domestic banking regulation. Chapter 6 concluded that the problems are likely to be magnified by the international character of the arrangement, while the potential benefits of international coordination are unlikely to be substantially realized. This bifurcation of the domestic and international merits of the A-IRB approach may have seemed somewhat artificial, given that one of Basel II's notable features is that it has generated domestic capital rules from an international process. But it is at least possible that the most favorable mixture of advantages and problems lies in a regime that does not attempt this degree and method of harmonization among national regulatory requirements.

Thus, the search for plausible alternatives involves two questions. First, is there a different approach to capital regulation that could be substituted for the A-IRB approach in a harmonized international regime? Second, might the best option instead be a regime that takes a different approach to the relationship between domestic capital regulation and an international arrangement? The possibilities range from eschewing any effort at substantive harmonization to establishing simpler international rules that coexist with more sophisticated domestic rules all the way to displacing domestic capital regulation entirely in favor of a supranational system for supervising capital levels in internationally active banks.

This chapter begins by considering three possible alternative regulatory models: retaining a standardized risk-based capital approach, substituting market-based discipline for regulatory capital requirements, and instituting a precommitment approach to regulatory capital. At least at present, none seems promising as a self-contained domestic regulatory model for maintaining minimum bank capital levels, much less as the basis for a harmonized international standard. The chapter continues with brief consideration of the first and third possibilities mentioned in the preceding paragraph for reworking the relationship established in Basel II between domestic capital regulation and an international arrangement. Not surprisingly, these seem unpromising as well.

In short, no single regulatory model or straightforward institutional mechanism presents an obviously better alternative to Basel II. The remaining inquiry, then, is whether some mix of substantive features and a realigned relationship between the domestic and international spheres might be a better—though obviously less elegant—solution. The next and final chapters proposes such a mix. However, it is worth noting here that this proposal comprises what are, in essence, variations on many of the self-contained alternatives discussed here. In part for economy of presentation and in part because policy books should generally not have surprise endings, these variations are introduced in this chapter.

Retaining a Standardized Approach

For the same reason physicians are enjoined "first, do no harm," so policymakers should be particularly careful in changing the regulatory scheme of the last two decades. Sound policy analysis requires consideration of whether, in spite of its widely recognized shortcomings, a standardized approach to risk-based capital requirements is nonetheless the best of an inevitably imperfect set of alternatives. Until recently, the Basel I regulatory regime was associated with unusual stability in the banking systems of Basel Committee countries, other than Japan. As implemented by national banking authorities, Basel I raised bank capital levels, which presumably contributed to overall stability among major banks that is all the more noteworthy considering the dramatic changes in the structure of the industry and the various shocks suffered by the financial system during this period (Asian crisis, Long-Term Capital Management, subprime debacle, etc.).[1]

---

1. Needless to say, the coexistence of Basel I and higher capital levels, on the one hand, and general banking stability, on the other, does not itself establish a causal relationship. It is, for example, highly likely that more sophisticated risk management and the wider availability of such risk-mitigating devices as credit derivatives contributed to the greater stability of banks during the recent shock than during 1990–91, before Basel I was fully implemented. Still, the correlation between a fully operative Basel I and banking stability should at least make policymakers pause to consider whether there *is* a significant causal relationship.

There are several extant variants on a standardized approach. One, of course, is Basel I itself, as modified formally with the market risk capital requirement and a series of more modest amendments. A second is Basel I as supplemented by national authorities. In the United States, for example, regulators have added extensive provisions on, among other things, the treatment of derivatives and the use of collateral or other devices to mitigate credit risk. A third variant is the standardized approach of Basel II, which incorporates changes similar to those heretofore applied unilaterally by the United States, as well as the other features described in chapter 4. The most significant of these other changes is the use of ratings by external agencies for allocation of specific exposures into the various risk buckets.

Among these variants, it seems reasonably clear that Basel I is the least preferable. As to the Basel II standardized approach, there is much to applaud. However, the wisdom of its reliance on external rating agencies was always questionable. To the objections raised during the negotiations, as discussed in chapter 4, must now be added the experience with ratings of mortgage-backed securities during 2007. Whatever the reasonableness of the agencies' ratings given their purpose and constraints, the limitations of external ratings as a basis for regulatory capital requirements have again been highlighted. Thus, it is possible that the best variant on a standardized approach would exclude the external ratings feature, even at the cost of less risk sensitivity.

In the end, though, the differences among the standardized variants are not dispositive. It seems unlikely that any form of a static, risk-bucket model is the best practical approach to capital regulation of large banks today. The trouble with Basel II lies predominantly in its technical and institutional implications, not in its premise that the changing business profiles of internationally active banks, financial product development, and risk management technology have together created both challenges to the current regulatory system and some promising avenues to help address those challenges. The reliance on periodic snapshots of capital ratios based on the historic value of assets is a potentially dangerous anachronism in a world of large banks that regularly securitize and sell a significant proportion of their loans, write and purchase large amounts of credit derivatives and interest rate swaps, and in general turn their assets over more rapidly than in times past. While Basel II may not be the best available means to link state-of-the-art risk assessment with bank supervision, the Basel I method as refined in the standardized approach of Basel II does not even play in this game.

The widely recognized shortcomings of Basel I, detailed in chapter 3, were themselves the impetus for the reform efforts that culminated in the revised framework. Whatever the flaws of the A-IRB approach, reversion to a standardized approach would effectively signal surrender by banking supervisors in their efforts to successfully adapt to risks presented by the contemporary financial system. Some form of the standardized version that dealt with the more easily correctable problems in Basel I might have been a preferable interim measure, even for large banks, while work continued on an appropriate new approach.[2] This was the reasoning of some regulators and outsiders—this author included—when implementation of A-IRB was bogged down in the United States. But that reasoning never contemplated more than an interim role for a standardized approach while the Basel Committee worked on regulatory approaches that either improved or substituted for the A-IRB method.

If a standardized risk-based approach to capital regulation is too insensitive to the nature and pace of change of credit risks assumed by internationally active banks, a simple leverage ratio would hardly seem worth considering. Indeed, as the foundation of a domestic regime to ensure adequate capitalization, it would be a curious reversion to pre-Basel I days. However, its very simplicity makes it deserving of consideration as one element of an international capital regime.

Under current US and Canadian practice, the leverage ratio is an adjunct to the risk-based capital requirements of Basel I. In the United States, its most important role is as a trigger in the system of prompt corrective action instituted following the widespread savings and loan failures of the 1980s. As the leverage ratio declines, meaning that the proportion of capital to assets is shrinking, it provides an indication of just how close to insolvency a bank is. When the leverage ratio drops below 4 percent, supervisory intervention must ensue. When it drops below 3 percent, stronger supervisory measures are required. If the ratio drops below 2 percent, the bank is considered "critically undercapitalized" and must in most circumstances be shut down.

---

2. In the summer of 2006, following dissemination of the US banking agencies' joint notice of proposed rule making, four large US banks proposed that all US banks be allowed to adopt any one of the three Basel II methods for calculating capital. They accurately pointed out that the United States would be in full compliance with the letter of Basel II in allowing this scope for election of methodologies, since the revised framework does not explicitly require any specific bank—no matter what its size or complexity—to adopt any specific capital method. The motivation of the banks in making this proposal was not obvious. It was clearly a response to the indication by the banking agencies that the leverage ratio would be retained in the United States, that more conservative transition floors would be used, and that a presumptive limit of a 10 percent decline in aggregate capital for all covered banks would be established. What is less clear is whether the banks were simply indicating that, with these limits on regulatory capital reductions, the expense of what is essentially an artificial risk management exercise was simply not worth it. The alternative explanation was that the banks were trying to pressure the Federal Reserve Board and the Office of the Comptroller of the Currency to convince the other two regulatory agencies to drop the leverage ratio and other features of the proposed US regulations that would be stricter than the text of Basel II itself. As described in chapter 4, the compromise reached among the four US banking agencies in 2007 dropped the 10 percent aggregate decline floor but retained the leverage ratio and the more conservative transition floors.

The efficacy of this role for the leverage ratio is supported by empirical work showing a fairly robust correlation between declines in the leverage ratio below 2 percent and near-term bank failure (Estrella, Park, and Peristiani 2000). The bluntness of the leverage ratio makes it of considerably less value in comparing healthy banks. Thus, it would surely not provide a useful "common language" for supervisors and market actors. But it could serve as a common minimum capital level for all internationally active banks. To be a useful indicator, the leverage requirement would have to be set high enough to provide time for home supervisors to react and for supervisors from other countries to take any necessary measures to protect their own financial systems from the potential ill-effects of the foreign bank's failure. Thus it could be set at a level that is considered, in US regulatory terms, "adequate" capitalization.[3] In countries in which markets believe that the government safety net is so strong as to make bank insolvency unlikely in any case, the leverage requirement could also serve a very rough competitive equality purpose, since it would partially mitigate the capital cost advantage derived from the safety net.

The leverage requirement is not only simple, it is about as transparent a capital calculation as one can imagine, easily derived from a bank's balance sheet. It is also considerably more difficult to manipulate, certainly when compared with the A-IRB approach. The elements of tier 1 capital and the total assets of the bank are central to a bank's statement of financial position, as certified by its accountants. Misstatements of those numbers would likely indicate that a bank's shareholders, as well as supervisors, were being misled. The leverage ratio thus avoids most of the issues of discretion and monitoring that will bedevil Basel II, as described in the preceding chapters.

A significant shortcoming of the US leverage ratio, even for the limited purpose suggested here, is that it does not take account of the off-balance-sheet activities that constitute an important portion of the aggregate credit risk to which a large contemporary bank is exposed. While the leverage ratio will never be more than a blunt regulatory instrument, it would be considerably more useful if it were able to incorporate some off-balance-sheet exposures. There are several possible methods for doing so. First, the leverage ratio might borrow from the Basel I methodology for converting off-balance-sheet exposures into balance-sheet equivalents.[4] The advantages of

---

3. In the US regulatory scheme, a bank must be "well capitalized" in order to be affiliated with insurance companies, merchant banks, and certain other kinds of financial firms. One requirement for being well capitalized is a minimum 5 percent leverage ratio.

4. The Canadian Office of the Superintendent of Financial Institutions includes the notional amounts of certain off-balance-sheet items in its "assets to capital multiple," which is its version of a leverage ratio. However, it also includes an adjusted amount of tier 2 capital, whereas US law limits the numerator in the ratio to tier 1, or truly core, capital. Canada also permits netting adjustments to the off-balance-sheet items to be included as assets.

this approach are that it is known to banks and supervisors and that it is relatively straightforward.[5] However, as described in chapter 3, the Basel I methodology has presented significant opportunities for regulatory arbitrage. It remains to be seen whether the changes made in the standardized version of Basel II will eliminate these opportunities. Moreover, while not conceptually complicated, this methodology still requires exposure-by-exposure classification and calculation. Thus, some of the simplicity and transparency of the leverage ratio would be lost.

Second, the leverage ratio might incorporate a more sophisticated methodology for determining the asset equivalent of off-balance-sheet exposures that would limit the potential for regulatory arbitrage. The methodology of this sort that comes first to mind is that used in the A-IRB approach under Basel II, which permits banks to use their own estimates of appropriate credit conversion factors to transform the off-balance-sheet exposures into asset equivalents. Obviously, though, to use the complex Basel II approach would be to defeat the purpose of using a minimum leverage ratio in the first place. Whatever the technical merits of other methodologies for measuring off-balance-sheet leverage, such as that suggested by Breuer (2002), they share the same disadvantages in the context of devising a readily calculated and observed metric.

Third, rather than try to modify the leverage ratio, supervisors might supplement it with an equally simple calculation that at least roughly captures the magnitude of off-balance-sheet exposures. Estrella, Park, and Peristiani (2000) identified just such a complementary measure in their examination of capital ratios as predictors of bank failure. They found that the ratio of capital to gross revenue of a bank is, like the capital/assets ratio, about as good a predictor of failure over one-to-two-year time horizons as more complex, risk-weighted measures. They note that a capital/gross revenue ratio reflects off-balance-sheet activities as well as conventional bank assets. They further suggest that gross revenue includes a crude measure of risk, in that riskier activities are likely to be undertaken by a bank only if they yield larger revenue streams. Like the simple leverage ratio, the capital/gross revenue ratio is readily calculated from a bank's financial statements and thus conveniently transparent.

A capital/gross revenue ratio is not without its own difficulties. Many banks may engage in fee-generating activities that pose very low, or even zero, credit risks. Moreover, as Estrella, Park, and Peristiani (2000) acknowledge, gross revenues may be even more sensitive to changes in the business cycle than total assets. Finally, of course, the very novelty of this measure means that it has not been calibrated over time in response

---

5. This appears to be the approach that US regulators had in mind when they tabled the possibility of a "modified" leverage ratio for smaller US banks (US Department of the Treasury Office of the Comptroller of the Currency et al. 2000).

to supervisory assessments of its significance at different values. Even the empirical work of Estrella and his coauthors is of only limited use in evaluating the utility of the capital/gross revenues ratio, since that work examined the correlation between the ratio and failure of all US commercial banks between 1989 and 1993. In a Basel Committee context, the relevant observations would be of large, internationally active banks in a more recent period, so as to cover the mix of off-balance-sheet activities characteristic of such banks today.

Of course, many of these problems are analogous to those associated with the leverage ratio itself. Like that measure, it is a very blunt metric. As part of a simple, transparent rule for minimum capital levels, it would seem promising enough to pursue. Basel Committee agencies could easily calculate the capital/gross revenue ratio for their banks over the last decade or more, compare those results with other indicators of bank soundness, and determine if this ratio does in fact satisfy the need for a simple indicator that reflects off-balance-sheet exposures.

Market Discipline: Mandatory Subordinated Debt

Perhaps the best-developed alternative to capital adequacy as a bank regulatory paradigm is a set of proposals that banks issue subordinated debt of specified characteristics and a minimum amount. The core idea is to enlist market forces in pursuit of the regulatory end of bank safety and soundness. Holders of subordinated debt are presumed to have interests in the bank similar to the interests of depositors (or, more realistically in most cases, the insurer of deposits). They stand to lose some or all their investment if the bank becomes insolvent and, unlike equity investors, their potential return is contractually capped. Holders of subordinated debt should, accordingly, prefer relatively conservative strategies by bank management, since they have no hope of upside returns from higher-risk strategies. If the regulatory requirements for subordinated debt are artfully constructed, the incentives of investors owning this debt may be roughly aligned with the public interest in containing the moral hazard created by the system of bank safety nets. Proponents of mandatory subordinated debt expect that some combination of the monitoring, lobbying, and trading strategies of debtholders will achieve this end.

There are numerous variations on the mandatory subordinated debt idea, reflecting different judgments as to the most effective combination of direct and indirect market discipline.[6] *Direct* market discipline refers to

---

6. Many of these proposals are summarized and compared in Board of Governors of the Federal Reserve System and the US Department of the Treasury (2000). Some proponents of mandatory subordinated debt also posit the goal of increasing the capital cushion of banks.

the impact on bank managers' behavior of either corporate governance actions by bondholders or unfavorable movements in the price of the required debt issues. *Indirect* market discipline refers to the incorporation of changes in the price of the subordinated debt into the bank regulatory system—whether by generating additional data for supervisors to consider, by making the price changes into triggers for supervisory intervention, or both. In its more robust forms, the proposed mandatory subordinated debt requirement would invert the three pillars in Basel II. Supervisory efforts would remain important, but market discipline would displace minimum capital requirements at the top of the regulatory system. As a result, the regulatory complexity of the A-IRB approach would be avoided.

It is important to note at the outset that, like most proposals for increased "market" discipline on banks, the subordinated debt idea is not an example of laissez-faire thinking. Government action would be necessary to mandate the issuance of debt instruments with the requisite characteristics. As with mandated public disclosures of information, the proposal is to require certain standardized corporate practices that will induce actions by self-interested market participants to restrict bank risk taking. The intended consequence (intended by the regulators, not the market participants) is the enhancement of the broader public interest in bank safety and soundness.

Once again, this alternative presents two questions. First, is some form of market discipline on balance superior to the A-IRB approach of Basel II, or to risk-weighted capital requirements generally, as the principal means of safety and soundness regulation? Second, should mandatory subordinated debt or some other market disciplining device be required as an element of an arrangement addressing the safety and soundness of internationally active banks? As with standardized capital measures, the answers suggested here are negative for the first question and affirmative for the second.

Direct Market Discipline

Although market discipline might be exerted in a truly direct fashion through the enforcement by bondholders of covenants in the debt contract, this seems unlikely as a routine matter. Enforcement of covenants entails substantial transaction costs, along with free rider problems, which makes it a less-than-practical governance device. Most proposals

---

However, as explained below, most large banks (or the holding companies that own them) already issue subordinated debt in excess of 2 percent of their assets, the minimum level around which most proposals for mandatory debt seem to have converged. Thus, a requirement of this magnitude may have a negligible effect on capital cushions in the largest banks.

claiming significant benefits from direct market discipline instead argue that price mechanisms will link market assessments of bank riskiness to managerial behavior. If investors judge the bank excessively risky, they will demand higher interest rates or, perhaps, decline to purchase subordinated debt at all. The resulting pressure on the cost of capital would then, it is hoped, force management to change its behavior.

Thus, proposals for mandatory subordinated debt typically include features designed to enhance this kind of pressure. Some would require that the subordinated debt be issued at regular intervals.[7] This requirement of periodic issuance is expected to force bank management to follow prudent risk management practices so as to keep the interest rate on the debt at a reasonable level. Other proposals go further and would cap the interest rates that banks could pay on the mandatory debt.[8] Banks unable to issue debt at or below this rate would be subject to regulatory consequences. Another approach would give the bondholders a put option that, if exercised, would trigger significant consequences for the bank. One proposal, for example, would force the bank to issue new subordinated debt in order to meet its regulatory minimum as puts are exercised. If it could not do so, the debt holders would automatically obtain equity positions and the prerogative to sell or liquidate the bank.[9]

The efficacy of direct market discipline depends to a great extent on some of the same assumptions that underpin the rationale for mandatory subordinated debt as a source of indirect market discipline. Important qualifications on these assumptions are discussed below. There are, in addition, both theoretical and empirical reasons more specific to direct

---

7. See, for example, US Shadow Financial Regulatory Committee (2000), Evanoff and Wall (2001); and Litan and Rauch (1997).

8. See, for example, US Shadow Financial Regulatory Committee (2000). The idea is to prevent management from paying high premiums and, as a result, being tempted to engage in even riskier behavior in hopes of high returns (Calomiris 1997). A variation on this theme is the proposal by Kupiec (2002) to impose a maximum ex ante probability of default on the mandated debt. In practice, this would translate into an interest rate cap (e.g., no interest higher than that paid on investment-grade debt).

9. The reissuance/equity conversion variation is in Evanoff (1993). Other proposals would use puts differently. For instance, Cooper and Fraser (1988) suggest giving bondholders a put option at 95 percent of face value. The put would be exercised not against the bank but against the Federal Deposit Insurance Corporation, which would be compensated with nonvoting equity shares that the bank would have to repurchase within a certain time or else lose its charter. One concern with giving bondholders put options is the possibility that the exercise of puts by some bondholders would cascade into an exercise by all bondholders, leading to liquidity problems for the bank. This kind of "run" on unsecured debt could itself be destabilizing (Board of Governors of the Federal Reserve System and the US Department of the Treasury 2000, 53).

market discipline to be skeptical that this form of discipline can be the centerpiece of bank regulation.

There are significant threshold questions at the theoretical level. First, as has been pointed out by Levonian (2001), an increase in subordinated debt that came from a shift away from equity would increase leverage and hence might also increase the propensity for risk taking. Second, while the interests of subordinated bondholders are roughly congruent with the public interest, they are not identical. The bondholders' interest lies in preserving the value of their fixed-income investment. The public interest in bank regulation also includes containing systemic risk and, at least to a limited degree, preserving the going concern value of banks. These additional considerations will, in some circumstances, call for supervisory discipline more stringent than the market discipline that would be exerted by rational investors even in the absence of information or other transactions costs.

There is, in any case, relatively little empirical work to back up the theoretical claim that the price of subordinated debt will actually discipline bank managers with anything like the potency that would be necessary if market discipline were to replace capital adequacy regulation. Bliss and Flannery (2002) note the contrast between the substantial amount of empirical work suggesting that market prices reflect the risk profile of banks and the paucity of empirical studies demonstrating direct influence on managers, particularly outside extreme situations such as bankruptcy. Their own effort to conduct such a study yielded inconclusive results.

A study by staff of the Federal Reserve System (1999) concluded that there was evidence of direct market discipline during periods of financial difficulty, based on the finding that banks with unfavorable accounting-based risk measures did not issue subordinated debt during a period of bond market volatility in 1989–92. Yet even this conclusion must be qualified, insofar as the study did not directly examine the impact of market discipline on the relative riskiness of strategies pursued by bank management during this period. That is, the temporary inability or disinclination of a bank to issue subordinated debt does not itself show how much of an effect capital market constraints had on bank practices. One does not know, for example, whether banks were able to substitute other sources of capital—including insured deposits—during this period. Similarly, while Ashcraft (2008) finds that an increase in the amount of subordinated debt in regulatory capital is associated with bank recovery from financial distress and infers the exercise of positive influence by debt holders, he does not specify the mechanism by which this influence is exerted.

Some of the more thoughtful proposals for direct market discipline may, by packaging mandatory subordinated debt with other regulatory devices (including relevant indirect disciplinary effects), be implicitly acknowledging its limitations.[10] A degree of direct discipline may be a welcome byproduct of requirements for subordinated debt, disclosure, or other market-enlisting regulation.[11] Requiring regular issuance of subordinated debt, rather than leaving to the banks' discretion when to access that part of the capital markets, would enhance this salutary effect. But as a substitute for capital requirements, a mandatory debt proposal premised on direct disciplinary effects seems too much a leap of faith and too little grounded in experience.[12]

Indirect Market Discipline

Recent proposals for mandatory subordinated debt have rested more on indirect disciplinary effects than on direct discipline. As debt holders reach adverse conclusions about the condition of a bank, the primary and secondary prices of its debt issues should decline. In the more modest versions of indirect discipline proposals, these price movements add to the data available to supervisors, signaling that market actors have detected significant problems with the bank. The hope is that this additional data will facilitate timely supervisory intervention.[13] More muscular proposals would use the increasing spread of the bank's subordinated debt over a specified benchmark to trigger regulatory interventions similar to those currently in effect for capital levels under the US system of prompt corrective action.

---

10. See, for example, US Shadow Financial Regulatory Committee (2000).

11. The incremental amount of market discipline to be gained from instituting regulatory requirements such as subordinated debt issuance depends, of course, on the existing state of discipline imposed on banks from both market and supervisory sources. It is doubtless more difficult to get significant additional market discipline in the United States and other Basel Committee countries—where both capital markets and bank supervision are relatively well developed—than in many developing countries with undeveloped capital markets and limited supervisory capacities.

12. Lang and Robertson (2002) offer another reason to be skeptical that a mandatory debt requirement on the order of 2 percent of assets, or risk-weighted assets, will lead to materially more market discipline. They point out that the ratio of insured deposits to total bank liabilities has been steadily declining for the last decade. Banks with more than $1 billion in assets now hold barely a third of their liabilities in insured deposits. Hence, they reason, any mandatory debt requirement will likely lead these banks simply to substitute one form of uninsured debt for another (uninsured deposits). While they believe that indirect discipline might be enhanced, they doubt that the amount of direct market discipline will increase significantly.

13. It has also been suggested that subordinated debt holders have an incentive to pressure regulators to intervene promptly with capital-deficient depository institutions because, if an institution is saved from insolvency or closed at the exact time of insolvency, only stockholders lose, and the investments of subordinated debt are saved (Board of Governors of the Federal Reserve System and the US Department of the Treasury 2000).

One could either substitute yield spreads for risk-based capital ratios or add yield spreads as an additional trigger.[14]

A proposal to substitute bond yield spreads for capital ratios presents an alternative regulatory approach, particularly where—as proposed by the US Shadow Financial Regulatory Committee (2000)—risk-based capital requirements would be entirely eliminated, not just displaced as triggers for prompt corrective action.[15] The arguments for this alternative are several. First, the risk-weighted capital requirements are thought to be fundamentally flawed. In their Basel I form, they are too crude and invite regulatory arbitrage. Calculated on the basis of historic value of assets on the banking book, Basel I ratios are likely to lag significantly in revealing problems as assets deteriorate (and thus "real," as opposed to regulatory, capital shrinks).[16] In their Basel II form they are thought by critics to be too complicated and of uncertain administrative feasibility, for some of the reasons explained in chapter 5. By contrast, the use of subordinated debt would be relatively simple: Although the optimal configuration of debt features (e.g., amount, maturity, frequency of issue) may be somewhat elusive, once banks are actually issuing the debt, there is an attractive automaticity to the process.

Second, some proponents of subordinated debt-spread triggers believe that opportunities for regulatory forbearance will be reduced. Even if capital ratios are established as "automatic" triggers for supervisory action, regulators retain considerable discretion to accept a bank's self-serving calculations of loan-loss reserves, qualifying capital, classification of loans, and other factors relevant to capital ratios. Market prices of subordinated debt are, obviously, less susceptible to manipulation through short-term, confidential supervisory judgments.

Third, substitution of yield spreads for capital ratios would broaden the triggering stimulus for prompt corrective action to include all significant risks. At their best, capital ratios capture only a limited part of the bank's risk profile. The controversy over operational risk capital requirements in Basel II and the liquidity problems of financial institutions dur-

---

14. The US Shadow Financial Regulatory Committee (2000) would eliminate risk-weighted capital requirements entirely, including from the prompt corrective action system, but would retain simple leverage ratio requirements, perhaps at higher levels than in current US regulatory practice. Evanoff and Wall (2001) do not make an explicit policy proposal but suggest reasons for "supplementing" the capital triggers under the prompt corrective action system.

15. In a later statement, the US Shadow Financial Regulatory Committee (2001) spoke of its subordinated debt proposal as a "supplement to the existing Basel capital framework." But the more comprehensive 2000 statement explicitly included a proposal for elimination of regulatory risk weights on capital.

16. The US General Accounting Office (1996) found that asset quality and management tend to deteriorate well before capital levels are adversely affected in troubled banks.

ing the subprime crisis bear out this observation. Subordinated debt yields, on the other hand, will reflect all information about the bank that is material to the risk of default on the bonds. Consequently, the prompt corrective action trigger will be more closely aligned with the overall safety and soundness aims of bank regulation.

Fourth, there is considerable empirical work establishing that yield spreads are sensitive to banks' risk profiles.[17] At least one study finds that those spreads are considerably *more* sensitive to risk than risk-weighted capital ratios. Evanoff and Wall (2001) compared subordinated debt spreads, simple leverage ratios, and risk-based capital ratios as predictors of later supervisory ratings by US regulators.[18] Yield spreads were slightly better predictors than simple leverage ratios but substantially better than any of the risk-based capital ratios. The most arresting finding was that a bank's capital classification under the current prompt corrective action system was essentially unrelated to the examination rating it would subsequently receive. Another notable finding was that yield spreads identified more banks as high-risk than did subsequent supervisory examinations. In a follow-up study, Evanoff and Wall (2002) conclude, albeit tentatively, that at least some of the banks received higher ratings than warranted by their actual condition. They suggest that these results are a sign of regulatory forbearance and thus further indication that spreads are preferable to capital ratios as triggers for supervisory action.[19]

A related line of empirical work examines the disclosure practices of banking organizations that issue subordinated debt. Covitz and Harrison (2004) find that bank managers issue public debt in part to convey positive information not previously disclosed and refrain from issuance in part to hide negative information. They suggest that the incentives for disclosure or withholding of information are particularly strong among banking firms because of their enormous reliance on various forms of borrowing (bonds, commercial paper, federal funds, eurodollar, etc.). Further, the relative opacity of banks may increase the potential payoff of measures to induce disclosure or create incentives for due diligence. The latter factor seems particularly important, in that rating agencies and others appear to focus more intensively on issuers at the time they issue

---

17. Much of the literature is reviewed in Flannery and Nikolova (2004), Bliss (2001), and Federal Reserve System (1999).

18. Three risk-based ratios were examined: the total risk-based capital ratio (i.e., incorporating both tier 1 and tier 2 capital); the ratio of tier 1 capital to risk-weighted assets; and the ratings assigned banks under current prompt corrective action regulations, which assign a capital category (well-capitalized, adequately capitalized, etc.) based on both leverage ratios and risk-weighted ratios.

19. A chronic problem in such studies is finding appropriate surrogates for the "true" condition of a bank. Evanoff and Wall used a variety of surrogates, including various accounting measures and subsequent examinations.

securities.[20] These findings—again subject to confirmation in subsequent research—reinforce the case for regular, mandatory subordinated-debt issuance in order to force negative private information into public view and thus strengthen market discipline.

There are also numerous questions about the potential effectiveness of indirect discipline. The importance of at least some of these questions is directly proportional to the degree of reliance on market signals to trigger mandatory regulatory intervention.

First, markets—whether for subordinated debt, uninsured deposits, or even equity—will price in any perceived safety net protections for the issuing banks. If, for example, all transactions of a bank were believed to be implicitly guaranteed by the government, then the interest rate demanded by purchasers of debt or certificates of deposit would not much exceed the risk-free rate of return for an instrument of similar maturity. More realistically, if markets perceive a reasonable probability that certain banks will be protected from insolvency by the central bank or other government entities, the prices of subordinated debt will not reflect the entire risk actually associated with the bank's operations.[21] A study by Nier and Baumann (2006) based on their large cross-country panel data set involving 32 countries over 1993–2000 provides some support for this hypothesis. They found, among other things, that the effects of market discipline are reduced when banks enjoy a high level of government support.[22]

As discussed in chapter 2, the strength of market suspicions of the existence of a too-big-to-fail policy and the potential for confining expectations of too-big-to-fail bailouts are among the most important, and con-

---

20. Covitz and Harrison place secondary emphasis on the disclosures required of issuers of new securities under the Securities Act of 1933. In practice, this increment of mandated disclosure may be relatively modest, insofar as the Securities Exchange Act of 1934 and associated regulations of the Securities and Exchange Commission already require substantial ongoing disclosure by any issuer whose securities are held by more than 500 investors. Obviously, this criterion captures all large banks in the United States. The incremental value of legal requirements for disclosure may, however, be greater in other countries, which tend not to have requirements for ongoing disclosure as extensive as those of the United States.

21. It is worth noting, in this regard, that Sironi (2002, 2003) found the spreads for public sector banks in Europe to be significantly lower compared with private banks judged by independent rating agencies to have roughly comparable risks. Benink and Wihlborg (2002) explain the limitations created on the potential effectiveness of subordinated debt as a disciplining device by market perceptions that European regulators have close relationships with their banks.

22. Similarly, Covitz, Hancock, and Kwast (2004) found that the risk sensitivity of spreads associated with the subordinated issues of US banks increased beginning in the late 1980s, as the Federal Deposit Insurance Corporation shifted its bank resolution policies toward mechanisms such as purchase and assumption transactions, which could effectively rescue a bank's ongoing deposit and lending functions without protecting all its creditors. However, they also found that, even where implicit government support is assumed to be strong, there is some risk sensitivity reflected in subordinated debt prices.

troversial, issues in contemporary banking regulation (Mishkin 2006). Some infer from the very sensitivity of subordinated debt prices to bank riskiness that holders of this debt must not believe it to be implicitly guaranteed (Federal Reserve System 1999). Others believe that the existence of *some* perception of investment risk does not indicate the elimination of *all* expectation of a too-big-to-fail bailout, particularly in light of other evidence of such expectations (Stern and Feldman 2004).[23] One distinguished commentator regards investor expectations of government support for troubled large banks as a sufficiently serious consideration that he doubts subordinated debt issues would actually yield the market discipline intended by their proponents.[24]

Second, the spreads between a particular bank's subordinated debt issue and some benchmark rate will be affected by more than just the relative riskiness of the bank's operations. The "noisiness" of the spreads reflects liquidity constraints, surpluses and shortages of particular issues, and general macroeconomic conditions (Board of Governors of the Federal Reserve System and the US Department of the Treasury 2000).[25] The body of evidence finding a correlation between spreads and measures of riskiness might be read to suggest that the noise does not drown out all messages from changes in spreads. Still, the impact of these other factors may limit the reliability of spreads as an indicator of bank riskiness, particularly in turbulent market conditions where secondary market bond prices are overwhelmed by macroeconomic factors. Indeed, the capital market turmoil attendant to the 2007–08 subprime crisis raises the prospect that banks would simply be unable to reissue specified amounts of subordinated debt, as contemplated in various policy proposals. Under these conditions, information about a specific bank's risks may be completely drowned out by broader market fears and uncertainties. A related problem is addressed in a study by Krishnan, Ritchken, and Thomson (2005) that focused specifically on the degree to which *changes* in bank risk are reflected in changes in credit spreads. While not dismissing the idea that

---

23. Morgan and Stiroh (1999) conclude from an examination of bond issues between 1993 and 1998 that the relationship between spreads and the riskiness of portfolios is weaker for larger banks, a finding they interpret as a reflection of a perceived implicit insurance phenomenon.

24. See Flannery (2005). He proposes that banks instead be required to issue reverse convertible debentures, debt instruments that would automatically convert to common equity if a bank's market capital ratio falls below some stated value. This ingenious proposal, which would reduce leverage and increase core equity at times of stress, raises its own issues, some of which are identified by Flannery himself and by Raiv (2004). But it is another idea that would bear more extensive inquiry by academics and regulators.

25. For a summary of studies finding influence on bond spreads by nondefault, risk-related factors, see Bliss (2001, 30–31).

there may be such a correlation, the authors did not find "strong and consistent evidence" of its existence.[26]

Another possible problem is the reliability of the price data from which subordinated debt yields in the secondary market are calculated. Many subordinated debt issues are not publicly traded or otherwise authoritatively priced on a regular basis. Hancock and Kwast (2001) found that price data from the two principal available sources—Bloomberg and Interactive Data Corporation—varied in statistically significant ways. Of course, as suggested by Evanoff, Jagtiani, and Nakata (2007), implementation of comprehensive subordinated debt requirements would make relevant markets deeper and information flows better.

Third is the question of exactly what information about bank risk is included in subordinated-debt yield spreads. More specifically, given the opaqueness of banks' assets and activities, do markets have adequate information to see early signs of trouble? Some cross-sectional studies seek to determine if supervisory judgments are reflected or anticipated (before those judgments have been made public) by bond markets. Others compare spreads with various accounting measures of riskiness, such as nonperforming loans, that are also available to supervisors. The former kind of study tells us nothing about what markets could *add* to the information already available to supervisors. Indeed, Bliss (2001) suggests that the studies he surveyed show only that bond yields provide redundant information. The latter kind of study, however, may reveal something about the ability or willingness of supervisors to incorporate available information into their supervisory judgments. This point is emphasized by Evanoff and Wall (2001), who worry about regulatory forbearance.

It is also possible that investors could rely on ratings of subordinated debt issues provided by external rating agencies, rather than expend resources for direct monitoring activities. As revealed in the unhappy experience with ratings of debt issued by structured investment vehicles, agency ratings may themselves be seriously flawed evaluations of the risk associated with a particular issue. While we might expect sophisticated investors to alter their reliance on rating agencies—at least pending convincing evidence that the latter have become substantially more predictive—the possibility of investor reliance on conflicted or unreliable third parties remains.

There is some limited evidence for the proposition that market participants may develop information that is not reflected in supervisory judg-

---

26. The authors did find that credit spreads tend to reflect firm-specific risks more for banks regularly issuing subordinated debt, though changes in market variables continued to be the dominant source of change.

ments but would be useful in predicting future performance by banking organizations (Berger, Davies, and Flannery 2000). If borne out in additional research, this fact may be explained by the more forward-looking perspective of market participants compared with regulators, a comparative advantage of market participants in quickly assimilating large quantities of information, or other factors. As of now, however, even one of the authors of this study subsequently concluded from a review of all available studies that "market information adds rather little to the explanatory power of models that rely exclusively on accounting information" (Flannery and Nikolova 2004, 93).

Fourth, there have been various concerns about the cost of requiring banks to issue mandatory debt, along with other practical considerations. Underwriting and other issuance fees are apparently significantly lower for subordinated debt than for equity issued by banks or bank holding companies (Board of Governors of the Federal Reserve System and the US Department of the Treasury 2000; US Shadow Financial Regulatory Committee 2000). More significant may be a potential liquidity premium for issues of less than about $75 million, which the Federal Reserve staff found to be the minimum size necessary to assure adequate liquidity. Depending on its size, a bank required to issue such subordinated debt regularly may not reach this dollar threshold and, accordingly, will be forced to pay a higher interest rate for non-risk-related reasons.

A somewhat different cost concern is that of false positives—circumstances where changes in yield spreads trigger supervisory inquiries or interventions that prove to have been unnecessary. That is, markets may mistakenly perceive problems that are not in fact present in the bank, or nonrisk factors may drive prices enough to force an intervention. One paper that addressed this problem assessed the resulting costs as modest and, in any case, worth incurring for the benefit of identifying problems that would otherwise have gone undetected (Krainer and Lopez 2003).

These and other considerations have led to considerable debate over the configuration of any mandatory subordinated debt system. For example, while current regulatory requirements for qualifying tier 2 capital create an incentive for banks to issue subordinated debt of longer maturity, some studies find that shorter-maturity debt is more sensitive to bank risk (Hancock and Kwast 2001).[27] Thus, the capital cushion purpose of subordinated debt conflicts somewhat with the potential disciplining purpose of that same debt.

---

27. Under existing regulations, qualifying tier 2 capital can include a limited amount of subordinated debt with an initial maturity of at least five years. Qualifying capital is reduced by one-fifth in each of the last five years before maturity, a restriction that accounts for the frequency with which bank holding companies exercise call options on outstanding subordinated debt instruments five years from maturity.

Role of Market Discipline

The abundance of proposals to use subordinated debt as a regulatory device testifies to the importance, and potential, of using market disciplines in banking supervision. It also highlights the uncertainty as to how the third, market-discipline pillar of the Basel II framework will work in practice. By enlisting scores, perhaps hundreds, of sophisticated investors—many of them institutions with extensive research capabilities—a mandatory subordinated debt system promises at a minimum to supplement the limited resources of banking supervisors in watching for incipient problems at large banking organizations. Many of the subordinated debt proposals would also facilitate oversight of the performance of the supervisors by creating a visible and standardized gauge of a bank's condition other than that formulated by the supervisors themselves.

The intuitive appeal of *direct* market discipline is undeniable. As the centerpiece of bank regulation, however, market discipline will almost surely fall short. The very factors that necessitate bank regulation in the first place—asymmetric information, high leverage ratios, financial interrelationships, and government deposit insurance—mean that market failures and the divergence of private from social costs will, for the indefinite future, remain significant. Even as an alternative to capital requirements, the direct market discipline associated with subordinated debt is too speculative to serve as a key regulatory tool. There is, at present, little evidence to show that managers of large, complex banking organizations will be effectively constrained by market forces from pursuing strategies that engender societally suboptimal levels of risk, although one can certainly imagine further research and experience leading eventually to an important ancillary role for direct discipline.

The potential effectiveness of *indirect* market discipline is better supported by existing empirical work. It is conceivable that the questions raised in the preceding section might some day be sufficiently answered to make a system of supervisory intervention based solely on changes in yield spreads viable. Of course, almost by definition, indirect market discipline operates as an adjunct to other regulatory and supervisory devices. In its weaker forms, indirect discipline is simply an additional piece of data for supervisors. Even if spreads were to replace capital levels as the triggers for supervisory intervention, the question of what actions the supervisors should take would remain. Presumably, the answer will be to require some combination of increases in capital, changes in bank strategies, and improvement in risk management practices. That is, the substance of bank requirements will either be specified in other regulations or devised on an ad hoc, discretionary basis by supervisors.

Yet this apparent limitation on the role of indirect market discipline may actually be an advantage, since it can be combined with other regulatory and supervisory elements in a variety of configurations. The US

Shadow Financial Regulatory Committee (2000) has, as mentioned earlier, proposed abandoning risk-weighted capital requirements in favor of higher leverage ratio requirements and the use of subordinated debt yield spreads as the trigger for prompt corrective action. This approach has the advantage of being relatively simple without being simplistic. It would retain minimum capital levels as an important piece of banking regulation. The mandatory subordinated debt feature would help signal supervisors when the bank was falling below desirable levels of economic capital and, in the process, make regulatory forbearance more difficult (or at least more obvious). All this could be achieved at substantially less cost than the A-IRB approach, since banks would be relieved of the costs of complying with regulatory requirements that are additional to, or independent of, the costs of sophisticated internal-risk management.[28] Given the extensive questions about the A-IRB approach detailed in chapter 5, the US Shadow Financial Regulatory Committee's proposal has considerable appeal.

Still, there are questions as to how effectively a mandatory subordinated debt system would promote some of the aims of the A-IRB approach, as nested in the larger revised framework. Perhaps the most important are the degree and speed with which change in a bank's risk profile is reflected in the market price for that bank's subordinated debt. If investors do not have access to information giving early signs of problems, or if the noise from broader economic developments drowns out the bank-specific signal contained in a bond price, the utility of the subordinated debt price as a supervisory tool will be limited.

In addition, there is a question of whether, in the absence of the incentives provided by the A-IRB approach, banks will continue to improve their risk management techniques in order to provide management, supervisors, and potentially even markets with a better gauge of bank risk. Of course, as discussed earlier, the tension between this incentive and the possible quid pro quo of lower capital is itself potentially problematic. But the steps taken by banks to improve their risk management systems in preparation for Basel II, while not yet adequate for that specific regulatory model, have undeniably been substantial. An argument can be made that,

---

28. If the US Shadow Financial Regulatory Committee's proposal were applied only to banks that will use the A-IRB model, the incremental costs associated with the issuance of subordinated debt would be very modest. Each of the large US banks (and, as discussed later in the text, European and Japanese banks) that will likely use the A-IRB approach already has an amount equal to at least 2 percent of its assets in outstanding subordinated debt (Board of Governors of the Federal Reserve System and the US Department of the Treasury 2000, 45–48). Moreover, the size of these banks is such that the apparent optimal liquidity threshold of $75 million should not be a problem. Actually, much of this debt is issued at the holding company level rather than at the bank level. Since the virtues of both direct and indirect market discipline are obviously greater when the debt is issued by the bank itself, there would be costs in converting to issuance by a bank subsidiary that has likely not previously issued securities directly.

with properly mandated disclosure, the indirect market discipline of yield spreads will reflect market assessment of banks' risk management performance and thus motivate managers to commit the necessary resources (and harness operating units with other incentives) to follow best practice. This argument is necessarily speculative. Moreover, the very advantage of yield spreads in reflecting all kinds of bank risks means that this discipline may be less effective in promoting a specific brand of risk mitigation.

Eliminating risk-weighted capital requirements entirely will, by definition, render nugatory the Basel II aim of aligning regulatory capital requirements more closely with actual risk. A higher simple leverage ratio requirement can itself induce regulatory arbitrage, arguably more serious than that prompted by Basel I. This, of course, was an original justification for moving to risk-weighted capital requirements in the 1980s. Again, proponents of mandatory subordinated debt can argue that yield spreads will, with proper bank disclosure, reflect risk capital relationships that may be cause for concern. In theory, this is a reasonable argument and, as indicated earlier, in practice yield spreads have performed better than risk-weighted capital ratios in anticipating bank problems. However, the more precise risk calibration under the IRB methodologies could make the risk-weighted ratios more meaningful and thus somewhat better predictors.

In truth, one's conclusions as to which committee—the Basel Committee or the US Shadow Financial Regulatory Committee—has the better of the argument mean little in immediate practical terms. The A-IRB approach will be implemented in the next couple of years, though likely with ongoing changes induced by the subprime crisis and attendant revealed inadequacies of the original Basel II formulas and standards. Nonetheless, among the recommendations in chapter 8 is a proposal that a mandatory subordinated capital requirement be imposed on all large, internationally active banks, regardless of whether the A-IRB approach is retained. The rationale and proposal are somewhat more limited than that of the Shadow Committee, since—at least for the present—using the subordinated debt spreads as triggers for supervisory action is not part of the recommendation. Instead, the recommendation favors the adoption of a mandatory subordinated debt requirement to help monitor the performance of bank supervisors and to explore further—in a real world context—the potential of market discipline to assume a greater role in bank regulation.

International Implications

Before leaving the alternative of market discipline, it is important to examine the international implications of adopting a mandatory subordinated debt requirement. As a factual matter, there is widespread issuance of subordinated debt by banks throughout the Basel Committee countries (Basel Committee 2003e). Nearly half of all the banking assets in these countries are held by banks that issue subordinated debt. On average, subordinated debt is held in an amount equal to about 3.6 percent of the risk-weighted assets of the banking organizations, well above the 2 percent limit of subordinated debt that can currently be used for regulatory capital purposes. The market for subordinated debt is about as deep in the rest of the Basel Committee countries as in the United States, although the *public* market for subordinated debt is considerably larger in the United States and United Kingdom than elsewhere.[29]

Thus, the imposition of a subordinated mandatory debt requirement would not require a major and costly innovation in the capital market activities of Basel Committee banks. As in the United States, it would not seem a major difficulty for the large banks that are likely candidates for the A-IRB methodology to issue subordinated debt on a quarterly basis so as to have outstanding an amount equal to at least 2 percent of assets outstanding. Compared with research on US banks, there have been relatively few studies of the sensitivity of European and Japanese banks' subordinated debt spreads to bank riskiness. Thus, one cannot say with assurance that the potential for indirect market discipline is as great elsewhere as in the United States. Perhaps, for example, there is too much noise in the spreads of universal banks to use bond yields as a reliable mechanism for evaluating portfolio riskiness. The relatively undeveloped character of public debt markets in some countries may also be an impediment. Still, these differences in national markets seem no more significant than the banking and regulatory differences relevant to the adoption of the A-IRB approach. Indeed, they appear rather less significant, insofar as research may reveal fairly robust risk sensitivity, and the very mandating of regular debt issues will presumably accelerate the development of public debt markets.

As an institutional matter, implementation of a subordinated debt requirement is manifestly easier to monitor than the A-IRB approach. In reality, this regulatory requirement would facilitate monitoring by each Basel Committee member of the overall performance of the other Basel Committee regulators, since subordinated yield spreads would be a low-cost means of gauging the condition of foreign banks that is relatively independent of supervisory influence. To be sure, the subordinated debt requirement would not promote the common regulatory language that may come from the extensive time spent by Basel regulators on the revised framework. As discussed in chapter 8, however, there are ways to foster more trust and information sharing among regulators well short of the massive A-IRB undertaking.

---

29. Sironi (2002) finds that, controlling for default risk, US banks pay a modest but statistically significant lower average spread on their subordinated debt. Sironi attributes this difference to the greater liquidity of the US market, although on average US banks pay somewhat higher spreads because of the number of public sector banks in Europe that presumably benefit from implicit safety net guarantees.

Precommitment Approach

The precommitment approach to capital requirements had its origins a decade ago in a paper by two Federal Reserve Board economists offering an alternative to the market-risk capital requirement then under discussion, and eventually adopted, by the Basel Committee (Kupiec and O'Brien 1995).[30] While policy development work for the succeeding few years was focused exclusively on market risk, at least one Federal Reserve official suggested at the time that the precommitment approach could also be applied to credit risk.[31] During the Basel II process this suggestion was taken up by Charles Taylor, who characterizes his proposed "new general approach" to capital adequacy as a "lineal descendant" of the original Kupiec and O'Brien proposal (Taylor 2002).

The precommitment approach is an example of an incentive-compatible regulatory scheme. A bank would determine the amount of capital it would hold against market risk for securities in its trading book and commit to manage its portfolio so as to keep its trading losses below that amount during some interval specified by the regulator. The bank could increase or decrease its capital allocation at the end of each interval. If the bank's actual market losses exceeded its capital allocation, a penalty would be imposed on the bank. Various penalties were proposed, including monetary penalties, punitive capital charges, public disclosure of the bank's breach of its loss target, or mandatory initiation of prompt corrective action.

The Federal Reserve Board formally requested comment on the idea at the same time that US banking agencies proposed the rules implementing the Basel agreement on market risk.[32] Reaction was mixed. Perhaps predictably, large New York banks were favorably disposed to the idea, while some regional and smaller banks had reservations. By late 1995, the Fed indicated it had decided to take no action, ostensibly on the basis of the public comments it had received. However, the proposal seemed ill-timed from the outset, insofar as the other Basel Committee countries had just agreed to the value-at-risk (VaR) approach to market risk. European Union countries needed to reach agreement on the EU's capital directive and thus were not disposed to reopen the market-risk question. This incident may thus represent a modest example of the influence of international institutional arrangements on domestic regulatory choices.

---

30. The authors refined and elaborated on their proposal in Kupiec and O'Brien (1997).

31. The suggestion was made by Federal Reserve Governor Susan Phillips, then chair of the Fed's committee on bank supervision and regulation. See Jaret Seiberg, "The Fed Considers Sweeping Changes In Risk-Based Capital Requirements," *American Banker*, December 13, 1996, 1. Later, however, Fed Chairman Alan Greenspan explicitly excluded its potential application to the banking book, as opposed to traded assets (Greenspan 1998).

32. The proposal was included in Board of Governors of the Federal Reserve System (1995).

Notwithstanding its abandonment of formal consideration of the pre-commitment approach, the Fed continued to support intellectual work on the idea.[33] The appeal of such an approach is not hard to understand. Like an internal models approach, precommitment builds on the bank's use of sophisticated risk assessment technologies. Unlike the market risk amendment to Basel I, however, precommitment would have permitted incorporation of the subjective judgments of bank risk managers into their capital calculations. Among other things, this feature would have allowed banks to adjust for the fact that the internal models approach effectively extrapolated the short-term VaR figures produced by the model into a much longer time horizon. Furthermore, proponents of precommitment argued that it could be effectively tailored to each bank's situation, while avoiding the imposition of standardized parameters imposed in an internal ratings approach. At the same time, the inherently difficult task of supervisory validation of internal models would be substantially mitigated, insofar as the penalty scheme created an incentive for banks to make their models as accurate as possible. Finally, the approach can be applied to cover all risks associated with a particular set of assets—operational and legal, as well as market.

The New York Clearing House Association, whose membership at the time consisted of 11 large banks, conducted a one-year pilot study to "provide further information and experience" on the precommitment approach for national regulators in the United States, Japan, and Switzerland (Fuji Bank and Swiss Bank Corporation having also participated).[34] The participating institutions concluded that precommitment was a viable approach and a preferable alternative to the Basel Committee's VaR-based capital requirement for market risk. In particular, the banks argued that the multiplier requirement for the VaR approach—which is applied to compensate for the limited time horizon of the internal model—was shown to be too high.

The most obvious difficulty with the precommitment approach for market risk lies in calibrating the penalty to be imposed when a bank's losses exceed its stated capital set-aside. The penalty must be adequate to offset the incentive of bank managers to set the capital level quite low, but it cannot be so punitive as to cause banks to hold inefficiently high levels

---

33. For example, a February 1998 conference on capital regulation cosponsored by the Board of Governors (along with the Federal Reserve Bank of New York, the Bank of Japan, and the Bank of England) included several papers addressing the precommitment approach. At that conference, Chairman Greenspan referred to the approach as a "potentially promising" application of the principle that supervisors should incorporate market advances into regulatory policies (Greenspan 1998).

34. The pilot program is described in Considine (1998). Although they conducted the study at their own initiative and expense, the participating banks consulted extensively with their regulatory agencies in deciding on the structure of the pilot program.

of capital that could otherwise be put to productive use.[35] If the calibration is off, the incentives on which the scheme rests will by definition be improperly aligned. Moreover, because there is no ex ante specification of capital levels, a bank that finds itself already in shaky circumstances may be both tempted and able to set a very low capital level for a given interval, betting that it will make rather than lose money.

These problems would be as or more serious if the precommitment approach were applied to credit risk for assets on the banking book. Because banking book assets still account for higher proportions of total assets than traded securities, supervisors would face an exacerbated time-inconsistency problem in the case of credit risk (Jackson and Perraudin 2000). That is, while a bank whose market losses have exceeded its capital allocation may still be fundamentally sound, a bank whose credit losses are substantially above a comparable capital allocation may well be facing serious liquidity or solvency problems. Under these circumstances, a supervisor may be reluctant to impose a penalty (whether monetary or in the form of mandatory disclosure of its above-capital losses), since the penalty could itself tip the bank into insolvency. An additional problem would be the absence of a transparent pricing mechanism to calculate credit "losses" during a given interval, in contrast to the readily available daily prices for traded securities. While write-offs or additional reserves are relatively transparent, the deterioration in credit quality of loans that are still being serviced is essentially opaque. This circumstance, of course, is one of the reasons for turning to credit risk models. Thus, as applied to credit risk, the precommitment approach is in this respect not obviously superior to the Basel II IRB approach.

Charles Taylor, responding to the complexity of the emerging A-IRB approach, attempted to solve the core problem of properly aligning incentives in a precommitment system by creating two yardsticks for regulatory sanctions whose triggering effects are inversely related (Taylor 2002). Each bank would propose a capital threshold for all its lines of business combined. Any bank whose capital fell below this threshold would be subject to supervisory action. At the same time, regulators would establish a loss parameter, denominated as a percentage of a bank's capital threshold. A bank suffering losses above the resulting loss threshold would also be subject to supervisory action.[36] Thus, if a bank proposes to maintain a relatively low capital threshold—thereby freeing up capital for lending—it will be bound by a relatively low loss threshold.[37]

---

35. An explication of this problem, presented at the February 1998 conference on capital regulation mentioned in footnote 33, is found in Kobayashi (1998).

36. Taylor eschews monetary penalties in favor of prompt corrective action as the sole sanction for breach of either the capital or loss thresholds.

37. Taylor subsequently recast his 2002 proposal as a "modernized leverage ratio," but his core concept appears unchanged. See Charles Taylor, "For a Better Risk Gauge, Update Leverage Ratio," *American Banker*, May 18, 2007, 10.

Taylor's proposal has significant attractive features. First, it allows banks to make their own decisions on the trade-off between risk and capital, within the regulatory structure constraint created by the loss parameter. Taylor notes that his approach thus avoids the excessive prescriptiveness of Basel II. Indeed, he argues that Basel II does not create an incentive for banks to implement state-of-the-art risk management techniques beyond those required for the A-IRB calculations. Under his approach, by contrast, a bank would have an ongoing incentive to improve its risk management techniques so as to optimize the capital threshold/loss threshold trade-off. Furthermore, because this approach permits diversity in risk management, concerns about herd behavior under Basel II should be mitigated.

Second, as suggested by its characterization as a "general" approach, the Taylor proposal is potentially applicable to all bank risks. This feature greatly simplifies capital regulation. It avoids the kind of artificiality found in the Basel II requirement for operational risk, for example. More fundamentally, it promises to take full account of the complexity of bank operations without creating a regulatory system that is itself so complex as to make compliance costs inefficiently high, effective monitoring difficult, and the accountability of regulators elusive. It also promises that the regulatory system will not have to be more or less continuously revised, in contrast to the apparent intention of the Basel Committee to regularly overhaul A-IRB requirements.

Third, because of its universal applicability and relative simplicity, the new general approach may better promote competitive equality among banks than Basel II. Taylor particularly emphasizes that it does not distinguish between different kinds of financial activities or institutions. It is wholly applicable to everything from a community bank in rural America to a universal bank in Switzerland and should, accordingly, reduce the competitive advantages that might accrue to the latter under Basel II.

Fourth, again because of its relative simplicity, it promises institutional advantages over Basel II. Domestically, it could facilitate the monitoring of bank supervisory authorities, insofar as actual bank losses would presumably be derived from the bank's regularly published financial statements. Similarly, national regulators could monitor relatively easily the performance of foreign banks against their loss thresholds. Taylor acknowledges that national regulators might seek competitive advantage for their banks by implementing the new general approach in an excessively liberal fashion. But he believes that "outlier" loss parameters would soon become apparent to other regulators, who could apply moral suasion against the permissive regulator in the Basel Committee.

Unfortunately, the Taylor proposal—at least in its current form—does not appear to deliver on its conceptual promise. Indeed, closer inspection suggests that it has not solved the key problems identified in the original precommitment proposals. In the earlier versions, calibration of the penalty for excessive losses was essential to creating proper incentives. In

Taylor's approach, calculation of the loss parameter assumes a corresponding importance. While he suggests factors that should be considered in establishing the loss parameter and gives some examples, he has not proposed an actual parameter value. Indeed, he has not even chosen among various possible approaches—a single loss parameter to be applied "globally" within the Basel Committee countries, different national parameters based on local conditions, or even bank-by-bank parameters based on factors such as a specific institution's potential for creating systemic risk. One suspects that, although the parameter itself may be stated as a simple percentage of capital, its derivation will require much work and empirical testing, maybe of the same order of magnitude as has been required for the A-IRB formulas. Without doing this work and then running simulations analogous to the various quantitative impact studies of the A-IRB formulas, the new general approach is obviously not anywhere near ready for adoption.

The problem of the opaqueness of credit "losses" that have yet to be realized as write-offs also afflicts the Taylor proposal, insofar as he postulates the use of "true," rather than historic, capital. Taylor defines true capital as the difference between assets and liabilities valued at fair, or marked-to-market, value. Sound as that choice is theoretically, it requires extensive adjustment to the value of nontraded assets such as loans. Taylor rather downplays the difficulty of making these "common-sense adjustments," but in practical terms the process might require something similar to the very credit risk models that provide the starting point for the A-IRB approach. At the very least, supervisors would need to assess and approve the accounting processes by which banks valued their nontraded assets.

Finally, as Taylor acknowledges, while his dual-trigger approach deters gaming the system in most circumstances, it does not prevent bank management that "wanted to go for broke and gamble the future of the institution" from setting a low capital threshold for a single regulatory period. If management were lucky, the gamble would pay off and the loss threshold would not be breached. But if things didn't turn out so well, the bank's capital could well be inadequate to cushion the losses. Taylor's response is that his approach is not "slavishly mechanical" and that supervisors would need to review the proposed capital thresholds of banks before accepting them. This is a wholly reasonable response, but when added to the complications created by the choice of loss parameter and the calculation of true capital, it suggests that the new general approach is considerably less straightforward than it may at first have appeared. As a result, some of the benefits of transparency, cost effectiveness, and management flexibility will inevitably be lost.

Taylor's effort to give banks maximum incentive to refine risk assessment and management within a manageable regulatory framework is an admirable one. It is in some sense unfair to hold his proposal to the same critical standard as the revised framework. After all, the latter has been developed by scores of bank supervisors over a period of decades, while the former is one analyst's solo effort to rationalize approaches to capital regulation. Like the subordinated debt proposals, the Taylor approach might—with expenditure of comparable time and resources—have evolved into a superior alternative to Basel II. The Basel Committee may be faulted for failing to develop these alternatives sufficiently to make a more informed choice as among regulatory paradigms. In its present state, however, the new general approach is not an immediate, realistic alternative for bank capital regulation.

Establishing an International Supervisory Role

Thus far this chapter has considered alternatives to the A-IRB approach that rest on different substantive paradigms for the regulation of bank capital levels or, to some extent, bank safety and soundness more generally. Because we are considering optimal *international* bank regulatory arrangements, and because some important shortcomings of Basel II inhere in its specifically international character, it is also worth evaluating alternatives that focus on significantly different relationships between the national and international regulatory systems. It may be that the net benefits of Basel II (or, for that matter, other regulatory paradigms) could be increased by addressing some of the governance problems encountered in chapters 5 and 6—the absence of national expertise in evaluating sophisticated bank models and the difficulties in monitoring the performance of national regulators in an A-IRB system.

One possibility is the transformation of the Basel Committee from a group of cooperating national regulators into an international banking regulator. In its strongest form, this transformation would entail the equivalent of a supranational bank regulatory agency in Basel. Such an agency would directly supervise banks in Basel Committee member countries—or, perhaps, supervise the large banks that will be adopting the A-IRB approach. Simply to state this possibility is to reveal how farfetched it is under present circumstances. The political hurdles to national governments ceding direct regulatory authority over their banks are simply insuperable in the foreseeable future. If the nations of the European Union—with their shared institutions and substantial harmonization of financial law—are unable to agree on consolidation of supervisory authority in a single regulator, prospects for an international innovation of this sort seem exceedingly dim.

Furthermore, it is by no means clear that, even were such a consolidation of regulatory authority within the realm of political possibility, the change would be desirable as a policy matter. In the context of efforts to achieve substantive harmonization, concerns have been expressed over the loss of regulatory flexibility to respond to local conditions (including macroeconomic conditions), the suppression of possibly healthy regulatory experimentation or competition, and the removal of regulatory authority further away from points of democratic accountability. All these concerns would apply to an international bank supervisory body. Coupled with the enormous operational uncertainty attendant to a leap from national to international supervision, these considerations would almost surely and substantially outweigh any benefits accruing from overcoming the governance problems mentioned earlier.

A more promising, if more modest, direct role for an international agency would be to assess the use of internal risk-rating systems of banks covered by the A-IRB approach to capital adequacy, or successor approaches in which bank credit risk models play an important role. The agency might evaluate all banks covered by an A-IRB or successor approach or, perhaps more realistically, selected banks from each Basel Committee country. The international entity would be composed of technically sophisticated bank examiners and experts in credit risk modeling. These examiners and experts would regularly monitor the banks to assure both technical competence and good faith in the implementation of those models. The international entity could be housed at the Bank for International Settlements in Basel and would formally report to the Basel Committee itself, as well as reporting its specific examination findings to the appropriate national supervisors. Rather than substitute for national regulation of capital adequacy, such an international body would constitute a governance device for the arrangement among committee nations by giving increased assurance to Basel Committee countries that the A-IRB (or successor) approach was being rigorously, competently, and consistently implemented.[38]

Thus, this variant on an international regulatory authority does not really present an alternative paradigm for capital adequacy regulation, even if we broaden that concept to include administrative and enforcement considerations as well as substantive principles of bank regulation. Still, like some versions of market discipline proposals, an international bank examination arrangement could be a useful element of a modified Basel II. There appear to be several potential benefits.

First, it would pool the best supervisory talent available for the daunting task of overseeing implementation of the A-IRB approach to capital regulation. As suggested in earlier chapters, at least in the near term there is considerable reason to doubt the capacity of some national supervisors to adequately evaluate banks' use of credit models for regulatory pur-

---

38. One obvious question is whether the international agency would also examine banks in countries other than the United States that adopt the foundational IRB approach. The answer would probably depend on some combination of the number of such banks and the technical expertise of the national supervisors that regulate them.

poses. An international agency to which top supervisors and credit model experts were detailed by national supervisory agencies could provide more thorough examination of A-IRB banks in countries that are relatively inexperienced in such assessments, while at the same time imparting experience and expertise to the examiners detailed to the international agency from those same countries. As examiners and experts return to their home agencies, they in turn would be able to pass on the state-of-the-art supervisory techniques that would develop within the international agency.

Second, an international agency would minimize the incidence of inconsistent interpretations of the requirements and standards of the revised framework. While such inconsistency can arise even within a single agency, divergences are likely to be less significant and shorter-lived than where a dozen or more national supervisors are operating largely independently of one another. Thus, this approach would contribute modestly to the goals of competitive equality.

A third, related benefit would be a more efficient process for adjusting the supervisory requirements and practices—both substantive and procedural—that are contained in the A-IRB approach. The complexity of the revised framework and the ongoing evolution of risk management techniques ensure that regular adjustments will need to be made. A single entity will be both better informed on the varieties of developments to which supervision must respond and better placed to implement such responses consistently. Although it is possible that the existence of an international examining agency would push all the Basel Committee countries toward prematurely or unwisely standardizing application of the A-IRB to different banks, and thus would foreclose the advantages of experimentation with different administrative techniques, this risk does not seem particularly troubling here. The examiners will obviously be able to particularize both their examinations and their interpretations where warranted. More importantly, the retention of supervisory authority by national agencies would ensure that good reasons for variations in interpretation and administration would be heard.

Fourth, an integrated international authority should substantially remove doubts as to whether national supervisors are exploiting the relative opaqueness of an A-IRB or successor approach to capital regulation in order to give competitive advantage to their own banks. The multinational character of the international examination teams will foreclose the opportunity for national regulators to be excessively lenient in evaluating a bank's credit model in operation. While national regulators could still forbear from acting after being informed of problems by the international examination team, this forbearance would be apparent to the international agency itself (and the examiners' countries). The monitoring function is thus inherent in the international agency's activities.

On the other hand, even an international agency of limited scope would have disadvantages, quite apart from any reflexive objections based on formal notions of sovereignty. First, creating a separate—and distant—agency to conduct a critical part of the examination of large banks would likely entail some duplication of regulatory resources and inefficiency in the examination process. Because national regulators would continue to have supervisory responsibility for the large banks, they would almost surely feel obliged to examine the bank's credit risk model that forms the basis for computing its regulatory capital. Obviously, this function would be necessary if the international agency examines only selected banks in any given year. Furthermore, the line between review of a bank's overall risk management systems and its qualifications and use of the A-IRB approach will surely be a fuzzy one in practice. The international examination team and the primary domestic supervisory agency would likely both evaluate some of the same processes. Finally, the need for domestic supervisors to maintain the requisite expertise even as they detail some of their most sophisticated examiners to the international agency could lead to a net increase in the resources required to conduct satisfactory examinations of A-IRB banks and, at the same time, a dilution of those potentially scarce resources.

Second, banks and their national supervisors may be reluctant to enter an arrangement that would result in potentially sensitive and/or proprietary bank information being available to examiners whose permanent affiliation is with the supervisory agencies of other nations. There is reason to believe, though, that this problem may be less serious than it at first appears. For one thing, current plans for enforcement of the revised framework already contemplate a supervisory role for nations that host significant operations of multinational banks based elsewhere, even as the Accord Implementation Group will seek to minimize instances of duplicative or inconsistent capital regulation. Thus, the international examination agency under consideration here would be more of an incremental than quantum change in the kind and amount of information available to foreign regulators. Banks themselves may nonetheless fear that proprietary information about their models or cost structures might be leaked to banks based in countries from which members of an examination team have been detailed. The professionalism of bank regulators and existing levels of trust among at least the Basel Committee members are such as to make this relatively unlikely.[39]

A more plausible concern is that members of an international examination team who become aware of serious problems in a bank may report those problems to their home supervisory agencies. They need not communicate specifics, much less proprietary information such as the bank's

---

39. National regulators in areas such as antitrust and securities already provide one another with confidential and business proprietary information in connection with enforcement of these laws, usually under formal confidentiality agreements.

experience with particular borrowers, in order to alert their home agencies to the possibility of a disruption in that bank's activities. The home agencies, in turn, might quietly counsel their own banks to reduce exposures to the troubled bank. In the worst case, a bank that might otherwise have resolved its problems could be driven into a more serious position by these individually rational but collectively damaging responses. National banking regulators already have such concerns, a fact that probably limits the extent of their information sharing with their counterparts. It is difficult to say whether scrutiny of an A-IRB bank's credit risk modeling would reveal the kinds of immediate risks that would fuel these concerns. Moreover, of course, the number of such cases is likely to be extremely limited. Still, the potential scope of damage to a large bank and the financial system generally may make national regulators reluctant to participate in an integrated international examination process for reasons beyond parochialism and chauvinism.

Eliminating International Cooperation on Safety and Soundness

At the other end of the spectrum from proposals to create an international bank supervisory entity is the alternative of eliminating international cooperation on bank safety and soundness regulation. This option might appeal to those who believe that national regulators have resorted to international cooperative arrangements in order to preserve their own bureaucratic power and position, even though the public interest may be better served by more regulatory competition.[40] Those who find public choice analysis helpful but not usually dispositive might still consider this option.

The substantive regulatory paradigm fashioned in an international harmonizing effort will almost inevitably deviate from that which is optimal from a purely domestic standpoint. Differences in policy choices and in regulatory contexts mean that compromise is necessary. The more detailed the harmonized standards, the more likely it is they will include elements that are suboptimal as a matter of domestic regulation.

---

40. Macey (2003) cites Basel I as an example of "regulatory cartelization" by national banking supervisors seeking to avoid competing for "market share"—meaning, in this context, the share of banking activity regulated by a particular supervisor. The idea is that the bureaucratic and career interests of supervisors will influence their actions more than the public interest. While there is almost always something to these concerns, the actual history of Basel II provides little support for the regulatory cartelization hypothesis. Moreover, to the degree that the supervisors' institutional interests are aligned with the public interest of protecting the government deposit insurance system, avoiding financial crises, and containing moral hazard, then the rather negative connotation of "cartelization" is somewhat misleading. Even nationalistic competition, though potentially corrosive in some of its effects, reflects the shared belief that some form of banking regulation is necessary.

The institutional implications of an international arrangement may render the regulatory scheme less adaptable than a self-contained national approach would be. The question, then, is whether the resulting costs for the efficient and effective regulation of banks outweigh the incremental benefits of the international arrangement for international financial stability, competitive equality, and supervisory facilitation.

It is possible that the foregoing question would be answered in the negative for every plausible international arrangement. In that case, the option of no international cooperation would be a solid one. Realistically, the issue is whether the potential public gains from international cooperation are substantial. If they are, then it is very likely that *some* arrangement will yield nontrivial net benefits. The close interconnections among major banks and national financial systems create the possibility of major negative externalities from the failure of a large bank. Indeed, much of the history of the Basel Committee can fairly be written as a series of responses to the failures of such institutions as Franklin National Bank, Banco Ambrosiano, Herstatt Bank, Continental Bank, Barings, and the Bank of Commerce and Credit International. In each case, systemic dangers appeared sufficiently possible as to galvanize national supervisors into cooperative action. Though no major commercial bank has failed during the subprime crisis,[41] this development has likewise underscored the potential for contagion among banks across national borders—both in the traditional sense of counterparty weakness and, in a new wrinkle, in the additional sense of bank emulation of practices by foreign (in this case, US) banks that yielded great profits for a time but that actually masked large risks. The Basel Committee's 2008 proposals to modify the revised framework ensued. All these actions—historical and contemporary—look less like the classic public choice story of an effort to preserve bureaucratic prerogative or to resist a healthy flight from unnecessary regulation than an effort to fulfill the task given the supervisors by their national governments.

That said, there is still good reason to scrutinize closely any particular proposed form of cooperative arrangement. We have already seen how special interest accommodations, the felt need to "succeed" in creating an arrangement, and other factors may induce smart supervisors in good faith to adopt an arrangement that may fail the test set forth in chapter 1.

Conclusion

Suppose the Basel Committee had proceeded very differently after it concluded in 1999 that a modified Basel I approach was not an adequate

---

41. The failures of Northern Rock, a UK bank, in 2007 and of IndyMac, a US thrift, in 2008 were certainly significant, but neither institution was among the largest in their respective countries.

long-run approach to capital regulation for large banks. Instead of immediately adopting a more or less single-minded commitment to an internal ratings–based approach, the committee might have taken six to 12 months to put in place an interim arrangement that generalized the application of incremental advances in capital regulation, including those already implemented by the United States, United Kingdom, and others during the first decade of the capital accord. This "Basel I½" might, for example, have included provisions on securitization, credit enhancements, derivatives, and credit risk mitigation measures, along with some adjustments to the risk buckets themselves (e.g., eliminating membership in the Organization for Economic Cooperation and Development as the basis for determining the relative creditworthiness of a sovereign).

At the same time, the committee could have launched serious inquiries into the feasibility of the internal ratings, market discipline, and precommitment approaches. It might also have expressly solicited new ideas to address the already-apparent shortcomings of each of these approaches. It is at least possible that an investment of substantial official and private resources in analyzing the other paradigms might have revealed modifications to one or both of the latter two approaches that would have made them more viable alternatives than they actually are today. At the least, there would have been fairer competition among the competing paradigms than has actually been the case, with only one of the three having benefited from years of intense efforts to improve it.

In retrospect, a course of action closer to that suggested in the preceding paragraph may have produced better policy decisions. One wishes that, for example, Flannery's (2005) proposal for using reverse convertible debentures as a market discipline device had been more thoroughly explored when he first suggested it several years earlier. Still, while it should be clear from the history of Basel II that the process was considerably less well-planned and executed than would have been desirable, it is not clear how much blame *can* be fairly apportioned to the committee in its basic decision. It is possible that officials from committee countries—individually or collectively—assessed in good faith the prospects for developing viable approaches other than one based on internal ratings and concluded those prospects were minimal (though we have no evidence of such a determination having been made). In addition, supervisory officials may have believed that banks would take the prospect of reform seriously—and thus devote the resources necessary both to refine reform proposals and to get ready for implementation—only if the banks believed the supervisory officials to be committed to one approach. Perhaps it was necessary for the A-IRB approach to be fully developed in order to reveal just how problematic it would be.

In any case, the question of how much fault may fairly be assigned to the Basel Committee for its failure to develop other possible approaches is largely irrelevant to the question of how best to proceed now, given the alternatives as they currently stand. A standardized approach does not seem adequate in the long run to manage the risks associated with large internationally active banks. Whatever their ultimate promise, neither a market discipline nor a precommitment approach is anywhere close to viability as a substitute for capital regulation. It may well be ill-advised as a policy matter to delay basic reforms for another five years while alternative paradigms are more fully developed into detailed, well-scrutinized proposals. At some point the costs of a regulatory limbo could exceed the costs of even a flawed reformed system of capital regulation. In any case, members of the Basel Committee are moving forward with implementation of Basel II, albeit with the addition of the agenda for change occasioned by the subprime crisis. To be taken seriously, policy recommendations must take account of current realities as well as future possibilities.

8

Conclusions and Recommendations

The advent of the subprime crisis triggered a debate over whether a fully implemented Basel II would have mitigated or exacerbated the risk associated with securities backed by subprime mortgages. Important as the merits of this debate are, the most significant argument is one that neither side can make credibly—that *any* capital regulation regime could have sufficiently contained these risks so that the subprime situation would have been merely a problem rather than a crisis. After a decade in which supervisory attention was mainly focused on capital regulation and banks' own risk management systems, policy debate inside and outside of the official sector has broadened to other subjects.

The Basel Committee has, in the wake of the crisis, acknowledged the need for more attention to liquidity risk. The unhappy experience of many banks with off-balance-sheet entities has suggested that reputational risk may need to be taken more seriously, since the actual risks to a bank resulting from such entities seem to have exceeded the contractual obligation of the bank to support them. Perhaps most interesting and potentially far-reaching, some actual and proposed responses to the crisis have focused on limiting the use of certain financial products. Mortgages and mortgage products will be more regulated after the crisis than they were before. Regulators and banks have been reassessing securitization practices more broadly, including consideration of alternatives such as covered bonds. Some market participants have themselves questioned whether financial institutions should be creating and trading financial instruments whose complexity makes assessment of the risks they pose, particularly in a down market, highly speculative. While eventual supervisory action may include relatively few outright prohibitions or significant restrictions on bank products, it will almost surely entail increased scrutiny of their use.

The current agenda for reforming bank regulation is thus far broader than that pursued by Basel Committee members over the past decade. While the analysis of Basel II in this book does not, of course, address these newly added issues, it does yield one relevant conclusion. The questions raised here about the efficacy of Basel II, both as a paradigm for domestic regulation and as an international arrangement, strengthen the case for more robust supervisory attention to, and action on, areas other than capital regulation. It seems improbable that *any* form of capital regulation will be able to bear the regulatory weight that, in fact if not in intention, the Basel Committee placed on it over the past decade. There is an undeniable attraction to a conceptually elegant mode of regulation that calibrates bank capital precisely to the risks associated with whatever credit exposures a bank may assume, whatever instruments it may trade, and whatever operations it may conduct. This attraction has perhaps come dangerously close to being a Siren song for at least some Basel II authors and defenders. One hopes that the subprime crisis has, if nothing else, injected sufficiently dissonant notes to catch the attention of Basel II believers.

But if capital regulation is fated to be less effective than was hoped by some, it will—and should—remain an important part of financial regulation. Indeed, the partial rescue of Bear Stearns by the Federal Reserve in March 2008 has set in motion a debate that may well lead in the United States to commercial bank–like capital requirements being extended to other financial institutions whose failure might pose a systemic risk. Thus, the fashioning of effective capital requirements remains a very important part of financial regulatory reform. So too, as the most highly-developed international process to harmonize an important field of domestic economic regulation, Basel II provides important evidence on the utility of this approach not only for capital regulation but for other areas of financial regulation. This chapter draws conclusions from the analysis in previous chapters, provides recommendations for changing Basel II, and ends with some thoughts on the lessons of this arrangement for regulatory cooperation and harmonization in other areas.

To recapitulate the approach set forth in chapter 1 and applied in subsequent chapters, assessment of international harmonization efforts requires analysis of both the appropriateness of the harmonized regulation for domestic purposes and the benefits arising from domestic application of those same rules by other participating countries. As part of the latter inquiry, it is obviously necessary to examine whether and how the international arrangement can assure implementation by all participating countries. For this reason, among others, the efficacy of a harmonizing effort depends to a considerable extent on the compatibility of the harmonized rules or regulatory procedures with the institutional capacities and features of the international arrangement. Finally, because most harmonizing efforts—certainly including Basel II—are nested in a broader structure of international cooperation, one must ask how such efforts will affect the overall pattern of cooperation.

The analysis in chapter 5 raised serious questions as to the appropriateness of the Basel II advanced internal ratings–based (A-IRB) model for minimum domestic capital requirements. Not all its shortcomings are intrinsic to the A-IRB approach. For example, the potentially sizable reduction in minimum capital requirements is attributable to the specific formulas developed by the Basel Committee in the then-prevailing political context for banking regulation, not to the idea of an A-IRB approach as such. But other problems—notably those associated with model reliability and monitoring—are inherent in any A-IRB or full-model approach to capital regulation, at least for the present. Whether these problems are serious enough to render A-IRB an unwise or infeasible model for banking regulation is a close question. The chief reasons for answering in the negative are, first, the absence of any compelling alternative model and, second, the expectation of some supervisors that they can ultimately adequately refine the model based on their experience to make the approach workable. The next several years may reveal whether this expectation is well-grounded, although the opaqueness of the A-IRB supervisory process and the unfortunate history of regulatory failures appearing only after disaster strikes may extend the test period.

When we turn to its specifically international character, Basel II appears more clearly ill-advised. The Basel II *process* has made some significant contributions to safety and soundness regulation. It focused banking supervisors—in the Basel Committee countries and around the world—on the need to align capital requirements and related regulation more closely to the complex and sometimes novel risks being assumed by internationally active banks. The supervisors, in turn, encouraged the banks to improve their risk management systems and, more generally, to do a better job of understanding the risks faced by their own institutions. It may be that it was easier for national supervisors in each Basel Committee country to prod their own banks in this direction as part of an international process, though the possibility that there was an implicit deal of significantly lower capital in return for more attention to risk management would suggest otherwise. Even with this qualification, these outcomes are accomplishments.

In addition, the introduction of the three-pillar concept was an important contribution to domestic banking regulation and an advance in international supervisory cooperation. Pillar 2 incorporated domestic supervisory practices into the carefully articulated shared expectations that define the Basel Committee as an international institution. Similarly, pillar 3 established the principle that market discipline should be enlisted as an element of an overall strategy for safety and soundness supervision. The very complexity of an internationally active bank's risks places a greater premium than ever on the firmness and sophistication of bank supervision. It also argues for enlisting, to the degree possible, the assistance of market judgments. Regrettably, though, pillars 2 and 3 received less emphasis than they deserved, and each is less ambitious than would have been desirable. There is little in the way of institutional apparatus or procedures to develop either of these important elements of modern banking supervision.

These benefits for international banking supervision are more than outweighed by the drawbacks of the A-IRB model as the basis for a cooperative arrangement. As explained in chapter 6, questions about the appropriateness of A-IRB as a model for US regulation become more serious in the context of the G-10 countries, much less the 82 other countries that are adopting Basel II. And, regardless of the supervisory capabilities of all these countries, the difficulties in monitoring implementation of the IRB approaches will compound questions of whether the Basel II regime is in fact enhancing the safety and soundness of internationally active banks. More speculatively, there is some concern that the ongoing extensive work elaborating or refining the IRB approaches will slow progress in the Basel Committee on important matters such as the definition of tier 1 capital and the management of liquidity risks. As markets for securitized mortgages imploded during 2007, one could not help wondering whether some of the time devoted by central bankers and other bank regulators to the Basel II exercise over the last decade would not have been better spent in collective assessments of emerging risks to internationally active banks.

Nor is it likely, given the amount of discretion granted national supervisors, that Basel II will produce greater competitive equality among banks from different countries than did Basel I. Nonetheless, the development and publication of highly specific capital adequacy rules have given banks an opportunity to complain on competitive equality grounds when national supervisors consider supplementing or strengthening those rules as applied domestically. These industry critics have attempted to transform what is supposed to be a floor for regulatory capital requirements into a ceiling. Although the proposition would be difficult to establish with any certainty, the trade negotiation dynamic of the Basel process negotiations may have enhanced the effectiveness of industry lobbying grounded on these sorts of complaints—to the detriment of the policy aims of financial stability and containing moral hazard.

Recommendations

The reality is that, for all its uncertainties and flaws, the revised framework has been agreed upon. With its belated implementation by the United States, Basel II completed its three-year sojourn in limbo and will soon be the applicable capital standard for at least the largest banks in all

Basel Committee countries.[1] It is highly unlikely that the Basel Committee will abandon the A-IRB approach anytime soon. Quite apart from the substantive judgment of participating agencies that it is the best approach and needs time to be fully developed, few members of the Basel Committee will be eager to start over after a decade of painstaking work. The doggedness with which the Federal Reserve Board and some other members of the committee pursued the A-IRB approach in the face of its obvious problems suggests that this disinclination will be very strong. Indeed, the criticisms of Basel II appear to have induced a certain defensive obstinacy on the part of some, though by no means all, of the officials involved.

This, then, is the point at which to confront the predicament of outside policy analysts commenting on what they believe to be a deficient newly-minted policy. One response, of course, is to call for a substantially different policy that an analyst believes clearly preferable. For the reasons suggested in the preceding paragraph, such a call is even less likely to be heeded, at least in the near to medium term, than a similarly ambitious proposal for overhauling a long-established policy. But this response can help maintain a critical focus on the new official policy as it is implemented and perhaps in some cases contribute to changing it sooner rather than later. A second option is for the policy analyst to state misgivings about the overall policy but then suggest only incremental changes. This kind of proposal is presumably more likely to be received favorably by policymakers (though how much more favorably varies greatly), but its potential policy relevance comes at the cost of blurring what the commentator may believe to be important analytical and normative problems in the newly adopted policy.

Given the analysis of the preceding chapters, the choice in making policy recommendations in this area is not so binary. While one may wish that the Basel Committee had pursued other approaches with more vigor a decade ago, chapter 7 concluded that none of the existing options is at present a sufficiently developed regulatory model to be readily substituted for the A-IRB approach of Basel II. Even if an alternative were available, there would remain the question of whether detailed harmonization is the optimal basis for an international arrangement. Thus the recommendations that follow do not comprise a "Basel III." Neither, though, are they mere glosses on Basel II. They may be better understood as "Basel II½." With US regulators having committed as part of their interagency compromise on implementation to a review of Basel II after it has been in operation for two years, there may now be a built-in opportunity to consider these and other proposed modifications.

As the use of a fraction implies, this package is an intermediate proposal. It has three aims. First, it is intended to put the international

---

1. As of this writing, US banking agencies have not published their proposal for amending capital requirements for banks not required or not choosing to adopt the A-IRB approach. In the European Union, all banks are now subject to one of the three Basel II approaches.

arrangement on a sounder footing by compensating for some of the more glaring problems with an international arrangement founded on a harmonized A-IRB approach. Second, it creates mechanisms that could evolve into more cohesive approaches both to domestic capital regulation and to Basel Committee arrangements, including the critical task of freeing senior Basel Committee officials to focus on evolving risks to the international banking system. Third, it provides for regular and rigorous assessments of the regulatory and institutional mechanisms included within the package, both to reinforce the second aim and to provide a greater measure of regulatory transparency.

Five recommendations are made here. The first is for the Basel Committee to accelerate its work on redefining the kinds of capital that qualify as tier 1 or tier 2 types. The second and third are proposals for an international leverage ratio and subordinated debt requirement, which are based on the discussion in chapter 7. These proposals could be adopted without forsaking the IRB approaches, although they are offered because they provide a more workable basis for an international arrangement. The fourth recommendation is for eliminating the harmonized, detailed rules of the IRB approaches in favor of a set of best supervisory practices, including some form of risk-based capital regulation and a requirement that each internationally active bank of a certain size establish and maintain a validated credit risk model. The fifth and final proposal is directed at improving the monitoring processes for both supervisory oversight of banks' risk management and international peer scrutiny of this supervisory oversight in each Basel Committee country. All these measures would be desirable whether or not the specific IRB approaches of Basel II are retained, although obviously their emphasis and role would shift were the third recommendation eventually adopted.

Were all these recommendations adopted, Basel II½ would rest on four, rather than three, pillars. Pillar 1 would be significantly scaled back to include a leverage ratio requirement and a requirement for some form of risk-sensitive capital requirement. Pillar 2 would include principles applicable to risk management by systemically important banks, including a requirement for maintenance of a credit risk model, as well as supervisory oversight and expected interventions. Pillar 3 would be expanded to include a subordinated debt requirement; its disclosure requirements would also be revisited and refined. Finally, a new pillar 4 would strengthen the monitoring capacities of the Basel Committee.

Recommendation 1: Accelerate Work on Redefining Capital

The Basel Committee has long recognized the need to revisit the definitions of tier 1 and tier 2 capital. Although the committee decided not to address this topic in Basel II, it has included the definition of capital as part of its post-Basel II work program. Thus this first recommendation is endorsement of the committee's agenda, rather than a call for a change of course. However, the rather deliberate pace with which the committee has begun this review should be accelerated. The fallout from the subprime crisis has again underscored the importance of ensuring that regulatory capital truly possesses the stable buffering characteristics that should define core capital.

In addition, the crisis has—at least for a time—altered the political environment for financial reform by placing banks on the defensive, just as the Latin American debt crisis of the 1980s did. Now, as then, domestic reformers may have the upper hand if they move quickly. Similarly, nationalistic competitive considerations will be more muted for a time within the Basel Committee, as supervisors focus more on shared prudential goals in the face of the massive failure of risk management by many of the world's largest financial institutions. Once the crisis recedes, though, the domestic political economy of normal times will return, and with it an international negotiating dynamic more sensitive to national considerations.

As a substantive matter, of course, neither national nor international rules on minimum capital ratios mean much if the amount of capital designated as the numerator of those ratios is spurious. Chapter 3 recounted how some of the key substantive compromises in the Basel I negotiations involved accommodating the wishes of some countries to include in the definition of capital such questionable items as unrealized gains from stock holdings. In the intervening years, Basel Committee countries have permitted their banks to include as tier 1 capital various hybrid financial instruments that were not included in the original Basel I definition of qualifying capital.

It is also worth noting that, in contrast to the extreme detail of the A-IRB portion of Basel II, a negotiated definition of the permissible components of tier 1 and tier 2 capital can be relatively straightforward. Unlike A-IRB, the capital of a bank should be reasonably transparent, with its certified financial statements providing an opportunity for any interested party to calculate the tier 1 and tier 2 levels. While there will surely be occasions for the exercise of national supervisory discretion to determine if a financial instrument qualifies, these occasions should be infrequent enough to be reported to and, where necessary, discussed in the Basel Committee.

Recommendation 2: Adopt an International Leverage Requirement

A leverage ratio requirement should be added to pillar 1. Its principal virtue would be to set a transparent floor for bank capital levels that is difficult to manipulate. Its simplicity and relative transparency mean that compliance can be much more easily monitored than an A-IRB approach. Thus, it is a particularly useful benchmark for supervisory intervention, as under the prompt corrective action system of US law. One striking characteristic of the otherwise Babel-like quality of the debate over Basel II in the United States was the near unanimity of present and former bank regulatory officials on the importance of retaining a leverage ratio requirement as a key supervisory tool. The only exceptions were two members of the Federal Reserve Board who briefly expressed sympathy for the view propounded by some banks that this requirement would be outmoded in a post-Basel II world.[2]

Of course, the flip side of a leverage ratio's simplicity is its bluntness. It is not relevant to a bank's calculation of its economic capital requirements. By definition, it excludes risk sensitivity. And under current US practice, it does not take account of off-balance-sheet activities that can, as shown by the fate of structured investment vehicles during the subprime crisis, pose enormous credit risks in the aggregate. Standing alone, a leverage ratio of any sort—and the current US requirement in particular—is surely insufficient for a prudent domestic capital regulation regime.

Yet when compared with the complexity, arbitrariness, and uncertainty of the A-IRB approach, the virtues of the leverage ratio shine brighter, especially as an element of an international arrangement on capital regulation. Its relative transparency is even more important in the international context. Basel Committee members, market actors, and virtually anyone else can readily determine the leverage ratio simply by inspecting a bank's balance sheet. As noted previously, the importance of certified financial statements for so many corporate and regulatory purposes reduces the chances that the reported numbers will have been manipulated, with or without the acquiescence of a bank's supervisors.

By adopting an international version of a leverage ratio, the Basel Committee would establish a requirement that, while certainly imperfect, helps provide at least moderate assurance that minimum capital levels are being maintained. In this regard, it is important to recall the discussion in chapter 6, which showed how a safety and soundness rationale for international capital standards rests in part on concerns that banking agencies in other countries may be tempted, or come under external pressure, to relax regulation of their own banks. This dynamic underscores

---

2. Then-chairman Alan Greenspan's expression of sympathy was more a conceptual musing than a concrete proposal to eliminate the requirement. The suggestion by Fed Governor Susan Bies that the leverage ratio would be eliminated was more significant, both because of its context as an effort to reassure banks during efforts to implement Basel II and because she was at the time the lead on bank regulatory issues on the board. As noted earlier, she subsequently pledged allegiance to the leverage ratio under pressure from influential members of Congress.

the importance of monitoring domestic enforcement of the international standard, since the very rationale for the international standard contemplates the possibility that national regulators may deviate from it. For this reason, the Basel Committee should adopt an international leverage ratio regardless of whether it retains the IRB approaches and regardless of whether these approaches to setting capital requirements prove technically reliable. The opaqueness of the internal ratings process and of related supervisory oversight makes international monitoring of IRB enforcement a continuing problem. There will inevitably be a trade-off between the sophistication of the capital standard and its transparency. A leverage ratio provides a useful, though imperfect, anchor.

While the leverage ratio will never be more than a blunt regulatory instrument, it can be better honed than the present US version. As discussed in chapter 7, the exclusion of off-balance-sheet items from the denominator of the ratio means that this metric misses entirely a large and growing part of the credit risk assumed by internationally active banks. None of the three options for redressing this circumstance is wholly satisfactory. Use of credit conversion factors, such as those in Basel I that turn off-balance-sheet items into "asset equivalents," obviously requires information about the off-balance-sheet exposures and thus loses much of the leverage ratio's simplicity and transparency. Moreover, while the story of how banks calculated capital requirements for their potential exposures to securitized assets in off-balance-sheet entities has yet to be fully told, there is some question as to whether all such exposures were in fact covered under the Basel I credit conversion rules still in effect for US banks in 2007. Yet the option of using a sophisticated methodology to capture potential exposures more comprehensively would only reduce transparency further.

Chapter 7 explained the conceptual promise of a capital-to-revenue ratio as a supplement to a conventional leverage ratio. The subprime mortgage crisis of 2007 reveals another potential advantage of this ratio, since it would reflect activities such as the servicing of legally independent structured investment vehicles that created severe reputational problems for Citigroup and other financial institutions. Obviously, though, an idea that has not even been backtested using available data is not ready for adoption.[3] It may be that a denominator other than gross revenue (but still related to income) would be more useful. It may be that no ratio of this sort provides even a blunt but workable indicator of credit risk from all activities of banks, including off-balance-sheet exposures. Yet the work required to address and answer these issues would be several orders of magnitude less than what was required to develop the A-IRB approach. This task should be undertaken. At the same time, in order to avoid the Basel Committee's 1999 mistake of committing itself to an undeveloped methodology, it is worth

---

3. Some of the committee's work on the simpler approaches to capital requirements for operational risk may provide a useful starting point.

revisiting the use of credit conversion factors and the informational issues surrounding off-balance-sheet exposures. It may be, for example, that the simple approach of a percentage of these exposures can serve the same purposes as the leverage ratio.[4]

Based on the current state of knowledge, then, the recommendation here is twofold. First, the Basel Committee should provisionally adopt a simple leverage ratio of the sort used in US and, in somewhat different form, Canadian bank regulation. Basel Committee members should commit to take corrective action for any internationally active bank whose ratio falls below the minimum.

Second, the committee should simultaneously undertake the analytical work needed to determine the utility of the capital/revenue ratio, a simple percentage of off-balance-sheet exposures, and any other similarly transparent alternative. If it turns out that the capital/revenue approach is promising, then a second minimum ratio should be adopted. If a basic percentage of off-balance-sheet exposures seems more predictive of bank problems, then that calculation should be incorporated into a revised leverage ratio, in which case the minimum percentage of balance sheet assets might need to be adjusted downward. If no option reveals itself to be useful, then the simple leverage ratio would be retained.

Setting the actual requirement of the provisional leverage ratio raises another problem. A plausible starting point might be the 5 percent level required under US law for a bank to be considered "well capitalized." Since the internationally active banks of special interest to Basel Committee members are generally part of the diversified financial services firms that US law requires to contain only well-capitalized banks, the 5 percent requirement would simply internationalize the rule already applicable to the likes of Citigroup and Bank of America. A conceptual rejoinder to this proposal is that a standardized international capital requirement should be truly a *minimum*. This would argue for the 4 percent level for a bank to be considered "adequately capitalized" under US law.

Here, though, one confronts the fact that the leverage ratios of many large European banks appear closer to 3 percent, and sometimes even less than that. Meanwhile, at least pending the effects of the 2007 subprime meltdown, the US counterparts of these banks generally maintained leverage ratios of 6 percent or higher (see appendix table 5A.1 in chapter 5). Some of this gap may be attributable to differences in applicable accounting standards, which affect the values of the numerator, denominator, or both. It may also be the case that differences in activities contained within banks

---

4. One obvious problem is how to assure useful and reliable disclosure of the off-balance-sheet exposures, so that the transparency virtues of the leverage ratio are replicated. Another is that the nature of these exposures arguably varies more than conventional loans to borrowers of different creditworthiness, and thus the use of a single percentage for the entire universe of exposures will be substantially cruder than a leverage ratio.

affect the comparative leverage ratios.[5] It seems unlikely, though, that these factors explain the entire disparity between US and European banks. Indeed, the traditional opposition of European regulators to an international leverage ratio may be based in no small part on the expectation that US regulators would insist on the US standard.

The practicalities of the situation thus present themselves: European regulators—notwithstanding the recent support for a leverage ratio and prompt corrective action system expressed by the European Shadow Financial Regulatory Committee (2006)—will likely continue to resist an international leverage ratio, at least partly out of concern that its level would force some European banks to reduce assets or increase capital. The recent decision by the Swiss Federal Banking Commission to impose a leverage ratio requirement on large banks may, however, signal that European regulators will be more receptive to such a requirement in the aftermath of the subprime crisis.[6] Even if the Federal Reserve Board agrees with the other banking agencies that an international leverage ratio is a good idea, the US agencies may be reluctant to agree to anything less than 4 percent, or even 5 percent. Having seen the efforts of some US banks to turn what were supposedly capital floors in Basel II into ceilings, the agencies may fear that a lower international standard will set off another round of complaints about competitive disadvantage. Short of technical explanations accounting for most of the current disparity in leverage ratios across the Atlantic, both sets of regulators will need to compromise.

One possibility would be to establish the leverage ratio at 3 percent. Technically, this is the US minimum for banks that are otherwise highly rated by their supervisory agencies,[7] although in practice the agencies require the higher levels. Setting the requirement at this level should not require wholesale adjustment by European banks. The US agencies

---

5. The leverage ratio requirement is also applicable to bank holding companies in the United States, so theoretically, financial activities that must be conducted only in affiliates of commercial banks (and not in the banks themselves) are still covered. There is some ambiguity on this point, since the 1999 law that permitted affiliations of commercial banks with virtually any other kind of financial institution specified that the Federal Reserve Board should not apply banking law capital requirements to affiliates whose capital is regulated by other agencies, such as the Securities and Exchange Commission.

6. The decision of the Swiss authorities is reported in Daniel Pruzin, Swiss Regulators to Hike Capital Requirements for Biggest Banks, *BNA's Banking Report*, July 7, 2008, 30. Because UBS and Credit Suisse suffered some of the largest losses of any European banks during the subprime crisis, the views of the Swiss supervisor may not portend a more general change of heart among European regulators.

7. As a formal matter, the 3 percent level applies to banks that have the highest composite rating under the so-called CAMELS ratings (based on capital, asset quality, management, earnings, liquidity, and sensitivity to market risk).

could maintain, in turn, that the Europeans were enacting a requirement where none had existed before and that, in any case, this was the same bare minimum as technically exists under US banking regulation.[8]

Recommendation 3: Add a Subordinated Debt Requirement

For all that greater supervisory cooperation and a common leverage ratio might bring in the way of more effective supervision, the complexity and speed of transactions in large banks will continue to pose great challenges in terms of obtaining and evaluating information about the condition of banks. For the reasons detailed in chapter 7, market discipline is a natural candidate to complement supervision in these circumstances. Thus, pillar 3 should be strengthened to include a requirement for systemically significant banks to issue subordinated debt. As noted earlier, there are sufficient uncertainties about even the most nuanced subordinated debt proposals to make principal reliance on that approach ill-advised. Indeed, an alternative market disciplinary device such as reverse convertible debentures might prove superior, since it has the potential not only to signal bank infirmities but also to provide an automatic compensatory addition of equity capital when the bank's position deteriorates (Flannery 2005). However, this promising idea raises its own conceptual questions and is thoroughly untested in practice. Subordinated debt proposals have been refined over years of academic and policy debate. As an adjunct to supervision, the approach seems well worth trying.[9]

To be a useful basis for comparison among banks, there would need to be standardization of maturity, frequency of issue, and as many other terms as possible. These details would have to be negotiated, of course, although empirical and policy work has already provided some starting points for discussion. As suggested in chapter 7, requirements might include issuance on a quarterly basis so as to have outstanding subordinated debt in an amount equal to at least 2 percent of the bank's assets. There would have to be a prohibition against credit enhancements or guarantees, as well as restrictions on ownership of the debt by affiliates and other parties with an incentive to prop up a bank's capital position.

The debt requirement would apply only to banks above a certain size. One possibility is the dual threshold of $250 billion in assets or $10 billion in on-balance-sheet foreign exposures used by the US banking agencies to

---

8. The key to the success of this tactic would probably be for the agencies to enlist the support of key congressional actors beforehand, something they did not do with Basel II. With congressional support for the move established, the banks would have nobody influential left to whom to complain, even were they so inclined.

9. Depending on experience with this requirement, it may later be appropriate to use subordinated debt prices as a trigger for supervisory intervention in some circumstances.

determine the "core" banks required to adopt A-IRB. Ultimately, though, the criteria chosen should be those that capture all banks whose activities have international systemic implications. Technically, both Basel I and Basel II already apply only to "internationally active banks" (Basel Committee 2006g, paragraph 20). However, the widespread adoption of Basel I as a generally applicable bank regulation in many countries created an assumption that subsequent Basel Committee measures would apply de facto to all banks. Making the subordinated debt requirement (and the requirement of a credit risk model set forth below) applicable only to banks whose scope and activities have international systemic implications does not rest on a similar assumption—on the contrary, it would be inappropriate and impractical to require most banks to issue subordinated debt. Though there is nothing wrong with the Basel Committee attending to generally applicable banking regulation, its primary focus and activity should be with banks whose weakness or failure could disrupt the banking systems of other countries.[10]

As noted in chapter 7, the impairment of credit flows to financial institutions during the subprime crisis raises an important question about the utility of an ongoing subordinated debt requirement for major banks. In a financial crisis, investors may be unable to distinguish among the risks faced by different banks. Prices of outstanding issues of subordinated debt may similarly reflect generalized market fears, rather than assessments of the specific circumstances of an issuing bank. In this eventuality, the subordinated debt requirement will be essentially useless, at least during the pendency of the crisis. This possibility, however, does not negate the value of the subordinated debt requirement, properly understood as a supervisory adjunct. The greatest value of a subordinated debt requirement is likely to be as a source of early warnings about problem banks. Adverse responses of analysts and investors to developments at a bank should prod supervisors to look more closely and, where appropriate, take corrective action. Supervisors do not need to be told to scrutinize major banks more thoroughly during a major financial dislocation—they are almost surely already nervously monitoring those institutions on something like a real-time basis and devising potential responses if conditions worsen. In these circumstances, the "canary in a coal mine" function of subordinated debt is hardly necessary; everyone knows the atmosphere has become toxic.

---

10. It is worth noting that domestic practice in the United States creates a precedent for imposing a subordinated debt requirement only on large banks. This is one of the requirements for a bank to own a "financial subsidiary" that is permitted to engage in certain activities otherwise forbidden to banks and their subsidiaries. Only if the bank is one of the 50 largest insured banks is it required to hold qualifying subordinated debt (Title 12 of the United States Code, paragraph 24a).

To realize the potential contribution of market discipline to financial safety and soundness, the issues surrounding the pillar 3 disclosure requirements discussed in chapter 5 would need to be resolved. Without adequate disclosure, the value of market reactions to bank conditions will be severely circumscribed. As a means to refine these requirements in a manner that strikes an appropriate balance of informational benefit to markets and manageable costs for banks, the Basel Committee should establish an advisory group consisting of representatives from national securities commissions, banks, and market actors that invest in or analyze subordinated debt issues. With the advice of that group, the committee should revise the pillar 3 requirements.

This proposal has the dual purpose of immediately providing regulators with additional information on market perceptions of bank risk and of determining whether subordinated debt prices could be used as a more formal part of bank regulation. There should be three institutional measures to ensure that these purposes are fulfilled.

First, like the other elements of this Basel II½ proposal, national implementation would need to be monitored and refined by the Basel Committee in a context of a more rigorous peer process. The more general quarterly review process proposed in the fifth recommendation could include reporting on the price movements of the debt issues and discussing anomalies or shortcomings in the requirement. The committee could modify the requirements as needed.[11]

Second, the advisory committee proposed in the preceding paragraph should be retained to provide ongoing independent views on the utility of, and possible improvements to, the subordinated debt requirement.

Third, after an appropriate period of experience with the requirement, the committee should commission an evaluation by respected nongovernmental experts. This evaluation should examine whether, when, and how movements in subordinated debt prices are indicative of problems in a bank and as such warrant supervisory attention. The conclusions of the evaluation, which ought to be publicly available, would provide the starting point for an analysis by the committee of whether a subordinated debt requirement is likely to add anything useful to supervisory practice, is useful only as an additional information input for supervisors, or has promise as a more formal trigger for supervisory attention.

---

11. Of course, regulators from one country may want to inquire of their counterparts in another country as to whether a significant decline in the price of subordinated debt of a bank in the second country presents a reason for immediate supervisory attention. However, such an inquiry would presumably be made immediately, rather than waiting for scheduled Basel Committee meetings.

Recommendation 4: Substitute International Principles for Detailed Pillar 1 Requirements

There are significant questions whether an A-IRB approach is a desirable model for domestic regulation. It is simply misplaced as a basis for international regulatory convergence, and there is thus a good argument for removing the IRB rules from pillar 1. This proposal obviously runs counter to the direction of the Basel Committee in the past decade, though not to the extensive and continuing skepticism of academics, policy observers, and, to some degree, banks. Thus, this recommendation is not made in the expectation that it will receive consideration from the Basel Committee in the near term but rather to illustrate how a more manageable—and thus effective—international arrangement on capital adequacy might be structured.

In place of the IRB rules would be a simple pillar 1 requirement for *some* form of risk-based capital requirement applicable to systemically important banks and a set of pillar 2 principles addressing both bank risk-management and supervisory oversight of bank capital. As to the pillar 1 requirement, it would be up to each national regulator, subject to ongoing consultations within the Basel Committee, to decide which regulatory capital rule should apply to its banks. Despite the misgivings here about an A-IRB approach as a regulatory model, there is no reason to forbid Basel Committee countries from using some form of this approach or, indeed, a full model approach. Though there is reason to be skeptical that the A-IRB approach will ever be the optimal form of capital regulation, experience with the approach in actual operation may allow for sufficient adjustment to make it a workably reliable regulatory model. Supervisors might even become comfortable with allowing each bank to use its own credit risk model, rather than formulas devised by the supervisors themselves. On the other hand, national regulators should also be free to elect a simpler risk-based approach, including one of the variants on a standardized approach, with all its limitations. Precisely because each existing approach has so many shortcomings, it seems reasonable to allow national regulators to make their own choice within the context of general oversight by the Basel Committee.

Pillar 2 sets forth four principles of supervisory review:

1. Banks should have a process for assessing their overall capital adequacy in relation to their risk profile and a strategy for maintaining their capital levels.

2. Supervisors should review and evaluate banks' internal capital-adequacy assessments and strategies, as well as their ability to monitor and ensure their compliance with regulatory capital ratios. Supervisors should take appropriate supervisory action if they are not satisfied with the result of this process.

3. Supervisors should expect banks to operate above the minimum regulatory capital ratios and should have the ability to require banks to hold capital in excess of the minimum.

4. Supervisors should seek to intervene at an early stage to prevent capital from falling below the minimum levels required to support the risk characteristics of a particular bank and should require rapid remedial action if capital is not maintained or restored.

These principles are unobjectionable as far as they go. However, they are underdeveloped even as a complement to the detailed rules of pillar 1 and even as elaborated in the rest of pillar 2. A return to simpler, more readily verifiable rules, as suggested here, should be accompanied by considerably more specific expectations for supervisory action to oversee bank risk management in general and capital levels in particular. This recommendation is consistent with the movement away from a narrow "regulatory" approach and toward a more "supervisory" approach to banking law that has been embraced by US, UK, and other national banking agencies. That shift has rested on the premise that risks associated with the complexity and pace of large bank activities cannot be effectively contained even with sophisticated rules. Instead, the emphasis increasingly has been on fostering robust risk management systems within the banks themselves. But a necessary adjunct to this approach is an equally robust and expert supervisory process. If Basel Committee arrangements are to provide assurance that the risks posed to international financial stability by banks of all member countries are adequately contained, then more international attention to the supervisory process is essential. Thus, while some of the additional principles recommended here will be relevant only if the pillar 1 IRB rules are abandoned, many could usefully be added to pillar 2 in any event.

The proposal here to remove the IRB rules from the Basel Accord is motivated not by rejection of the premise underlying the movement toward a more supervisory approach to banking law but by skepticism that the IRB methods for capital rules are well-advised and a conviction that embedding these methods in a detailed international arrangement is misguided. Removing those rules should be accompanied by increased, not less, attention to banks' calculations of their own risk. To the current first supervisory principle in pillar 2 should be added a requirement that each bank covered by the subordinated debt requirement maintain credit and operational risk models as part of its strategy for assessing and maintaining adequate capital levels. A set of best practices on incorporating the output of these models into bank capital maintenance should be developed in consultation with banks and the outside vendors that market such models. The resulting guidelines would then be included in pillar 2.

The second supervisory principle in pillar 2 would have to be substantially augmented with best practices for validating the integrity of the models used by banks. Some of the existing pillar 1 guidance on qualifications for the IRB approaches could be imported into this expansion of pillar 2. This might be adequate for supervisors who retain an IRB method for determining regulatory capital. However, where supervisors have elected a different method—either a standardized approach or a full-model approach—the guidelines for validation will need to be broad enough to apply to any model a bank might reasonably use. This quite fundamental step away from the pillar 1 rules is intended to reconnect the Basel process with the original aim of better aligning supervisory activities with bank expertise in assessing risk sensitivity. The monitoring problems identified in chapter 5 remain; indeed, they may be compounded, insofar as each bank will use its own credit model (just as it will for business purposes as A-IRB is implemented). The next recommendation responds in part to that problem, but only in part. Although the elimination of A-IRB as a separate regulatory capital requirement would also eliminate the invitation to regulatory arbitrage that attaches to something banks regard as an artificial measure, the potential for bank mistakes and supervisory uncertainty are surely present in the Basel II½ proposal presented here, though arguably no more so than under Basel II.

Regardless of the fate of the IRB approaches as elements of the Basel II international arrangement, certain elaborations of the second, third, and fourth supervisory principles of pillar 2 are called for. For reasons discussed in chapter 6, there should be more specificity in expectations for the supervisory oversight process, including the nature and extent of bank examinations. Supervisors should be expected to receive and review on a regular basis the raw output of the credit and operational risk model of banks, along with an explanation of any discrepancies in the amount of capital actually held by the banks against particular risks and the amount that would be indicated by the model. This practice would enhance both the rigor of supervisory evaluation under the second principle and the foundation for action under the third principle, stating the expectation that banks will operate above minimum levels of capital.[12] The fourth supervisory principle—on regulatory intervention to prevent or remedy capital declines below minimum levels—should be considerably more developed. While all the specifics of the US system of prompt corrective action may not be suitable for all Basel Committee members, there must be clearer expectations concerning the timing and scope of regulatory interventions in

---

12. Where a country maintains an IRB method for setting risk-based regulatory capital requirements, there should be little or no divergence between model output and capital requirement; thus the impact of this additional requirement would be limited in these circumstances.

response to declines below the minimum levels of either the leverage ratio or applicable risk-based requirements. In addition, as experience is gained with market activity in the required issues of subordinated debt, the Basel Committee should draft guidance concerning appropriate supervisory reactions to price changes that could indicate problems in a bank.

Recommendation 5: Strengthen the Monitoring Functions of the Basel Committee

For all its working groups and meetings, the Basel Committee has shied away from monitoring or even discussing the capital positions of banks within the Basel countries. In its early years, the relative informality of the committee was one reason for its success. Even today, there are good reasons not to make capital adequacy accords binding as a matter of international law. The notion of adjudicating "violations" of such an arrangement sits uncomfortably with both the aim of promoting cooperation among national supervisors and the need for supervisors to exercise regulatory judgment in light of a bank's external as well as internal circumstances. It is probably unhelpful to think in terms of demanding "compliance" with a capital accord, because the overtly adversarial posture that could be generated by an emphasis on international legal obligations and enforcement could erode the cooperation among supervisors that is critical to all the activities of the Basel Committee.[13]

Still, the presence of nationalistic as well as cooperative incentives for national supervisory agencies argues for institutional arrangements within the committee to uphold the shared expectations reflected in its capital agreements. As suggested earlier, the most effective means of achieving this end may be to combine monitoring activities with other functions such as information sharing, analysis, problem solving, and work on new proposals. That is, the monitoring task should be embedded in peer review, rather than an adjudicatory context. The peer review function should itself be blended with cooperative endeavors. In addition to the institutional features of the subordinated debt proposal, two innovations that follow these precepts are recommended here—one modest and the other fairly far-reaching.

First, the committee should institute a quarterly review and report on capital levels of the large, internationally active banks covered by the requirements for subordinated debt and the use of internal models. The report, which could be either an appendix to the existing BIS *Quarterly*

---

13. The reluctance of US banking agencies to cast the Basel capital accords as legally binding is also connected to the potential domestic legal and constitutional issues that would be raised, since it is doubtful that the agencies have authority to bind the United States as an international legal matter.

Review or a freestanding Basel Committee publication, would have both a quantitative and qualitative section. The former would contain the leverage and risk-based capital ratios of these banks,[14] as well as information on the price movements of banks' subordinated debt described in the second recommendation. The qualitative portion would include the committee's analysis of the condition of these banks and an account of steps taken by national regulators to strengthen any bank whose capital ratios fell below the regulatory minimum or whose debt price movements gave other grounds for concern.

The requirement of a report will obviously provide information to markets, policy analysts, academics, and other interested parties. While much of this information will already have been available from other sources, its quarterly release in aggregated form will create a regular occasion for these groups to focus on the capital condition of internationally active banks. This focus may, in an admittedly modest fashion, provide some oversight of the Basel Committee and the national supervisors. More significant could be the attention paid to the information and analysis by Basel Committee members themselves as the report is prepared. National supervisors will need to explain significant changes in their banks' capital positions or subordinated debt prices to the rest of the committee. This process will allow other members to make further inquiries on the conditions of a specific bank or banks, as well as to bring to the fore trends that may require regulatory attention or adjustment. While this reporting requirement obviously cannot guarantee closer attention by the Basel Committee to the quality of minimum capital regulation in its member countries, it at least provides an opportunity for appropriate review. The prospect of scrutiny by nongovernmental parties (including ex post scrutiny if potential warning signs have been ignored) may itself prompt greater committee activism.

Second, the committee should establish an inspection unit, charged with independently assessing the capital management practices of large, internationally active banks from Basel Committee countries. One or more teams of experts would conduct on-site model validation and oversight of a limited number of these banks in any given year. The inspection unit would, within the constraints of its resources, examine banks from different countries each year. Initially, at least, the experts in the inspection unit would be drawn from the bank regulatory agencies in the Basel Committee countries, detailed for a sufficiently long period that they could function as part of a team of examiners. The inspection unit teams would indirectly monitor how national agencies were performing in model supervision. The experience would also provide members of the team the opportunity to profit from what other national supervisors had learned in their own model validation and examination efforts and, hopefully, build

---

14. The risk-based capital ratios would not, of course, be directly comparable, since under the foregoing set of recommendations each country would select its own measure.

trust and a true "common language" among the relevant experts from different countries.

Regardless of whether an IRB or other common risk-based capital approach is required, these banks will maintain complex risk management systems, including the use of credit risk models. If the IRB approaches of Basel II are retained, assessment of a bank's internal ratings system and associated capital calculation is obviously central to the success of the regulatory approach. If the IRB approaches are dropped from the international arrangement, some countries may nonetheless retain them. Banks in countries that do not would still be required, as stated in the third recommendation, to maintain appropriate models as an integral part of their risk management systems. If there is no national or international capital requirement, supervisors would still be able to use a bank's credit risk model and the larger risk management system of which it is a part, in evaluating whether a bank's capital levels are adequate for its risk profile.

As emphasized earlier, the opaqueness of both the operation of the bank credit risk models and their supervision by national regulators are key contributors to the monitoring difficulties associated with Basel II. The proposal for review and reporting of bank capital positions does not ameliorate these problems. Although the Accord Implementation Group and its various subgroups will create at least some indirect opportunities for peer review of certain aspects of IRB implementation, there is nothing in existing Basel Committee plans that will extend peer oversight into the bank-specific supervisory process. This kind of supervision will be just as important in a non-IRB regime. An inspection unit would assume this role and, thereby, mitigate one of the greatest obstacles to effective monitoring of supervisory oversight of sophisticated bank risk management systems.

As a practical matter, the unit would likely be able to review only a modest fraction of even the largest banks in any given year. But this level of activity should be sufficient to give the Basel Committee as a whole an indication of how each member country's banking agencies are administering the IRB approach or, in the absence of a common risk-based capital requirement, how they are supervising the risk management systems of large banks. Following each of its examinations, the inspection unit should have a debriefing process with the relevant national supervisor. There would be no direct legal or regulatory consequences of these examinations. However, where the inspection unit uncovered significant problems that national supervisors had failed to correct or of which they were unaware, there would be opportunity for discussion and, as appropriate, remedial action by the national supervisor. The results of each year's reviews should be discussed within the Basel Committee as a whole and an edited description of the inspection unit's annual activities published by the committee as part of one of the quarterly reports proposed earlier.

An obvious hurdle to this recommendation is the concern of banks and national supervisors with the proprietary information—both risk management and customer-based—available to supervisors validating a credit risk model. In this context, the concern probably would not extend to the greatest worry of a bank regulator—that a hint of a problem in a bank becomes a self-fulfilling prophecy as counterparties rush to exit relationships with the troubled bank. This worry is expressed by supervisors as an explanation for why they may not immediately tell other national supervisors that one of their banks has encountered a problem. The model validation and examination process would only by chance coincide with an incident of vulnerability for a specific bank.

As to broader confidentiality concerns, these are real but need not be insuperable. Regulators in other areas—including competition and securities—have found ways to share information about internationally active firms during investigations, while maintaining appropriate levels of confidentiality about proprietary information. There seems no reason why similar arrangements could not be developed in the banking area. Indeed, the greater problem may be that the officials on detail—knowing the performance of their home agencies is subject to scrutiny and their individual actions may affect their careers once they return to their permanent jobs—will pull their punches in evaluating supervisory performance.

There is an argument for gradually converting the inspection unit from a group of detailees to a permanently staffed entity that employs its own experts. Over time these experts might be recruited directly from sources other than bank supervisory agencies. The resulting autonomy and continuity of the staff would help guard against the problems anticipated in the preceding paragraphs, while not resulting in any transfer of direct regulatory authority from those national agencies. Even short of this more permanent status, the inspection unit could be expanded to involve experts from, and examination of bank models in, non-Basel Committee countries.

Implications Beyond Capital Regulation

Because the work of the Basel Committee is the exemplary case of a form of international economic arrangement that has been variously described as "soft law," a government regulatory network, or international regulatory convergence, the question arises whether it contains lessons for other economic areas inevitably arise. The Basel Committee has been exemplary both in its range of cooperative activities, which include coordinating supervision of internationally active banks as well as harmonizing capital requirements, and in the degree to which agreement within the committee has been incorporated into national regulatory practice. In its idealized form, such an arrangement is a system of structured international activities carried out by national government officials with domestic regulatory responsibility, intended to make national laws and regulations more congruent and to facilitate coordinated enforcement of similar national laws. The arrangement is not binding as a matter of international law—unlike trade agreements, for example. Accordingly, there is no formal dispute settlement mechanism. The informality and flexibility are consistent with the underlying assumption that the participating officials have a shared, ongoing interest in the effective regulation of private actors involved in international economic activity.

The ongoing cooperation of banking officials in the Basel Committee, including the Basel II effort, and the remarkable influence of Basel I outside the G-10 countries suggested that a new mode of international economic governance was emerging, in which national regulation would be efficaciously coordinated internationally. Enthusiasm for this new approach arose partly from its promise as a means of managing a global financial system in a world of nation states. Inevitably, there has arisen the question whether the Basel Committee should prefigure a broader set of arrangements for supervisory cooperation and substantive convergence among national financial regulators. As dramatically shown by the financial problems unleashed by the collapse of the US subprime housing market, there are close links not only between commercial banks around the world but also between banks and other financial market actors. Yet other international arrangements among financial supervisors—such as those under the auspices of the International Organization of Securities Commissions and the International Association of Insurance Supervisors—have to date been considerably less robust than those of the Basel Committee.

Going even farther afield from banking regulation, some have wondered whether the Basel Committee arrangements provide a viable alternative to trade agreements for dealing with commercial arenas in which divergent domestic regulation creates impediments to trade in goods or services. Trade agreements usually address such circumstances by creating international obligations that limit the permissible scope of national regulation directed against foreign interests, either in the form of national treatment provisions or as more general procedural and substantive regulatory requirements. These alternative approaches in trade agreements each pose significant difficulties. National treatment obligations are notoriously difficult to apply to many forms of domestic regulation; treatment of a foreign firm that appears discriminatory is often justified by reference to the peculiarities of that firm's product or conduct. Imposition by trade agreements of binding obligations to observe specified procedural or substantive requirements can, particularly in the context of dispute settlement, embody a deregulatory bias that elicits negative political reaction. The question is whether regulatory convergence could eliminate most discriminatory or costly differential treatment of foreign firms without undermining the foundational aims of the regulatory area.

Of course, there has long been both skepticism and enthusiasm about the Basel Committee's efforts. Some have disparaged these efforts as nothing more than a bureaucratic effort at self-protection in the face of regulatory competition (Macey 2003). Others, beginning from a different ideological orientation, have offered an interestingly complementary critique of the Basel Committee as a triumph of technocrats over democratically accountable legislatures (Alston 1997). Experience with the Basel II process to date suggests that, whatever one's views of the desirability of nonformalized modes of coordinating national regulation, the potential of highly developed harmonization efforts may be more limited than both enthusiasts and critics have expected, though perhaps for different reasons.

In fact, the best answer to questions about the lessons of Basel II for other areas—financial and nonfinancial—is that they are limited. One cannot, of course, reasonably infer general principles about the utility of a given form of international arrangements from a single case, no matter how interesting and important. The analytical emphasis in this book on the interaction between the particulars of a substantive regulatory approach and the institutional capacities of a specific arrangement underscores the perils of applying these conclusions elsewhere. Furthermore, the history of the Basel Committee itself reveals the importance of specifics in determining the appropriateness of the regulatory convergence approach. While some of these specifics are fairly durable—such as the complexity or ease of monitoring compliance with the harmonized arrangement—others are highly contingent, such as the political domestic political environments prevailing at the time the arrangement is negotiated.

Although specifics are ultimately determinative, some elements of the Basel II experience do suggest certain considerations relevant to the promise of regulatory convergence arrangements in international financial regulation and, more broadly, other international economic spheres.

First, the importance of building the international arrangement on an efficacious regulatory model is, for all its obviousness, difficult to overstate. Unless the model provides at least a workably sound basis for domestic regulation, the international arrangement is unlikely to be a net benefit for participating countries. The conclusion here that Basel II is misguided is closely connected to the conclusion that the A-IRB approach is problematic as a domestic regulatory model. In the case of Basel II, one can argue that the officials who drove the process made some basic mistakes in fixing on an approach to capital regulation that was completely untested. However, costs associated with a suboptimal regulatory model will usually be incurred in an international negotiation for a harmonized arrangement, even where the basic model is a sound one for all participating countries. The negotiation will yield a regulatory approach different from that which would have been generated in a purely domestic process, as countries accommodate one another's preferences in order to reach agreement. In most instances, as in Basel II, the effect will be a domestic regulatory regime inferior to one that would emerge from a solely domestic process. Thus, to be a worthwhile policy initiative, this "optimality gap" between the internationally harmonized rules and domestically generated rules must be offset by other benefits, such as those discussed in chapter 6. The greater the optimality gap, the greater must be these other benefits.[15]

Arrangements with highly detailed negotiated rules are almost sure to enlarge the optimality gap. In some instances, the gap will increase because the greater the detail in the rules, the greater the chance that some of these detailed rules will be unsuitable for the domestic regulatory environments of one or more participating countries. For industries such as financial services, in which innovation and changing practices require regulatory suppleness, the detail in the international arrangement may slow proper supervisory responses because the international renegotiation of these details may be difficult to complete expeditiously.

Second, the Basel II experience suggests that the success of international regulatory convergence efforts depends on successfully matching a regulatory model to institutional capacities and incentives. This is among the most important ways in which the specifics of an arrangement determine its efficacy. The A-IRB approach of Basel II presents substantial difficulties not only for domestic regulators supervising banks but for other Basel Committee members monitoring the quality of oversight by each national supervisor. Even a model that is a sound basis for domestic regulation in participating countries may not align well with an international arrangement's institutional features. Accordingly, there may be situations in which no regulatory model is both sensible policy in participating countries and compatible with an effective international arrangement.

The recommendations presented earlier in this chapter illustrate the two strategies for achieving greater compatibility between the substantive and institutional elements of a regulatory convergence arrangement. Either the substantive points of harmonization can be adjusted to better fit the capacities of an international arrangement or the institutional features of the arrangement can be adjusted so as to augment its capacities and change the prevailing incentive structure. As with the Basel II recommendations, these strategies may be combined to produce a more effective international arrangement. Indeed, the Basel II experience raises the possibility that too ambitious an effort at harmonizing rules might undermine some of the salutary effects of the Basel Committee's other activities. A somewhat counterintuitive implication of these observations

---

15. It is possible that, in a particular case, an international process could yield a pattern of regulation that serves the public interest of some, or even all, participating countries better than would a domestically generated regulatory model. This could happen if, for example, the international configuration of negotiating parties reduced the influence of a domestic interest group that was able to capture the national regulatory process. Similarly, an international arrangement might exercise oversight of national regulators that is valuable but underprovided within the nation's domestic system. However, such instances are likely to be considerably fewer than those in which there is an optimality gap.

is that simpler international rules will sometimes, maybe frequently, be more valuable than a comprehensive scheme in achieving specified regulatory ends, even where the activities regulated are themselves complex.

A corollary to this point is more far-reaching, though even more speculative. While an assessment of Basel II should engender a measure of skepticism toward ambitious efforts at detailed international regulatory harmonization, it may simultaneously recommend bolder institutional initiatives. Such boldness need not and, in many cases, should not lead to even the limited supranational functions contained in the foregoing recommendations for modifying Basel II. But to the degree that financial (or other) markets are significantly and progressively globalized, it seems unlikely that conventional international arrangements will be effective. There appear to be significant constraints on the use of international arrangements to provide a global regulatory framework for financial activities, and perhaps other transnational economic activities as well. In addition to the problems associated with detailed negotiated common rules, an arrangement composed of multiple national regulators may pose chronic incentive and efficiency problems. Effective and efficient regulation of global economic activities may require development of appropriate *supra* national governance mechanisms to help monitor implementation of the rules and standards agreed upon internationally and, eventually, to play a direct (if limited) role in supervision of private economic activity.

Third, the history of Basel I and Basel II counsels a good deal of attention to the political economy prevailing in an issue area for which a regulatory convergence arrangement is contemplated.[16] While it is axiomatic that the outcome of any process involving governments will be shaped by politics, the relevant politics may vary substantially depending on factors such as the timing and scope of the initiative. This observation applies both to the prevailing political economy within each participating nation and, at the international level, to interactions between government officials and private interests. That is, even within a particular issue area, there is likely not a fixed set of political dynamics shaping the initiative and thus its outcome. The greater the potential fluidity of these forces in an issue area, the more consequential will be the choices of those who launch such an initiative.

It is true that retrospective criticism often overlooks the contemporaneous uncertainties and nuances that confronted policymakers. However, even an examination of Basel II more sympathetic to policymakers suggests that the initiative was launched with less of a plan—both substantive and political—than would have been advisable. Though a simplification of the Basel I and II histories, one point of contrast between the two

---

16. It may be more precise to say political "economies," since the relevant political dynamic may differ significantly from country to country. However, as in the case of Basel II, during any negotiation there will usually be exogenous forces that have parallel effects, even where there are differences in the relevant politics of participating countries.

negotiations is illustrative of the importance of the prevailing political dynamic to the outcome of an exercise in international regulatory convergence: The initiation of Basel I when most banks were on the defensive in the aftermath of the Latin American debt crisis led to a regime that required higher regulatory capital floors, whereas the tortured development of the A-IRB approach of Basel II during a period of high bank profits and self-confidence led to a regime that promised significantly lower regulatory capital requirements. One suspects that Basel II would have looked very different had the subprime mortgage crisis occurred during, rather than after, the negotiations.

With respect to initiatives in other areas, one lesson may be that in international negotiations as in much of life, timing is very important. At the very least, officials contemplating an international initiative to compensate for perceived inadequacies in the regulation of financial activity would be wise to consider, in light of the Basel II experience, how they can navigate the political seas so as to maximize chances of achieving the aims that motivate them to seek an international arrangement.

These tentative inferences from the Basel II experience lend some support to commentators such as Leebron (1996) who have been skeptical of international proposals for detailed harmonization of domestic regulation in all but unusual cases. The history of Basel II bolsters the common criticisms of such initiatives as too likely to be maladapted to conditions in each country and too difficult to modify in response to changing external circumstances. The Basel II experience also suggests that the effort required to complete and sustain a complex harmonized arrangement may come with high opportunity costs, as other more productive modes of international cooperation remain comparatively undeveloped. Yet none of the foregoing is meant to suggest that informal cooperative mechanisms among national regulators, or even more fully elaborated modes of regulatory convergence, are presumptively misguided. On the contrary, where a regulatory sphere includes significant transnational activity, the effectiveness and efficiency of national regulation may increasingly depend on bilateral, multilateral, or even supranational cooperation. Basel II reveals the potential hazards as well as benefits of one approach to such arrangements. But its ultimate lesson is that something different must be tried, not that sustained and structured cooperative efforts should be abandoned.

References

Acharya, Viral V. 2003. Is the International Convergence of Capital Adequacy Regulation Desirable? *Journal of Finance* 58, no. 6: 2745–781.

Aite Consulting Group. 2007. Basel II or Basel Who: Risk Management Initiatives in the U.S. Boston, MA: Aite Consulting Group.

Acharya, Sankarshan, and Jean-François Dreyfus. 1989. Optimal Bank Reorganization Policies and the Pricing of Federal Deposit Insurance. *Journal of Finance* 44, no. 5: 1313–33.

Alexander, Gordon J., and Alexandre M. Baptista. 2006. Does the Basle Capital Accord Reduce Bank Fragility? An Assessment of the Value-at-Risk Approach. *Journal of Monetary Economics* 53, no. 7: 1631–660.

Allen, Franklin, and Douglas Gale. 2003. Capital Adequacy Regulation: In Search of a Rationale. In *Economics in an Imperfect World: Essays in Honor of Joseph E. Stiglitz*, eds. Richard Arnott, Bruce Greenwald, Ravi Kanbur, and Barry Nalebuff. Cambridge, MA and London: MIT Press.

Allen, Linda, and Anthony Saunders. 2003. *A Survey of Cyclical Effects in Credit Risk Measurement Models.* BIS Working Paper 126. Basel: Bank for International Settlements.

Allen, Linda, and Anthony Saunders. 2004. Incorporating Systemic Influences into Risk Measurement: A Survey of the Literature. *Journal of Financial Services Research* 26, no. 2: 161–92.

Allen, Linda, Gayle DeLong, and Anthony Saunders. 2004. Issues in the Credit Risk Modeling of Retail Markets. *Journal of Banking & Finance* 20, no. 4: 727–52.

Alston, Philip. 1997. The Myopia of the Handmaidens: International Lawyers and Globalization. *European Journal of International Law* 8, no. 2: 435.

Altman, Edward I., and Gabriele Sabato. 2005. Effects of the New Basel Capital Accord on Bank Capital Requirements for SMEs. *Journal of Financial Services Research* 28, no. 1–3: 15–42.

Amato, Jeffrey D., and Craig H. Furfine. 2003. *Are Credit Ratings Procyclical?* BIS Working Paper 129. Basel: Bank for International Settlements.

Ambrose, Brent W., Michael Lacour-Little, and Anthony B. Sanders. 2005. Does Regulatory Capital Arbitrage, Reputation, or Asymmetric Information Drive Securitization? *Journal of Financial Services Research* 28, no. 1–3: 113–33.

Ashcraft, Adam. 2001. Do Tougher Bank Capital Requirements Matter? New Evidence From the Eighties. Federal Reserve Bank of New York. Photocopy.

Ashcraft, Adam. 2008. Does the Market Discipline Banks? New Evidence from Regulatory Capital Mix. *Journal of Financial Intermediation* (forthcoming).

Aspinwall, Richard C. 1983. On the "Specialness" of Banking. *Issues in Bank Regulation 7*, no. 2: 16.

Ayadi, Rym, and Kristin Ross. 2003. The Changing Regulatory Capital Regime in Europe: A Challenging New Business Concept. Summary of a Conference Hosted by the Centre for European Policy Studies, PriceWaterhouseCoopers, and the Federation of European Securities Exchanges, Brussels, November 12–13.

Bank for International Settlements. 1989. *Annual Report*. Basel.

Barajas, Adolfo, Ralph Chami, and Thomas Cosimano. 2005. *Did the Basel Accord Cause Credit Slowdown in Latin America?* IMF Working Paper 05/38. Washington: International Monetary Fund.

Bardos, Jeffrey. 1987. The Risk-Based Capital Agreement: A Further Step towards Policy Convergence. *Federal Reserve Bank of New York Quarterly Review,* 12 no. 4: 26–34.

Barr, Michael S., and Geoffrey P. Miller. 2006. Global Administrative Law: The View from Basel. *European Journal of International Law* 17, no. 1: 15–46.

Barrios, Victor E., and Juan M. Blanco. 2003. The Effectiveness of Bank Capital Adequacy Regulation: A Theoretical and Empirical Approach. *Journal of Banking & Finance* 27, no. 10: 1935–58.

Barth, James R, Gerard Caprio, Jr., and Ross Levine. 2006. *Rethinking Bank Regulation.* Cambridge, MA: Cambridge University Press.

Barth, James R., Gerard Caprio, Jr., and Daniel E. Nolle. 2004. *Comparative International Characteristics of Banking.* Office of the Comptroller of the Currency Economic and Policy Analysis Working Paper 2004-1 (January). Washington: US Office of the Comptroller of the Currency.

Basak, Suleyman, and Alex Shapiro. 2001. Value-at-Risk Based Risk Management: Optimal Policies and Asset Prices. *Review of Financial Studies* 14 (Summer): 371–405.

Basel Committee on Banking Supervision. 1988. *International Convergence of Capital Measurement and Capital Standards.* Basel: Bank for International Settlements.

Basel Committee on Banking Supervision. 1990a. *Report on International Developments in Banking Supervision.* Basel: Bank for International Settlements.

Basel Committee on Banking Supervision. 1990b. *Information Flows Between Banking Supervisory Authorities.* Basel: Bank for International Settlements.

Basel Committee on Banking Supervision. 1991. *Amendment of the Basle Capital Accord in Respect of the Inclusion of General Provisions/General Loan-Loss Reserves in Capital.* Basel: Bank for International Settlements.

Basel Committee on Banking Supervision. 1992a. *Report on International Developments in Banking Supervision.* Basel: Bank for International Settlements.

Basel Committee on Banking Supervision. 1992b. *Minimum Standards for the Supervision of International Banking Groups and their Cross-Border Establishments.* Basel: Bank for International Settlements.

Basel Committee on Banking Supervision. 1993. *The Supervisory Treatment of Market Risks.* Basel: Bank for International Settlements.

Basel Committee on Banking Supervision. 1994a. *Amendment to the 1988 Capital Accord: Recognition of Collateral.* Basel: Bank for International Settlements.

Basel Committee on Banking Supervision. 1994b. *Amendment to the Capital Accord of July 1988.* Basel: Bank for International Settlements.

Basel Committee on Banking Supervision. 1994c. *Basel Capital Accord: The Treatment of the Credit Risk Associated with Certain Off-Balance-Sheet Items.* Basel: Bank for International Settlements.

Basel Committee on Banking Supervision. 1994d. *Report on International Developments in Banking Supervision.* Basel: Bank for International Settlements.

Basel Committee on Banking Supervision. 1995a. *Basel Capital Accord: Treatment of Potential Exposure for Off-Balance-Sheet Items*. Basel: Bank for International Settlements.

Basel Committee on Banking Supervision. 1995b. *Planned Supplement to the Capital Accord to Incorporate Market Risks*. Basel: Bank for International Settlements.

Basel Committee on Banking Supervision. 1996. *Amendment to the Capital Accord to Incorporate Market Risks*. Basel: Bank for International Settlements.

Basel Committee on Banking Supervision. 1998. *Amendment to the Basel Capital Accord of July 1988*. Basel: Bank for International Settlements.

Basel Committee on Banking Supervision. 1999a. *Credit Risk Modelling: Current Practices and Applications*. Basel: Bank for International Settlements.

Basel Committee on Banking Supervision. 1999b. *A New Capital Adequacy Framework*. Consultative Paper Issued by the Basel Committee on Banking Supervision. Basel: Bank for International Settlements.

Basel Committee on Banking Supervision. 2001a. *Overview of the New Basel Capital Accord*. Consultative Document. Basel: Bank for International Settlements.

Basel Committee on Banking Supervision. 2001b. *The New Basel Capital Accord*. Basel: Bank for International Settlements.

Basel Committee on Banking Supervision. 2001c. Results of the Second Quantitative Impact Study. Basel: Bank for International Settlements.

Basel Committee on Banking Supervision. 2001d. *Potential Modifications to the Committee's Proposals*. Basel: Bank for International Settlements.

Basel Committee on Banking Supervision. 2001e. *The New Basel Capital Accord*. Explanatory Note (January). Basel: Bank for International Settlements.

Basel Committee on Banking Supervision. 2002a. Overview Paper for the Impact Study. Basel: Bank for International Settlements.

Basel Committee on Banking Supervision. 2002b. *Quantitative Impact Study 3: Technical Guidance*. Basel: Bank for International Settlements.

Basel Committee on Banking Supervision. 2003a. *The New Basel Capital Accord*. Consultative Document. Basel: Bank for International Settlements.

Basel Committee on Banking Supervision. 2003b. Supplementary Information on QIS-3. Basel: Bank for International Settlements.

Basel Committee on Banking Supervision. 2003c. Quantitative Impact Study 3—Overview of Global Results. Basel: Bank for International Settlements.

Basel Committee on Banking Supervision. 2003d. *High-Level Principles for the Cross-Border Implementation of the New Accord*. Basel: Bank for International Settlements.

Basel Committee on Banking Supervision. 2003e. *Markets for Bank Subordinated Debt and Equity in Basel Committee Member Countries*. Basel Committee on Banking Supervision Working Paper 12 (August). Basel: Bank for International Settlements.

Basel Committee on Banking Supervision. 2004a. *Modifications to the Capital Treatment for Expected and Unexpected Credit Losses in the New Basel Accord*. Basel: Bank for International Settlements.

Basel Committee on Banking Supervision. 2004b. *Changes to the Securitisation Framework*. Basel: Bank for International Settlements.

Basel Committee on Banking Supervision. 2004c. *International Convergence of Capital Measurement and Capital Standards: A Revised Framework*. Basel: Bank for International Settlements.

Basel Committee on Banking Supervision. 2004d. *Implementation of Basel II: Practical Considerations*. Basel: Bank for International Settlements.

Basel Committee on Banking Supervision. 2005a. *Update on Work of the Accord Implementation Group Related to Validation Under the Basel II Framework*. Newsletter no. 4. Basel: Bank for International Settlements.

Basel Committee on Banking Supervision. 2005b. Guidance on Paragraph 468 of the Framework Document. Basel: Bank for International Settlements.

Basel Committee on Banking Supervision. 2005c. *Validation of Low-Default Portfolios in the Basel II Framework*. Newsletter no. 6. Basel: Bank for International Settlements.

Basel Committee on Banking Supervision. 2005d. *The Treatment of Expected Losses by Banks Using the AMA Under the Basel II Framework*. Newsletter no. 7. Basel: Bank for International Settlements.

Basel Committee on Banking Supervision. 2005e. *The Application of Basel II to Trading Activities and the Treatment of Double Default Effects*. Basel: Bank for International Settlements.

Basel Committee on Banking Supervision. 2006a. *Use of Vendor Products in the Basel II IRB Framework*. Newsletter no. 8. Basel: Bank for International Settlements.

Basel Committee on Banking Supervision. 2006b. *Home-Host Information Sharing for Effective Basel II Implementation*. Basel: Bank for International Settlements.

Basel Committee on Banking Supervision. 2006c. *Report for the G-7 Summit on the Activities of the Basel Committee*. Basel: Bank for International Settlements.

Basel Committee on Banking Supervision. 2006d. Results of the Fifth Quantitative Impact Study (QIS-5). Basel: Bank for International Settlements.

Basel Committee on Banking Supervision. 2006e. *Studies on Credit Risk Concentration*. Basel Committee on Banking Supervision Working Paper 15. Basel: Bank for International Settlements.

Basel Committee on Banking Supervision. 2006f. *The IRB Use Test: Background and Implementation*. Newsletter no. 9. Basel: Bank for International Settlements.

Basel Committee on Banking Supervision. 2006g. *International Convergence of Capital Measurement and Capital Standards: A Revised Framework Comprehensive Version*. Basel: Bank for International Settlements.

Basel Committee on Banking Supervision. 2007a. *History of the Basel Committee and Its Membership*. Basel: Bank for International Settlements.

Basel Committee on Banking Supervision. 2007b. *Progress on Basel II Implementation, New Workstreams and Outreach*. Newsletter no. 11. Basel: Bank for International Settlements.

Basel Committee on Banking Supervision. 2008a. *Liquidity Risk: Management and Supervisory Challenges*. Basel: Bank for International Settlements.

Basel Committee on Banking Supervision. 2008b. *Principles for Sound Liquidity Risk Management and Supervision*. Basel: Bank for International Settlements.

Basel Committee on Banking Supervision Joint Forum. 2001. *Risk Management Practices and Regulatory Capital: Cross-Sectoral Comparison*. Basel: Bank for International Settlements.

Benford, James, and Erlend Nier. 2007. *Monitoring Cyclicality of Basel II Capital Requirements*. Bank of England Financial Stability Paper no. 3. London: Bank of England.

Benink, Harald, and Clas Wihlborg. 2002. The New Basel Capital Accord: Making It Effective with Stronger Market Discipline. *European Financial Management* 8, no. 1: 103–15.

Benston, George J., and George G. Kaufman. 1995. Is the Banking and Payments System Fragile? *Journal of Financial Services Research* 9, no. 3–4: 209–40.

Berger, Allen N. 2006. Potential Competitive Effects of Basel II on Banks in SME Credit Markets in the United States. *Journal of Financial Services Research* 29, no.1: 5–36.

Berger, Allen N., Sally M. Davies, and Mark J. Flannery. 2000. Comparing Market and Supervisory Assessments of Bank Performance: Who Knows What When? *Journal of Money, Credit, and Banking* 32, no. 3: 641–70.

Berger, Allen N., Richard J. Herring, and Giorgio P. Szego. 1995. The Role of Capital in Financial Institutions. *Journal of Banking & Finance* 19, no. 3–4: 393–430.

Bernanke, Ben S. 1983. Nonmonetary Effects of the Financial Crisis in the Propagation of the Great Depression. *American Economic Review* 73, no. 3: 257–76.

Bielicki, Piotr, and Grzegorz Bednarski. 2006. Home and Host Supervisors' Relations from a Host Supervisor's Perspective. In *Cross-Border Banking: Regulatory Challenges*, eds. Gerard Caprio, Jr., Douglas D. Evanoff, and George G. Kaufman. Singapore: World Scientific.

Bliss, Robert R. 2001. Market Discipline and Subordinated Debt: A Review of Some Salient Issues. *Economic Perspectives* (Federal Reserve Bank of Chicago) 25, no. 1: 24–45.

Bliss, Robert R., and Mark J. Flannery. 2002. Market Discipline in the Governance of US Bank Holding Companies: Monitoring vs. Influencing. *European Finance Review* 6, no. 2: 361–95.

Blum, J. 1999. Do Capital Adequacy Requirements Reduce Risks in Banking? *Journal of Banking & Finance* 23, no. 5: 755–71.

Board of Governors of the Federal Reserve System. 1982. *Federal Reserve Bulletin* 68 (January): 33–34.

Board of Governors of the Federal Reserve System. 1983. *Bank Capital Trends and Financing.* Staff Study no. 122. Washington.

Board of Governors of the Federal Reserve System. 1986. Proposed Rulemaking, Banking Holding Companies and Change in Bank Control; Capital Maintenance; Supplemental Adjusted Capital Measure. *Federal Register* 51 (January 31): 3976–83.

Board of Governors of the Federal Reserve System. 1987. Proposed Rule, Capital Maintenance; Revision to Capital Adequacy Guidelines. *Federal Register* 52 (February 19): 5119–39.

Board of Governors of the Federal Reserve System. 1995. Proposed Rule, Capital Requirements for Market Risk. *Federal Register* 60 (July 25): 38142–44.

Board of Governors of the Federal Reserve System, Division of Banking Supervision and Regulation. 1999. Assessing Capital Adequacy in Relation to Risk at Large Banking Organizations and Others with Complex Risk Profiles. Staff Report 99-18 (July 1). Washington.

Board of Governors of the Federal Reserve System and the US Department of the Treasury. 2000. The Feasibility and Desirability of Mandatory Subordinated Debt. Report submitted to the Congress, December. Washington.

Bookstaber, Richard. 2007. *A Demon of Our Own Design: Markets, Hedge Funds, and the Perils of Financial Innovation.* Hoboken, NJ: John Wiley & Sons.

Borio, Claudio. 2008. *The Financial Turmoil of 2007-?: A Preliminary Assessment and Some Policy Considerations.* BIS Working Paper 251. Basel: Bank for International Settlements.

Breuer, Peter. 2002. Measuring Off-Balance-Sheet Leverage. *Journal of Banking & Finance* 26, no. 2–3: 223–42.

Buerkle, Tom. 2003. Basel Under Threat. *Institutional Investor* 32 (July).

Calem, Paul S., and James R. Follain. 2005. An Examination of How the Proposed Bifurcated Implementation of Basel II in the US May Affect Competition among Banking Organizations for Residential Mortgages. Photocopy (January 14).

Calem, Paul, and Rafael Rob. 1999. The Impact of Capital-Based Regulation on Bank Risk-Taking. *Journal of Financial Intermediation* 8, no. 4: 317–52.

Calomiris, Charles W. 1997. *The Postmodern Banking Safety Net: Lessons from Developed and Developing Countries.* Washington: American Enterprise Institute.

Calomiris, Charles, and Joseph Mason. 2004. How to Restructure Failed Banking Systems: Lessons from the U.S. in the 1930s and Japan in the 1990s. In *Privatization, Corporate Governance and Transition Economies in East Asia,* eds. Takatoshi Ito and Anne Krueger. Chicago: University of Chicago Press, 375–420.

Cargill, Thomas F., Michael M. Hutchison, and Takatoshi Ito. 1997. *The Political Economy of Japanese Monetary Policy.* Cambridge, MA: MIT Press.

Chan, Yuk-Shee, Stuart I. Greenbaum, and Anjan V. Thakor. 1992. Is Fairly Priced Deposit Insurance Possible? *Journal of Finance* 47, no. 1: 227–45.

Committee on Banking Regulation and Supervisory Practices. 1975. *Report to the Governors on the Supervision of Banks' Foreign Establishments.* Basel: Bank for International Settlements.

Committee on Banking Regulation and Supervisory Practices. 1981. *Report on International Developments in Banking Supervision, 1980.* Basel: Bank for International Settlements.

Committee on Banking Regulation and Supervisory Practices. 1982. *Report on International Developments in Banking Supervision, 1981.* Basel: Bank for International Settlements.

Committee on Banking Regulation and Supervisory Practices. 1983a. *Report on International Developments in Banking Supervision, 1982.* Basel: Bank for International Settlements.

Committee on Banking Regulation and Supervisory Practices. 1983b. *Principles for the Supervision of Banks' Foreign Establishments.* Basel: Bank for International Settlements.

Committee on Banking Regulation and Supervisory Practices. 1984. *Report on International Developments in Banking Supervision, 1983.* Basel: Bank for International Settlements.

Committee on Banking Regulation and Supervisory Practices. 1987a. *Proposals for International Convergence of Capital Measurement and Capital Standards.* Consultative Paper. Basel: Bank for International Settlements.

Committee on Banking Regulation and Supervisory Practices. 1987b. *Report on International Developments in Banking Supervision, 1986.* Basel: Bank for International Settlements.

Committee on Banking Regulation and Supervisory Practices. 1988. *Outcome of the Consultative Process on Proposals for International Convergence of Capital Measurement and Capital Standards.* Basel: Bank for International Settlements.

Committee on the Global Financial System. 2005. *Stress Testing at Major Financial Institutions: Survey Results and Practice.* Basel: Bank for International Settlements.

Considine, Jill. 1998. Pilot Exercise—Pre-Commitment Approach to Market Risk. *Federal Reserve Bank of New York Economic Policy Review* 4, No. 3: 131–36.

Cooper, K., and R.D. Fraser. 1988. The Rising Cost of Bank Failures: A Proposed Solution. *Journal of Retail Banking* 10 (Fall): 5–12.

Covitz, Daniel M., and Paul Harrison. 2004. Do Banks Time Bond Issuance to Trigger Disclosure, Due Diligence, and Investor Scrutiny? *Journal of Financial Intermediation* 13, no. 3: 299–323.

Covitz, Daniel M., Diana Hancock, and Myron L. Kwast. 2004. *Market Discipline in Banking Reconsidered: The Roles of Funding Manager Decisions and Deposit Insurance Reforms.* Federal Reserve Board Finance and Economics Discussion Series Paper 2004-53. Washington: Federal Reserve Board.

Cowan, Adrian, and Charles Cowan. 2004. Default Correlation: An Empirical Investigation of a Subprime Lender. *Journal of Banking & Finance* 28, no. 4: 753–71.

Crouhy, Michel, Dan Galai, and Robert Mark. 2005. The Use of Internal Models: Comparison of the New Basel Credit Proposals with Available Internal Models for Credit Risk. In *Capital Adequacy Beyond Basel: Banking, Securities, and Insurance,* ed. Hal S. Scott. Oxford, UK and New York: Oxford University Press.

Cull, Robert, Lemma Senbet, and Marco Sorge. 2004. *Deposit Insurance and Bank Intermediation in the Long Run.* BIS Working Paper 156. Basel: Bank for International Settlements.

Dale, Richard. 1984. *The Regulation of International Banking.* Cambridge, UK: Woodhead-Faulkner.

Daníelsson, Jón. 2003. On the Feasibility of Risk Based Regulation. *CESifo Economic Studies* 49, no. 2: 157–79.

Daníelsson, Jón, Hyun Song Shin, and Jean-Pierre Zigrand. 2004. The Impact of Risk Regulation on Price Dynamics. *Journal of Banking & Finance* 28, no. 5: 1069–87.

Daníelsson, Jón, Paul Embrechts, Charles Goodhart, Con Keating, Felix Muenniche, Olivier Renault, and Hyun Song Shin. 2001. *An Academic Response to Basel II.* London School of Economics Financial Markets Group Special Paper No. 130. London: London School of Economics.

de Carmoy, Hervé. 1990. *Global Banking Strategy: Financial Markets and Industrial Decay.* Cambridge, MA, and Oxford, UK: Basil Blackwell.

de Swaan, Tom. 1998. Capital Regulation: The Road Ahead. *FRBNY Economic Policy Review* 4, no. 3: 231–35.

DeFerrari, Lisa, and David E. Palmer. 2001. Supervision of Large Complex Banking Organizations. *Federal Reserve Bulletin* (February): 47–57.

Dell'Ariccia, Giovanni, and Robert Marquez. 2006. Competition Among Regulators and Credit Market Integration. *Journal of Financial Economics* 79, no. 2: 401–30.

Demirgüç-Kunt, Ash, Enrica Detragiache, and Thierry Tressel. 2006. *Banking on the Principles: Compliance with Basel Core Principles and Bank Soundness.* World Bank Policy Research Working Paper 3954. Washington: World Bank.

Dietsch, Michel, and Jöel Petey. 2004. Should SME Exposures Be Treated as Retail or Corporate Exposures? A Comparative Analysis of Default Probabilities and Asset Correlations in French and German SMEs. *Journal of Banking & Finance* 28, no. 4: 773–88.

Drage, John, and Fiona Mann. 1999. Improving the Stability of the International Financial System. *Financial Stability Review* (Bank of England) 8 (June): 40–77.

Estrella, Arturo. 1995. A Prolegomenon to Future Capital Requirements. 1995. *Federal Reserve Bank of New York Economic Policy Review* 1, no. 2: 1–12.

Estrella, Arturo. 2001. Regulatory Capital and the Supervision of Financial Institutions: Some Basic Distinctions and Policy Choices. In *Challenges for Central Banking*, eds. Anthony M. Santomero, Staffan Viotti, and Andres Vreddin. Boston: Kluwer Academic Publishers.

Estrella, Arturo. 2004. The Cyclical Behavior of Optimal Bank Capital. *Journal of Banking & Finance*, 28, no. 6: 1469–98.

Estrella, Arturo, Sangkyun Park, and Stavros Peristiani. 2000. Capital Ratios as Predictors of Bank Failure. *Federal Reserve Bank of New York Economic Policy Review* 6, no. 2: 33–52.

European Shadow Financial Regulatory Committee. 2006. *Basel II and the Scope for Prompt Corrective Action in Europe.* Statement no. 25 (November 20).

Evanoff, Douglas D. 1993. Preferred Sources of Market Discipline. *Yale Journal on Regulation* 10, no. 2: 347–67.

Evanoff, Douglas D., and Larry D. Wall. 2001. Sub-Debt Yield Spreads as Bank Risk Measures. *Journal of Financial Services Research* 20, no. 2/3: 121–45.

Evanoff, Douglas D., and Larry D. Wall. 2002. Measures of Riskiness of Banking Organizations: Subordinated Debt Yields, Risk-Based Capital, and Examination Ratings. *Journal of Banking & Finance* 26, no. 5: 989–1009.

Evanoff, Douglas D., Julapa A. Jagtiani, and Taisuke Nakata. 2007. *The Potential Role of Subordinated Debt Programs in Enhancing Market Discipline in Banking.* Federal Reserve Bank of Kansas City Research Working Paper 07-07.

FDIC (Federal Deposit Insurance Corporation). 1981. Statement of Policy on Capital Adequacy. *Federal Register* 46 (December 28): 62693–94.

FDIC (Federal Deposit Insurance Corporation). 1997. *History of the 1980s—Lessons for the Future. Volume I: An Examination of the Banking Crises of the 1980s and Early 1990s.* Washington: Federal Deposit Insurance Corporation.

FDIC (Federal Deposit Insurance Corporation). 2003. *Estimating the Capital Impact of Basel II in the United States.* Staff Study (December 8). Available at www.fdic.gov (accessed July 16, 2008).

Federal Reserve System, Study Group on Subordinated Notes and Debentures. 1999. *Using Subordinated Debt as an Instrument of Market Discipline.* Staff Study 172 (December). Washington: Federal Reserve Board.

Financial Stability Forum. 2008. *Report of the Financial Stability Forum on Enhancing Market and Institutional Resilience* (April 12). Basel: Financial Stability Forum.

Financial Stability Institute. 2006. *Implementation of the New Capital Adequacy Framework in Non-Basel Committee Member Countries.* Occasional Paper no. 6. Basel: Financial Stability Institute.

FitchRatings. 2004. *Demystifying Basel II: A Closer Look at the IRB Measures and Disclosure Framework* (August 25). Available at http://images.to.camcom.it/f/tofinanza/I_/I_08.pdf.

FitchRatings. 2008. *Basel II Correlation Values: An Empirical Analysis of EL, UL, and the IRB Model* (May 19). Available at www.fitchresearch.com.

Flannery, Mark J. 2005. No Pain, No Gain? Effecting Market Discipline via Reverse Convertible Debentures. In *Capital Adequacy Beyond Basel: Banking, Securities, and Insurance*, ed. Hal S. Scott. Oxford, UK and New York: Oxford University Press.

Flannery, Mark J. 2006. *Likely Effects of Basel II Capital Standards on Competition within the 1–4 Family Residential Mortgage Industry.* Mortgage Bankers Association White Paper. Washington: Mortgage Bankers Association.

Flannery, Mark J., and Stanislava Nikolova. 2004. Market Discipline of US Financial Firms: Recent Evidence and Research Issues. In *Market Discipline Across Countries and Industries*, eds. William C. Hunter, George G. Kaufman, Claudio Borio, and Kostas Tsatsaronis. Cambridge, MA: MIT Press.

Freixas, X., and Rochet, J.C. 1995. Fair Pricing of Deposit Insurance. Is It Possible? Yes. Is it Desirable? No. University of Pompeu Fabra, Barcelona. Photocopy.

Fukao, Mitsuhiro. 2003. *Financial Strains and the Zero Lower Bound: The Japanese Experience.* BIS Working Paper 141. Basel: Bank for International Settlements.

Furfine, Craig. 1999. Bank Portfolio Allocation: The Impact of Capital Requirements, Regulatory Monitoring, and Economic Conditions. *Journal of Financial Services Research* 20, no. 1: 33–56.

Goodhart, Charles, Boris Hofmann, and Miguel Segoviano. 2004. Bank Regulation and Macroeconomic Fluctuations. *Oxford Review of Economic Policy* 20, no. 4: 591–615.

Gordy, Michael, and Bradley Howells. 2006. Procyclicality in Basel II: Can We Treat the Disease Without Killing the Patient? *Journal of Financial Intermediation* 15, no. 3: 395–417.

Greenspan, Alan. 1998. The Role of Capital in Optimal Banking Supervision and Regulation. *Federal Reserve Bank of New York Economic Policy Review* 4, no. 3 (October): 163–68.

Hancock, Diane, and Myron L. Kwast. 2001. Using Subordinated Debt to Monitor Bank Holding Companies: Is It Feasible? *Journal of Financial Services Research* 20, no. 2/3: 147–87.

Hancock, Diane, Andreas Lehnert, Wayne Passmore, and Shane M. Sherlund. 2005. *An Analysis of the Potential Competitive Impacts of Basel II Capital Standards on US Mortgage Rates and Mortgage Securitization.* Federal Reserve Board Paper. Washington: Federal Reserve Board.

Hannon, Timothy H., and Steven J. Pilloff. 2004. *Will the Proposed Application of Basel II in the United States Encourage Increased Bank Merger Activity? Evidence from Past Merger Activity.* Federal Reserve Board Finance And Economics Discussion Series Paper no. 2004-13. Washington: Federal Reserve Board.

Hempel, George H. 1976. *Bank Capital.* Boston: Bankers Publishing Company.

Hendricks, Darryll. 2004. Commentary on Rebalancing the Three Pillars of Basel II. *Federal Reserve Bank of New York Economic Policy Review* 10, no. 2 (September): 23–26.

Herring, Richard. 2005. Implementing Basel II: Is the Game Worth the Candle? *Financial Markets, Institutions & Instruments* 14, no. 5: 267–87.

Herring, Richard, and Til Schuermann. 2005. Capital Regulation for Position Risk in Banks, Securities Firms, and Insurance Companies. In *Capital Adequacy Beyond Basel: Banking, Securities, and Insurance,* ed. Hal S. Scott. New York and Oxford, UK: Oxford University Press.

Heyward, Peter. 1992. Prospects for International Cooperation by Bank Supervisors. *International Lawyer* 24, no. 3: 787–801.

Himino, Ryozo. 2004. Basel II—Towards a New Common Language. *BIS Quarterly Review* (September): 41–49.

Hohl, Stefan, Patrick McGuire, and Eli Remolona. 2006. Cross-Border Banking in Asia: Basel II and Other Prudential Issues. In *Cross-Border Banking: Regulatory Challenges,* eds. Gerard Caprio, Jr., Douglas D. Evanoff, and George G. Kaufman. Singapore: World Scientific.

Holloway, Niegel. 1987. A Hidden Asset: Japanese Banks Win Victory Over Capital-Adequacy Proposals. *Far Eastern Economic Review* 138, no. 52. 62–64.

Hoshi, Takeo, and Anil K Kashyap. 2004. *Solutions to the Japanese Banking Crisis: What Might Work and What Definitely Will Fail.* Hi-Stat Discussion Paper Series d04-35. Institute of Economic Research, Hitotsubashi University.

IBCA Banking Analysis, Ltd. 1994. *Real Banking Profitability.* London: ICBA Banking Analysis, Ltd.

IMF (International Monetary Fund). 1989. *International Capital Markets.* Washington.

IMF (International Monetary Fund). 1999. *International Capital Markets.* Washington.

IMF (International Monetary Fund). 2003. *Germany: Financial System Stability Assessment.* IMF Country Report no. 03/343. Washington.

Institute of International Finance. 1998. *Report of the Working Group on Capital Adequacy: Recommendations for Revising the Regulatory Capital Rules for Credit Risk.* Washington: Institute of International Finance.

Institute of International Finance. 1999. *Report of the Working Group on Capital Adequacy: Response to Credit Risk Modeling: Current Practices and Applications*, a Consultative Paper Issued by the Basel Committee on Banking Supervision. Washington.

Institute of International Finance. 2003. *IIF Response to the Third Consultative Paper of the Basel Committee on Banking Supervision*. Washington.

Ito, Takatoshi, and Yuri Nagataki Sasaki. 2002. Impacts of the Basle Capital Standard on Japanese Banks' Behavior. *Journal of the Japanese and International Economies* 16, no. 3: 372–397.

International Swaps and Derivatives Association. 1998. *Credit Risk and Regulatory Capital*. New York.

Jackson, Patricia. 2006. Basel II Home Host Issues. In *Cross-Border Banking: Regulatory Challenges*, eds. Gerard Caprio, Jr., Douglas D. Evanoff, and George G. Kaufman. Singapore: World Scientific.

Jackson, Patricia, and William Perraudin. 2000. Regulatory Implications of Credit Risk Modelling. *Journal of Banking & Finance* 24, no. 1: 1–14.

Jackson, Patricia, Pamela Nickell, and William Perraudin. 1999. Credit Risk Modelling. *Financial Stability Review* (Bank of England), Issue 6: 94–121.

Jackson, Patricia, William Perraudin, and Victoria Saporta. 2002. Regulatory and "Economic" Solvency Standards for Internationally Active Banks. *Journal of Banking & Finance* 26, no. 5: 953–76.

Jackson, Patricia, Craig Furfine, Hans Groeneveld, Diana Hancock, David Jones, William Perraudin, Lawrence Radecki, and Masao Yoneyama. 1999. *Capital Requirements and Bank Behaviour: The Impact of the Basle Accord*. Basel Committee on Banking Supervision Working Paper no. 1 (April). Basel: Bank for International Settlements.

Jagtiani, Julapa, Anthony Saunders, and Gregory Udell. 1995. The Effect of Bank Capital Requirements on Bank Off-Balance-Sheet Financial Innovation. *Journal of Banking & Finance* 19, no. 3/4: 647–58.

Jeitschko, Thomas D., and Shin Dong Jeung. 2005. Incentives for Risk-Taking in Banking—A Unified Approach. *Journal of Banking & Finance* 29, no. 3: 759–77.

Jiménez, Gabriel, and Jesús Saurina. 2006. Credit Cycles, Credit Risk, and Prudential Regulation. *International Journal of Central Banking* 2, no. 2: 65–98.

Joint Forum on Financial Conglomerates. 1999. Capital Adequacy Principles. In *Supervision of Financial Conglomerates*, documents jointly released by the Basel Committee on Banking Supervision, the International Organization of Securities Commissions and the International Association of Insurance Supervisors (February). Basel: Joint Forum on Financial Conglomerates.

Jones, David. 2000. Emerging Problems with the Basel Capital Accord: Regulatory Capital Arbitrage and Related Issues. *Journal of Banking & Finance* 24, no. 1–2: 35–58.

Kahn, Charles M., and João A. C. Santos. 2005. Allocating Bank Regulatory Powers: Lender of Last Resort, Deposit Insurance and Supervision. *European Economic Review* 49, no. 8: 2107–36.

Kahn, Charles M., and João A. C. Santos. 2006. Who Should Act as a Lender of Last Resort? An Incomplete Contracts Model: A Comment. *Journal of Money, Credit, and Banking* 38, no. 4: 1111–18.

Kaltofin, Daniel, Stephan Paul, and Stefan Stein. 2006. *Retail Loans & Basel II: Using Portfolio Segmentation to Reduce Capital Requirements*. ECRI Research Report no. 8. Brussels: European Credit Research Institute.

Kane, Edward J. 1991. Incentive Conflict in the International Regulatory Agreement on Risk-Based Capital. In *Pacific Basin Capital Markets Research*, eds. R. P. Chang and S. Ghon Rhee, volume II. Amsterdam: Elsevier, 3–21.

Kane, Edward J., Haluk Unal, and Asli Demirguc-Kunt. 1991. Capital Positions of Japanese Banks. In *Pacific Basin Capital Markets Research*, volume II, eds. R. P. Chang and S. Ghon Rhee. Amsterdam: Elsevier, 125–41.

Kapstein, Ethan. 1994. *Governing the Global Economy: International Finance and the State.* Cambridge, MA: Harvard University Press.

Kapstein, Ethan. 2006. *Architects of Stability? International Cooperation Among Financial Supervisors.* BIS Working Paper 199. Basel: Bank for International Settlements.

Kashyap, Anil K., and Jeremy Stein. 2004. Cyclical Implications of Basel II Capital Standards. *Economic Perspectives* (Federal Reserve Bank of Chicago), First Quarter: 18–31.

Kim, Daesik, and Anthony M. Santomero. 1988. Risk in Banking and Capital Regulation. *Journal of Finance* 43, no. 5: 1219–33.

Kleff, Volker, and Martin Weber. 2005. *How Do Banks Determine Capital? Evidence from Germany.* ZEW Working Paper. Available at http://medici.bwl.uni-mannheim.de (accessed July 16, 2008).

Kobayahsi, Shuji. 1998. Designing Incentive-Compatible Regulation in Banking: The Role of Penalty in the Precommitment Approach. *Federal Reserve Bank of New York Economic Policy Review* 4, no. 3 (October): 145–53.

Krainer, John, and Jose A. Lopez. 2003. How Might Financial Market Information Be Used for Supervisory Purposes? In *Federal Reserve Bank of San Francisco 2003 Economic Review.* Available at www.frbsf.org (accessed May 20, 2008).

Krishnan, C.N.V., P.H. Ritchken, and J.B. Thomson. 2005. Monitoring and Controlling Bank Risk: Does Risky Debt Help? *Journal of Finance* 60, no. 1: 343–78.

Kupiec, Paul. 2002. *Internal Models, Subordinated Debt, and Regulatory Capital Requirements for Bank Credit Risk.* IMF Working Paper 02-157. Washington: International Monetary Fund.

Kupiec, Paul. 2006. *Basel II: A Case for Recalibration.* FDIC Center for Financial Research Working Paper 2006-13. Washington: Federal Deposit Insurance Corporation.

Kupiec, Paul H., and James M. O'Brien. 1995. *A Pre-Commitment Approach to Capital Requirements for Market Risk.* Board of Governors of the Federal Reserve System Finance and Economics Working Paper no. 95-36. Washington: Federal Reserve Board.

Kupiec, Paul H., and James M. O'Brien. 1997. *The Pre-Commitment Approach: Using Incentives to Set Market Risk Capital Requirements.* Board of Governors of the Federal Reserve System Finance and Economics Working Paper no. 97-14. Washington: Federal Reserve Board.

Laeven, Luc. 2002. *Pricing of Deposit Insurance.* World Bank Working Paper no. 2871. Washington: World Bank.

Lang, William W., and Douglas D. Robertson. 2002. Analysis of Proposals for a Minimum Subordinated Debt Requirement. *Journal of Economics and Business* 54, no. 1: 115–36.

Lang, William W., Loretta J. Mester, and Todd Vermilyea. 2007. *Competitive Effects of Basel II on US Bank Credit Card Lending.* Working Paper no. 07-9. Federal Reserve Bank of Philadelphia.

Leebron, David W. 1996. Lying Down with Procrustes: An Analysis of Harmonization Claims. In *Fair Trade and Harmonization,* volume 1, eds. Jagdish Bhagwati and Robert E. Hudec. Cambridge, MA: MIT Press.

Levonian, Mark. 2001. *Subordinated Debt and the Quality of Market Discipline in Banking.* Federal Reserve Bank of San Francisco. Available at www.bis.org (accessed May 20, 2008).

Litan, Robert, and Jonathan Rauch. 1997. *American Finance for the 21st Century.* Washington: Brookings Institution Press.

Lopez, J.A., and Saidenberg, M. 2000. Evaluating Credit Risk Models. *Journal of Banking & Finance* 24, no. 1-2, 151–65.

Lucas, André, Pieter Klaassen, Peter Spreij, and Stefan Straetmans. 2002. Extreme Tails for Linear Portfolio Credit Risk Models. In *Risk Management and Systemic Risk: Proceedings of the Third Joint Central Bank Research Conference.* Basel: Bank for International Settlements.

Macey, Jonathan R. 2003. Regulatory Globalization as a Response to Regulatory Competition. *Emory Law Journal* 52, no. 3: 1353–79.

Majnoni, Giovanni, and Andrew Powell. 2006. Basel II and Home versus Host Regulation. In *Cross-Border Banking: Regulatory Challenges*, eds. Gerard Caprio, Jr., Douglas D. Evanoff, and George G. Kaufman. Singapore: World Scientific.

Martin, Pamela. 2003. Preparing for Basel II Implementation. *RMA Journal* 85, no. 6: 52–53.

Milne, Alistair. 2002. Bank Capital Regulation as an Incentive Mechanism: Implications for Portfolio Choice. *Journal of Banking & Finance* 26, no. 1: 1–13.

Milne, Alistair, and A. Elizabeth Whalley. 2001. *Bank Capital Regulation and Incentives for Risk-Taking*. Working Paper. London: City University Business School.

Mingo, John J. 2000. Policy Implications of the Federal Reserve Study of Credit Risk Models at Major US Banking Institutions. *Journal of Banking & Finance* 24, no. 1-2: 15–33.

Mishkin, Frederic S. 2006. How Big a Problem Is Too Big to Fail? *Journal of Economic Literature* 44, no. 4: 988–1004.

Montgomery, Heather. 2005. The Effect of the Basel Accord on Bank Portfolios in Japan. *Journal of the Japanese and International Economies* 19, no. 1: 24–36.

Morgan, Donald P. 2002. Rating Banks: Risk and Uncertainty in an Opaque Industry. *American Economic Review* 92, no. 4: 874–88.

Morgan, Donald P., and Kevin J. Stiroh. 1999. *Bond Market Discipline of Banks: Is the Market Tough Enough?* Federal Reserve Bank of New York Staff Study no. 95.

Morris, S., and Hyun Song Shin. 1999. Risk Management with Interdependent Choice. *Oxford Review of Economic Policy* (Autumn): 52–62.

Nakaso, Hiroshi. 2001. *The Financial Crisis in Japan During the 1990s: How the Bank of Japan Responded and the Lessons Learnt*. BIS Working Paper no. 6. Basel: Bank for International Settlements.

Nier, Erlend, and Ursel Baumann. 2006. Market Discipline, Disclosure and Moral Hazard in Banking. *Journal of Financial Intermediation* 15, no. 3: 332–61.

Nolle, Daniel E. 2003. Bank Supervision in the US and the G-10: Implications for Basel II. *The RMA Journal* 85, no. 9: 38–42.

Norton, Joseph Jude. 1995. *Devising International Bank Supervisory Standards*. Dordrecht, Netherlands: Martinus Nijhoff.

Orgler, Yair E., and Benjamin Wolkowitz. 1976. *Bank Capital*. New York: Van Nostrand Reinhold Company.

Pecchioli, R.M. 1987. *Prudential Supervision in Banking*. Paris: Organization for Economic Cooperation and Development.

Peek, Joe, and Eric S. Rosengren. 1995. The Capital Crunch: Neither a Borrower Nor a Lender Be. *Journal of Money, Credit and Banking* 27, no. 3: 625–38.

Peek, Joe, and Eric S. Rosengren. 1997. The International Transmission of Financial Shocks: The Case of Japan. *American Economic Review* 87, no. 3: 495–505.

Peek, Joe, and Eric S. Rosengren. 2000. Collateral Damage: Effects of the Japanese Bank Crisis on Real Activity in the United States. *American Economic Review* 90, no. 1: 30–45.

Peek, Joe, and Eric S. Rosengren. 2005. Unnatural Selection: Perverse Incentives and the Misallocation of Credit in Japan. *American Economic Review* 95, no. 4: 1144–66.

Pennacchi, George G. 2005. Risk-Based Capital Standards, Deposit Insurance, and Procyclicality. *Journal of Financial Intermediation* 14, no. 4: 432–65.

Persaud, Avinash. 2008. Banking on the Right Path. *Finance & Development* 45, no. 2: 34–35.

Peura, Samu, and Esa Jokivuolle. 2004. Simulation Based Stress Tests of Banks' Regulatory Capital Adequacy. *Journal of Banking & Finance*. Forthcoming.

Peura, Samu, and Jussi Keppo. 2006. Optimal Bank Capital with Costly Recapitalization. *Journal of Business* 79, no. 4: 2163–201.

Powell, Andrew. 2004. *Basel II and Developing Countries: Sailing Through the Sea of Standards*. World Bank Policy Research Working Paper 3387. Washington: World Bank.

PriceWaterhouseCoopers. 2005. *The Capital Requirements Directive: Non-Capital Compliance Costs*. Published as Annex 3 to Financial Services Authority, Consultative Paper 06-3, Strengthening Capital Standards 2. London: Financial Services Authority.

Putnam, Robert. 1988. Diplomacy and Domestic Politics: The Logic of Two-Level Games. *International Organization* 42, no. 3: 427–60.

Raiv, Alon. 2004. Bank Stability and Market Discipline: Debt-for-Equity Swap Versus Subordinated Notes. Photocopy.

Rebonato, Riccoardo. 2007. *Plight of the Fortune Tellers: Why We Need to Manage Financial Risk Differently.* Princeton: Princeton University Press.

Reinicke, Wolfgang H. 1995. *Banking, Politics and Global Finance: American Commercial Banks and Regulatory Change, 1980–1990.* Washington: Brookings Institution.

Richardson, Jeremy, and Michael Stephenson. 2000. *Some Aspects of Regulatory Capital.* Occasional Paper Series no. 7. London: Financial Services Authority.

Rochet, Jean-Charles. 2004. Rebalancing the Three Pillars of Basel II. *Economic Policy Review* 10, no. 2: 7–21.

Saidenberg, Marc, and Til Schuermann. 2004. The New Basel Capital Accord and Questions for Research. In *The New Basel Capital Accord,* ed. Benton E. Gup. Mason, OH: South-Western.

Santomero, Anthony M., and Ronald D. Watson. 1977. Determining an Optimal Capital Standard for the Banking Industry. *Journal of Finance* 32, no. 4: 1267–82.

Santos, João A. C. 2001. Bank Capital Regulation in Contemporary Banking Theory: A Review of the Literature. *Financial Markets, Institutions and Instruments* 10, no. 2: 41–84.

Santos, João A. C. 2006. Comments on Jackson, Bielicki and Bednarski, and Majnoni and Powell. In *Cross-Border Banking: Regulatory Challenges,* eds. Gerard Caprio, Jr., Douglas D. Evanoff, and George G. Kaufman. Singapore: World Scientific.

Saurina, Jésus. 2008. Banking on the Right Path. *Finance & Development* 45, no. 2: 32–33.

Schuermann, Til. 2004. Why Were Banks Better Off in the 2001 Recession? *Federal Reserve Bank of New York Current Issues in Economics and Finance* 10, no. 1: 1–7.

Scott, Hal S., ed. 2005. *Capital Adequacy Beyond Basel: Banking, Securities, and Insurance.* Oxford, UK and New York: Oxford University Press.

Scott, Hal S. 2006. An Overview of International Finance Law and Regulation. In *Handbook of International Economic Law,* eds. Andrew T. Guzman and Alan O. Sykes. Cheltenham, UK: Edward Elgar.

Scott, Hal S., and Shinsaku Iwahara. 1994. *In Search of a Level Playing Field: The Implementation of the Basel Accord in Japan and the United States.* Occasional Paper no. 46. Washington: Group of Thirty.

Shimizu, Yoshinori. 2000. Convoy Regulation, Bank Management, and the Financial Crisis in Japan. In *Japan's Financial Crisis and Its Parallels to U.S. Experience,* eds. Ryoichi Mikitani and Adam Posen. Washington: Institute for International Economics, 57–99.

Singer, David Andrew. 2004. Capital Rules: The Domestic Politics of International Regulatory Harmonization. *International Organization* 58, no. 3: 531–56.

Sironi, Andrea. 2002. Strengthening Banks' Market Discipline and Leveling the Playing Field: Are the Two Compatible? *Journal of Banking & Finance* 26, no. 5: 1065–91.

Sironi, Andrea. 2003. Testing for Market Discipline in the European Banking Industry: Evidence from Subordinated Debt Issues. *Journal of Money, Credit, and Banking* 35, no. 3: 443–72.

Spero, Joan E. 1980. *The Failure of the Franklin National Bank: Challenge to the International Banking System.* New York: Columbia University Press.

Standard & Poor's. 2003. *Basel Committee on Banking Supervision Third Consultation Paper: Standard & Poor's Response.* Available at www.bis.org (accessed on May 15, 2008).

Standard & Poor's RatingsDirect. 2007. *Greater Basel II Pillar 3 Disclosure Would Enhance Transparency and Comparability in the Global Banking Sector* (July 11).

Stern, Gary H., and Ron J. Feldman. 2004. *Too Big to Fail: The Hazards of Bank Bailouts.* Washington: Brookings Institution Press.

Taylor, Charles. 2002. *A New General Approach to Capital Adequacy: A Simple and Comprehensive Alternative to Basel 2.* London: Center for the Study of Financial Innovation.

Thomas, Hugh, and Zhiqiang Wang. 2005. Interpreting the Internal Ratings-Based Capital Requirements in Basel II. *Journal of Banking Regulation* 6, no. 3: 274–89.

Treacy, William F., and Mark S. Carey. 1998. Credit Risk Rating at Large US Banks. *Federal Reserve Bulletin* (November): 898–921.

UK Financial Services Authority. 2004. *Procyclicality of Capital Requirements Under Basel II: Aide Memoire*. Available at www.fsa.gov.uk.

UK Financial Services Authority. 2006. *Strengthening Capital Standards 2*. Consultative Paper 06/3 (February). London.

US Department of the Treasury. 1991. *Modernizing the Financial System: Recommendations for Safer, More Competitive Banks*. Washington.

US Department of the Treasury. 2008. *The Department of the Treasury Blueprint for a Modernized Financial Regulatory Structure*. Washington.

US Department of the Treasury Office of the Comptroller of the Currency. 1985. Final Rule, Minimum Capital Ratios; Issuance of Directives. *Federal Register* 50 (March 14): 10207–219.

US Department of the Treasury Office of the Comptroller of the Currency, Federal Reserve System, Federal Deposit Insurance Corporation, US Department of the Treasury Office of Thrift Supervision. 2000. Simplified Capital Framework for Non-Complex Institutions, Advance Notice of Proposed Rulemaking. *Federal Register* 65, no. 214 (November 3): 66193–97.

US Department of the Treasury Office of the Comptroller of the Currency, Federal Reserve System, Federal Deposit Insurance Corporation, US Department of the Treasury Office of Thrift Supervision. 2003. Risk-Based Capital Guidelines; Implementation of New Basel Accord, Advance Notice or Proposed Rulemaking. *Federal Register* 68, no. 149 (August 4): 45900–48.

US Department of the Treasury Office of the Comptroller of the Currency, Board of Governors of the Federal Reserve System, Federal Deposit Insurance Corporation, US Department of the Treasury Office of Thrift Supervision. 2006a. Risk-Based Capital Standards; Advanced Capital Adequacy Framework, Proposed Rule and Notices. *Federal Register* 71, no. 185 (September 25): 55830–958.

US Department of the Treasury Office of the Comptroller of the Currency, Board of Governors of the Federal Reserve System, Federal Deposit Insurance Corporation, US Department of the Treasury Office of Thrift Supervision. 2006b. Risk-Based Capital Guidelines; Capital Adequacy Guidelines; Capital Maintenance: Domestic Capital Modifications. *Federal Register* 71, no. 247 (December 26): 77446–518.

US Department of the Treasury Office of the Comptroller of the Currency, Board of Governors of the Federal Reserve System, Federal Deposit Insurance Corporation, US Department of the Treasury Office of Thrift Supervision. 2006c. *Summary Findings of the Fourth Quantitative Impact Study*. Washington.

US Department of the Treasury Office of the Comptroller of the Currency, Federal Reserve System, Federal Deposit Insurance Corporation, US Department of the Treasury Office of Thrift Supervision. 2007. Risk-Based Capital Standards; Advanced Capital Adequacy Framework—Basel II, Final Rule. *Federal Register* 72, no. 235 (December 7): 69288–445.

US General Accounting Office. 1988. *International Finance: Market Access Concerns of US Financial Institutions in Japan*. GAO Report NSIAD-88-108BR. Washington.

US General Accounting Office. 1994. *International Banking: Strengthening the Framework for Supervising International Banks*. GAO Report CGD-94-8. Washington.

US General Accounting Office. 1996. *Bank and Thrift Regulation: Implementation of FDICIA's Prompt Regulatory Action Provisions*. GAO Report GGD-97-18. Washington.

US Senate, Committee on Banking, Housing, and Urban Affairs. 1987. Senate Report 100–19, Competitive Equality Banking Act of 1987. Washington.

US Shadow Financial Regulatory Committee. 2000. *Reforming Bank Capital Regulation*. Washington: American Enterprise Institute.

US Shadow Financial Regulatory Committee. 2001. *The Basel Committee's Revised Capital Accord Proposal.* Statement no. 169 (February 26).

Van den Heuvel, Skander. 2002. Banking Conditions and the Effects of Monetary Policy: Evidence from US States. Photocopy.

Wagster, John D. 1996. Impact of the 1988 Basle Accord on International Banks. *Journal of Finance* 51, no. 4: 1321–46.

Wagster, John D. 1999. The Basle Accord of 1988 and the International Credit Crunch of 1989–1992. *Journal of Financial Services Research* 15, no. 2: 123–43.

Wall, Larry D., and Pamela P. Peterson. 1996. Banks' Responses to Binding Regulatory Capital Requirements. *Economic Review* (Federal Reserve Bank of Atlanta) (March/April): 1–17.

Wellons, Philip A. 2005. Enforcement of Risk-Based Capital Rules. In *Capital Adequacy Beyond Basel: Banking, Securities, and Insurance,* ed. Hal S. Scott. Oxford, UK and New York: Oxford University Press.

White, Lawrence J. 1994. On the Harmonization of Bank Regulation. *Oxford Review of Economic Policy* 10, no. 4: 626–42.

Wilmarth, Arthur. 2002. The Transformation of the US Financial Services Industry, 1975–2000. *University of Illinois Law Review*, no. 2: 215–476.

Wilson, Ian. 2004. Implementing Basel II: A Case Study Based on the Barclays Basel II Preparations. *Journal of Financial Regulation and Compliance* 12, no. 4: 297–305.

Zimmer, Steven A., and Robert N. McCauley. 1991. Bank Cost of Capital and International Competition. *Quarterly Review of the Federal Reserve Bank of New York* 15, no. 3/4: 33–59.

Index

ABN Amro, 99
Accord Implementation Group (AIG), 3*b*, 206, 219–22, 254, 278
accounting policy, international variation in, 211–12
advanced internal ratings–based approach (A-IRB), 9, 28
  advantages of, 10, 150–66, 225
  basis of, 107
  versus capital redefinition, 265
  centrality of, 16, 198
  commitment to, 263
  common language and, 172–75
  competitive equality and, 127, 182–89
  consultative paper proposals for, 105, 117
  costs of, 167*n*, 167–68, 222, 222*n*
  domestic regulation and, 139–93
  elimination of, 273–76
  impact on capital levels, 103, 160–66
  implementation of, 166–77
  incentive for banks to adopt, 160
  as international approach, 10–11, 140, 201, 218–19
  versus leverage ratio requirement, 229, 266
  mandatory requirements for, 128–29, 204
  versus mandatory subordinated debt, 232, 243–44, 245
  modifications of, 203
  monitoring difficulties, 168–69, 204–206, 213–14, 262, 275, 278
  multinational banks and, 216
  national differences inherent in, 212, 219, 219*n*
  negative effects of, 10, 177–89, 225, 261–62
  versus precommitment approach, 248–49
  procyclical impact of, 178–82
  qualification for, 108, 128–29, 155–57, 275
  reliability of, 152–59
  risk management improvement and, 175–77, 243
  risk sensitivity and, 150–66
advanced measurement approach (AMA), 163
AIG (Accord Implementation Group), 3*b*, 206, 219–22, 254, 278
alternative regulatory models, 11, 225–58
American Bankers Association, 90
Asia, Basel II implementation in, 208, 208*n*
Asian financial crisis
  Basel I and, 80, 80*n*, 91*n*, 92
  Basel II and, 96–98
  versus subprime crisis, 132

299

risk-weight categories, 55, 55*n*, 57–59, 58*b*–59*b*
changes in, 61, 61*n*
three-pillar approach (*See* three-pillar approach)
Basel IA proposal, 119*n*, 128*n*, 188, 257
Basel II
aims of, 7, 189
alternatives to, 11, 225–58
assessment of, 5*n*, 5–7, 260
versus Basel I, 1–3, 9, 151, 195, 226
as domestic regulatory model, 5–7, 10, 139–93
as international arrangement, 10–11, 140, 195–224, 251, 261–62 (*See also* international harmonization)
policy recommendations, 262–79
capital definition, 118*n*, 264
competitive equality and, 127, 182–89, 190, 200–202, 209–14, 262
document size, 169, 169*n*
implementation of, 126–30
difficulties in, 166–77, 263
high-level principles for, 219, 220*b*
timing of, 13–14
lessons learned from, 281–84
main elements of, 105–107, 123, 124*b*–125*b*
minimum capital level requirements, uncertainty over, 162–64
monitoring difficulties, 166–77, 204–206, 205*n*, 213–14, 262, 275, 278
national discretion provisions, 123*n*, 201, 212*n*, 212–13
negotiation of, 8–9, 13–14, 87–137, 149, 161–62 (*See also* consultative papers)
policy recommendations, 11–12
as regulatory cartelization, 255*n*
release of, 122–23, 137
subprime crisis and, 10–12, 14, 137, 190, 259–60
Basel II½, 263–64
Basel III, 263
"Basel-plus" measures, unilateral, 203
basic indicator approach, 108
Bear Stearns, 22*n*, 260
Belgium, banking regulation in, 42
Bernanke, Ben, 129, 214*n*
best-practice operational requirements, for A-IRB approach, 156–57, 275
BIS. *See* Bank for International Settlements
bondholders, subordinated, 233, 233*n*
bond yield spreads, substitution for capital ratios, 236–45

Bretton Woods system, 4*b*, 33
Bush (George W.) administration, 132

CAMEL/CAMELS system, 31*n*, 269*n*
Canada
banking regulation in, 40–42, 42
leverage ratio requirement, 228–31, 229*n*, 268
capital
measurement of, common framework for, 53–54, 56–57
redefining, 12, 264–66
tier 1, 55*n*, 55–57, 57*b*, 69, 71–72, 164*n*, 264
tier 2, 55–57, 57*b*, 164*n*, 264
tier 3, 63*n*
Capital Adequacy Directive (CAD), 61–62, 64, 118, 206, 246
capital/asset ratio, 28, 29, 30, 43–44
capital charges
calculation of, 118*n*
market risk, 62, 62*t*
capital cushion
determination of, 144
effects on cost of debt, 18–19
mandatory subordinated debt and, 231*n*–232*n*, 241
capital definition
in Basel I, 55–57, 57*b*, 118*n*
in Basel II, 118*n*, 264
modification of, 12, 264–65
variation in, 42, 44, 51–52, 56
capital/deposit ratio, 29
capital/gross revenue ratio, 230–31
capital levels
above minimum requirements, 143–45
Basel II process and, 92*n*, 92–93, 102*n*, 102–103
under CP-2 proposal, 111–13
decline in, 31*f*, 31–33, 32*t*, 53, 188–89
determined by market forces, 141–50
divergence between actual risk and, 83–84, 84*n*
effect of Basel I on, 67
impact of A-IRB approach on, 160–66
median, 142
capital ratios
international variation on, 39–42, 44
of largest banks, 48, 48*t*
as predictors of bank failure, 230–31
substitution of bond yield spreads for, 236–45
types of, 28–29
regulatory discrepancies between, 29–31, 39

international supervision of, 252–55
policy recommendations, 12
regulatory arbitrage and, 108, 171–72, 189, 215
shift to, 104–13, 196n
"use test," 170–71
International Association of Insurance Supervisors, 280
international banks. *See* multinational banks
International Convergence of Capital Measurement and Capital Standards: A Revised Framework. *See* Basel II
international harmonization, 10–11, 140, 195–224
amendment difficulties with, 202n, 202–203
beyond capital regulation, 279–84
domestic costs of, 201–203
elimination of, 255–56
versus flexibility, 223
indirect benefits of, 222–23
mandatory subordinated debt and, 244–45
political economy of, 135–37, 283n, 283–84
potential benefits of, 6–7, 196, 204–209, 260–61
stickiness of, 203
International Lending Supervision Act (ILSA), 38n, 46n, 52, 52n
International Liaison Group, 3b
International Monetary Fund (IMF), 2b, 4b, 206, 207n
on CP-1 proposal, 98
US quota at, 38, 46
International Organization of Securities Commissioners, 62n, 123n, 280
international supervisory role, establishment of, 13, 251–55, 276–79
International Swaps and Derivatives Association, 99
international variation
in capital definition, 51–52, 56
on capital ratios, 39–42, 44
in capital regulation, 45
in cost of equity capital, 211
interstate branching, prohibitions on, 34
investment banks, restrictions on, 34–35
investment preferences, international variation in, 211–12

IRB approach. *See* internal ratings–based approach
Italy, banking regulation in, 40–41, 41n

Japan
bank examinations in, 204n
banking regulation in, 40n, 40–41, 41n
Basel I negotiation and, 48–50, 54
capital definition in, 52, 56, 56n
financial crisis in, 69–72, 74–75, 213
savings rate in, 49
subordinated debt in, 245
Japanese banks
asset accumulation by, 46–48, 47t, 48n
Basel I compliance by, 66, 66n, 68, 68n, 70–72
capital levels of, 142n
capital ratios of, 48, 48n, 48t
US competitive concerns about, 49, 49n, 76–77, 85
Joint Forum on Financial Conglomerates, 217n

keiretsu relationships, 49
Köln Summit, 96–97

Latin American debt crisis, 36–37, 38, 46, 265, 284
versus Basel I outcome, 73, 91n, 190
status of loss provisions and, 60, 60n
"least cost alternative" rule, 23n
lender of last resort, government as, 19–22, 199
lending
to developing countries, 36–37
higher-risk, by non-IRB banks, 183–84
mortgage (*See* mortgage lending)
procyclical nature of, 77–79, 79n, 117–18, 143, 178–82, 202
to small and medium-sized enterprises, 116, 185n, 185–86
letters of credit. *See* off-balance-sheet items
leverage ratio requirement, 12, 145–48, 228n, 228–31
arguments against, 148, 229–30
versus bond yield spreads, 237, 243–44
international adoption of, 265–70
setting of, 268–69
LGD (loss-given-default), 179n, 219n, 221n
LIBOR rates, 131–32
liquidity premium, for mandatory subordinated debt, 241

liquidity risk, 28, 262
    subprime crisis and, 131–35, 135*n*, 259
loan-loss reserves
    in Basel I, 60, 60*n*, 118*n*
    in Basel II, 118*n*
    countercyclical, 182
    definition of, variation in, 51
Long-Term Capital Management (LTCM),
        19*n*, 91*n*, 92, 153
loss-given-default (LGD), 179*n*, 219*n*, 221*n*
Luxembourg, banking regulation in, 41*n*,
        42

macroeconomic conditions
    Basel I and, 73, 77–79, 84, 178
    Basel II and, 178–82, 202
    decline in capital levels and, 33–34
Madrid compromise, 121, 121*n*
mandatory subordinated debt, 231–45
    international implications of, 244–45
    international requirement for, 270–72
    market discipline and, 242–44, 270–72
    threshold for, 270–71
market discipline, 231–45, 258. *See also*
        pillar 3 (market discipline)
    direct, 231–35, 242–44
    effect of Basel I on, 73
    indirect, 232, 235–42
    mandatory subordinated debt and,
        242–44, 270–72
market forces, capital levels determined
        by, 141–50
market risk, 27
    Basel I amendments incorporating,
        61–64, 62*t*, 82
material deficiencies, 129–30
McDonough, William, 91, 121, 161
    on Basel I review, 91–92, 92*n*
    on high capital levels, 144*n*
    on IRB approach, 99, 112
    on securitization, 88*n*
    support for IRB approach, 103–104
Mellon Bank, 116
Mexico default, 37, 61*n*
minimum capital rules. *See* capital
        requirements; pillar 1 (minimum
        capital rules)
minimum ratio of capital to income, 12
Models Task Force, 95–96
money market funds, 33*n*, 33–34, 35
monitoring
    of Basel I compliance, 67–68
    of Basel II compliance, 166–77, 204–206,
        221, 262, 275

history of, 29
incentives for, 19*n*
international agency responsible for, 13,
        251–55, 276–79
of mandatory subordinated debt, 245,
        272
mortgage lending. *See also* subprime crisis
        (2007)
    under A-IRB approach, 188
    competition for, 186, 186*n*
    originate-to-distribute model of, 132
    riskiness of, 14, 182, 259
    risk weighting of, 114, 159, 227
multinational banks
    asset accumulation by, 47*t*, 47–48
    capital levels of, 46
    cooperative supervision of, 214–22
    minimum capital requirements applied
        to, 37*n*, 37–38
multiple gearing, 217*n*

National Bank Act, 29
national discretion, Basel II provisions
        granting, 123*n*, 201, 212*n*, 212–13
national policy goals, Basel II in relation
        to, 5–7, 10, 139–93, 212
negative externalities, 21–22, 143
    required capital levels and, 24–27, 198
Netherlands, banking regulation in, 42
New York Clearing House Association,
        247, 247*n*
non-Basel countries
    Basel I adopted by, 65–66
    Basel II adopted by, 127, 206–207, 210
nongovernmental actors, benefits of
        international harmonization for, 196
non-IRB banks, disadvantages of Basel II
        for, 183–87
Northern Rock, 132, 256*n*

off-balance-sheet items
    included in capital rules, 39, 39*n*, 81, 82
    leverage ratio requirement and, 229*n*,
        230–31, 266–68, 268*n*
    risk-weighting of, 55–56, 59–60, 60*t*
    subprime crisis and, 131–32, 259
oil embargo, 33
operational risk requirement, 27–28,
        215*n*–216*n*
    approaches to, 108
    Basel I and, 87*n*, 92
    Basel II and, 93, 98, 103, 108
    in consultative paper proposals, 111–13,
        116, 117

Other Publications from the Peterson Institute

WORKING PAPERS

Managing Official Export Credits: The Quest
for a Global Regime*　　　　John E. Ray
July 1995　　　　ISBN 0-88132-207-5
Asia Pacific Fusion: Japan's Role in APEC*
Yoichi Funabashi
October 1995　　　　ISBN 0-88132-224-5
Korea-United States Cooperation in the New
World Order* C. Fred Bergsten/Il SaKong, eds.
February 1996　　　　ISBN 0-88132-226-1
Why Exports Really Matter!* ISBN 0-88132-221-0
Why Exports Matter More!* ISBN 0-88132-229-6
J. David Richardson and Karin Rindal
July 1995; February 1996
Global Corporations and National
Governments　　　　Edward M. Graham
May 1996　　　　ISBN 0-88132-111-7
Global Economic Leadership and the Group of
Seven　　　　C. Fred Bergsten
and C. Randall Henning
May 1996　　　　ISBN 0-88132-218-0
The Trading System after the Uruguay Round*
John Whalley and Colleen Hamilton
July 1996　　　　ISBN 0-88132-131-1
Private Capital Flows to Emerging Markets
after the Mexican Crisis* Guillermo A. Calvo,
Morris Goldstein, and Eduard Hochreiter
September 1996　　　　ISBN 0-88132-232-6
The Crawling Band as an Exchange Rate
Regime: Lessons from Chile, Colombia,
and Israel　　　　John Williamson
September 1996　　　　ISBN 0-88132-231-8
Flying High: Liberalizing Civil Aviation
in the Asia Pacific*　　　Gary Clyde Hufbauer
and Christopher Findlay
November 1996　　　　ISBN 0-88132-227-X
Measuring the Costs of Visible Protection
in Korea*　　　　Namdoo Kim
November 1996　　　　ISBN 0-88132-236-9
The World Trading System: Challenges Ahead
Jeffrey J. Schott
December 1996　　　　ISBN 0-88132-235-0
Has Globalization Gone Too Far?　Dani Rodrik
March 1997　　　ISBN paper 0-88132-241-5
Korea-United States Economic Relationship*
C. Fred Bergsten and Il SaKong, editors
March 1997　　　　ISBN 0-88132-240-7
Summitry in the Americas: A Progress Report
Richard E. Feinberg
April 1997　　　　ISBN 0-88132-242-3
Corruption and the Global Economy
Kimberly Ann Elliott
June 1997　　　　ISBN 0-88132-233-4
Regional Trading Blocs in the World
Economic System　　Jeffrey A. Frankel
October 1997　　　　ISBN 0-88132-202-4
Sustaining the Asia Pacific Miracle:
Environmental Protection and Economic
Integration　　　Andre Dua and Daniel C. Esty
October 1997　　　　ISBN 0-88132-250-4
Trade and Income Distribution
William R. Cline
November 1997　　　　ISBN 0-88132-216-4

Global Competition Policy
Edward M. Graham and J. David Richardson
December 1997　　　　ISBN 0-88132-166-4
Unfinished Business: Telecommunications
after the Uruguay Round
Gary Clyde Hufbauer and Erika Wada
December 1997　　　　ISBN 0-88132-257-1
Financial Services Liberalization in the WTO
Wendy Dobson and Pierre Jacquet
June 1998　　　　ISBN 0-88132-254-7
Restoring Japan's Economic Growth
Adam S. Posen
September 1998　　　　ISBN 0-88132-262-8
Measuring the Costs of Protection in China
Zhang Shuguang, Zhang Yansheng,
and Wan Zhongxin
November 1998　　　　ISBN 0-88132-247-4
Foreign Direct Investment and Development:
The New Policy Agenda for Developing
Countries and Economies in Transition
Theodore H. Moran
December 1998　　　　ISBN 0-88132-258-X
Behind the Open Door: Foreign Enterprises
in the Chinese Marketplace　Daniel H. Rosen
January 1999　　　ISBN 0-88132-263-6
Toward A New International Financial
Architecture: A Practical Post-Asia Agenda
Barry Eichengreen
February 1999　　　　ISBN 0-88132-270-9
Is the U.S. Trade Deficit Sustainable?
Catherine L. Mann
September 1999　　　　ISBN 0-88132-265-2
Safeguarding Prosperity in a Global Financial
System: The Future International Financial
Architecture, Independent Task Force Report
Sponsored by the Council on Foreign Relations
Morris Goldstein, Project Director
October 1999　　　　ISBN 0-88132-287-3
Avoiding the Apocalypse: The Future
of the Two Koreas　　　Marcus Noland
June 2000　　　　ISBN 0-88132-278-4
Assessing Financial Vulnerability:
An Early Warning System for Emerging
Markets　　　　Morris Goldstein,
Graciela Kaminsky, and Carmen Reinhart
June 2000　　　　ISBN 0-88132-237-7
Global Electronic Commerce: A Policy Primer
Catherine L. Mann, Sue E. Eckert, and Sarah
Cleeland Knight
July 2000　　　　ISBN 0-88132-274-1
The WTO after Seattle　　Jeffrey J. Schott, ed.
July 2000　　　　ISBN 0-88132-290-3
Intellectual Property Rights in the Global
Economy　　　　Keith E. Maskus
August 2000　　　　ISBN 0-88132-282-2
The Political Economy of the Asian Financial
Crisis　　　　Stephan Haggard
August 2000　　　　ISBN 0-88132-283-0
Transforming Foreign Aid: United States
Assistance in the 21st Century　Carol Lancaster
August 2000　　　　ISBN 0-88132-291-1

WORKS IN PROGRESS

DISTRIBUTORS OUTSIDE THE UNITED STATES

Australia, New Zealand,
and Papua New Guinea
D. A. Information Services
648 Whitehorse Road
Mitcham, Victoria 3132, Australia
Tel: 61-3-9210-7777
Fax: 61-3-9210-7788
Email: service@dadirect.com.au
www.dadirect.com.au

India, Bangladesh, Nepal, and Sri Lanka
Viva Books Private Limited
Mr. Vinod Vasishtha
4737/23 Ansari Road
Daryaganj, New Delhi 110002
India
Tel: 91-11-4224-2200
Fax: 91-11-4224-2240
Email: viva@vivagroupindia.net
www.vivagroupindia.com

Mexico, Central America, South America,
and Puerto Rico
US PubRep, Inc.
311 Dean Drive
Rockville, MD 20851
Tel: 301-838-9276
Fax: 301-838-9278
Email: c.falk@ieee.org

Asia *(Brunei, Burma, Cambodia, China,*
Hong Kong, Indonesia, Korea, Laos, Malaysia,
Philippines, Singapore, Taiwan, Thailand,
and Vietnam)
East-West Export Books (EWEB)
University of Hawaii Press
2840 Kolowalu Street
Honolulu, Hawaii 96822-1888
Tel: 808-956-8830
Fax: 808-988-6052
Email: eweb@hawaii.edu

Canada
Renouf Bookstore
5369 Canotek Road, Unit 1
Ottawa, Ontario K1J 9J3, Canada
Tel: 613-745-2665
Fax: 613-745-7660
www.renoufbooks.com

Japan
United Publishers Services Ltd.
1-32-5, Higashi-shinagawa
Shinagawa-ku, Tokyo 140-0002
Japan
Tel: 81-3-5479-7251
Fax: 81-3-5479-7307
Email: purchasing@ups.co.jp
For trade accounts only. Individuals will find
Institute books in leading Tokyo bookstores.

Middle East
MERIC
2 Bahgat Ali Street, El Masry Towers
Tower D, Apt. 24
Zamalek, Cairo
Egypt
Tel. 20-2-7633824
Fax: 20-2-7369355
Email: mahmoud_fouda@mericonline.com
www.mericonline.com

United Kingdom, Europe
(including Russia and Turkey), **Africa,**
and Israel
The Eurospan Group
c/o Turpin Distribution
Pegasus Drive
Stratton Business Park
Biggleswade, Bedfordshire
SG18 8TQ
United Kingdom
Tel: 44 (0) 1767-604972
Fax: 44 (0) 1767-601640
Email: eurospan@turpin-distribution.com
www.eurospangroup.com/bookstore

Visit our website at:
www.petersoninstitute.org
E-mail orders to:
petersonmail@presswarehouse.com